Dictionary of Ancient Magic Words and Spells

"Lecouteux is a genius. I have been gratefully following his research—which provides information I have never found in other locations—for years."

MAJA D'AOUST, WITCH OF THE DAWN
AND AUTHOR OF *FAMILIARS IN WITCHCRAFT*
AND *ASTROLOGY OF THE SHADOW SELF*

Dictionary of Ancient Magic Words and Spells

From Abraxas to Zoar

Claude Lecouteux

Translated by Jon E. Graham

Inner Traditions
Rochester, Vermont

Inner Traditions
One Park Street
Rochester, Vermont 05767
www.InnerTraditions.com

Copyright © 2014 by Éditions Imago
English translation copyright © 2015 by Inner Traditions International

Originally published in French under the title *Dictionnaire des Formules magiques* by Éditions Imago, 7 rue Suger, 75006 Paris
First U.S. edition published in 2015 by Inner Traditions

All biblical references are from the Latin Vulgate Bible.

All rights reserved. No part of this book may be reproduced or utilized in any form or by any means, electronic or mechanical, including photocopying, recording, or by any information storage and retrieval system, without permission in writing from the publisher. No part of this book may be used or reproduced to train artificial intelligence technologies or systems.

Volume I
of
The Sorceror's Scholar
Collector's Edition Boxed Set

Dictionary of Ancient Magic Words and Spells

Printed and bound in India by Nutech Print Services

10 9 8 7 6 5 4 3 2 1

Text design and layout by Virginia Scott Bowman
This book was typeset in Garamond Premier Pro and Gill Sans.

Inner Traditions wishes to express its appreciation for assistance given by the government of France through the National Book Office of the Ministère de la Culture in the preparation of this translation.

Nous tenons à exprimer nos plus vifs remerciements au gouvernement de la France et au ministère de la Culture, Centre National du Livre, pour leur concours dans la préparation de la traduction de cet ouvrage.

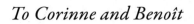

To Corinne and Benoît

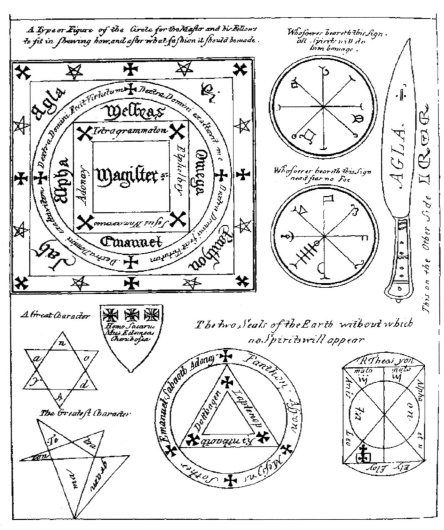

From Reginald Scot, *Discoverie of Witchcraft*, 1584

CONTENTS

Acknowledgments   ix

Praeambulus: Words That Possess a Power   **xi**

Dictionary of Ancient
Magic Words and Spells   1

From Abraxas to Zoar

APPENDIX ONE
Use of *Caracteres* in Magic   354

APPENDIX TWO
Cryptography   381

APPENDIX THREE
List of Magic Words Appearing in the Spells   385

Bibliography   393

Elijah conjuring, thirteenth-century manuscript

ACKNOWLEDGMENTS

It is with great pleasure that I offer thanks to the individuals who helped me complete this task: Daiva Vaitkevičienė (Vilnius, Lithuania) and Ronald Grambo (Kongsvinger, Norway), without whose help I would have been unable to grasp many dialectical turns of phrase in the Scandinavian grimoires; Emanuela Timotin (Bucharest, Romania), who introduced me to Romanian charms; Gian Marco Mondino (Torino) who was able to procure a copy of the *Libro de secreto,* Ane Ohrvik (Oslo) and Julien Véronèse (Paris) who sent me their studies on charms.

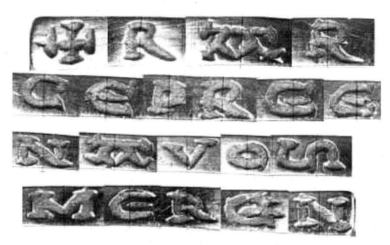

Magical inscription on a sixteenth-century ring

PRAEAMBULUS

WORDS THAT POSSESS A POWER

From *Abracadabra* to the *Avada Kedavr** and *Rennervate* used in the Harry Potter books,[1] everyone has become familiar with magic words, although novels, films, and comic books can provide only a simplified, distorted version of them. Shouted, whispered, chanted, recited, or muttered by a magician, sorcerer, or witch—using peculiar and even incomprehensible words to obtain supernatural effects—these perpetually evolving spells come down to us from the dawn of time. Thanks to the efforts of the scholars from a variety of disciplines, we now have a corpus consisting of tens of thousands of accounts at our disposal.[†] These phrases can be found in charms (from the Latin *carmen*, meaning "song"), orisons, blessings, conjurations, and medical prescriptions.

SOME DEFINITIONS

Orisons are magic prayers that conceal their true nature behind a Christian exterior, most often through references to Jesus, Mary, the evangelists, and so on. Blessings can be pagan or Christian, but either way they share the same structure: they are used to summon good

---

*In which we can recognize *Abracadabra*.
[†]The Adolf Spamer Collection at the Humboldt University in Berlin, for example, has twenty-two thousand.

fortune on an individual; they are the opposite of curses. Conjurations are used to summon supernatural beings whose assistance is required as well as to perform the exorcisms necessary to banish the malevolent entities embodied in misfortunes. These entities are most often encountered in remote solitudes and deserted regions where men rarely travel. As for the short notes still known today as *brevets* in France, they are most often found on amulets of parchment or paper that contain Kabbalistic phrases that have been encrypted through the use of characters known as "Solomonic writing," "Ephesian letters,"* or "unknown scripts."† All these strange signs are called *caracteres*[2] in Latin, a term I will use to avoid creating any confusion. A scholar wrote this about *Ephesiae litterae* in 1717: "They plunge the soul of those who hear them into terror."[3] Hebrew letters were also used because, according to the Pseudo–Arnaldus de Villanova,‡ they were the most effective ("*Si habet literas hebraycas, efficassisimum est opera*").[4] But Saint Jerome had already spoken in his own time about magicians who used every means to impress their customers: the less these customers understood, the more they found admirable.[5]

PAGANISM AND CHRISTIANITY

While the bulk of the charms are intended to provide protection and to heal illnesses affecting men and livestock—and are thus suggestive of what we might customarily describe as medical prescriptions—some are truly magical because of the entities they call on through strange phrases and words. Like the pagans, medieval Christians believed that disease was sent by the devil or by demons,[6] and they only added the notion of sin to this concept. God is the great, all-powerful physician, per the saying "*Diabolus ligavit, Angelus curavit, Dominus salvavit*" (the devil bound, the angel cured, God saved).§ The cross and Christ's wounds became beneficial aids: "*crux et passio Christi sint medicina mei*" (the

---

*It is believed that the name "Ephesian" comes from the Babylonian *epêsu*, "enchanter."
†The original terms are *salmoniacas scripturas*, *Ephesia grammata* (or *Ephesiae litterae*), *barbara nomina*, and *litterae ignotae*. They are also referred to as *voces magicae*. Thomas Aquinas called such signs *ignota nomina*, "unknown words."
‡Arnaud de Villeneuve in French.
§Christ is regarded as a doctor; see Matthew 4:32.

cross and the suffering of Christ are my medicine). An English charm dating from the second half of the fourteenth century also invokes the tears of the Virgin, the Three Magi, and the secret names of God:

> *Sint medicyna mei pia crux et passio Christi*
> *Vulnera quinque dei sint medicyna mei!*
> *Virginis et lacrime mihi sint medicamina trina,*
> *Her mihi portanti succurrant febricitanti! Amen*
> *† A † g. † l. † a. † Jaspar † Melchysar † Baptizar †*[7]

Another account from this same country, a benediction intended to encourage a good labor and delivery, provides an accurate image of the blend of the Christian sacred and the pagan profane in this kind of prescription:

> *Boro berto briore † Vulnera quinque dei sint medicina mei †*
> *Tahebal †† ghether ††† guthman †††††*[8]

Here the five wounds of Christ are framed by magical pagan phrases.

It can be noted in passing that every affliction is a bond, that demons are binders, and that the Christian figures undo these bonds. Sometimes these demons' names are given to us. They are dwarves and elves, trolls and gnomes who shoot invisible arrows at you.[9] In 348, Cyril of Jerusalem noted, "As long as man lives within a body, he will have to fight off countless wild demons,"* and Porphyry stated that the demons would be free to choose where they wanted to dwell. It was therefore necessary to find protection as well from their human auxiliaries, such as magicians and sorcerers, and to do this, people resorted to esoteric practices that enlisted invisible beings, the foremost of which were the gods or God.

THE USEFUL NATURE OF THE SPELLS

One of the purposes of magical phrases and words was the protection of people and property. It involved preventing something from happening or halting an action already at work—a fire or the effects of a curse, projectiles (arrows, then bullets) or the bite of bladed weapons. An entire series

---

*This is reminiscent of what Paul expresses in his letter to the Galatians 5:29.

of apotropaic (protective) charms aimed at providing shelter from evil spells, the sudden death of livestock, and theft, and here a large number of recipes indicate how to uncover a thief by subjecting him to a magic test or by forcing him to return his booty. A subcategory of these recipes, which is suggestive of black magic, teaches how to blind a thief in one eye from a distance, paralyze him, or otherwise get one's revenge on him.

The bulk of the spells come from healing charms. Johann Weyer (1515–1588) provides a good overview of these in his *Cinq livres de l'imposture des diables, des enchantements, et sorcelleries* (Five Books on the Imposture of Devils, Enchantments, and Sorceries), published in Paris in 1570, from which I have drawn this example:

> There are some who to staunch the flow of blood take a cup of cold water, into which they drip three drops of blood, and at each drop say the dominical orison with the angelic salutation. They then give it to the patient and ask him: "Who will help you?" The patient answers it will be the Holy Mary. They then say: "*sancta Maria hunc sanguinem firma,*" meaning, "Saint Mary, stop this blood flow." Others write on the patient's forehead with the blood that drips out: "*Consummatum est,*" meaning: "All is achieved." Others to stop the blood flow say these words: "*sanguis mane fixus in tua vena sicut Christus in sua poena: sanguis mane fixus sicut Christus quando fuit crucifixus.*" This means: "Blood remain in your vein like Christ in his torment; blood remain still like Christ when he was crucified." They say this should be repeated three times. Another says "*De latere eius exiuit sanguis et aqua,*" meaning, "blood and water come out his side." Others think that the flow of blood from several parts of the body can be stopped with these words: "Christ was born in Bethlehem and suffered in Jerusalem; his blood is troubled; I tell you to stop it by the power of God and by the aid of all the saints; just as in the Jordan in which Saint John baptized our Lord Jesus Christ, in the name of the Father and the Son and the Holy Ghost." Hold the nameless finger in the wound and make three crosses on it; say five Our Fathers and Hail Marys, and once the Apostles' Creed in honor of the five wounds.[10]

Then there are the spells intended to grant one's wishes. These range from desires for wealth—through the discovery of hidden treasures!—

to catching fish, and doing so with a net or a line is spelled out, to winning the love of a person one lusts after, by way of curious spells such as the one that helps a woman weave a blouse, makes her dance, or makes an entire household dance against its will. Oddly enough, spells for invisibility rarely accompany magical phrases and words.

The fact that the phrases may have been incomprehensible was irrelevant since their use was based on an act of faith, relying first on the magic and authority of the text, then on the tradition. If they have been handed down, it is because they work, and the more impenetrable they seem, the more effective they are! In this regard, we may speak of the notion of "mystification."

Let's look at one example. Who today would guess that *XV XR XI* means "Christ is victorious, Christ rules, Christ commands" (*imperat*)? Entire phrases are reduced to a series of letters whose meaning generally escapes us. Only Christian series have been partially deciphered. I am thinking here of *Zacharias's Benediction* against the plague, which contains eighteen uppercase letters, each of which refers to a passage from a psalm, or of the *Charm of Saint Agatha*, used against fires, which includes nine, each of which is the initial for a word.

THE RECOURSE

The use of spells by this means requires divine or diabolical aid. To get all luck on one's side, one would accumulate the names of supernatural beings based on an extremely ancient belief: to possess the true name of one of these beings compels their obedience. To name is to master, to lift a corner of the veil covering the mystery and force the creature or power to bend to our will because *numen est nomen* (a spirit's power is embedded in its name), an idea that can be found almost everywhere, especially in the legends of changelings, those children who had been replaced by demons or fairies.[11] If the true name was not known, one would gather together all the known names to form a veritable litany, in the hopes that the right one might be among them.* A very fine Greek text recommends this:

---

*The ancient Egyptians invoked *Phnô eai Iabôk* this way and the Jews *Adonai Sabaôth*. Horus-Knuphi is also called Arbath, Abaoth, and Bakchabre, and in a Greek plant conjuration, Chronos, Hera, Ammon, Isis, Zeus, Helion, Osiris, Hermes, Mnevis, Horus, Pan, Ares, and Athena are all called upon!

Only invoke the Great Name when in great distress, in situations of life and death.... Say *Jao* three times, then the great name of God. I invoke you, *Ptha hra iè Phta oum emêcha erôth Barôch thorchtha thôm chai eouch archandabar ôea eô yneôch èra ôn èloph bom phta athabrasia Abriasôth barbarbelôcha barbariasô*...*¹²

During the Middle Ages, this accumulation procedure was picked up anew by Christian magic, which informs us that God has seventy-two ways of being named.† This number kept growing because people were not satisfied with only the Latin names, but also sought out those in Greek, Hebrew, and sometimes even Arabic. The variety of these names is explicable if we remember what Origen (ca. 185–253) said: "The names that possess a power in one language, lose it when they are translated."¹³ Therefore people took all the names and nicknames of God from the Bible as well as all the descriptive phrases, metaphors, and symbols that applied to him. For good measure, the names of the Three Magi, the patriarchs, the apostles, the archangels, and so on were all added to the list. The same was done with the Holy Trinity and the Virgin Mary. In other words, the entire Christian pantheon was mobilized. This was how only the licit white magic proceeded. The *ars notoria*, illicit black magic, did likewise with demons and planetary spirits, for, as the author of *Picatrix* notes, "There are certain words among the names of God that compel the spirits of heaven to come down to earth."¹⁴ Starting in the sixteenth century, esoteric writings circulated the hierarchy of hell, with a multitude of names ranging from Lucifer and Satan to Belial and Belzebuth. Spells and prayers were then made in the name of the devil, the Adversary, the Evil One!

RITUALS AND INGREDIENTS

For the word or spell to be effective, it had to be written at a time previously indicated. Among the days of the week, Thursday was most auspicious in the Scandinavian countries, followed by Saturday and Wednesday.

---

*This word appears frequently in Greek charms, for example in the Greek Magical Papyri (PGM IV, 88–93).

†A large number of charms are based on Biblical and hagiographical elements, such as the Charms of Saint Peter, Saint Agatha, Saint Anne, Longinus, the Jordan, Saint Suzanne, Saint Apollonia, and so forth.

This precision is rare for charms with phrases in other lands. Throughout Western Europe, they had to be drawn before sunrise as the underlying idea is that magic is the daughter of darkness. The choice of the day is based on the astrological traditions of classical antiquity, which drew a distinction between lucky and unlucky days, but this background disappeared as magic became more popular and was no longer solely performed by scholars. Only a few signatures (coded depictions of the heavenly bodies and constellations) from all this survive among the spells.[15]

The oldest charms sometimes include rituals, but this is rare for a very simple reason: the scribes or authors did not really want everyone to be able to use them without the services of a "specialist." The scribes and copyists therefore censored their texts.

We should not forget that during the Middle Ages, and even long after, the people who knew how to read and write were clerics and churchmen, and they drew a supplemental income from the writing or copying of charms. They could make a little money on the side, to put it in modern terms, by selling them or performing them. The proof? This is supplied by the penitential books, which continually denounce the magicians or sorcerer priests, reminding people that the "notorious arts" were forbidden by the Church. Primarily all that remains of charms is the way they were used: this spell should be hung around the neck, this other one diluted in water and given to the patient to drink. And the patient should lap it up, then spit it out . . .

We can learn a bit more about the ingredients and everything that accompanies the magic words and phrases: blood of a bat or black dog, a piece of your baptism taper, or a piece of cheese, bread, or lead, or a hazel wand. One ties knots or sticks a certain nail in a wall, or carves a notch in the ear of a black cat . . .

The value of these details is, among other things, that they reveal a practically boundless imaginal realm that is quite solidly anchored in reality and daily life. The animals and instruments are the same ones you come across or use every day.

SPELLS FOR EVERYTHING

What is most noticeable in the magic phrases is their multiple functionality. It would only be a slight exaggeration to say that none of them are truly specialized, treat but one illness or type of curse, or even serve as protection against any one form of attack, whatever that aggression may be. This multifunctional character arises from their ability to be combined together, and this is especially true of the Christian or Christianized texts. All evidence points toward the fact that a stock of set phrases existed from which magicians, witches, or healers drew what they needed at will. The material collected in the dictionary provides ample documentation for this situation.

Another conclusion becomes obvious: the accumulation of spells in a single text tends to show that doubt persisted as to the effectiveness of each spell taken separately. For this reason, the people of the Middle Ages and their descendants juxtaposed them, blending truly pagan elements together with them, such as invocations to the sun and moon.

As best we can judge, pagan charms were first given a mere Christian veneer; clerics then developed Christian charms on the pagan models, replacing gods like Odin and Thor with figures from the dominant religion. In the third stage, these two kinds of prescriptions merged together to form texts in which Christianity and paganism were neighbors. This is how we can find the magic square *Sator Arepo Tenet Opera Rotas* next to Christ and the Our Father next to the spell *poro pota,* and so on.

Over a thousand-year stretch, we can see a clear reduction of magic spells—both developed and abbreviated—in the grimoires. When compared to medieval manuscripts, *La poule noire* (The Black Hen) or *Le petit Albert* (The Little Albert) come off as poor relations. Several have survived into the present, but not the oldest ones. They are direct descendants of the books printed in the seventeenth century, especially those that cast anathema against superstitions. Jean-Baptiste Their's *Traité des superstitions* (*Treatise on Superstitions*; 1679) provides a good example. The content seems to have been decanted over the years with the elimination of the more obscure spells, but this proceeded at varying paces in different countries. On the other hand, everything that fell under the heading of Christian magic continued to be handed down, which tends to show that the church had managed over the long haul to divert pagan folk magic to its own benefit—at least in part. This development should not come as any surprise: every plant cut off from its roots will die. What endures is the belief in a cure, an acquisition, or a form of protection through supernatural means. In this regard people's minds have scarcely evolved, and just as they did in earlier times, men and women continue to make pilgrimages, visit healers, and wear amulets.

With magic words and phrases, we enter into a specific world where the opening of the Gospel of John holds complete sway: "In the beginning was the Word"— and when John tells us that "the Word was God," this means that it was all-powerful. If we just stick to contemporary accounts, I can add that it will still hold true *in saecula saeculorum,* and beyond all religions, cultures, and eras. The main lesson that can be taken from this is humanity's immense need for transcendence, the irrepressible need to place above it beings that govern our lives for both good and ill.

ELEMENTS OF LANGUAGE

From a linguistic perspective, magic spells come in a wide variety and can be separated into three basic types. We first have elements of the Christian liturgy—extracts from the Bible, especially the Psalms,* prayers, litanies, and the Mass. Second we have Greek, Hebrew, and Latin words,† often including words from the local dialect that are so twisted as to be unrecognizable, for what seems to be most important is the sound, which is often based on alliterations and homophones. The use of sounds prompts a series of variations on a single word, such as, "festella, festelle, festelli festello festello, festella festellum," used to banish all kinds of fistulas.[16]

There are also variations on a specific concept. A German charm intended to compel the return of a fugitive opens with the phrase:

Peda inpeda. Prepeda. Conpeda prepedias Inpediae. Conpedia.

---

*Johann Weyer writes: "Another washes his hands with the patient during the rise of the fever and at its onset, he whispers the psalm, which begins, '*Exaltabo te Deux meus rex*' [Blessed be the Lord, my strength, Psalm 144]. Another says while taking the patient's hand, '*Aeque facilis tibi febris hac sit, atque Mariæ virgini Christi partus,*' in other words, 'This fever will be as easy to bear as the birth of Christ was to Mary'" (*Cinq Livres de l'imposture,* IV, 4).

†Or alternately, in the case of Romanian charms, the magical character of the text often comes from the use of the Slavonic liturgical language.

The words are derived from the verbs *impedio* and *prepedio,* "to shackle, to hinder," and the term *compedus,* "that which binds the feet together." The fugitive's feet are bound together at a distance by means of words.

Lastly, we find sequences of letters that can be the initials of words. We are all familiar with I.N.R.I., meaning "Jesus of Nazareth, King of the Jews," or VRS (*vade retro satanas*). Such words are sometimes composed of a phrase or abbreviations, like the one found in the work of Rabelais, where Pantagruel is written P.N.T.G.R.L.[17] A passage from the *Gesta imperatorum* suggests this; in fact we read there the sequence "P P P, S S S, R R R, F F F," meaning, "*Pater patriae perditur, sapientia secum sustollitur, ruunt regna Rome ferro, flamma, fame.*"[18] The series of letters would therefore be a mnemonic means used to retain whole phrases, but in charms it also serves as a way to keep things secret: only the initiate, mage, or sorcerer knows what it means.

Otherwise, we are generally confronted by amulet "texts" in which we find crosses, numbers, and signs mixed in with the letters. The meanings of these series of letters have been long lost, if there ever were meanings, because obscurity strengthens their magical nature, at least for the profane. When we have several variations of the same phrase, we can see that it was not understood by the individuals who copied it, who were clerics for the most part. There are two causes for these transcription errors: either the spell was written in writing that was hard to decipher, or else it was misheard when used by a third party or dictated to the cleric. This is the conclusion that is drawn from the almost phonetic transcriptions of prayers like the Our Father, or the change of the word *artifex* to *artifaehs,* or the Provençal spelling *dixitz* for *dixit,* or *penitensia.*

It is worth citing Julien Véronèse's pertinent observations on the transmission of texts. He writes:

> Revelations were in fact made in certain reputedly sacred languages—Egyptian in Greek tradition, Hebrew or "Chaldean" [Aramaic] in the Judeo-Christian tradition—the knowledge of which, from one era to the next, tended to get lost. Over the course of time, the revealed word became increasingly resistant to all attempts to decode it. But this progressive loss of meaning is far from being a handicap

in this domain. To the contrary, it becomes, especially with respect to the invocations that form a large part of magic rituals, a token of their effectiveness. Words whose meanings have become unknown [if they were ever known] . . . more easily appear to belong to the very language of the deity. . . . In other words, the secret nature of magical language is a guarantee of its power.[19]

THE SPELLING OF THE SPELLS

A word should be said about the written aspect of the spells, as this will enable us to get a better sense of the changes that were made over time by the copyists and users. In medieval manuscripts, the letters themselves were frequently a source of confusion. Here are a few examples of letters and pairs of letters that could be mistaken for one another:

u ↔ o	ni ↔ m	r ↔ t	l ↔ t
u ↔ n	rn ↔ m	r ↔ z	c ↔ t
st ↔ h	in ↔ m	r ↔ c	d ↔ ol
p ↔ f	iu ↔ m/in	l ↔ t	

A transcription is based on the pronunciation; this is how we get the notation /ngn/ for /gn/, or why /x/ becomes /xs/. The first letters of words can be omitted—*abriel* for Gabriel, *erba* for *herba*, while others are doubled up—*vinccit* for *vincit*. Words can be dislocated, as in *An An Jzapla* for *Ananizapta*, *su † per* for *super*, and *ad jutor* for *adjutor*, and then words can even be compounded, for example *saname* for *sana me* (heal me). We have words stuck together, such as *Kuiaesinnceliss* for *qui est in Coelis* (who art in heaven), or contracted, for example, *alfaetho* for *alpha et omega*. Words are abbreviated, such as with *ysros* for *ischyros* (strong), and letters vanish, as in *fia volua* for *fiat voluntas* (thy will be done). The list of examples of cacography and other linguistic phenomena that leave their mark on the manuscripts is much longer, but we should also mention the variations made with uppercase and lowercase letters, for example, *a † G † l.a* or even *teneBRArum*—elements that I have scrupulously respected in this dictionary. May this overview give the reader a small idea of the difficulties encountered by the researcher!

What we can deduce from an overall view of these linguistic

phenomena is that the important thing was the prosody of the charms and the inclusion of terms with strange sounds that strengthened their magic aura. To test the accuracy of this conjecture, it is enough to pronounce them out loud while respecting the rules of their accentuation, record it, and then listen to it. What you will hear is a kind of a highly rhythmic, monotonous chant that cannot help but bring to mind that of the Altaic shamans. The reader can try this experiment using this extract from a spell to banish cankers: *"canckera canckere canckere canckeri canckero canckera canckerum;"*[20] or even better, with this extract from a summoning of air spirits by Peter D'Abano (1250–1316):

Adonai, Zabaoth, Amioram, Sadai, El, Aty, Titeip, Azia, Hyn, Minosel, Achadan, Vay, Ey, Haa, Eye, Exe, a El, El, a Hy, Hau, Hau, Hau, Minosel, Achadan, Va, Va, Va, Va.[21]

WRITING AND CODING

To write magic words or phrases, we are sometimes told it is necessary to use one's own blood or that of animals—the most often cited animals are bats, cats (preferably black ones), roosters, and dogs—and to write on paper, wax, or virgin parchment, meaning it came from a stillborn animal. Other support materials are cited on which the required *caracteres* are drawn in ink. These include fruits, bread, cheese, a communion wafer, or an object used to drink or eat, such as a bowl or goblet. In healing procedures, the phrases are drunk after being dissolved in a liquid; in procedures of persecution, they prevent the individual from swallowing, such as when the intention is to uncover a thief.

The texts can be coded. A twelfth-century manuscript preserved in Paris gives us a few keys, for example, the replacement of vowels with dots:

A = .   e = :   i = :.   o = ::   u = :.:[22]

But other variations exist as well. Consonants may also be substituted for the vowels: *b* represents *a*, *f* for *e*, *k* for *i*, *p* for *o*, and *x* for *u*. Or all the letters of a word can be replaced by those letters that follow them (say, two places later) in the alphabet: *viuit* (he lived) thereby becomes *xkxkx*. The alphabet can be written backward, using *z* for *a*, *y* for *b*, and so forth. The vowels can be numbered from 1 to 5 (1 = *a*, and so on), or from 5 to 1 (5 = *a*, and so on). A dot can be used for *a*, a line for *e*, a Δ for *i*, and a ∇ for *u*. And of course, alphabets were invented.[23] The reader can try to decipher some phrases with the help of the clues found in appendix 2.

The local idiom can also be transliterated into Greek letters, especially in Italy, often in an approximate way, as shown in the following example from a *bref* for healing animals:[24]

TEXT	TRANSLITERATION
χίστινομουραρού πλασχρίζι σιλουμάλι ἐστιδιαβάντιτζιλισχριβίτιἐττάαχχάτιλι ἀλουχόδδου χουν Γ Πάτερνοόστερ ἐδ τρι ἀβι–μαρί ἐδ σι ἐστι διααρρέρι τζιλι ἀτταχά–τι ἀλαχούδα διλαββέστια	Kristinomourusou plaskhritzi siloumali esti diavanti tzili skhriviti ettakhkhatili aloukhoddou khoun G Pater noster eth tri avimari eth si esti diarreri tzili attakhati alakhouda dialabbestia
TRANSCRIPTION (SOUTHERN ITALIAN):	**TRANSLATION**
Kisti nomu ora suplascrizzi, si lu mali esti di avanti, cili scriviti e 'ttacatili allu coddu cun tri Pater noster e tri Avi Mari. Ed si esti di arreri cili attacati all cuda dilla bestia.	These words written here above, if the evil is in front, write them down and attach them to the neck while saying three Our Fathers and three Hail Marys, and if the evil is behind, attach them to the animal's tail.

In medieval Ireland, this kind of coding is also used, and in a charm against bladder diseases, we read: PRECHNYTΦcANω MNYBVc:-KNAATYω NIBVS:- FINIT:-, meaning *"prechnytosan (praedicent) omnibus nationibus"* (preach to all nations).

Another way to encrypt is, quite simply, by abbreviating. A spell from an Italian grimoire explains how this was done.

Eloim, Ariel e Jehova, Agla, Tagla, Mathon,
Oarios, Almouzin, Arios, Membrot, Varios,
Pithona, Magots, Salphae, Gabots, Salamandra,
Tabots, Gnomus, Terra, Coelis, Godend,
Aqua, Guingua, Jauna, Etitnamus, Zariatnatmick, etc.

A. E. A. J. A. T. M. O.
A. A. M. V. P. M. S. G. S. T.
G. T. C. G. A. C. J. E. Z., etc.[25]

Each letter represents a word. When similar series of letters are found, it is quite difficult to discover what they represent. Also, these letters can be used to form new magic words. Often such series are poorly deciphered. For another attestation with variants, see the entry for *Agla* in this dictionary.

SIGNS AND ALPHABETS

All the ancient grimoires contain so-called Kabbalistic signs called Ephesian letters (*Ephesia grammata*) and *caracteres,* taken from secret alphabets or else reused from Heinrich Cornelius Agrippa's *Occult Philosophy* or inspired by it.

In fact, it could be said that everything constituted a sign. Magic works when letters and figures are unknown to the profane. Until the nineteenth century, runes were used in the Scandinavian countries, and Ancient Greek and Hebrew letters were used there and elsewhere in Europe, including Great Britain (since at least the ninth and tenth centuries). This is how the name Veronica came to be written as Bepponike. The use of Ancient Greek remains rare, just as it is rare to find people capable of reading and writing it. When this language is encountered in a charm or prescription, you can be sure that it involves a scholarly tradition rooted in antiquity. Sometimes a simple phrase in a language foreign to the scribe became a magic spell. This is why there are so many Latin terms (almost always disfigured) that appear in the vernacular charms. In Scandinavia, in addition to the Latin words we find German, English, and Celtic words. It is obvious that some words were invented or coined from Latin models, and that terms in the local dialect were Latinized through the addition of Latin declensional endings.

LATIN CHARMS

Contrary to what one might think at first glance, the languages of charms are not "exotic tongues" like Greek or Hebrew, which are those of the spells from high magic rituals—the Kabbalah, *The Lesser Key of Solomon,* Heinrich Cornelius Agrippa's *Occult Philosophy*—that are known only to scholars. Greek provided a number of terms along with its alphabet, which served to transliterate the common tongue, and Hebrew supplied several names and words that were most often drawn from the scriptures. The major language of magic from the Middle Ages into the nineteenth century was Latin, which remains a mysterious language for many people, the language of the liturgy. We need to recall that the people who attended sermons given in this language often did not understand a word of them. They knew the responses, canticles, hymns, and so forth by heart, which is shown in the transcriptions of biblical passages for magical purposes. The words and expressions are therefore frequently skewed Latin terms or else common words that have been Latinized, or even Latin-sounding fabrications, or ultimately, Latin terms that were misunderstood, poorly deciphered, or extremely disfigured, which does not facilitate their comprehension and produces spells that are impenetrably obscure.

For example, the phrase, "Continuing on his way, Jesus passed close to them," which in Latin is *"Jesus autem transiens per medium illorum ibat"* (Luke 4:30), was frequently used by travelers during the period from the Middle Ages to the nineteenth century. Here is a glance at its evolution:

In 1789: *Jesus Hutem Abrasius rer medrum I lov rum ibat*
In 1800: *Jesu en fentrans tius Poe mer dium Horum ibat*
Thesus outrem trans sniper medium poramilet
In 1827: *Jesus aut antrocius † per Medium † Senum telb*[26]

Ultimately, the Latin charms worked through the melody and the prosody of the language, and the researcher should pronounce these words disregarding the written form if he wishes to move forward. When they exist, the variants are of great assistance because by comparing them it is sometimes possible to reconstruct the original meaning.

We have to believe that their appeal still works, as J. K. Rowling has Harry Potter speak spells such as *"Levicorpus! Muffliato, Reparo! Lumos! Impedimenta! Sectumsempra! Petrificus!"* But long before this author, a radio series from the 1960s offered this incantation:

Chaviro
Rotentacha
Chamipataro
Rogrillapatacha
*Chalacharo.**

The extraordinary if not extravagant world of magic spells reflects a way of thinking that has endured through the centuries and continues to fuel cinematographic and fictional works.

---

*The radio series was *Signé Furax* created by Pierre Dac and Francis Blanche, and the incantation means: "The cat sees the roast, the roast tempts the cat, the cat puts its paw on the roast, the roast burns the cat's paw, the cat drops the roast!" In the folktale collection *Trésor des contes*, vol. 2, Henri Pourrat records a version of the same spell collected in Auvergne in the 1950s, but with a different ending: "Cat shakes paw and abandons the roast." The folktale titled "Le Desservant nouveau" (p. 64 in the same volume) also offers a good example of French spells moving from Latin into the oral tradition.

HOW THE DICTIONARY IS ORGANIZED

My dictionary is the result of the scrutinizing of more than seven thousand magic spells from western and northern Europe. This corpus continues to grow as a result of the ongoing analysis of medieval manuscripts and the fortuitous discoveries of grimoires, like that of Vinje, Norway (found hidden beneath the floorboards of the local church), or that of Elverum in the same country (found in a farmhouse attic), or again in the documents found in the *Sachet accoucheur* (birthing pouch) owned by a family in Auvergne, France. There is also the extraordinary library of the sorcerer and quack doctor Joseph Wetzel, which was discovered during a search of his premises in 1894. It contained 123 books![27] In 1760, Johann Wallberger supplied a list of sixty-eight titles.[28] I cannot claim this to be an exhaustive list, because collecting magical words and spells is an immense task that calls for a team of researchers, if only for the many languages that need to be mastered. My book's essential purpose is to provide a glimpse of the fruits of magical thought from the Middle Ages into the nineteenth century.

The entries of this dictionary are arranged by single magical words and spells. When the spells are short, the entire phrase is used for the entry; if they are long, only a portion of the phrase is used. The other entries are abbreviated spells, and they are presented following the same principle.

Some entries provide information about the grimoires I studied, and others gather together the data on a theme.

I have strictly respected the spellings of the manuscripts, so it should come as no surprise to sometimes find what looks like gibberish, such as *vicit* for *vincit,* and so on, as well as variants for proper names (Semiphoras, Schemhamphoras, Shem ha-mephorash).

When there are several accounts offering variations of the same spell, all will be included. Some items are synthesized overviews combining the names of God, demons, and so forth.

In the Middle Ages, magic spells and words were passed on within medicinal and pharmaceutical codices, or else transmitted in manuscripts that had empty space left over, but from the sixteenth century onward into the nineteenth century, thanks to printing and peddling, they spread almost everywhere in the form of grimoires whose compilers drew their contents from everything they could get their hands on. Therefore, this dictionary does not confine itself to the Middle Ages, and it charts the evolution of these prescriptions, allowing us to distinguish the ancient traditions from the newer ones.

The commentary directly follows the names of the charms and prescriptions and seeks to decipher them whenever possible. The Biblical references are based on the Vulgate Latin translation.

Due to typographical limitations, I had to leave out some spells filled with Kabbalistic signs. All the original uses of uppercase and lowercase letters, italics, and staggered letters have been faithfully respected.

I have limited the bibliographical indications (marked 📖) to the source of the charm cited in the order of its appearance in the entry and, when necessary, to the most pertinent studies.

The ✦ symbol refers to other entries that make it possible to get a better grasp of the spell or word.

To avoid multiple entries that simply repeat the same information, I have provided an appendix that indicates in which spell the principal magical word can be found (see appendix 3 on pp. 385–391).

This dictionary rounds off the work that appears in two other publications of mine: *The Book of Grimoires* (2012) and *The High Magic of Talismans and Amulets: Tradition and Craft* (2014).

It is my hope that this tool, which lays no claim to being exhaustive, will make it easier to identify the magic legacy common to the countries included in this book and to give the reader a better idea of its true circulation.

CLAUDE LECOUTEUX

GAGNY, SEPTEMBER 1997–EASTER 2010

NOTES

1. Rowling, *Harry Potter and the Half-Blood Prince*, 536, 556.
2. Cf. Grévin and Véronèse, "Les 'caractères' magiques au Moyen Âge (XIIe–XIVe siècle)."
3. Arpe, *De prodigiosis naturae et artis operibus talismanes et amuleta dictis*, 17. On the "Ephesian letters," cf. also Wessely, *Ephesia grammata*.
4. Pseudo–Arnaldus de Villanova, *Opera*, folio 215 v°.

5. *Epistola* LXXV, 3.
6. Cf. Lecouteux, *The Book of Grimoires*, 57–62.
7. Holthausen, "Rezepte, Segen und Zaubersprüche aus zwei Stockholmer Handschriften," 80.
8. Ibid., 85.
9. Honko, *Krankeitsprojektile: Untersuchung über eine urtümliche Krankheitserklärung*, 178.
10. Weyer, *Cinq livres de l'imposture des diables, des enchantements et sorcelleries*, IV, 4.
11. Doulet, *Quand les démons enlevaient les enfants: Les changelins, étude d'une figure mythique*.
12. Bartsch, *Die Sachbeschwörungen der römischen Liturgie*, 170.
13. *Contra Celsum*, I, 45.
14. *Picatrix*, IV, 4.
15. Lecouteux, *The Book of Grimoires*, 181–87.
16. Van Haver, *Nederlandse incantatieliteratuur, een gecommentarieerd compendium van Nederlandse bezweringsformules*, no. 549, 206.
17. Rabelais, *Gargantua and Pantagruel*, II, 23. Cf. Rabelais, *The Works of Francis Rabelais*, vol. 2, 168 .
18. Dick, Die Gesta Romanorum nach der Innsbrucker Handschrift vom Jahre 1342, chap. 92.
19. Véronèse, "Secret," in Sallmann, ed., *Dictionnaire historique de la magie et des sciences occultes*, 656.
20. Van Haver, *Nederlandse incantatieliteratuur*, no. 549, 206.
21. D'Abano, *Heptameron*, in Agrippa von Nettesheim, *Opera*, vol. 1, 570.
22. Paris, Bibliothèque Nationale de France, new Latin acquisitions 7743, folio 251.
23. Cf. Lecouteux, *The Book of Grimoires*, 181–87. For more on the various encryption methods, see Bischoff, *Übersicht über die nichtdiplomatischen Geheimschriften des Mittelalters*, 1–27. See appendix 2.
24. Pradel, *Griechische und süditalienische Gebete*, 14.
25. *La Grande clavicola di Solomone*, 20. This has to do with a spirit summoning.
26. Bang, *Norske Hexeformularer og magiske Opskrifter*, no. 1095; Ohrt I, *Danmarks Trylleformler*, no. 1263.
27. Cf. Beck, "Die Bibliothek eines Hexenmeisters."
28. Wallberger, *Berühmtes Zauberbuch oder aufrichtige Entdeckung bewährter ungemeiner Geheimnisse*.

Page from a seventeenth-century Icelandic grimoire

Dictionary of Ancient Magic Words and Spells

From Abraxas to Zoar

*Whoever seeks to grasp this book
shall learn from it fine reason,
and several things he may hear from it
are good to keep in mind.*

          Thirteenth Century

You who wish to read this book, keep it secret the best you can and only divulge it to the one who merits it, who is worthy and well prepared for this art.

          Picatrix IV, 9, 26, anno 1256

May he who wishes to know the secrets, know to keep them secret and not give bread to dogs or pearls to swine.

      De electro [treatise on amber], circa 1570

A A A B E D Y E O H R ATT: To cause a girl to pursue you, you should write these letters on her clothing.

📖 Ohrt II, 79.

A A G G: Inscribed on wax in the shape of a cross, these letters allow a prisoner to free himself from his bonds; this seal should also be carried when one wishes to be invisible.

📖 Heidelberg, Germany, University Library, Cpg 369, folio 168 r°.

A : 2 X3 : H : X : I : R : 2 : m: To uncover the identity of someone who has stolen something from you, you should write these words and place them beneath your head for the whole night: the face of the thief will appear.

📖 Ohrt, II, 438.

ABA: This term appears in the spell + *Aba* + *Aluy* + *Abafroy* +*Agera* + *Procha,* and so on, which the person should speak when wishing to win at cards or another game, or he should carry it on his person, written on virgin parchment.

📖 Thiers I, 356, 410.

A B A D E P G P Ψ † † 2 A † P † β X: To find love, you should write these letters on your hand.

📖 Ohrt II, 79.

A. B. A. G. A. P.: To win the love of a young woman, write these letters on her right hand on a Thursday evening, then take the maiden's hand and press it over her chest.

📖 Bang, no. 1123.

ABARA BARBARICA BORDON CABRADU BRABARSABA: This spell is used to soothe bladder pain. It should be written on a male pig's bladder for a man and a sow's bladder for a woman, then attached over his or her belly. It is a variant of *Abracadabra*.

📖 Önnerfors, 27.

ABAS † ELIM † ABRATO † AGEBAT PROCHA: This must be written on a piece of tin and placed beneath the headboard of the person whose love you wish to win.

📖 *Secrets magiques pour l'amour*, no. XVII.

ABBAC, ABDAC, ISTAC: This is the opening for a lengthy spell convoking the spirits when the individual wishes to no longer be mocked or scorned:

Abbac, Abdac, Istac, Audac, Castrac, Cuac, Cusor, Tristator, Derisor, Detestator, Incantator.

We can probably take the names ending in *-or* for those of demons meaning "Smiter, Mocker, Curser, Enchanter."

📖 *Clavicules*, chap. 16.

ABBA † THEOS † BEHETIMYHAT: The opening words (the *Incipit*) of the twenty-second orison of the *Liber iuratus* (Book of Consecrations), in which the individual asks God to fortify his discernment and soul:

abba † theos † behetimyhat † hehem † ruhos † bethar † husurnhunt † hetarius † theos †

We can recognize several Greek words (*abba,* "father," *theos,* "God"); *ruhos* is most likely the "Greekified" Hebrew word *ruach,* meaning "spirit."

📖 *Liber iuratus,* chap. 33.

A, B, C, H, G: To reconcile individuals living in the same house but who hate each other, the following spell would be written on a piece of paper that was then placed beneath the doorsill over which all them had to cross:

A, b, c, h, g, g, T, g, v, x, o, o, g, k, F, s, z

📖 Vaitkevičienė, no. 1630 (spell from Poland).

ABEK/HABEK: A magic word that appears in an eleventh-century spell against epilepsy (*morbus comitalis*): *Horner Larci Habek Cisius elaoro hodier laciaon Virtus coeli libera pellet.* It can be found in later spells intended to stop hemorrhaging.

✦ *Abek, Wabek.*
📖 Heim, 226.

ABEK, WABEK, FABEK: Opening phrase for the Dutch and German *Charm of the Three Roses;* it should be repeated three times to stop bleeding.

📖 Van Haver, no. 40.

A B G D K E: These *caracteres* form the start of a long series found in the *Note* or *Bref of Charlemagne,* a text believed to have been written by Pope Leo III and given to Charlemagne in order to protect him "from enemies, swords, potions, serpents, and poisons." This phrase reappears in several Latin charms, most notably in the *Note of Saint Columban.* It is said that God gave it to the abbot Colomban and that the priest requested it before leaving for war. Skeptical, the priest experimented on a criminal to test the virtues of the spell, and the villain emerged unscathed from all the ordeals imposed on him. A copy made its way to Charlemagne by way of Pope Leo III. The *Note of Saint Columban* offers protection from thieves, curses, bad weather, epilepsy, and fire.

📖 *Galdrakver*, folio 9r°–10v°; Aymar, 331–32, 335, 339; Romano, "Guaritrici tradizionali nel Bresciano"; Zingerle, *Sitten, Bräuche und Meinungen*, 67, no. 573.

A B H Z P O B L 9 H B M G N: First part of a prescription for soothing the pains of childbirth. This must be written on a piece of paper with the name of the birth mother in the center:

A b h z P O b L 9 h b m g n
Subratum nome nex gr.

followed by these other words: † *Ecgitar* † *circabato* † *Bessiabato* † *Argon* † *vigora* † *tänet*. The paper is then placed in a leather pouch whose seam is on the right side. It must not have any knot or ribbon and should be attached to the individual during an odd-numbered hour.

📖 *Egyptian Secrets* II, 138.

ABIA: A term used in alliterative phrases such as *Abia Obia Sabia* or *Abia Dabia Fabia* (*Egyptian Secrets* has *Abiam, Dabiam, Fabiam*), which should be written or carved on a staff when seeking to strike someone from a distance, mainly a witch who attacks livestock, or when shoeing a wild horse. *Abia* is probably the abbreviation of a sentence from the Bible or the names of God. At the beginning of the eighteenth century it can be found in a spell for preventing hailstorms: † *AB* †† *IA* † combined with *SAB* † *Z*, *NDSMB* and *Agla*. *Z* is believed to refer to Zachariah and *B* to Benedict. Jean-Baptiste Thiers, who lived during the seventeenth century, was of the opinion that this word is derived from Abraxas, but other scholars believe its origin is Hebrew and offer the following interpretation: A(b), "father," B(en), "son," and Rua(ch), "spirit."

In early-nineteenth-century Switzerland and Germany, *Abia, Dabia, Fabia* was inscribed on a gun barrel in order to ensure its target was struck.

✦ *Hola Noa*.

📖 *Egyptian Secrets,* I, 149, 221; Thiers I, 364; Spamer, 369.

ABLA, GOT, BATA, BLEU: These words should be spoken to cause a weapon to dysfunction. *Abla* could represent the four letters of the beginning of the Jewish morning prayer: *aleph, beth, lamed* and *aleph*.
 📖 Honorius, 65.

ABLANATHANALBA: A word that means "you are our father"; it is endowed with magical properties and commonly used on Greek amulets and papyri. One example in the collection of the National Library of France (no. 177) depicts an armed spirit with serpents for legs and a rooster's head over the palindrome *Ablanathanalba* on one side. On the opposite side there is a winged god standing on the back of a reclining lion, with magical letters. This was all intended to protect the bearer from fear. A Greek papyrus, or curse tablet, dating from the second to fourth centuries, places it at the top of a series of words arranged in a triangle that shrinks one letter every line: *ablanathanalba; aeêiouô; iaeôbaphrenemoun; ôuoiêea; akrammachamarei.*

The phrase is also used in a reductive formula to combat fever:

ABLANATHANABLANAMACHARAMARACHARAMARACH
BLANATHANABLANAMACHARAMARACHARAMARA
LANATHANABLANAMACHARAMARACHARAMAR
ANATHANABLANAMACHARAMARACHARAMA
NATHANABLANAMACHARAMARACHARAM
ATHANABLANAMACHARAMARACHARA
THANABLANAMACHARAMARACHAR
ANABLANAMACHARAMARACHA
NABLANAMACHARAMARACH
ABLANAMACHARAMARA
BLANAMACHARAMAR
LANAMACHARAMA
ANAMACHARAM
NAMACHARA
AMACHAR
MACHA
ACH
A

It can also be found in a Greek charm for obtaining victory in the phrase: *ABLANATHANALBA AKRAMMACHAMARI PEPHNA PHO'ZA PHNEBENNOUNI NAACHTHIP... OUNORBA.*

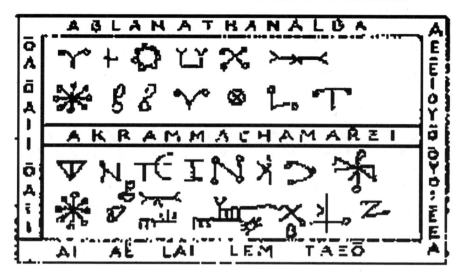

A Coptic amulet on papyrus that may date from the fourth century, found in Egypt, bears this phrase: *AKRAMMAJAMARI AABLANAPHANALBAA.* On a gem intended to inspire love, *Ablanathanalba* is written in a circle around the first name Faustina. A curse tablet found in Cypress shows the compound *ABLANATHANALBASISOPETRON.* On a phylactery discovered in Germany that was intended to protect several people, we read:

> *OYDAEAGANFOZL ... UNI Ia Ia Iai Sabaôth Adônai Ablanathanalba* Akramachari Semeseilam Sêsêngembarpharangês, io io io.*

📖 PGM III, 633–34; IV, 307ff; XIc, 107–121; XII, 107–121; XXXIII, 1–25 ; XXXVI, 187–88 and 211–30; Martinez, *Michigan Papyri XVI*; Mastrocinque, "Metamorfosi di Kronos," 118.

ABRA: Word of a spell intended to provide protection against a dwarf who was believed to transmit illnesses. † *Abra Iesus* † *Alabra Iesus* †

---

*A variant form is *Ablanaianabla.*

Galabra Iesus. This phrase is preceded by the equally widespread *thebal guttatim*.

📖 Berthoin-Mathieu, 155; Deonna, "Abra, abraca. La croix talisman de Lausanne."

AB : RA : CA ≡ D.A: — B. R: A.: To chase away a cold fever, these words are written on a piece of bread that is then given to the patient to eat. The letters form the word *Abracadabra!*

📖 Bang, no. 1150.

Ab. Ra: Ca≡ D.: A:= C.R: a

ABRAC: To reconcile people who hate each other, the words *Abrac, amon, filon* should be written on a piece of bread and given to them to eat.

✦ *Arac*.

📖 Weyer, *Opera Omnia*, IV, 7.

ABRACADABRA: This term was already known as a magical word in the second century BCE. It appears in an amulet from that era in the form of *a ba ga da* in Greek letters. According to some, this could be the acrostic form of the Hebrew *Ha brakha dabra*, "The blessing has spoken"; הברכה דברה others maintain it is a derivative of Abraxas. It is used in a shrinking pattern against fevers and pains. By making the word shorter and shorter, the pains or illness are encouraged to gradually diminish:

Abracadabra
Bracadabra
Racadabra
Acadabra
Cadabra
Adabra
Abra
Bra
Ra
A

The Greek papyri offer some interesting variations, such as the sequence based on *Akrakanarba* (Ακρακαναρβα, κρακαναρβα, καναρβα,

αναρβα, αρβα, ρβα, βα, βα, and κρακαναρβα, καναρβα, ρακαναρβα, ακαναρβα, καναρβα, αναρβα, καρβα, αρβα, ρβα, α). It was basically passed down by the doctor of Sulpicius Severus (in the third century), Quintus Serenus Sammonicus, in his *Liber Medicinalis* (verses 935–39), which prescribes its wearing when one is stricken with double tertian fever. It should be noted that this spell enjoyed wide use during the Great Plague of London (1665–1666).

In medieval Italy, in Venetian, we find the spell: † *Arabra* † *Arabrum* † *Brototin* † *Soromi* † *Bretotiamin* †. And we find in Columbia: *Brac Cabrac Cabra Cadabrac Cabracam.*

The Lesser Key of Solomon (II, 8) offers the following variation in the conjuration of the sword used in magical operations: *Abrahach, Abrach, Abracadabra*. This spell is found again in the "Consecration of the Athame (ritual dagger)" in *The Book of Shadows* of the neopagan Wiccan movement, created by Gerald Brousseau Gardner around 1940–1950:

> I conjure thee,
> O Athame
> By these names, Abrahach, Abrach, Abracadabra,
> That thou servest me for a strength and
> defence in all magical operations
> against all mine enemies, visible and invisible . . .

The novelist Dan Brown believes this word comes from an ancient Aramaic magic spell—*Avrach Ka Dabra*—that means "I create by speaking" (*The Lost Symbol,* chap. III, 3). Everyone sees things their own way.

This prescription is offered in Lithuania for treating erysipelas: spread some butter on bread, and on it write this word, subtracting two letters each time, recite three Hail Marys, sign oneself three times, and eat the bread at dawn, dusk, and at dawn again.

> *Abracadabra*
> *bracadabr*
> *racadab*
> *acada*
> *cad*
> *a*
> *Fikus Mikus Arabikus*

✦ *Triangle.*

📖 Dornseiff, 64; Heim, 491; PGM II, 1ff, 64ff; Werner, no. 8, 197; Vaitkevičienė, no. 1372.

ABRACH: The following variation of the spell *Abracadabra* can be read on an amulet meant to be worn around the neck:

† *Abrach* † *lam* † *Abrahc* † *la* † *Abrach* † *l* † *Abrach* † *Abrach* † *Abrac* † *Abr* † † *ab* † *A* † *B* †

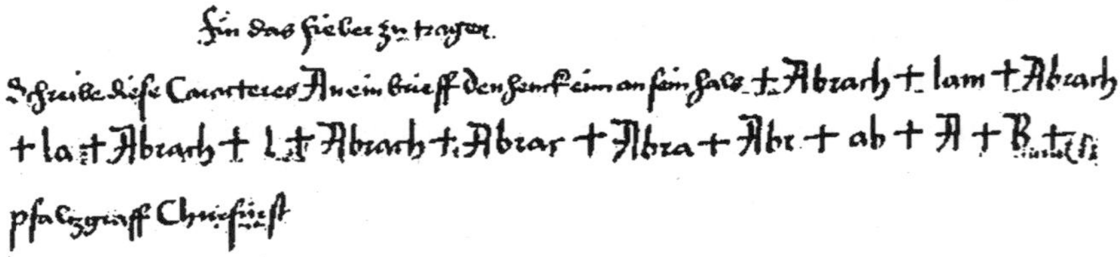

[handwritten manuscript text]

📖 Heidelberg, Germany, University Library, Cpg 267, folio 11 r°.

ABRACHA † ABRAC LAUS: Invocation addressed to God to cure fevers. The spell is spoken over the patient and an Our Father is added: *Abracha* † *Abrac Laus* † *Agyos* † *Sanctus* † *Sanctus* † *Sanctus Fortis Et Immortalis*. It can be found in this form in the *Sachet accoucheur:*

> plenesmo. *Abrocala* ✡ *Abra* ✡ *Abraca* ✡ *Abracalaps* ✡ *Abralaps* ✡ *Abracalas* ✡ ✡ ✡ *Abracalaps* ✡ *Abrocalaps*. *Abraca* ✡ *Abracala* ✡ *Abra*. F.G. ✡ ✡ ✡ *Naqui nostros castatunta mihi Jhesus Christus bris quod dedit bris quod tulitz bris quod dedit* טט *Christus ursim in nomine Domini*. May the Lord be with you, the Father, the Son, and the Holy Ghost. He who carries this note on his person, fevers shall flee, and if he is stricken, the fever will weaken immediately.

📖 Braekman, 66; Aymar, 334.

ABRACULA/ABRACULUS: A word featured in a reductive spell intended to cure fever. It should be written on a note to be worn around the neck. It appears in a wide variety of forms in the manuscripts. A conjuration in the *Book of Incantations* gives a related term, *Abracalos,* in this spell: *abini abyndo abyncola abracalos pyel thyel syel* (folio 49 v°).

📖 Heidelberg, Germany, University Library, Cpg 267, folio 12 r°; 16 v°.

Für das fieber

Schreib an ein zettell diese wordt + Abzzarula + Bzarula + Auzarula + Zarula Arula + Cula + ula + la + a + den solstu eim an sein halß henken, neun dage Er soll an dem ersten dage neun pr ñr vnd neun aue Mia beden dornach alle dage eins mrnder Bis die neun dage umb sein dan verbren den zettell h Z Cc̄r̄.

Ein segen für den fröser

Diese wordt los ein an sein halß dragen An ein zettell geschrieben funffzehen dage Er soll auch bedten vff Reßen knien den ersten dage funfftzehen pr ñr vnd xv aue Mia Vnd alle dage eins mrnder V, an den leitzten dag Chr im den zettell von dem halß Vnd verbren in doch soll er garr nit in den zettell sehen Nun volgen die wordt Abramlauũ + Abramlaũ + Abramla + Abramil + Abraru + Abrar + Abra + Abr + ab + A + Auch des kranken nauff namen darzu hanßell. Jilge ẽr̃.

Ein Segen für das fieber

Schreibe vff Capier + + + + Abramlus Abramla Abraru Abrara Abra.
+ + + + Vnd henckts den siechen an halß Er wirdt gesunt hinaw.

ABRAHAM JULITA: Magic words to be used against fever in reductive diagrams in the same way as *Abracadabra*.

ABRAHAM TE ALLIGAT † YSSAC TE TENEAT † IACOB TE OSTENDAT † (May Abraham bind you, Isaac seize you, Jacob reveal you): To prevent a thief from getting away it is necessary to draw four crosses at the four outside corners of all doors and to write the phrase cited above on the inward facing side of these doors. This spell dates from around 1500.

  Variants: *Abraham † liga † Isacc † Retinet † Jacob † Retuzet* ; *Enovia Abraham ligarit Jsacia Jacobs et ußit Redutaat.*
  📖 Ohrt I, no. 1246; Spamer, 248.

ABRAXAS, ABRASAX: This divine, cosmic name appears in the magical papyri of ancient Greece and on a large quantity of amulets, on so many amulets in fact that they have become synonymous with this term. In the *Abrasax* form, which designates the god of the year, it contains seven letters representing the seven days of the week, of which the *pséphos,* meaning the sum of the numbers represented by their constituent letters, is 365—the number of days in a year. Its use goes back to the Basilidian sect (second century).

A lead tablet conserved in the Louvre Museum contains an adjuration of the spirit of a dead man "by Barbaratham Cheloumbra Barouch Adonaï and by Abraxas," in which a fragment of the Jewish prayer "*barouch aththa Adonai*" (blessed by the Lord) can be recognized. Another one housed in the Cairo Museum contains a charm and an adjuration "by Abrathabrasax." A later one dating from the fifth century includes the phrase "Lord Sisirô Sisiphermou Cnouôr Abrasax."

The name is also found on a phylactery intended to provide protection against demons and fevers: ABRASAX ABRASICHO'OU.

This is what François-André-Adrien Pluquet (1716–1790), archbishop of Albi, then Cambrai, tells us:

> Basilides, who adopted Pythagorean philosophy, concluded that nothing was more apt at attracting the beneficial influences of this Intelligence, that the expression of the number three hundred sixty-five and as numbers were expressed using the letters of the alphabet, he chose from the alphabet the letters whose sequence could express three hundred sixty-five and this sequence of letters formed the word Abraxas. As the word Abraxas has the virtue of powerfully attracting the influence of the producing intelligence of the world, this name was carved on stones that were called Abraxas, a prodigious number of which can be found in studies throughout Europe. As Pythagoras presumed the producing intelligence of the world resided in the sun, the word of Abraxas was joined with the image of the sun as an explanation of the virtues attributed to it. People of this era were stubbornly obsessed with the virtue of Talismans, and this is how Abraxas spread almost everywhere & instead of the sun, different symbols were carved on the Abraxas that were most apt at depicting its characteristics and finally the favors one expected of it & which one wished granted, as can be see by an Abraxas that depicts a man mounted of a bull with this inscription: restore this woman's womb to its proper place you who govern the course of the sun.

📖 PGM LXXXIX, 1–27; Heim, 481, 537, 542ff.; Bernant, 289, 291, 341ff.; Dieterich; Pluquet, 471; Barb, "Abraxas Studien"; Harrauer; Sallmann, 17ff.

ABRE ET ABREMON ET ABRENDE ET CONSECRAMINA: These spells were hung at the necks of fearful men and women. *Abrende* is the deformation of *Abremonte*.

📖 Aymar, 346.

ABREMONTE: The beginning of an exorcism intended to free a possessed individual. The exorcist places his left hand on the individual's head and his right hand over his or her mouth, then speaks this into both ears (*ambas aures*):

> *Abremonte Abrya, Abremonte consacramentaria, Ypar Ypar Ytumba opote celacent alaphie.*

Then firmly grasping the possessed individual, he speaks the incantation that opens with these words: "I conjure you, evil spirit, by the terrible name of God Agla and by Agla Helene, all-powerful name of God . . ."

◆ Abre.
📖 Franz II, 569.

ABRIA SOLLITIE OAT: To cause the return of a stolen piece of property, a person would write these words on a piece of lead, then break the lead in two and place one piece above the door and the other below it: *Abria Sollitie Oat I Sachi Redempt, Jacob Vomun, Redugbit.* The first part of the phrase can be interpreted as, "You must return the property/the thing."

📖 Bang, no. 1118.

ABRIDO ÆRIGETU SAEP RETE OBRIGAT: Phrase intended to stop bleeding in an Old English charm. It can also be found in a tenth-century English charm in Latin in the form: *abrido ærigetu saep rete obrigate.*

📖 Berthoin-Mathieu, 155ff.

ABROKOŁYOTUM: In Poland when a dog is rabid, these words should be written on paper that it is then given to the dog to eat with bread:

Abrokołyotum
Brokołyotum
Rokołyotum
Okołyotum
Kołyotum
Ołyotum
Łyotum
Yotum
Otum
Tum
Um
M

📖 Vaitkevičienė, no. 1374.

ABRUTIM ABRUTIM GEBRUTIM GEBRUTIM: This phrase forms part of a complex ritual that takes place when the moon is in Gemini, and it must be repeated twenty times. It is accompanied by the slaughter of a rooster and with fumigations. The purpose is to cause "a figure" to appear who will grant the wish that is asked of it.

📖 *Picatrix*, Book IV, chapter 3: *Gáyat al-Hakîm*, 311.

ABTAN, ABYNISTAN, ZORATAN: These are allegedly the words God spoke to Moses when he ascended the mountain: *Abtan, Abynistan, Zoratan Juran Nondieras, Potarte Faijs Alapeina Pohnij Sacrofcium.* With these words the prophet speaks to the angels that seal the four quarters of the world. If one wishes to perform miracles, it is necessary to fast for three days and to be chaste and pure before uttering these words.

📖 *Semiphoras* II, chapter 2.

ABUENOP: When an individual has crushed into powder the hippomane of a mare in order to win someone's love, one fills an apple with this powder and places a skin over it on which one writes the name of the person desired along with this word and a *caractere*.

📖 *Clavicules: Les véritable clavicules de Salomon*, 66.

AB UMASIS: To make a garter that will let you travel seven leagues in one hour, you must capture a young wolf and slit its throat with a new knife at the hour of Mars. Its hide should be cut into thumb-sized garters, and on one side you will write with the animal's blood and on the other, your own: *Ab umasis cadis anba carit in fortitudine cibi illius.* This is a corruption of the biblical phrase: *Qui cum surrexisset comedit et bibit et ambulavit in fortitudine cibi illius* (I Kings 19:1).

Variant: *Le dragon rouge: Adhumatis cados ambulavit fortitudine cibi illius.*

📖 *Libro de segretto e di magia,* 5. (see entry for LIBRO DE SEGRETTO)

AC : P : X : ☉ : When someone wishes to find hidden treasure, he must have in his possession a hazel wand that has been cut two days before the new moon. This wand is used to draw a circle (see illustration below) with crosses on the border.

In order to be protected against the devil or spirit that comes at your request, it is necessary to have in your possession a long sequence of *caracteres*:

Ac : P : X : ☉ : y3 : V : N : y : Ac : y : Z : X : M : A : 4 : K : y : 72 K 36 X Ø : X ... B.

📖 Black Book of Jeløen; Bang no. 1443.

†. A. C. D. A. S. †.: According to a legend found in many grimoires, Pope Leo III allegedly wrote a short spell including *caracteres* that offered protection from the plague, demons, poison, serpents, and curses, which he allegedly sent to Charlemagne. Here is the version from the *Sachet accoucheur:*

> †. *a. c. d. a. s.* †. *p. c. e. aa. N. S. e. b. a. n. m. a. e. n. p. ofc. n. n. p. ofc. n; p. el. x. p. h..* He who bears these caracteres shall not die by weapons † *Jotha* † *Adonai* † *Christus* † *Job* † *Ethaphon. t. x. o. a. n. e. p. p. t. m. a. ee. x.* Christ vanquishes † Christ reigns † Christ governs † Lord God is my aid, [my] foundation †. R. † R. X.

A manuscript from London's British Library gives an entirely different composition that does not contain these letters but only divine names and titles.

📖 Aymar, 331, 339; London, British Library, Sloane 2584, folio 45 v°.

ACE ROMEIE ECLENN NECEROM: To counter a toothache, these words would be written down, then tossed to a dog.

📖 Bang, no. 1108.

ACHIT, PACKEIT, ALMACIT: These three words form part of a ritual dating from around 1752 whose purpose is the recovery of stolen property. The words are written on a note, then the note is placed inside the incision made with a knife in a piece of smoked lard, then the entire thing is burned with a candle while reciting the incantation five times. The operation is repeated for five days in a row in the morning, and the individual writes *Peda peet moum Segum Calia* over his door and *omnes morche* under it.

📖 Spamer, 236.

ACHIZECH: To prevent birds from eating freshly sown seed, a toad and a bat are buried in a pot of fresh dirt and then this word is written on the inside of the lid with the blood of a crow. The object is then buried in the freshly sown field.

📖 *Petit Albert,* 335.

ACKO: The following spell is written on paper to heal fever. It should be written on virgin parchment and the ink used diluted in water that is given to the patient to drink.

  acko MENEIBOS cvpω aaopNe avτvRa. Fekevιωιk

 📖 *Antidotarium Bruxellense* 23–29, 368.

ACOTOS EXFETEN CANABO: Spell from a ritual intended to summon a person whose presence is desired.
 Variant: *Actor, Actus, Exfeton, Canaba.*
 📖 Werner, no. 1, 195.

ACRÆ. ÆRCRE. ÆRNEM.: The opening of a long phrase intended to protect one from empoisoned breath and all swellings caused by poison. It is necessary on a Friday to churn butter not blended with any water that comes from a cow or doe that is all one color while chanting the litany over it, then the Our Father nine times and the following phrase nine times:

> *Acræ. ærcre ærnem. nadre. ærcuna hel. ærnem. nipærn. ær; asan; buipine. adcrice. ærnem. meodre. ærnem. æpern. em. allum. honor. ucus. idar. adceri. cunolari. raticamo. helæ. icas cpita. hæle. tobær.; tera. fueli. cui; robater. plana. uili.*

The first three words could mean "declaration against blood, against poison," and *nadre ærcuna hel* could mean "slay the viper with a magic spell." Scholars have suggested the following translation: "May my magic spell heal, that which healed the Christ in whom is the spell, he who had all the pains" for *raticamo . . . tera fueli.*

In an abbreviated format that contains some variations, we find this incantation on the creation of a "holy onguent:" *Acre arcre arnem nona ærnem beoðor arnem nidren arcun cunað ele harassan fidine.*

 📖 Berthoin-Mathieu, 56, 106.

ACRIUZ, FENDEYUZ: To win the love of a sovereign, make a wax doll with his name on it and stick a new silver needle in it while saying: *Acriuz, Fendeuyz, Nephalez, Feyeduz.*

The wax doll is then buried and a suffumigation made. When

the smoke begins rising, say these words: *Acderuz, Madurez Feyleuz, Hueryreliz*. Then request the help of the spirits in order to inspire the king's love and friendship.

In the Arabic source of the *Picatrix*, the *Gâyat al-Hakîm*, the magic words take the following form:

1. *Aqarjûs, Ġidâjûs, Jâlihâs, Jahîdûs*
2. *Akârûs, Mandûrâs, Fîlâhûs, Warmâlîs*

📖 *Picatrix* III, 10, 14; *Gâyat al-Hakîm*, 266.

ACTATOS: The first word of the spell *Actatos Catipla Bejouran Itapan Marnutus*, to be spoken to learn the plans of the infernal powers and be given the means to fight and overcome them. One must have possession of a talisman on which *Actatos Bejouran Marnutus* is carved.

📖 *Trésor*, 184b–85b.

† ADA † † ABA EBE †† THANAT DO † ZONCHA AGOLA † ZABOHA †: By writing these words on a parchment with wolf's blood, then wrapping it in a cloth with argental mercury, and then carrying it on one's person, one will be honored and all his wishes shall be granted; if this object is held before a lock, it shall open. This recipe can be found in the Danish *Cyprianus,* a widespread grimoire, but the words are presented in a slightly altered arrangement:

† *Ada* † *A Ba* † *ebe* † † *Tanat do* † *Zoncha Agola* † *Za Boha* †.

📖 *Egyptian Secrets* II, 123.

ADABRA † DRABRA † RABRA † ABRA † BRA † RA † A: This phrase is valuable for all kinds of afflictions; it should be worn at the throat for five, six, or nine days, during which time seven Our Fathers should be spoken each day. This is one of many variations of *Abracadabra*. See also *Aladabra*, which falls into the same category.

📖 Braekman, no. 76.

ADAM: The name of the first man according to biblical tradition is used in many spells and was once used as an amulet. It can also be found in a benediction intended to ensure a good birth: *Adam Bedam*

Alam Betur Alam Botum, or also: † *Adam* † *Adam* † *Adam* † *veni foras* † *Christi te vocat* † *sancta Maria, libera ancillam tuam N.* For Marcellus of Bordeaux, the term was good for protecting dovecotes, and the *Geoponika* of Emperor Porphyrogenitus explicitly states that Adam, in this case, should be written at the four corners of the structure. According to Jean-Baptiste Thiers, it was still used in the seventeenth century. According to Maiolus (1520–1599), when a woman was in labor, the Jews wrote *Adam havah Chutz Lilith* on all the walls of her room and the names of the three angels, Senoi, Sansenoi, and Samangeloph, on the inside of the door. This name can be found connected with that of Eli in a prescription for protection against any enmity that combines Kabbalistic symbols, the names of the Three Magi, and the opening of Luke 4:30: *Jesus autem transiens per medium horum ibat.*

✦ Birth.

📖 Franz II, 201; Heim, 353; Thiers I, 361; Bang, no. 1089.

† A DANDA † LIBERANDA † PRO VERMIS † ESTOMACA †: Phrase from an Occitan medical prescription dating from the fourteenth century, intended for healing a toothache. It was written on paper and then dissolved in water. The pain would disappear as the letters of the words faded. We should note that there is no connection between this phrase and the desired purpose. In fact, it can be translated as, "To give for deliverance from stomach worms."

📖 Princeton, New Jersey, Princeton University, Garret 80, folios 5 v°–6r°.

AD : CER : RUB: To see in dream the person who has robbed you, this must be written on a piece of paper that is then placed beneath your right ear.

📖 Bang, no. 1091.

ADIBAGA SABAOTH ADONAY: This is the start of a phrase whose purpose is to destroy all spells and summon the individual who caused all the harm. One takes the heart of a dead animal, places it on a clean plate, and then sticks nine hawthorn spikes into it while saying:

Adibaga Sabaoth Adonay contrà ratout prisons prerunt fini unixio paracle gossum. Then two more thorns are stuck in it while saying: *Qui fussum mediator agros gaviol valax,* two others declaimed: *Landa zazar valoi sator saluxio paracle gossum,* then two following with the words: *Mortus cum fine sunt et pert flagellationem Domini noseri Jesu Christi,* and the last two while saying: *Avir sunt devnat vous paracletur strator verbonum offisum fidando.* One then makes his request and pierces the heart with a nail.

📖 Honorius, 80.

ADNÂLÎS: To part a man from a woman and inspire enmity between them, make two hollow *volts,* or dolls, bearing their names and prepare a mixture for both that consists of the bile of a black cat and a pig, and so on, which is then poured inside them. For that of the woman, blend various ingredients that one then melts, then the chest of the doll is pierced with a needle while saying: *Adnâlîs, Baljûrâs, Mandûris, Ba'jûlis.*

Then prepare bdellium, opoponax (resins) and the fat of a black cat and a black dog, and suffumigate the *volt,* or doll, while saying a spell that opens with: *Mimûrâs, Handânûs, Bahwâlûs.*

✦ *O Hûdis.*
📖 *Gâyat al-Hakîm,* 269–71.

ADONAI, ADONAY (אדני): This means "Supreme Teacher" in Hebrew. It is one of the names of God in the Old Testament, and the Jews pronounced Adonaï, the ineffable Tetragrammaton, *YHWH.* It was much used in magic during the Hellenic era, and it remains quite popular today. It frequently appears in the lists of divine names for spells. For example, it is used in this fifteenth-century spell for healing eye problems: Blow then upon his eyes and say: "*Christus vincit, Christus regnat, Christus imperat. Ayos Ayos Ayos, Adonay Sabaoth, Adonay Emmanuel. Benedictio partis, etc., descendat, et introeat spiritus tecum et liberet te ab omni malo. Amen. Sana, domine, oculos famuli tui N. sicut sanasti oculos Tobye.*"

📖 Heim, no. 523, 532; Franz I, 409, 430; II, 169, 497; Dalman, *Der Gottesname Adonaj eine seine Geschichte.*

ADONAY SABAOTH, CADAS ADONAY AMARA: The third *Semiphoras of Solomon*. Adam used it when he spoke with the spirits and the dead; when he questioned them they would give him the answers he sought when constrained by these words (*Semiphoras*).

The spell can be found in more complete form and including two series in the *Conjuration of Monday* in the *Liber incantationum* (The Book of Incantations).

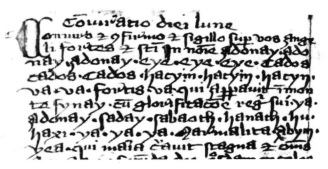

1. *Adonay. Adonay. Adonay. Eye. Eye. Eye. Cados. Cados. Cados. Hatyn. Hatyn. Hatyn. va. va.*
2. *ya. Adonay. Saday. Sabaoth. Hanath. hu. Haxi. ya. ya. ya. Marmalita. Abym. yea.*

📖 *Liber incantationum,* Bavarian National Library, ms. Clm 809, folio 88 v°.

ADRA ADRATA ADRATTA: In the fifteenth century, if a prisoner wanted to free himself of his chains, he needed to write this phrase on the padlock and follow it with the letters: *f. A.K. O. q. t.*

📖 Heidelberg, Germany, University Library, Cpg 369, folio 168 r°.

ADRA ADRATA, ASDRA, BILLAL BELIAL, ALIAL: This phrase is included in a prayer intended to drive away all evil spirits from the house as well as "the damnable enchanters and enchantresses." The conjuration that follows is made with divine names.

 📖 Van Haver, no. 1031.

ÆAS AIAET AIAS IN AOM INI IL BULI: This is a phrase to be written on a piece of paper and then placed under one's pillow in order to uncover the identity of a thief; the guilty party will appear in a dream.

 ✦ *Ad.*
 📖 Espeland, § 7.

AEÊIOUÔ: A magic word that was carved on numerous Greek amulets discovered in Egypt.

 📖 Bonner, *Studies in Magic Amulets Chiefly Graeco-Egyptian*, no. 2.

† ÆGRIN THON STRUHT: These words are the opening to a long phrase in an Old English charm intended to halt nosebleeds:

> + *Ægrin thonn struht fola ærgren. tart strut onntria enn piathu morfona onnhel. ara ca leo þ gruth veron. +++. fil cron /></ inro cron aer crio ærmio aær leno.*

Several terms have been identified as coming from a highly distorted Old Irish: *sruth fola,* "bleedings"; *gruth,* "curdled milk"; the Old English *onhæl,* "sick." +++ meanwhile is an Irish spelling for *neither* or *in.*

 📖 Berthoin-Mathieu, 154; Storms, no. 77.

AETE BANDTE, ZU BRANTE BEDE. † † †: When a horse has thrown someone, one must say these words very softly three times while passing the left foot over the painful area.

 📖 *Egyptian Secrets* II, 163.

AFA AFCA NOSTRA: To ensure that rifles and muskets fail, it is necessary to speak these words while looking down their barrels. Saying these words backward will cancel what you have done.

 📖 *Egyptian Secrets* II, 32.

AFRIASS, AESTEIAS: This is the start of a phrase intended to kill the "worm" gnawing on the digit of a man or horse. The following phrase is written on a paper to be wrapped around the ailing limb:

> *Afriass, aesteias, Srus, Srus, Sras,*
> *Atestoos, Xaaja † se do † da da †*
> *Abia Am bles † Greem Er A. ran † C y y † Um † † †*

The "worm" is the given interpretation of the disease's origin. It always represents a malefic entity.

📖 *Egyptian Secrets* II, 108.

A. F. S.: To cause a cold fever to vanish, these letters are written on almonds. The patient should eat them one after another at the onset of the illness:

> *A. F. S.*
> *F. S. A.*
> *S. A. F.*

These letters, which include an error, are most likely abbreviations for *Artus, Pratus, Sartus,* a phrase that appeared in 1790 in a prescription against apoplexy.

✦ *Artus.*
📖 Bang, no. 1157.

AGALRIA PIDHOL GARIA ANANUS QEPTA: In order to prevent an enemy from replying, speak these words to him. The first word is a distortion of *Agla,* the abbreviation of four Hebrew words—*aieth, gadol, leolam, Adonaï*—that form the phrase: "You rule for eternity, Lord." This comes from the Jewish prayer *Shemoneh esreh.* The last two words are probably a version of *ANANIZEPTA,* an acrostic of the phrase: *Antidotum Nazareni auferat necem intoxicationis santificet alimenta poculaque trinitas Amen,* which is, among other things, a protective spell against the plague. The following words can be read on a fifteenth-century lozenge-shaped pendetive found near Middleham Castle in 1985:

> *Ecce agnus dei qui tollit peccata mundi—Tetragrammaton—Ananizapta.*

✦ *ANANIZEPTA, Agla.*
📖 BaK, no. 75.

AGATA † SAGATA † AMEN: "These letters or *caracteres*" should be written on a piece of buttered bread and given to the patient to eat in the evening. They combat a toothache.
    📖 Bang, no. 1148.

1 AGERAM 2 SARAGOEN 3 ALAGON 4 SALAGON: To fight against a toothache, these words are written on a piece of bread that is given to the patient to eat for four mornings in a row. This is why the Black Book (grimoire) from Fron, Norway, numbers them.

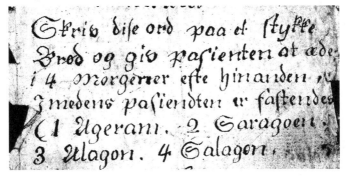

AGERIN NAGERIN VAGERIN JAGERIN IPAGRIN SIPIA: To contend against a toothache, one should write these words on a piece of paper. This paper should then be cut into three pieces and the first piece should be placed on the sufferer's tooth at night. The paper should be spit into the fire the following morning. Repeat the operation with the other two pieces and the tooth will be cured. This prescription can be found in various Scandinavian grimoires dating from 1780 on, with *Spagerin-Sepia* as the final words. Another instructs the individual to write *Jageron* on bread the first day, *Ageron* the second, *Nageron* the third, *Vageron* the fourth, and *Sepia* the fifth and to toss the last one into the forest or to a dog.

✦ *Ageron.*
📖 BBE, 85; Bang, no. 998, no. 1016; no. 1022; Espeland, no. 31.

AGERON JEGERON NEGERON SIPIA: These words need to be written on a bank note that is then placed on the ailing tooth to cure it. The word *Sipia* is then tossed to a dog. This phrase is also used in the form of *Ageront, Nageront Seheont* against apoplexy.
- ✦ *Agerin, Artus.*
- 📖 BBE, 87; Bang, no. 1127.

AGIA: ADULLA AULLA: A phrase whose purpose is to cause a woman or girl to love you. It is to be written on a ribbon that is then handed to the desired woman with your right hand.
- 📖 Bang, no. 1129.

A. G. J. A. B. J. C. A. E. S. Q. S. L.: For an epileptic's epilepsy. These *caracteres* should be drawn on a silver ring and worn on the index finger of the right hand. The first four letters are a deformation of *Agla,* one of the secret names of God.
- 📖 Braekman, no. 35.

AGLA: It is common knowledge that these four letters are most likely the initials of four Hebrew words—*aieth, gadol, leolam, Adonaï,* or *Atlah Gabor Leolam Adonay*—which form a phrase that means, "You rule for eternity Lord." This phrase comes from a Jewish prayer, the *Shemoneh esreh.* Like many magic words, *Agla* can be found in a variety of spells; in the tenth century it could be found in the form *Ogla,* in an ordeal spell—in the exorcism of the possessed—and it enters into the manufacture of various phylacteries. The following phrase can be read on a fifteenth-century silver ring:

AG
LA   AVEMARIA GRACIA PLE.

We find inscribed on another ring, this time of English origin: *AGLA. THALCVT. CALCVT. CATTAMA.* A fourteenth-century gold Italian ring is carved with: + *AGLA* + *AD///OS* + *VDROS* + *IDROS* + *THEBAL* + *GVT* + *G////////*

The word is used in charms against spells and against fevers, in which case it would be written on a Host, and against unclean spirits. To stop a nosebleed, *Agla* would be written on the patient's forehead and a prayer recited to the Virgin.

To stop a hemorrhage, it is necessary to write, for example: *Consummatum est* † *agla,* with one's own blood, which can also be seen in the *Charm of Longinius,* where it should be written on the hand and accompanied by two crosses: † *agla* †.

Agla works against fevers in the following way. You should take three Hosts and write on the back of the first one and on its outer perimeter: † *on* † *Jhesus* † *on* † *leo* † *on* † *filius* †, then † *A* † *g* † *l* † *a* in the middle. On the second write: † *on* † *omg* † *on* † *aries* † *on* † *agnus* †, and in the middle: † *te* † *tra* † *gra* † *ma* † *ton* †. The third Host should bear these phrases: † *on* † *pater* † *on* † *gloria* † *on* † *mundus,* while on the back *Jhesus nazarenus* † *crucifixus* † *Rex* † *judeorum* † *sit medicina mea* should be written. "Each day you should recite five Our Fathers and five Hail Marys."

A fifteenth-century German manuscript includes the following magical prescription against poisoning:

> For one who has been poisoned by poison. Write the following words on three sheets of virgin parchment and swallow them, one in the morning, one at noon, and one in the evening. And if one has been victim of a poisoner, the poison will leave at once and he will be healed. Here are the words: † *Agla* ††† *effrecga* ††† *agla* † *refoa* †††

In *The Lesser Key of Solomon, Agla* also appears on the fourth pentacle of Mars.

For a difficult birth, *Agla* can be found in the *Charm of Saint Suzanne,* combined with a very popular phrase: *Christus vincit † Christus regnat † Christus imperat † a † g † l † a † Amen.* A birthing charm from Upper Auvergne, whose contents partially date from the early Middle Ages, was opened in 1925, and our phrase was discovered in the following form:

† *a † G † l a agyos † o theos † yskyros † emanuel † omnipotens virtus in terra celum omnipotens olimphi . . .*

In the *Charm of Job,* which is intended to kill worms, in other words, certain forms of the disease entity, *Agla* appears in the terminating phrase: *in nomine Patris alaia agla†et filij messyas†et Spiritus sancti†sorchistin†Amen.*

Against sacred fire one must say: *Jot † het † agla † hayman † hewaw†;* the words that delivered the children from the furnace (Daniel 3:51–90).

In a fifteenth-century divination ritual cited by Jean-Baptiste Thiers, it is necessary to say *Aglati, Aglata, Calin, Cala* when summoning the seraphim Uriel. Thiers also provides other phrases featuring *Agla*. Here is one that spares its bearer from all danger:

† *Agla Pentagrammaton † On † Athanatos † Anafarcon †, des armes Barnasa † Leutias † Bucella † Agla † Agla † Tetragrammaton † etc. Conjuro vos omnia arma, etc. Obsecro te Domine Fili Dei, etc. Abba Pater, miserere mei, etc.*

Agla is used to dull the cutting edge of a blade: after one has spoken the incantation in the name of the blood of the Lord, one must say four times: † *panthon † genton † Aglay † pater noster.*

Agla has been written on amulets since the Middle Ages to provide protection from fire. In a Dutch phrase against conflagrations, *Agla* forms part of the invocation and is one of the names of God.

Heli, Heloim, Sothar, Emanuël, Saboath, Agla, Tetragrammaton, Hagios, Othuos, Ischyros, Athanatos, Jehova, Adonai, Sasay, Messias

This should be written on the house, which is then sprinkled with holy water.

But a slightly richer version of the same phrase can be found in the *Thesaurus exorcismorum,* where it is used to determine if a person is being tortured by unclean spirits (*vexatur a spiritibus immundis*). From the fourteenth to fifteenth century era we find the following conjuration in a German manuscript written in Latin:

> Take the head of the possessed individual into your left hand and place the thumb of your right hand in his mouth while speaking these words in both ears: *"Abremonte abrya, abremonte consacramentaria ypar ypar ytumba opote alacent alaphie."* Then grasp the individual firmly and recite these incantations: I conjure you, evil spirits, by the terrible name of God Agla and by the very powerful name of God Agla Helene . . .

In another fifteenth-century exorcism ritual, the exorcist must place the possessed on top of a cross drawn in chalk in front of the altar and encircled by the three magic names: Agla, Gaba, Emmanuel.

Agla is also used against evil spells and demons. For example, one long charm contains the "sacred words" (*heijlich woort*): agla † ende tetragrammaton †.

To communicate with a spirit, it is summoned and the "sacred words" that follow are then spoken: *ala drabra ladra dabra rabra afra brara agla et alpha et omega.*

Toothaches can be cured by wearing a note with † *Agla* † *Tetragrammaton* † *Emanuel* † followed by "Christ vanquishes," and so forth around the neck.

A sixteenth-century charm uses this magic word to uncover the identity of a thief with the help of a sieve or a strainer and scissors. The spell caster addresses the utensil with a triple incantation: to the three individuals of the Trinity; then to the Virgin Mary, to the patriarchs, prophets, apostles, evangelists, martyrs, confessors, virgins, and widows; and finally to the four elements and to the four cardinal points, followed by the coercive phrase: "I command you by the powerful name Agla..."

The *Agrippa*, a pamphlet of magic that was once widespread in the French countryside and the subject of legend, has passed down an "Exorcism of the aerial spirits" that offers us some interesting information. Lot allegedly heard the name *Agla*, which is what spared his life as well as that of his family (*per nomen Dei Agla quod Loth audivit, et factus salvus cum sua familia*). *Agla* also forms part of the three secret names (*per haec tria nomina secreta Agla, On, Tetragrammaton*). These two details can also be found in the Grimoire of Pope Honorius (*Le livre des conjurations*), printed in Rome in 1670. *Agla* is also cited in the *Agrippa* as part of an invocation of the angels of the four parts of the world. Their names must be written inside a magic circle, then the following incantation must be spoken:

> *O vos omnes, adjuro atque contestor per sedem Adonay, per Agios, Otheos, Ischyros, Athanatos, Paracletus, Alpha et Omega, et per haec tria nomina secreta, Agla, On, Tetragrammaton, quod hodie teneatis adimplere quod cupio.*
>
> [I implore you, all of you, and summon you by the throne of Adonay, by Agios, Otheos, Ischiros, Athanatos, Paracletus, Alpha, and Omega, and by the three secret names Agla, On, Tetragrammaton, that you come forth today to do my will.]

The *Agrippa* finally uses our magic name, deformed as *Agia*, in a charm intended to provide protection to the flock. First a pentacle must be made on virgin parchment, and then written on it are *Autheos, Anastros, Noxio, Bay, Gloy, Aper, Agia, Agios, Hischiros*, and an orison, then a mass should be said over it. "The parchment should be trampled by the sheep by being placed between two boards at the exit of the sheepfold so that the herd crosses over it, then this parchment should be pulled out and kept in a clean location."

The *Enchiridion Leonis Pape*, generally attributed to Pope Leo III, who was elected to the Holy See in 795, used *Agla* in a charm intended to provide for a good journey. This charm opens with the following phrase: "*Agla, Tetragrammaton, on athanatos, Anasarcon, on, Pantateon, Janua...*" An orison from the same collection is preceded in the following manner: "... and it must be noted that this one contains the name of Christ, which is Agla, which is used to be armored in ice against all adversities, of which it is said that when seen and worn every day one cannot die of an evil or sudden death." With other sacred names, Agla serves also, according to the *Grimoire of Pope Honorius,* to expel the demons in hell, to convoke Bechet, the demon of Friday, and to make Lucifer or one of his acolytes appear "in beautiful human form, without any mishape or ugliness, to respond to the true desires of all that I request of him without having the power to harm either my body or my soul." The *Libro de segretto e di magia* (p. 9), uses *Agla,* which it says refers to the *Key of Solomon,* in the summoning of a spirit:

agla tagla Mathon oarios almonsin arios menbrot varios pithonco magots salphe gabats salamander tabots [or *jabots*] *quomas lerve celis godens aqua quinqua sama eritscamus zariat nat mik E per.*

Followed by the *caracteres:*

The frequent use of this word has brought about many corrupted versions, such as *Aiglo, Aglodt, Aglati / Aglata, Abgla.* Muslims believe that *Agla* makes it possible to read the future and to find lost objects if it is spoken when facing east.

Agla is also featured in a spell to blind a thief in one eye: the spell caster would use the following material and *caracteres:*

This simple overview of *Agla* in the grimoires and large collections of charms collected in Western Europe informs us that this name of God created from a phrase can be used in countless different situations. It enters into lists and services as reinforcement to an invocation because it is a sacred name. It should be noted that *Agla* is absent in the charms that are written in Old English and Old German, and that it was introduced into the magical cultural milieu after the year 1000. We have one proof in an eleventh-century charm that is a parallel of one I cited above and should be written on four sacred Hosts:

> *Scribe in .IIII. oblatis contra febres*
> † *Hely.* †† *Heloy.*†
> † *Heloe.* †† *Heloen.*†
> †*ye ;* †† *ya.*†
> † *Sabaoth.* †† *adonai.*†

📖 Franz I, 294; II, 65, 369, 397, 569, note 3; Hunt, 98, 284, 360; Braekman, no. 5; London, British Library, Royal 12 G IV, folio 175 v°; Karlsruhe, Germany, Baden State Library, Donaueschingen 792, folio 138 v°; Heidelberg, Germany, University Library, Cpg 369, folio 168 v°; Braekman, no. 49, no. 145; Ohrt I, no. 315; Thiers I, 142; Sébillot, III, 133; Van Haver, no. 483, 679, 1016; Braekman, no. 388; Dresden, Germany, Saxon State and University Library, ms. M. 206, folio 66 r°; Paris, National Library, new Latin acquisition 7743, folio 251; *Grimoires*, no. 22, 33, 77, 108, 148, 191, 198, 302; *Clavicula*, 32, 55 (repeated four times).

† AGLA † AGLALA: To stop hemorrhaging, this should be written on the patient's forehead using his own blood:

> † *agla* †
> † *aglala* †
> † *aglalata* †

📖 Amati, *Ubbie. Ciancioni e ciarpe del sec. XIV,* 31.

AGLA, GARNAZE, EGLATUS, EGLA: For protection against all fever, these words must be written on a small note that is swallowed for three days in a row.

📖 Honorius, 65.

AGLAS, AGLANOS, ALGADENAS: The opening of a phrase, featuring Jesus and the two thieves on the cross, that must be written in one's own blood and swallowed in order to avoid being made to suffer under the question, which during the Inquisition meant under torture.

 📖 Honorius, 72; *Enchiridion* 1633, 166.

AGLATHEOS: This is a zodiac amulet, in this case Pisces, described by the doctor and astrologer Armand de Villeneuve (1235–1311). It bears this word in the center surrounded by the phrase in Latin: "He who believes in me, even if he were dead, shall live. All is consummated." This phylactery is useful against all skin diseases (boils, cankers, and so forth).

 📖 Pseudo–Arnaldus de Villanova, *Opera*. Lyon, 1509, folio 302 r°.

AGLATI: The phrase *Aglati Aglata Calin Cala* appears in a ritual intended to hold fast Uriel, the first seraphim, as well as other spirits. In order for these beings to speak truthfully to you, the moon must be in conjunction with Saturn.

 📖 Thiers I, 189, 191.

AGLOROS † THEOMYTHOS † THEMYROS: The opening of the twenty-third orison of the *Book of Consecrations:*

> *Agloros † theomythos † themyros † sehocodothos † zehocodos † hattihamel † sozena † haptamygel † sozihenzia † hemya † gettahol † helyna † sothoneya † geherahel † halimyz † zezoray † gezetiz † gerehona † hazihal † hazai † megnos † megalos . usyon † saduht. Amen.*

Two Greek words can be recognized in this spell: *megalos* (large) and *theomythos* (myth, divine speech).

 📖 *Liber iuratus*, chap. 34.

AGLOTAS: This is one of the seventy-two names of God. It is featured in the exorcism of Uriel: "I exorcise you, Uriel, by the seventy-two names of God, by Agios, Adonaï, Celin, Celes, Potas, Aglotas . . ."

 📖 Thiers I, 190.

AGNA AGILLA AGILLA: To win the love of a young woman, write these words on a piece of parchment that you will then use to jab her right jaw. She will then do what you will of her.

 📖 Bang, no. 116.

AGO, MAGO, MAGOLA: Used to contend against Saint Anthony's fire when it affects livestock, which is to say erysipelas. These words must be written on a piece of paper that is then given to the affected animal to eat.

 📖 *Egyptian Secrets* II, 245.

AGULA IGULA AGULET: These words must be written on a piece of cheese and given to someone suspected of theft to eat. If he is guilty, he will not be able to swallow it.

 📖 Ohrt I, no. 952.

AGUSTI, DECH, REGRITIOR ET MARTI PICATION HADOCH SAGENE: In order to win a case in court, you must leave home before sunrise and go to the door of your adversary, take a small piece of cloth, and spit in it three times and say: *"Non me Astarot."* When standing before the court, you should take the cloth into your right hand while clenching your thumb inside and look straight at your enemy and say:

> I, N. N., am looking at you with six eyes
> Two are mine
> Two are yours
> Two are those of the devil
> You shall shut up,
> Me, I wish to speak.
> With Lucifer's chain
> I bind your mouth and tongue
> So that you shall not be free
> Before I wish it;
> Too bad for you,
> Advantage is mine
> In the name of
> Agusti, Dech, Regritor and Marti Pication Hadoch Sagene.

If you follow the advice of this prescription, you will win the case and be acquitted of the crime or forfeit for which you are liable.

📖 Bang, no. 1409.

† AHA † MAHY † FROHA: When inscribed on a shelled hard-boiled egg that is eaten in three mouthfuls, these words cure fever.

📖 *Egyptian Secrets* II, 154.

AILIF, CASYL ZAZEHIT MEL MELAS: To strike whomever you choose with a *voult,* make a human effigy in wax on which this phrase is inscribed, then bury it. Reginald Scot indicates that it is also necessary to add specific *caracteres* that he does not reproduce.

📖 Scot, Book XII, chapter 16.

A. I. N. R. B.: This spell was used in France in 1744 for protection against fire; the phrase had to be written on charcoal.

📖 D'Abano, 81.

A.K.K.L.R.R.U.C.G.D.A.B.I.: To see a thief in dream, meaning to uncover his identity, write these letters on a Wednesday morning and place them beneath your right ear at night. ✦ D A B I is featured in other charms whose purpose is to heal epilepsy.

📖 Bang, no. 1109.

AKRAMMACHAMARI: Most likely, a derivative of an Aramaic expression, this word means "tears away the magic charm" and can be found combined with *Ablanathanalba* and *Sesengenbarpharangês* (see their respective entries). It is found on a tablet discovered in North Africa as *Achramachamarei,* "the god of the firmament."

📖 Gager, 55, 63, 104, 226.

ALADABRA † LADABRA †: This phrase against quartan fever should be written on a note using the following reductive spell: *aladabra † ladabra † adabra † dabra † abra † ra † a † abraca †.* It is then hung at the patient's throat with his or her name added to it. It also heals tertian fever.

This is one of the countless variations of *Abracadabra*. In a set of magical instructions showing how to speak with spirits, the phrase is: *ala drabra ladr(a) dabra rabra afra brara agla et alpha omega*. This is a wonderful variation of several phonemes that cries out to be spoken aloud!

 📖 Braekman, no. 82, 388; *Grimoires,* no. 50; Van Haver, no. 270.

ALAN: This word appears in a spell for protecting pigs: *Alan Tabalim Fugan ab omni malo. Exaudita est oracio tua,* or *Alan Fugan Saladdiel.* It is believed that *Alan* is the corruption of *Alam,* a Kabbalistic acrostic that when written correctly is *Tabalim* (Tob El), meaning "God is good." *Fugan* has been compared to the Greek *pyknos,* meaning "wise, skilled."

 📖 Franz II, 139.

ALAY † CALAN † FARAN † ETAN †: When worn on one's person, these names provide protection from storms and poison and heal sickness, according to a thirteenth-century manuscript. We should note that the *n* of the last three words could be a *u*.

 📖 Berlin, ms. Latin quart. 2, folio 25 r°.

ALBELLA: To cure a horse, one should whisper † *albella* † *abella* † *alpha* † *eloij* in its ear, and recite three Our Fathers and three Hail Marys in honor of the Holy Trinity.

 📖 Braekman, no. 213.

† ALBO † ALBOUT: In the *Benediction* or *Charm of Job,* we can find several phrases useful for expelling worms, such as the following:

> † *albo* † *albout* † *albubue* † *Zabulantes* † *ypedie* † *Transonie* † *abantroste.*

ALEDAR, LIIAZISLEA: This is the closing phrase for a Romanian charm against fever written in 1882: *Aledar, liiazislea, nomuserli, apcea, ebalt, șegoraba bojii NN.* It falls under the heading of incomprehensible *voces magicae* and immediately follows the fragment of a Greek prayer: "Hold us well, hold us with fear, Amen."

 ✦ *Stomen calcos.*
 📖 Bucharest, Romanian Academy Library, ms. 4458, folio 97 r°.

ALES-DALES-TOLAS: According to some, these words should be carved on one's right arm to provide protection in brawls; according to others, it is spoken aloud during a divination session.

Variant: † *Ales* † *Dales* † *Tales*

📖 *Enchiridion,* 1663, 158; Werner, no. 2, 196.

ALGA ACEKITA AULA: This magical phrase comes from around 1735. It was written on the right hand using the individual's own blood in order to obtain someone's love.

📖 Bang, no. 1039.

ALGA † ALGAT: These are the first words of a phrase for protecting an individual from all projectiles and spells. The individual had to write the following words on a piece of parchment to be carried beneath his right armpit:

† *Alga* † *Algas* † *Algat* † *Ana*
† *Sekretum* † *Essolatum* † *Dragor*
† *Mecsit* † *Arnols* † *Artesie*
† *Arthimei*

📖 Bang, no. 1041.

ALGA ALGATEM: The following phrase was used in Norway during the period of around 1750 to 1850 to protect sheep from death. It would be written on as many pieces of paper as there were sheep in the herd, and attached to them.

Alga algatem algus alge gogye algeti algoe algitind algtin alpha.

Another grimoire offers this variation: *Alga Algatem Algus Alge, Gagye, Agetie, Algna, Algitin, Dalgatie, Alpha,* and a third has this: *Alga Algatum alge Sago algaa algatim dalgetur siphe.*

📖 Bang, no. 1040.

ALGALAT. ESTNU: To part a woman or girl you love from someone else, write these words with your own blood on your hand and hold it out to her.

📖 Bang, no. 1130.

4. ALGAR, 4 ALTUM H. EBREH H. GRAMMAH AH: It was believed in the seventeenth century that if someone wrote this phrase and carried it on his person, it would render him invisible. A fragment of the Tetragrammaton has been identified in it.
📖 Ohrt II, 131.

† ALIA † NEC GLIA † NEC GALLINA †: In the ninth and tenth centuries, to cure leukoma, these words would be spoken aloud while making the sign of the cross and asking the aid of Christ. The spell turns up again in fifteenth-century Denmark in a slightly altered form.

† Alia † nec glia † nec alma †

Thanks to another account, we know today that it is a hen that was supposed to cure this disease.
📖 Ohrt I, no. 1158

† ALIA † NEC GLIA † NEC ALMA †: This phrase was the opening of a charm for healing eye problems, more specifically leukoma.
📖 Wickersheimer, 154ff.; Ohrt I, no. 1158.

ALIF LAFEIL ZAZAHIT MEL MELTAT LEUATAM LEUTACE: This evil phrase was meant to be written on a *voult dagyde,* in other words a doll of bewitchment, to be buried in a grave. The words had to be placed on its head and side.
📖 Weyer III, 9.

ALLAS, GALLI YNOMINAM: These words were written on one's right hand when wishing to speak to someone in a dream. The remnants of "In the name of (Saint) Gall" can be seen in this phrase.
📖 Bang, no. 1097.

ALOURI: To heal a child who is *en chartre* (suffering from a disease characterized by lethargy), make a sign of the cross over some bread dough and take a handful from the center to make a small loaf. Cook it in the oven, then give it to the first poor person whose path you cross while saying, "In the name of God and My Lord Alouri." The child will be cured.
📖 Thiers I, 381ff.

ALPHA and OMEGA: According to the Vulgate Holy Bible (John 1:8 and 11, 21:6, 22:13) this is the name of God. It designated the deity as encompassing everything (*Aion*) just as *alpha* and *omega* embrace the entire Greek alphabet. These two Greek letters are often used magically in charms, amulets, and pentacles.

 Franz I, 351, 430; II, 95, 482ff., 587; Heim, 543, 551.

ALRAX, ALGASMA, IURCHA, SYORCHA: To summon forth the demon that answers to these names, it is conjured in the name of God to show itself in a good and nonthreatening appearance. On Christmas night the spell caster must make his way to a crossroads and, in the name of the Trinity, draw two concentric circles with two diameters forming a cross. Each letter of I.N.R.I. is inscribed in the inner circle inside a quarter marked off by the cross. The four names above are placed on the perimeter of the other circle. The caster then stands inside the center of the circle and, while he holds the flesh and blood of Christ beneath his right foot inside his shoe, pronounces the incantation: "I conjure you Alrax, Algasma, Iurcha, Syorcha in the name of God ††† to show yourself here in good face without racket or horror, outside of this circle."

 Ohrt I, no. 988.

ALU: This is a runic magic word for which we have twenty accounts in the period from the third to the eighth centuries.

It appears alone or combined with other magic words, such as *laupu laukaR* (leek). Philologists relate it to the Hittite *alwanzahh* (to enchant). *Alu* could also be likened to "beer runes" (*ölrúnar*). This beverage causes an ecstatic trance regarded as magic.

 McKinnel and Simek, *Runes, Magic and Religion;* Saltveit, "Litt mer om laukaR og alu," 150-56.

AMACHA BORUM: This regressive phrase is used to combat toothaches and fevers. These two words are a corruption of two Hebrew terms meaning "illness, wound" and "health." Jean-Baptiste Thiers cites the phrase *Boris Borus* for stopping nosebleeds. Here is how the phrase must be written:

> AMACHA BORUM
> MACHA BORU
> ACHA BOR
> ACH BO
> AC B

📖 Thiers I, 365.

AMADAM, TAUSTOS, TAUSTAZO, BARACHETA, MEMOR, GEDITA: These are magic words appearing in the orison *Misericordissime Domine* by Pope Leo X. *Barach* is glossed in Latin by *fulgurans*.

📖 *Enchiridion*, 61.

AMALOR/AMELOR: This is a term in a phrase intended to heal cutaneous glanders in horses. Jean-Baptiste Thiers handed it down in an incomplete form. It is necessary to take three pieces of virgin wax, place them in a piece of . . . —certainly a piece of clean linen—tie them in three knots with a hemp rope and with each knot say this five times:

> Pater et Ave Maria, Christus + Christus vincit + Christus + Christus abicit + Amelor + Alcinor + descendat + in nomine, etc.

📖 Thiers I, 217.

AMAPOYLFAE/AMAPOLYLL AE: To obtain someone's love, one must make a copper medal that has *caracteres* carved on one side and Jeova de Nona (Ieova. Ae Nonna) on the reverse side. It should then be worn around the neck, and the person will say this word twelve times every day of October in front of the door of one's object of affection.

📖 *Clavicules: Les véritable clavicules de Salomon*, 67ff.

AMARA: This word has been regularly used in charms since the time of classical antiquity, and enters into unintelligible compositions like

> Amara † Tanta † Cyri;
> Amara † Thanta † Thirin Amara Tinta post hos . . .

During the Middle Ages, the phrase was corrupted, as seen in the German spell on page 41 for delivering a possessed person from the devil.

In 1237, an Italian exorcism of Filippo di Greve ended in *AMARA TANTA TYRI SYCALOS SYCALIRI.*

Amara is also found among the various names for God, such as in the beginning of this listing: *Tetragrammaton, Adonai, Agla, Sabaoth, Lali, Amara, Eli* . . .

📖 Heim, 558; Heidelberg, Germany, University Library, Cpg 268, folio 26 v°; Astori, 99.

AMARA TONTA TYRA:
This is the opening to a long spell that was used in the fifteenth-century Tyrol to question the demon that was possessing an individual.

> *Amara Tonta Tyra post hos firabis ficaliri Elypolis starras poly polyque lique linarras buccabor uel barton uel Tiram celi massis Metumbor o priczoni Jordan Ciriacus Valentinus.*

📖 Zingerle, 319.

† AMARITUDINE † FULGUR:
The opening of a spell found in a long ritual dated 1702, whose purpose is to compel a witch to come forth.

> † *Amaritudine* † *fulgur* † *Ador* ††† *queso* † *fulgur* † *fulgoris* † *Amen.*

The Latin words (meaning "bitterness," "lightning," and "request") make no sense.

📖 Van Haver, no. 1006.

AMICO CAPDINOPO ΦΙΦΡΟΝ ΙΔΡΑCACIMO:
This phrase is accompanied by a threefold appeal for Christ's aid (*Christus adjuva*) and another to Beronice or Veronica. It combines Greek and Latin letters, and it seeks to halt bleeding.

📖 Storms, no. 59.

AMISTA ASTERIT: To make a young girl lift up her shirt, write these words on a piece of parchment that should then be placed beneath the doorsill of her house.
    📖 Bang, no. 1111.

AMMARA SONTHA: In the fifteenth century it was believed that it was sufficient to show these words to a madman and he would be cured.
    📖 Heidelberg, Germany, University Library, ms. Cpg 369.

AMMATIA + VRA + VRI + CEDAT (αμματ‵α + υρα+ υρι + τζεδαδ): In order to freeze the arm of an enemy so that his dagger would not wound you, it was necessary to say these words three times. This phrase was used in Sicily during the early Middle Ages.
    📖 Schneegans, 586; Pradel, 32.

AMOL. ARIBILOP. ARNOL: This is a text found on amulets. To protect oneself from all kinds of projectiles, this was written on a piece of parchment that the individual would then carry on his person.
    📖 Bang, no. 1112.

AMOUZIN ABBO MATANOS: To heal wounds without balm, the person would write this phrase, take the shoe off his left foot, stand on his right leg, then extend his bare foot and make the sign of the cross over the wounded individual while saying † *Ante,* a second sign of the cross with † *Ante te,* and a third with † *Super ante te.*
    ✦ *Ante.*
    📖 Van Haver, no. 364.

† AMPLOTONN † RACHAS † VRIEL †: These are the opening words of a phrase intended to blind a thief in one eye. The individual casting the spell draws an eye that he then sticks with a nail while saying:

> † *Amplotonn* † *Rachas* † *Vriel* † *Vintarton* † *veh* † *Gabriel* † *Tetragon* † *Holltin* † *Rapahel* † *Tetragon* † *Richtor* † *Michael* †.

Then three Our Fathers and three Hail Marys are recited. This ritual is repeated three times. Angel names can be recognized: Richtor is coined

from the German *Richter*, "judge," and Rachas likely refers to *Rache*, "vengeance."

📖 *Magia de furto*; Leipzig, Municipal Library, ms. C.M. 66, folio 16 r°; Ohrt I, no. 966–67.

ANACHI JEHOVA, HŒLERSA: This is the opening of a long spell intended to give the illusion that one is accompanied by several people. It requires the individual to pick up a handful of sand and speak the following incantation:

> *Anachi Jéhova, Hœlersa, Azarbel, rets caras sapor aye pora cacotamo lopidon ardagal margas poston eulia Kephar, solzeth Karne phaca ghedolos salesetata.*

The sand is then mixed with snakeskin that has been reduced to a powder and then placed in an ivory box. When the individual wishes to produce this illusion, he casts a pinch of this sand mixture into the air while repeating the incantation. A variation of this spell puts the word *buget* between *eulia* and *Kephar*.

📖 Honorius, 63ff.

ANAFARCON: This name appears in the phrase † *Agla Pentagrammaton* † *On* † *Athanatos* † *Anafarcon* †, which Jean-Baptiste Thiers cites as offering protection against all kinds of danger. It can be found in an earlier English charm written in the eleventh century.

✦ *Arcum Conteret.*

ANAL AVNOL ARBITNPS PROLET UM: These words are written on a piece of parchment and kept on one's person to overcome one's enemies.

📖 Bang, no. 1115.

ANANI: This term appears in a fever-healing ritual dating from the beginning of the sixteenth century. The healer writes *Anani* three times on the patient's right hand while saying each time: "Christ vanquishes, Christ reigns, Christ commands," after which the healer writes *on pater on filius on spiritus sanctus* on the palm of the hand three times. The inscription is washed off with holy water that the fever sufferer must drink. On the second day, the healer writes *on aries on ouis on agnus* and repeats the same operation. On the third day he writes *on leo on vitulus on on vermis*. Once these divine names have been drunk, the patient is cured.

 📖 Ohrt I, no. 1144.

ANANIA† ANASSIA † EMISAEL † LIBERA NOS † DOMINE: For putting out a fire, these words should be spoken three times while signing where there are crosses. The three names are those of the three Hebrews in the furnace, for whom history has bequeathed two different sets of names. One consists of Ananias, Azarius, and Misaël, while the other is Shadrach, Meshach, and Abednego. The words are also featured in a procedure that involves a trial by boiling water.

 📖 Honorius, 69; Franz II, 62.

ANANIS ARSIMUS ARABOR EISUNUS: To win a game of cards or dice, use the blood of a black dog to write these words and attach them with a hemp thread spun during the Sunday sermon.

 In a very close form (*Aranis † Arsimus † Arabor † Ausus †*) and by taking the blood of a black cat to write this phrase that should then be attached beneath the left arm, a person can free himself from enchantment.

 ✦ *Arols.*
 📖 Bang, no. 1137, 1139.

ANANIZAPTA: Following in the footsteps of Guarinius (1491), it is believed that this word is an acrostic for the phrase: *Antidotum Nazareni auferat necem intoxicationis santificet alimenta poculaque trinitas Amen* (May the antidote of the Nazarene prevent murder by poisoning and may the Trinity sanctify food and drink). Among other things this is also a protection spell against the plague. This word offers protection from epilepsy, especially when engraved on a ring. On a gold ring from the fourteenth century now in the British Museum, we can read:

Dum dicitur Ananis3ata est mala mors capta
Ananis3atam ferit ile quem ledere querit.

In an incantation against the plague, *Ananizapta* is repeated five times. On the front of a cameo to be worn for protection against illness, the word is associated with *T*:

T
Anazapta Dei-Emanuel

T represents the Greek *tau*, which itself is the Egyptian hieroglyph symbolizing life, the *crux ansata*. This word appears in the lexicons of the early Middle Ages, such as the *Liber ordinus rerum*, for example.

Ananizapta ferit mortem, dum ledere querit,
Est mala mors capta, dum dicitur Ananizapta,
Ananizapta Dei nunc miserere mei.

Ananizapta smiteth death,
whiles harme intendeth he,
This word Ananizapta say,
and death shall captiue be,
Ananizapta ô of God,
haue mercie now on me.

Variants: *Amazapta, Ananigeptus, An An Jzapla, An An Qepta, Ananus Qepta.*

📖 Stockholm, Royal Library, ms. XIV in kl. 4°, folio 35; Ohrt I, no. 263 (*Ananzapta* with the "Five Wounds of Christ" listing); Dalton, no. 718, 870, 875; London, British Library, Sloane 73, folio 189 v°; Sloane 389, folio 92 v°; Sloane 1315, folio 97 v°; Sloane 2187, folio 17 r°; Oxford, Bodleian Library, Rawlinson C. 668, folio 74 r°; Thiers I, 355; Braekman, no. 98; *Grimoires*, no. 45, 108; Seligman, 1–25.

ANASAGES: This word needs to be spoken aloud to cure a toothache. Variations also exist, such as *Amazapta, Ananigeptus, An An Jzapla, An An Qepta, Ananus Qepta.*

📖 Thiers I, 361.

A. N. D. T. P. E.: Abbreviation for "In the name of the three princes of Hell," used in *Secrets magiques de l'amour en nombre de octante et trois.*

📖 *Secrets magiques pour l'amour*, 27.

ANEL ARTUS DUN: These words provide protection from bullets when written down and carried on one's person.

📖 BBE, 15.

ANEX ANEXIS ARABS: A person can win at cards and dice and other games by writing these words in the evening with blood from a wooden cup [*sic*] and attaching them beneath his right arm.

📖 Bang, no. 1142.

ANOEAM EMANEAN NATAN: To extinguish a fire, write these words on a sheet of lead and toss it into the flames.

✦ *Ansrand.*
📖 BBE, 19.

ANSA: This word appears in an eleventh-century spell intended to provide an individual with protection from the devil's arrows, in fact from demons: *O ligeo .ansa. amur.eus. Hieus. hus. Nom .liberatius .Geratius.* This incomprehensible gibberish can also be found in a charm against fever dating from the tenth or eleventh century: *ansa amuhus deus, hus mun, hus anger, liberazius ierosus.*

📖 Franz II, 484; Heim 551.

ANSRAND, EMANSRAN, NOTAN: To put out a conflagration, write these words on a piece of lead and toss it into the fire. There are numerous variations: *Anoran, Emaran Notan; Amior $\frac{9}{6}$ Nator; Amior † Natan; † amiorant † Emanuron † Nator. Notan* gradually transformed into *Natanieel.*

✦ *Anoeam.*
📖 Bang, no. 1118.

ANTE SUPERANTE: To heal the dislocated limb of a horse, one said: *Ante, patante, suparante in nomine Patris,* etc. Dominique Camus has collected a spell that was still in use only a few years ago for the purpose of protecting livestock:

> *Ante* †
> *Superante* ††
> *Superante te* †††

Another shorter spell instructs that the sign of the cross should be made with salt over each animal or at the entrance to the stable, sty, henhouse, or hutch. Simply by saying *Ante Superante Superante te* while making the sign of the cross, one could heal a sprain. The oldest recorded incidence of this spell is found in England in a fifteenth-century charm against the sprain of a horse (see *Zinupt*). In the Netherlands, † *Ante* † *Sus ante* † *Per Ante* † cures gout.

It was even claimed that a rooster could be made immortal by writing *Ante, Ante te, super Ante te* on a piece of paper and making him swallow it. This spell would then be repeated three times over his beak, then his head would be nailed to the table with a new nail, which would then be pulled out!

✦ *Amouzin*.

📖 Thiers I, 361ff.; Van Haver, no. 231, no. 491; Camus 1990, no. 77, 79, 81, 87ff.; Camus 2001, 101–4; Hunt, 96.

ANTHOS, ANOSTROS: To win the love of everyone, one should wear a note at his or her throat on which is written:

> *Anthos, Anostros, Noxio, Bay, Gloy, Apen.*

Anthos is also one of the words that should be inscribed on a note that is carried with relics and serves as a phylactery.

Variant: † *Anthos* † *â aortoo* † *noxio* † *bay* † *gloy* † *aperit.*

📖 Thiers I, 410; II, 313.

ANULA. SINULA. ADEA: These words are used in a conjuration against fever dating from the tenth century, or are reinforced by *vincit leo* and *Christus natus* (see these entries). The person reciting them is asking God to deliver his servant. *Anula* could be the Hebrew *Ani El*, "I am God."

📖 Franz II, 481.

ANUOLL, AORDA: To uncover the identity of a robber, this phrase should be written on a piece of cheese that is then given to the one suspected of having stolen from you: *Anuoll, Aorda, Laboro Dolor Paupertin. Giam Tuam.* The thief will be unable to swallow even a mouthful. The Latin words make no sense: *Giam* should be the accusative form of *Gloria; laboro* means "I work," *dolor,* "pain," *paupertin* "pauper."

📖 Bang, no. 1144.

† A. II: To facilitate a birth, these letters should be written on a parchment and placed on the woman in labor, then say: "In the beginning was the word" (the opening of the Gospel of John), followed by: "† *soter zz,* God was the word † *savoir.* This was in the beginning † *agios* † in God † *allocax.*"

📖 Aymar, 340.

APPACION: A Cambridge manuscript dating from 1044 contains a spell against gout: + *Appacion* ++ *Appria* + *Appremont et qua settuena* +. This must be written on a piece of parchment and worn around the neck to provide protection from the disease. *Appremont* is certainly related to *Abremonte.*

✦ *Abremonte.*
📖 Hunt, 73, 144.

A:P:S:3:X:F: Writing these *caracteres* on your right hand will allow you to see your wishes granted.

📖 Vaitkevičienė, no. 1631 (spell from Poland).

ARA: This is one of the components of the following magic phrase, whose nine words form a square:

> *Ara Ira Ora*
> *Ora Ara Ira*
> *Ira Ora Ara*

A connection has been made between *Ara* and *A(b)rac,* a word that appears in the phase *Abrac Abeor Aberer,* found in the *Heptameron* of astronomer Peter d'Abano (died in 1316). Jean-Baptiste Thiers notes a similar phrase: *Abrac Amon . . .*

📖 Thiers I, 361.

ARABA OMEL ALIFAL: When worn these words: *Araba Omel alifal Cuttar uden et armoen Trola Coblamot Fasteanus,* protect the bearer from sharp projectiles like arrows. The following variation dates from around 1750: *Araba. Omet. Arliful Cultaru om et Aruoru, Prole. Kablamat y all canus.*

Another charm recommends to a wounded individual that he carry on his person a long, incomprehensible phrase that contains the following elements: *Ababaomel Arli Ssus / Culteaum Armoem / Proba Cablanis / Wartilnum.*

Alas, comparisons of all the different variations have not made it possible to restore the original spellings.

📖 BBE, 15; Bang, no. 1095, 1113.

ARAGON SARAGON ATRAGON SUTAGON: To cure a toothache, it is necessary to write these words on four pieces of bread and give one to the patient to eat every morning. Variations include: *Ageram Saragoen Alagon Salagon, Arego Saragoen Alagon Salagon.* The Black Book of Jeløen, compiled in Norway around 1750, presents this phrase like this:

📖 Bang, no. 1152.

ARAKHA, ARAKHA, ARAKHAËL: Exorcism spell from the Coptic Prayer of Saint Gregorios.

📖 Lexa, t. 1, 109.

ARA LIEA: To heal three kinds of fever, nineteenth-century Romanians wrote this long spell on paper that the patient had to keep on his or her person: *ara liea, sadeleia, tracu, leovitu, inelegami, naşegon, isu, islugi, vaşah, abaset, bluşiaia, nemulea, raboja.* The patient should read it three times a day.

📖 Bucharest, Romanian Academy Library, ms. 4458, folio 94 r°.

ARAPS IASPER SCRIP: To capture snakes this following spell was used in England along with "in the name of the Father, and so forth":

Araps Iasper Scrib Porro Pontem Zoro Zehebete Zaraf Maras Spiritus Praclitus.

📖 London, British Library, Royal 12 B.XXV, folio 62 v°.

ARARACARARA: This is a magic word discovered carved on an enchantment tablet in the Carthage amphitheater and inserted in the spell: *araracarara eptiscere cycbacyc bacacicyχ bacaχieyc obrimemao saum obriulem patatnaχ apomspsesro iaω iossef ioerbet ioparcebet ioparcebet bolcoset.*

According to another source: *bacacicyχ bacaχieyc* would be the name of a demon: *erecisipte ararcarara eptiscere coggens enim vos enim et reges demoniorum bacaχicyχdemenon bacaχicyχ cogens enim vos et iudices exsenyium animarum qui vos in tachymorey vite iodicaveunt criny. arinchor*...

📖 Audollent, 345ff.

ARARITA: This is an acrostic of the Hebrew *Achad Rosh Achadotho Rosh Ichudo Tamaratho Achad*

אחד ראש אחדותו ראש ייחודו תמורתו אחד

which today would read *Ekhad rosh, Akhduto rosh, yekhudo temurahzo* ("One is his beginning; one is his individuality; his permutation is one"). This word is found in regressive phrases: it is copied, subtracting one letter every time.

Ararita
Ararit
Arari
Arar
Ara
Ar
A

It is necessary to carve a cross on the patient's forehead with a knife, say *consummatum est,* then next cut letter after letter with the knife. Heinrich Cornelius Agrippa cites it as a divine name. When carried carved on a gold strip, the word protects the bearer from sudden death (*Semiphoras*). In *The Lesser Key of Solomon,* it is a divine name spelled *Araritha,* and is accompanied by the following *caracteres:*

📖 *Grimoires,* no. 11; Agrippa, *De occulta philosophia,* III, 11; Clavicula, 28; *Semiphoras,* Schäuble edition, 300.

ARATALY: In thirteenth-century England, this regressive phrase written on a page would be attached to the patient's arm, where it would be left for nine days. During this time "Our Father in honor of the apostles Peter and Paul" would be recited three times. When the page was removed at the end of this period, the patient would be cured.

Arataly
Rataly
Ataly
Taly
Aly
Ly

📖 Thomas, *Religion and the Decline of Magic.*

ARATO: This is the beginning of a charm intended to open doors, recorded by Johann Weyer in the sixteenth century.

> To open closed doors, it is necessary to take a piece of wax that has been used in a baptism and print upon it flowers that are called bells of Our Lady and attach the whole of it to the front part of the shirt. Then when you wish to open you must blow three times while saying these words: *Arato hoc partiko, hoc maratarikin,* in your name I open this door, which I am obliged to break down just as you broke up the Hells, *In nomine Patris, et filij, et Spiritus sancti. Amen.*

📖 Weyer III, 9; Scot, Book XII, chapter 14.

ARC: To prevent a dog from biting and barking, say the following three times while looking at the animal: *"L'arc barbare, le cœur se fend, la queue se pend, la clef de saint Pierre te ferme la gueule jusqu'à demain."* ("The barbaric arch, the heart breaks, the tail hangs down, Saint Peter's key closes your mouth until tomorrow.")

 📖 Honorius, 70.

ARCHITRICLIN (Architeclinus, Archideclin, Archedechne): This pseudosaint was invoked for aid against horse diseases and against fever. The name originally designated the individual charged with organizing a feast. The architriclin of the wedding in Cana (John 2:1–11) even became the proper name of a rich lord and saint, Saint Agrias.

 📖 Braekman, 235–38; Stockholm, Royal Library of Stockholm, ms. XIV in kl. 4°, folio 137; Hunt, 360.

ARCUM CONTERET & CONFRINGET ARMA, &C.: Many borrowings from the scriptures have accumulated in this charm that aims to spare an individual from a host of dangers. The most prominent borrowings are from the Psalms and from Christian symbols and figures. This phrase, opening with *Arcum*, is taken from Psalm 45:10:

> *Arcum conteret & confringet arma, &c. Monstra te esse matrem, &c. Dextera Domini, &c. Miserator & misericors Dominus, &c. Sancte Deux, &c. Deus qui in tot periculis, &c. Deus autem transiens, &c. Domine Iesu Christe Fili Dei vivi qui hora, &c.* ✠ *Agla Pentagrammaton* ✠ *On* ✠ *Athanatos* ✠ *Anafarcon* ✠ *&c.* ✠ *Crux Christi salva me* ✠ *&c. Perscrutati sunt, &c. Ave Virgo gloriosa, &c. Hagios invisibilis Dominus, &c. Per signum* ✠ *Domine Tau libera me, In nomine Patris, &c. Adonay Iob Magister dicit, 91. O bone Iesu, &c.* ✠ *Ananizaptam* ✠ *Ihozath* ✠ *L A Laus Deo semper, O inimici mei ad vos nemo, &c. In nomine Iesu, &c.*

This phrase comes up in the *Grimoire of Pope Honorius:* "To prevent a dog from biting and barking, say the following three times while looking at the animal: *L'arc barbare, le cœur se fend, la queue se pend, la clef de saint Pierre te ferme la gueule jusqu'à demain* ("The barbaric arch, the heart breaks, the tail hangs down, Saint Peter's key closes your mouth until tomorrow").

Monstra te esse matrem ("reveal yourself as mother") comes from the lactation miracle of Saint Bernard of Clairvaux. When he spoke these words in front of a statue of the Virgin, it came alive and shot milk into his mouth. Painters have often illustrated this miracle. *Dextera Domini (fecit virtutem)* comes from Psalm 117:16. *Miserator & misericors Dominus* is taken from the First Epistle of James (5:11) or Psalm 144:8.

 📖 *Grimoires,* no. 108.

ARCUS SUPED ASSEDIT: A charm in Old English tells us that to heal a horse of boils it is necessary to chant Our Father nine times and one over a loaf of barley bread that is then given to the horse to eat: *Arcus suped assedit virgo cannabid lux et ure canabid.*

 Thanks to three similar incantations from the fourteenth and fifteenth centuries, scholars have discovered that this involves a corruption of the phrase: *Arcus super nos sedit, uirgo natabit, lux et (h)ora sedebit* ("The rainbow has laid over us, the Virgin [probably the sign of the zodiac, Virgo] has swum, the light [meaning the day] and the hour [of the birth] will be set").

 📖 Berthoin-Mathieu, 152, 488–91; Storms, no. 84; Olsan, 438–47.

AREBRODAS: A Kabbalistic word offering protection from dog bite. It is carried on the individual's person, written this way:

Arebrodas
Rebrodas
Ebrodas
Brodas
Rodas
Odas
Das
As

Some scholars believe that *Arebrodas* is a derivative of *Sator Arepo.*

AREX: The following phrase was used in a spell against fever in the thirteenth century: † *Cristus* † *arex* † *yre* † *artifex* † *ranx* † *yriorum*, and for those who "have worked at night," at the same time as the names of the seven sleepers of Ephesus.

 ✦ *Arox.*
 📖 Hunt, 84.

ARILL. AT. GOLL. GOTTZO: Formula for an amulet that one should wear to ensure protection from bullets.
  📖 *Egyptian Secrets* II, 304.

ARKE PIAS FERDACO SIRCARI: These words are used in a ritual intended to learn how a person from whom you have had no news is doing.
  📖 Werner, no. 5, 196ff.

ARMINI FARINI RESTINGUO: For protection from firearms, this would be written down on paper, then swallowed. One could then speak these words when danger threatened. These words are likely a corruption of *Arma ignifera restinguo* ("I extinguish firearms").
  📖 Werner, no. 6, 197.

AROLS, ARSINE, ARABOR, ASASUS: To win at cards or dice, write these words in your own blood on a paper that you attach to yourself using hemp string that has been spun during Sunday mass.
  ✦ *Ananis*
  📖 Bang, no. 1136.

AROS NEMOS HELY: These words should be written on a white sheep hide and accompanied by Jesus, *Alpha* and *Omega,* and the names of the seven sleepers of Ephesus. The hide is washed in water to be given to an individual suffering from quartan fever to drink.
  📖 Heidelberg, Germany, University Library, Cpg 267, folio 12 r°.

AROX AXAX APORTAXA: When written on a piece of virgin parchment and placed under the pillow, this phrase will ensure a good sleep.

✦ *Arex.*
📖 *Grimoires,* no. 29.

ARS NOTORIA: *The Notary Art of Solomon* is a thirteenth-century magic treatise of which fifty-three manuscripts have come down to us. It offers orisons that make it possible to assimilate the teachings of the liberal arts, in other words from the *Trivium* (grammar, rhetoric, logic) and from the *Quadrivium* (music, geometry, astronomy/astrology, theology). God is supposed to have revealed it to Solomon, the master of the spirits and keeper of a supernatural power.

According to the testimony of Flavius Josephus (first century), a book of incantations circulated under his name:

> He composed such incantations also by which distempers are alleviated. And he left behind him the manner of using exorcisms, by which they drive away demons, so that they never return; and this method of cure is of great force unto this day; for I have seen a certain man of my own country, whose name was Eleazar, releasing people that were demoniacal in the presence of Vespasian, and his sons, and his captains, and the whole multitude of his soldiers. The manner of the cure was this: He put a ring that had a Foot of one of those sorts mentioned by Solomon to the nostrils of the demoniac, after which he drew out the demon through his nostrils; and when the man fell down immediately, he abjured him to return into him no more, making still mention of Solomon, and reciting the incantations which he composed. And when Eleazar would persuade and demonstrate to the spectators that he had such a power, he set a little way off a cup or basin full of water, and commanded the demon, as he went out of the man, to overturn it, and thereby to let the spectators know that he had left the man; and when this was done, the skill and wisdom of Solomon was shown very manifestly. (*Antiquities of the Jews* II, 5)

According to others the true author would be Apollonius of Tyana. By reciting orisons made from long lists of divine names, angels, and

A page from the *Ars notoria*, 1295

Greek, Chaldean, and Hebrew words, and by examining geometrical figures called "notes" (whose number varies from thirty-five to forty in the manuscripts), one can obtain intellectual illumination and acquire knowledge. This grimoire has two parts. The first, the *Flores aurei*, has two series of orisons for developing the intellectual faculties and acquiring disciplines. It opens with, "Here beginneth the first Treatise of this

Art, which Master Apollonius calleth *The Golden Flowers,* being the general introduction to all the Natural Sciences, and this is Confirmed, Composed, and Approved by the Authority of Solomon, Manichaeus, and Euduchaeus." The second part contains ten orisons for the acquisition of learning. In the concluding part, nine orisons preceded the "notes." Some orisons are divided into several parts. Instructions are provided for how to recite them, and their relationship with the phases of the moon is established.

✦ *Assaylemath, De. el. x, Eliphamasay, Ezomamos, Gezemothon, Gezomelion, Hanazay, Hancor, Hely Scemath, Lamed, Lameth, Theon, Theos Pater.*

📖 Véronèse, ed. *L'Ars notoria au moyen âge*; *Ars notoria. The Notory Art of Solomon Shewing the Cabanistical Key of Magical Operations.* For more on the formation of words and names, see Daniel and Maltomini, *Supplementum magicum* I, 4–6; and Dornseiff, *Das Alphabet in Mystik und Magie,* 63–67.

ARSILIU ARZAMISU: To cure three kinds of fever, eighteenth-century Romanians wrote this spell on paper that the patient had to keep in his or her possession: *arsilisu arz misu pe murat, de dat, faraon.* The patient had to read it three times a day. *Dat* might mean "spell" (*fapt*), and *faraon* "pharaoh."

Another spell for the same fever is: *ara liea, sadeleia, tracu, leovitu, inelegami, nașegon, isu: islugi, vașah, abaset, blușaia, nemulea, raboja.*

📖 Bucharest, Romanian Academy Library, ms. 4458, folio 94 r°; ms. 4743, folio 184 v°.

ARTUS: This term forms part of two imperfect magic squares intended to offer protection from epilepsy.

| Artus, Pratus, Sartus |
| Pratus, Sartus, Artus |
| Sartus, Artus, Pratus |
| Vragen Ragen Seragen |
| Ragen Seragen Vragen |
| Seragen Vragen Ragen |

Ageront Nageront Sebeont

Artus can be found in a collection of Anglo-Irish spells from the Middle Ages, in which the term is used in a prescription against fevers.

Over a payment agreement it is necessary to write: ††† *hympnus* † *artus* † *arus* † *tremens* † *eloy* †, followed in Latin by "the wind chafes, the angel announces, the Christ frees †††." The note is bound to the right hand while reciting several prayers (Our Father, Apostles' Creed, Hail Mary), and it is left there for three days, during which time the individual fasts. The payment note is then removed, burned, and its ashes cast into flowing water to carry away the evil. *Artus* is also found in a short spell for protection against bullets.

◆ *Anel.*
📖 Black Book of Jeløen; Bang, no. 1127; *Grimoires*, no. 53.

ASCA BASCA RASTAIA SERE CERCER RECERCEL: To heal a breast canker, these words must be spoken into one's closed fists while performing a complicated procedure.
📖 *Antidotarium Bruxellense*, 383, 4ff.

ASKION, KATASKION, LIX, TETRAX, DAMNAMENEUS, AISIA: These are *Ephesia grammata* (Ephesian words) that are said to have been written on the statue of Artemis in Ephesus. This phrase was spoken to give oneself protection from evil. The last word is *asia* or *asion*. The oldest example dates from the fourth century BCE.
📖 Kotansky, 111; Ogden, 47; Flint, 45–50.

† ASLA † TARA † PENTA: This is a phrase that appears in a ritual for manufacturing a ring that grants victory. It is forged from seven metals and cast beneath the seven planets. Next it must be engraved with: † *Asla* † *Tara* † *Penta*. Once it has been slipped on the ring finger of the right hand on a Friday, one must say: *O Fuska—Criame—Lera*.
📖 Bang, no. 1042.

ASMALIOR: To bend a woman to your will, you must craft a gold ring set with a yellow stone in the thirteenth house of the moon and carve on it this *caractere*:

Then place the word *Asmalior* under the stone written with dove's blood on virgin parchment perfumed with aloe.

📖 London, British Library, Lansdowne 1202, 4to, folio 173.

ASMOT: The *Libro de segretto e di magia* (p. 5) offers this protection spell that is intended to paralyze any foes who wish you ill: *Asmot † Deo Vir † Birtir † Ligete in omnibus membris tujs quia te corumpere volo.*

ASSAYLEMATH: This is the opening to a prayer attributed to Solomon in the thirteenth century. It causes God to increase the memory, reason, and eloquence of the one who recites it. It is first given in an abbreviated form:

> *Assaylemath, assay, Lemeth, Azzabue*
> *AZzaylemath, Lemath Azacgessenio*
> *Lemath, Sebanche, Ellithy, Aygezo*

then in its complete form:

Ars notoria, 14ff.

Azay lemach azae gessemon thelamech azabhaihal sezyon traheo emagal gyeotheon samegon pamphilos sitragramon limpda jachim alna hasios genonagal samalayp camiel secal hanagogan heselemach getal sam sademon sebmassan traphon oriaglpan thonagas tyngen amissus coysodaman assonnap senaly sodan alup theonantriatos copha anaphial Azathon azaza hamel hyala saraman gelyor synon banadacha gennam sassetal maga halgozaman setraphangon zegelune Athanathay senach zere zabal somayel leosamach githacal halebriatos Jaboy del masan negbare phacamech schon nehooz cherisemach gethazayhy amilya semem ames gemay passaynach tagayl agamal fragal mesi themegemach samalacha nabolem zopmon usyon felam semessi theon, Amen

Liber iuratus, chap. XXI

Hazailzemaht uel Hasaylemath lemaht azac gessemon thelamoht hazab habatal haebal sezior sicromagal gigoro mogal gielotheon samagoy haphiles pamphilos sicragalmon lanpda iothun halnal hailos halna genenogal samanlay tacayhel thamiel secalmana hoesemolas hesemelaht gesatham cethal stilmon saibaiol semalsay crathon hanagnil panconuegos tyngeny hamyssitoy sebarnay hassinilop thenaly soday henaly halaco meahil crihicos sepha caphanal hazaron tezamahal haila saraumay gelior synoy bariachacha gehemizay ietrafagon .legelyme hathamathay senac gromyazay sothalmagaal iemazai zehemphagon hasihezamay legelime hacama ieizobol ierozabal symalyel seymaly seihel leosamaht gemyhacal halabre cyophagros theos phabos ycolmazay negen pharamepht nehihahon sehon gethorem nehehom helisemaht saratihai ierasiai hynaliha semem̄amos gezamay iecremai passamaht thagail hagamal fagamesy fagamesym themegoman zemegamary salamatha salamothono bon lon . sepizihon harion vsyon semession tegon. Amen

Liber iuratus, chap. XX

Assaylemaht uel Assailamath rasay semaht azahat araaht lameth hazabat hamat hamae gesemon grephemyon zelamye hazatha hamatha hazaremehal hazanebal helial zebial seziol semyhor hamissiton fintiugon tintiugethe hamissirion sebarnay halmoth alymyon gemail halimot sadail hehomail neomail cristos thiothot sepha taphamal paphalios sicromemior laupdau laupta iothileta lazahemor iemeamor letahemor saromegall haemor giseleccor giheleraton glereleon gamasgay semagar semalgay semasgyy balna atheton iesamahel gegemahelay hala hela iemay semethay may semnay geles syney iolehelney iesmar samennay bariaccoca cariactera tharietha socalmata getymay socalma socagamal helgezamay balma hailos halos zaynos ienenegal sarimalip sacramalaip tamygell thamal sathabynhel sathabmal samal maga samalanga saminaga satalmagu silymal salmana sagnaht silymythu semalsay gahit galiht gezamanay sabal zegahaton zehanphaton iezamycrathon iecnaphaton iezemo iezelem ioselimen hatanathos hathanathay semaht zemehet iezorahel chetorab helgezorabal craton hariobal hariagal hanagai hariagil parithomegos samaziel simazihel leosemaht leosamaty thenuathol genynatol gemizacol hebalthe halabee hamysschon sebanay halmye gemail sadail neomahil cristolepha caphanial hazaron gezamel haymal haihala sememay geliesmoy thanccha gemiazay zohanphaton ielesamen hathanathay gemaht iesomabelhaynosiel halabethen iabaioge halabeht ebalohe myphos phabos phelior phobos ydolmassay predolmassay pholior negioggen neginather pharamnee pharanhe stomicopten sohomythepoten hymaliassenon ymiamos manyhas geromay yemay ierathayazai passamaht thon beht bon sathamac hagynol naragal semozihot nerothinay ragnathi ranal ragnali ragahal hagmal hagamal sagomossyn .agemesym domogetha theomegen theromagen salmatha salamaht zalamatha hon bolon lialon sephezium sapinon saphiamon hamon harion vsyon gemessyon sepha phalymyt sebanay hamyssithon thnitingren harcon rogonbon vsyon. amen

The Greek word *crathon,* "power, potency," *theon / theos,* "God," *hathanathay* (i.e., *athanatos*) can be recognized in this.

✦ *Ars notoria;* Oraison.

📖 *Ars notoria,* 14ff., 106ff.

ASTAROTH: This name does not only designate the prince of Hell, who drew his name from the Semitic mother goddess Ashtoreth, the Phoenician Astarte, and the Babylonian Ishtar. It is also a magic word found on a gold ring attributed to Solomon; it is made in the moon's second house and bears a yellow stone carved with the *caractere* below. The word *Astarot* (variant of *Astaroth*) is placed under the stone, written with dove's blood on virgin parchment perfumed with amber, which makes it possible to obtain a spirit familiar.

📖 London, British Library, Lansdowne 1202, 4to, folio 172–73.

ATAY DE SATAY SURATAY AVALDE, MARCHE: When repeated three times, this phrase is used to heal twisted limbs and sprains in animals and humans.

📖 Honorius, 108.

ATHAGON: This word is effective for banishing the pain of a toothache. Write this word on a bread end and place it on the tooth. Once the pain has been soothed, spit the bread out into the fire and spit three times after.

📖 Bang, no. 1151.

ATHENA: This name, when written on an olive leaf and attached to the head, is effective against headaches. The connection with this goddess of antiquity is probably the following: when Hephaestus split Zeus's skull with an axe, Athena sprung out fully armed.

ATRACATETRACATI: Magic word carved on an enchantment tablet that was supposed to protect a tomb from grave robbers and is inserted in the spell: *Atracatetracati gallara precata egdarat hehes celata mentis ablata.*

📖 Audollent, 168ff.

† AUGUSTI † DECH † REQVITION † ET MORTI † FISCHATION † ITADOCH † SEGENE † AMEN X: To remain very strong, in other words to prevent anyone from causing you harm, it is necessary to speak these words and ask Lucifer to bind the arms and legs of any potential enemy.

📖 Black Book of Jeløen; Bang, no. 1371.

AULU SAURE (αυλου σαυρε): For protection against serious illness and disabilities, these words are etched on a gold tube inside of which the right foot of a lizard is placed. This phylactery is to be worn on the left arm, according to the Latin *Cyranides* of the twelfth century. The Byzantine manuscripts of this text give us: Εβλοὺ Σαυρε.

📖 *Cyranides*, Book II, letter Z.

AURATABUL: By writing this shrinking phrase three times above the door of a house that has been robbed, the thief is obliged to return, whereupon he can be captured.

Auratabul
Auratabu
Auratab
Aurata
Aurat
Aura
Aur
Au
A

📖 BBE, 29.

AUTHEOS †, ANASTROS † NOXIO: To protect one's flocks, the long spell below would be written above two pentacles drawn on parchment that is then rubbed on the animals before being placed in a way so that they will walk over it when leaving the sheepfold.

Autheos †, Anastros † Noxio † Bay † Gloy † Aper † Agia † Agios † Hischiros. Deus Tetragrammaton misericors et pius, per ista sanctissima nomina et per tua sanctissima attributa da mihi fortunam et horam bonam in omnibus meis factis, et libera me omni malo et perturbation. Amen. Then say three Apostles' Creeds, and so on.

📖 D'Abano, 87.

AVIGAZITOR: This magical word can undo the laces of the breeches (sexual magic) if written on a virgin parchment before sunrise.

    📖 Thiers I, 359, 413; IV, 590.

AVIS GRAVIS SEPS SIPA: These words are the corrupted forms of a Greek invocation of God. According to the Pseudo-Arnaldus de Villanova, they will unlace the crotch of a pair of breeches if written in the corners of a cross encircled by the opening words of the Gospel of John. The drawing is diluted with holy water or wine, which one then drinks. We can also find these words in this more intelligible form: *Anis otheus aius ageatus eleison*, and so forth.

    📖 Franz II, 481; Pseudo-Arnaldus de Villanova, *Opera*, folio 215 v°.

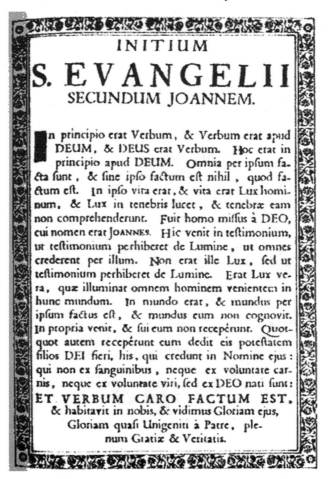

AX: To avoid pregnancy, Byzantines would resort to magic. When the moon was waning, they would write the following letters, which they then carried on their persons. The author of this prescription even offered a means to test their effectiveness: "Tie them to a tree, it will be sterile or wither." α ζ β δ σ θ ω ζ η θ γ ω π Ψ ε λ χ

📖 Tselikas, 73.

AXTU SVATUS SUTUS EIORTUS FIILKOUT ERTRATUS: This is a spell that a pig is given to swallow in order to cure it.

📖 Espeland, § 13.

AZARIEL! CAKARIEL! MESCA!: To put out a fire, one must cast rough salt that has been blessed into the four corners of the fire and say these words while holding one's arms stretched out in front. These three names are corruptions of those of the three Hebrews in the furnace— Shadrach, Meshach, and Abednego—who are regularly invoked during conflagrations.

✦ *Anania.*

📖 Van Haver, no. 684.

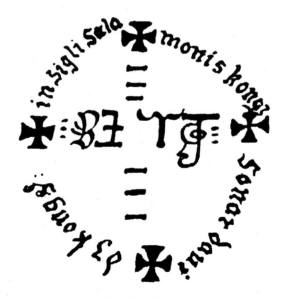

Scandinavian amulet

BACHANDE BELTZLIOR DEALZEHAT: According to *The Lesser Key of Solomon,* this phrase allows one to get revenge on his enemies.

BACTRA. BACTRUS. BACTRIM. A E I O U: This phrase, followed by five Kabbalistic signs, allows one to win at cards or dice if he has written it on his hand in dog's blood.

The signs correspond to the vowels, and the whole thing is therefore a decoding key. This series of vowels is found on a Genovese amulet of the seventeenth or eighteenth century that says: "A E I O U, to free one from one's bonds."

📖 Bang, no. 1138; Deonna, "Superstitions à Genève," 345.

BAGAHI, LACA, BACHAHÉ: These words are the beginning of the conjuration of the devil in *Le Miracle de Théophile* (The Miracle of Théophile) by Rutebeuf (thirteenth century):

> *Bagahi, Laca, Bachahé*
> *Lamac, Cahi, Achabahé*
> *Karrelyos*
> *Lamac, Lamec, Bachalyos,*
> *Cabahagi, Sabalyos,*
> *Baryolas,*
> *Samahac et Famyolas,*
> *Harrahya*

📖 Rutebeuf, v. 160ff.

BAHÂHAJÛS: In an operation meant to make a monarch treat a woman benevolently and give her undying love, two hollow wax effigies would be made, one of the woman and one of the king. A preparation consisting of numerous ingredients was poured into each one, then the figures were tied together facing each other and pierced with a silver needle while the caster said: *Bahâhajûs, Bâlîjâs, Ûdarijâs. 'Armûlîs.* The dolls were then wrapped in white cotton, then in new silk that was bound with seven knots while these words were spoken over each one: *Bahâhajûs, Bahâdajâs, Ûbalûs, Manâtis, Tûrânûs, Jâhîgâs Batûrâs.* A suffumigation was then performed while a conjuration was spoken that summons four spirits and opens with the magic words: *Algidûs, Maltâjâs, Hûlis, Minûrâs.*

 📖 *Gâyat al-Hakîm*, 269; Bissing, 23–27; for more on the number 7, see Roscher, *Über Alter, Ursprung und Bedeutung der Hippokratischen Schrift von der Siebenzahl*.

BALAM + NABAT + APASIA: These words, added to a figure that is supposed to represent an eye, make it possible to put the eye of a thief out at a distance. The phrase must be written on the drawing and an incantation spoken.

 📖 Bang, no. 1376 d.

BALBUCH: To catch a large number of fish, you must make a tin ring in the fifteenth house of the moon and set in it a crystal stone on which the sign below has been carved. Place under the stone the word *Balbuch* written with dove's blood on virgin parchment "perfumed with flies[?]."

$$\cdot\mathbf{V}\cdot$$

 📖 London, British Library, Lansdowne 1202, 4to, folio 175–76.

BALIDETH, ASSAIBI, ABUMALITH, AMEN: If girls or widows wish to see their future husbands in dream, they most recite the following orison at night:

> *Kyrios clementissime, qui Abraham servo tuo dedisti uxorem Saram, & filio ejus obedientissimo, per admirabile signum indicati Rebeccam uxorem: indica mihi ancillæ tuæ quem sim nup-*

tura virum, per ministerium tuorum spirituum Balideth, Assaibi, Abumalith. Amen.

[Most merciful master, you who gave your servant Abraham Sarah as wife, and to his most obedient son Rebecca as wife by an admirable sign, show your servant what man she shall wed. By the ministry of your spirits Balideth, Assaibi, Abumalith. Amen.]

On awakening the following morning, the girl must bring back to mind what she saw in her dreams during the night and if while sleeping she saw no man appear, she should continue trying for three Fridays in a row. If the girl still has not seen any man appear during these three nights, she has good cause to believe that she shall never wed. Widows can do this just like girls but with one difference. Girls should sleep by the head of the bed while widows should sleep at its foot, transferring the headboard there.

Abumalith is found in a spell that accompanies the creation of a garter that makes it possible to travel without fatigue. The phrase is *Abumalith cades ambulavit in fortitudine cibi illius.* The final five words mean, "He walked thanks to the strength of this food," which comes from the Bible (II Kings 19:8).

📖 *Petit Albert*, 27ff.

BALOM † HALFA: A Norwegian ritual used around 1770 for the purpose of blinding a thief in one eye starts with the following phrase:

Balom † halfa † Asio † Aliata † ligagarie Mantonie Akalib etu omni Cilli Mus Alde Nabau † bilial † Sadro † Asharo † go.

This phrase should be written around the eye that has been drawn previously by the caster of this spell.

✦ *Balam.*
📖 Bang, no. 1376d.

BALRUNG. BANRIOR. FLUXUEL: To bring an invincible horse to the race this spell must be written on a paper that is then attached to his left ear.

📖 Bartsch, *Sagen, Märchen und Gebräuche*, vol. 2, no. 2059.

BALSAMIAH: To heal all sorts of ills and wounds, you must make a silver ring in the fifth house of the moon and set in it a red stone on which the symbol below is carved. Beneath the stone, you will place *Balsamiah*, written with the blood of a white dove on virgin parchment perfumed with incense.

 📖 London, British Library, Lansdowne 1202, 4to, folio 174.

BAR KRABAR LLAI ALLA TETRAGRAMATON: This spell is used to compel the spirits to appear at a specific place on Saint John's Night.

 📖 Werner, no. 7, 196.

BARNAZA + LEURIAS + BUCELLA: This is the fragment of the beginning of an orison that is intended to provide protection from evil spells and diseases. The *Enchiridion Leonis Pape* incorporates it into an orison in the following way:

> *Barnaza, Lenitas, Buccella, Buccella, Agla, Angla, Tetragrammaton, Adonai.*

Another spell:

> *Barnasa + Leutias + Bucella + Agla + Agla + Tetragrammaton +*

appears in a spell targeting weapons. At the end of the eighteenth century, a grimoire from the Swiss canton of Vaud notes an "orison against all manner of weapon" that opens with:

> *Barnasa † levetas † bucella † agla † Tetragrammaton † adonnay †.*

The closing phrase offers this sequence of words:

> *† crux 4 Elj † Eloï † adonay † corpus christi Colchi † Sabot nomina Deus †.*

 📖 Thiers I, 313ff.; II, 474; *Enchiridion*, 73; Hervé, 362.

BARO BARTO BARTTA SELAMA: This phrase is to be written on a piece of paper that the individual then sticks up his nose to heal a nonspecified affliction, most likely a nosebleed.

 ✦ *Barto, Buri, Buria.*
 📖 Espeland, § 51.

BARTO, BERTO: To stop bleeding caused by an axe or knife, the individual writes these words on the weapon and holds it on the wound: *Barto, Berto I Dem Batio, Bruta Bruta Brixa.*
- ✦ *Buria.*
- 📖 Bang, no. 1125.

2 BARULA ✠ MISPIRATI IN EXA MELEN AUGENS FONS DECEDE BOLDAKŸE SEPARŸ: This incomprehensible phrase forms part of a citation (convocation) ritual of the spirits. This ritual requires the blood of a hoopoe for writing these words and a sword that is used to draw a squared magic circle (*circulum quadratum*), around which is written:

on ✠ *ely* ✠ *eloÿ* ✠ *agla* ✠

A knight will then appear on his steed with a kestrel on his wrist, and he will ask, "What do you want? What is your request? Why have you summoned me? I am ready to perform all that you ask." The caster must refrain from answering and keep his eyes averted, and the knight will leave. Then the caster must turn to face the east, repeating the *Barula* phrase, and a golden knight wearing a crown will appear and ask what he desires.
- 📖 Vinje, no. 9.

BASSOR † MASSON † AGAR: To contend with quartan fever, it is necessary to take three eggs and write: *Bassor † Masson † Agar † Quem † Ysa Res † Hytq Ad Matanor † Groner Hosa* on the first with: *In nomine Patri et Fili et Spiritus sancti. Amen.*
- 📖 Braekman, no. 84.

BASTAM BASTA BRIORA: You must say these words over a pair of dice before rolling them if you wish to win.
- 📖 Bang, no. 1164.

B B B: In Byzantium, the following incomprehensible spell would be written on laurel leaves that would be given to someone suspected of theft: βββτουρεορζφβ

That person would then be unable to use the stolen object and would confess the crime.
- 📖 Tselikas, 74.

BBPPNENA: For protection during a journey or for success at court, it is necessary to wear a ring on which this is written. It seems these letters represent the name of Saint Veronica.

✦ *Beppnniknettani.*

📖 King, 230.

+B+D+Z+K+Z+K+B+D+Z+00+K+: If these *caracteres* are written on a knife with a sharp point and it is used to stab someone, that individual will not bleed.

📖 Vaitkevičienė, no. 1393; Bang, no. 1164.

BEDE † NEBULA † PREBYLA †: This is the beginning of a long charm in bastard Latin that is barely comprehensible. Its purpose is to compel a thief to return stolen property.

> *Bede † nebula † prebyla † Abram † liguit † Jacob † religut † Jsaag † aoldomimum † redurit † dicens: Crux Christi reolucat te aberinte . . .*

This means, "May Abraham bind you! May Jacob hold you fast! May Isaac return you to the house while saying, 'May the cross of Christ bring you back from the East . . .'" The phrase, "May Christ call you back," is found repeated as many times as there are cardinal points. *Aoldomimum* can be read as *ad domum* (at the house) and *aberinte* as *ab Oriente* (of the East). These corrupted forms give an idea of the linguistic difficulties that are presented by charms.

📖 Ohrt I, no. 924.

BEGARISDON ALENGIPP HARIM: To leave a magic circle unscathed, one must say:

> *Begarisdon alengipp Harim gantal satai blaki imtil gilnach mekar Cairupp bermag sanus oganthon bedanki gragrim bestas teras argint.*

📖 Kornreuther, *Magia ordinis artium et scientiarum abtrusarum*, ms. 253.

BEHEYMEREZ AMAULIZ MENEMEYDUZ CAYNAUREZ:

This is an incantation to be performed during a suffumigation once one has manufactured a *voult* (doll) (for information on its manufacture, see *Deytuz*) intended to help an individual win the love of a woman. "I change the mind of the woman X and her feelings for that man by the virtue of these spirits and the power of these spirits Beheydraz, Metlurez, Auleyuz, Nanitaynuz."

📖 *Picatrix* III, 10.

BELL, PELOM, COCORESTU: To win the love of a young woman, these words should be written on a goblet that is given her to drink, filled with any kind of beverage.

📖 BBE, 47.

BENATIR CARARKAU DEDOS ETINARMI: To make oneself invisible and gain entry everywhere, a talisman mounted on a ring is used, and these words spoken: *Benatir* for the water, *Cararkau* for the seas, *Etinarmi* for the air and *Dedos* for the land.

📖 *Trésor*, 179a.

BENEDICTION OF JOB: This phrase is essentially used to conjure worms away and is accompanied by magical phrases such as *Job tridanson + Gruba + Zerobantis +*.

✦ *Job, Magulus, Albo.*
📖 Faggiotto, 249.

BEPPNNIKNETTANI: It is recommended in a tenth-century charm written in Old English to write this phrase in Greek letters:

† †. *A* † † *O* † *y*† *i F B y M* +++++ *B e p p N N I K N E T T A N I*

It is used as a form of protection against witches and the evil spells of elves. The first part of the word is the name of Saint Veronica. It should be noted that the end of the phrase is reminiscent of what is written on magic rings.

✦ *Beronix, Thebal, Gvttani.*
📖 Storms, no. 32; Berthoin-Mathieu, 64ff.

BERONIX, BERONIXA: *Beronix* is invoked to counter bleeding. This name designates Saint Veronica and refers to her biblical legend (Revelation 19:16), which tells us how she suffered blood loss, and it has commonly appeared in charms since the tenth century. In the case of a man bleeding, † *beronix* † was to be written on his right hand; if it was a woman, then † *beronica* † on her left hand. A Rouen manuscript dating from the eleventh century refers to Veronica for the healing of a hemorrhage, but another one from fifteenth-century Basel offers a prayer where Veronica (Feronica) steps in to fight fevers.

 📖 Braekman, 14; Rouen, Municipal Library, ms. 1407, folio 123 v°; Basel, University Library, ms. B. VII. 30, folio 34v°.

BESTARBESTO: See P459, F13192, C49947p92, 582, F3662.

† BESTERA † BESTIE: Around 1393 in France, this spell was written on a crust of bread to cure the bite of a rabid dog:

> † *bestera* † *bestie* † *nay* † *brigonay* † *dictera* † *sagragan* † *es* † *domina* † *fiat* † *fiat* † *fiat*

 📖 Breteton and Ferrier, *Le Mesnagier de Paris*, 788.

BETAT RELTA: These words allegedly cured a dislocation.

 📖 Pseudo Végetius, Book IV, chapter 26.

BIBLE: The Bible was used as an amulet. Verses or certain passages were copied from it to be worn or otherwise carried on the person. Psalm 90 was used this way as a phylactery into the twentieth century. The Gospel of John was one of the most popular texts for this purpose. It offered protection from nosebleeds and bad weather in combination with the *Consummatum est* (John 19:30), as well as against swellings, sprains, and limping (John 19:36). As for Jesus's cry in the Garden of Gethsemane, *"Eli, lamma sabacthani"* (Lord, why have you forsaken me?) from Matthew 27:46 and Mark 15:34, it was wisely used in exorcisms and weather charms. The citation from Luke 4:30, *"Jesus autem transiens,"* offers protection from enemies in the blessing of weapons; that from Jeremiah 10:2, *"a signis coeli quae timent* *gentes,"* from plague and wounds due to weapons; and that of Mark 5:6–9 prevents livestock from being bewitched.

✦ *Psalms.*
📖 Heim, 514ff.; Franz I, 469; II, 203, 431; Thiers I, 356, 366ff., 377, 406, 413; Bang, no. 1294.

† BIEN † BEN † AY † Y: To heal a toothache, these words are written on a small piece of paper to be worn around the neck. *Ay* most likely represents Adonay, and *Y,* Yehova or Yahwe.
📖 Braekman, 120.

BIRTH: Since antiquity numerous charms have been used to facilitate birth. The most widespread one since the thirteenth century is:

> *De viro vir, virgo de virgine. Vicit leo de tribu Juda, radix David. Maria peperit Christum, Elisabet sterilis Johannem Baptistam. Adiurate, infans, per patrem, etc., sive sis masculus an femina, ut exeas de uulua ista. Exinanite. Exinanite* (cf. Psalm 136:7).

Other forms of this charm have been found in England dating from the eleventh century on. The words of Psalm 1:34 and of John 2:43 (*veni foras*) have also been used since the tenth century. We should note that one hundred years earlier, people referred to Deuteronomy 2:21ff. and even to verses from Virgil's *Aeneid* (X, 1 and XI, 1). The Virgin, God, and Saint Margaret were believed to preside over births. Christians in the twelfth century also used the following charm, written on bread:

> Adam † Adam † Adam † come outside † God summons you † Saint Mary, free your servant N. By the mouths of infants and nursing children, you have achieved glory over your name in order to destroy the enemy and to allow the child to survive.

The bread is then given to the woman in labor, who then quickly delivers the baby.

✦ *Boro berto, A b h z P O b L 9 h b m g n, exi foras.*
📖 Thiers I, 472 (*Anna peperit…*); Eliade, 611–15.

BISMILLE ARAATHE: The crafting of the magic mirror known as Floron's Mirror, which allows one to know the past, present, and future, includes a long conjuration that opens with words behind which the first sentence of the Qur'an can be recognized: "In the name of Allah, the Most Gracious, the Most Merciful (بسم الله الرحمن الرحيم :)." The conjuration must partially consist of Arabic that has been corrupted to the point of unintelligibility.

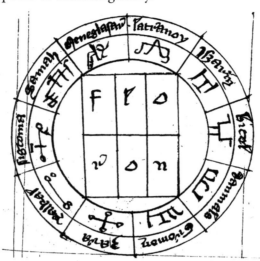

Bismille. Araathe. Mem. Bismissa. Gassim. Gisim. Galisim. Dergosim. Samaiaosim. Balim. Ausini. Taxarim. Zaloimi. Huyacabanay. Illete. Laytimi. Hehelmini. Bacoymi. Choma. Laminas. Unuchomin. Zonim. Narbanatorum. Azarethia. Thachitat. Hinanadom. Illemey sard. Hucatef. Ille megiptimi. Sitaginatim. Uiae. Hamtamice. Tamice. Catiala. Calcarini. Alaoht. Haleytum. Gaptametumij. Morto orfail. Geibel. Huabaton. Albical. Huale pin. Halmagrilie. Hualeon. Huastanie. Hualcamemech. Huatorzor. Illenie. Giptimi. Catgnie. Gacheaine. Lesuma. Lesanim. Apcasale. Albweroahit. Ulleath. Alferd. Usemech. Aptisile. Abfluwarch. Ullelath. Anc dulamoralie. Hahysitimi. Waleles. Lithimi. Caegine. Cacliegineles. Mirabolamini. Abcasile. Albiwahith. Alleath. Hala maton. Unicia. Gaycatalon. Hugia. Gaysoze. Cemeselis. Phalmorach. Bethathura. Huaba. Lagis. Illeme. Ammintini. Geligine. Gathegine. Lesmirapta libe. Albiwath. Ularith.

The caster will then see a knight in armor appear in the mirror, and he will be able to ask him questions.

The *Liber incantationum* provides a second version of this spell following the other one. As it differs on many points, it makes it possible to see how the spellings of magic texts evolved:

Brismissa. Cassini. Gossini. Gaissini. Gratagoasini.samalaosini. Raximi. Gertimi. Caraxini. Maraxini. Sobohini. Herura. Bauor. Allegalite. Alicisti. Alaro. Haletum. Hamaymon. Hyalermon. Bispellimi. Briste. Delmin. Hybelim. Bytho. Yhan. Bythoimin. Chosuma. Lanym. Lonynti. Corrimernum. Uicabanor. Atheretatat. Hyathet. Huyazalon. Ucairf. Illemegyptum. Biragyarius. Hyarice. Heramice. Heramenice. Conolor. Ganstraxumi. Aloryoli. Helytum. Gayta. Mementum. Montoro. Lazyabel. Hubaton. Albnetal. Hyxalepini. Almagarie. Hualeon. Hyalcanixe. Hualenyefet. Huatosor. Allemegistum. Cagine. Sacogyna. Lamyni. Lesymaybdo. Abtysilchi; alluhuait. Ualehat. Arfard. Huzeniecht. Aptihle. Abimerahit. Ullehach. Enzebula. Morabe. Balicum. Ueralesucum. Ceagyna. Lesmyro. Valanum. Aptalile. Asugnathetht. Ualleaach. Hyamacharon. Hyabia. Gayatalon. Hya. Yagapolozol. Phalmolmeth. Bethaura. Huaba. Laygip. Illenietentum. Caygine. Oragine. Deragimeles. Myrapcalile. Ulleytith. Setercaha.

The *Picatrix* (IV, 7, 23) mentions the crafting of a mirror intended to raise storms. The names of the seven planets were written on it—Zohal, Musteri, Marrech, Xemz, Zohara, Hotarid, Alchamar—their seven figures, their seven angels—Captiel, Staquiel, Samael, Raphael, Anael, Michael, Gabriel—and the seven winds—Barchia, Bethel almoda, Hanamar benabis, Zobaa marrach, Fide arrach, Samores maymon, Aczabi. Comparison of the texts makes it possible to understand how the incantation of Floron's Mirror was formed.

📖 *Liber incantationum*, ms. Clm 809, folios 37 r°–39 r°. For more on divination with mirrors, see Delatte, *La catoptromancie grecque et ses dérivés*.

BLAI: This word was found on the corpse of a Helvetian mercenary in the Trione Valley in Italy in 1779. He was interred in Groscavallo (Val Grande di Lanzo, province of Turin). He had carried it in his shirt, like an amulet.

📖 *Registro dei morti della parrocchia di Groscavallo,* anno 1779.

BLRURCION: To give assistance to a woman in labor, the following phrase should be written: *Blrurcion † blrurun † blutanno † bluttiono †*, followed by "Jesus of Nazareth, king of the Jews," and placed on her belly. Another manuscript suggests: *bhuron bhurinum bhitaono.*

 📖 London, British Library, Sloane 2584, folio 25 v°; Sloane 3160 (sixteenth century), folio 169r°.

+B:+N:+G:+N:+R:+4: For protection against any kind of damage in nineteenth-century Poland, the *caracteres* below would be written on a piece of paper to be carried on one's person:

+B:+N:+G:+N:+R:+4
O:+B:+C:+B:+4:+
C:+C:+M:+N:+S:+B+e

 📖 Vaitkevičienė, no. 1621.

B. O. K.: The beginning of a sequence of *caracteres* that must be worn on one's left hand if one wishes to regain his lord's favor and reconcile with him.

B.O.K. n. f. 9. R. S. P. b. C. O. H. D. A. A. l. q. P. 9 gg G ††† H. D. S. p. s. F. G. A. I. O. ω Gleon y y † R. R. R. o-S Cs C. t o r R.

 S.p.s. is probably "spiritus"; *Cs,* "Christus"; and *C.t or r R,* "creator."
 📖 Aymar, 332.

BOLUS † BOLUS † BOLUS †: To cure a toothache in twentieth-century France, the tooth would be lightly grazed with a new nail while whispering these words. The nail would then be hammered into a stump while repeating three Our Fathers and three Hail Marys. The ritual includes an example of an evil transferred to a plant, which was once quite common. In earlier times, sick children were passed through the fork of a tree in order to rid them of an illness.

 📖 Camus 2001, 93.

† BON † PEN † NA † ASON: According to a twelfth-century German manuscript, this phrase would expel worms.

 📖 Heim, 555.

BOR PHOR PHORBA: In a Greek exorcism featuring the use of olive branches as whips, the possessed, after the demon had been expelled, would be placed on a tin sheet inscribed with these words:

> *BOR Phor PHORBA Phor PHORBA BES CHARIN BAUBA TE Phor BORPHORBA PHORBABOR BAPHORBA PHABRAIE PHORBA PHARBA PHORPHOR PHORBA BOBORBORBA PAMPHORBA PHORPHOR PHORBA, protect N.*

The variant *BORHORB ABARBOR* can be found throughout the Mediterranean basin on curse tablets and amulets. It is generally associated with Hecate and Selene.

📖 PGM IV, 1227–64.

BORO BERTO BRIORE: A medical manuscript of English origin that has been preserved in Stockholm and dates from the fifteenth century has passed down a charm intended to free a woman who is awaiting a child. We can recognize the "standard" Christian phrases it contains, such as "Christ the doctor incarnate who is obedient until his death on the cross."

> *Boro berto briore † Vulnera quinque dei sint medicina mei † Tahebal †† gheter ††† Guthman †††† Purld cramper † Cristus † factus † est † pro † nobis † obediens † vsque † ad † mortem † autem † crucis †*

This is followed by an appeal addressed to Mary and the saints. *Obediens usque ad mortem* comes from Paul's Epistle to the Philippians. *Tahebal Gheter Guthman* is the corruption of the phrase "Thebal Guth Gutany." A gold ring dating from around 1500 that has been discovered in Denmark bears the inscription: *buro † berto † beriora.* The beginning of the phrase has been worn away.

📖 Stockholm, Royal Library, ms. XIV in kl. 4°, folio 143; Ohrt II, 96.

BRAC † CABRAC † CARABRA † CADEBRAC † CABRACAM † I HEAL YOU: These words are spoken three times in succession, then the speaker blows into the mouth of the ailing sheep to heal it of "ulcerous lesions" and fevers. It is a variant of *Abracadabra.*

📖 Honorius, 106.

BREF (short letter, note): This is the name given to various amulets in the Germanic regions (Middle High German *breve*) from the Middle Ages to today (*brief*). A *bref* often consists of images of the saints combined with prayers and relic fragments. All the component pieces are placed in a pouch that is then hung around the neck of a child. A bref can also be a piece of parchment or paper on which are written abbreviated spells, in which phrases are often reduced to a series of letters.

BRINTATÊN SIPHRI BRISCHULMA: This is the beginning of a Greek phrase from the fourth or fifth century for summoning the good demon Horus-Chnuphi and the saint Orion, who rests in the North:

> *Brintatên siphri brischulma arouaxar bamesen chriphi niptoumichmoumaôph*
>
> (Βρινταθην σιφρι βρισχυλμα αρουαξαρ βαμεσεν χριφι νιπτουμιχμουμαωφ)

The invocation closes with *Arbath, Abaoth, Bakchabrè*.

📖 PGM 1, 4ff.

B.R.O.D.L.Y.: To win at cards, one must write these letters on his right hand in his own blood.

📖 Bang, no. 1134.

BUD: This single syllable is to be spoken to prevent scorpions from causing harm.

📖 Scot, Book XII, chapter 16; Thiers I, 408.

†† BÜMA: Following the conjuring of an elven spirit or dwarf (*wichteleyn*), in which a spell is repeated three times to compel it to come, one must add this:

> †† *büma* † *lasa* † *lamina* † *yoth* † *Athana* †

This charm dates from the sixteenth century.

📖 A. E. Schönbach, "Eine Auslese altdeutscher Segensformeln," *Analecta Graecensia. Fechtschrift zur 42. Versammlung deutscher Philologen und Schulmänner in Wien*, 44ff.

BUONI JACUM: When one is compelled to fight in a duel, these words should be written on a ribbon that is then tied around the right wrist. The adversary's sword will not find its target.

 📖 *Dragon noir,* 165ff.; Werner, no. 9, 198.

BURI, BERTO, BERIG: To stop a nosebleed, write these words on a piece of paper, then place it in the nose. These spells were extremely popular in all the Scandinavian countries. *Buro † berto † beriora* can be found written on a fifteenth-century ring, and this phrase can be seen on one from the following century: *burabariaberioraiabaltesar.* They were used to stop bleeding.

 Variants: *Burot Bartot Bararot; Buro Bartte Beriora; Bure Berte Beria* (cf., Ohrt II, 96).
 ✦ *Barto, Buria.*
 📖 Bang, no. 1092.

BURIA BALTA BORIA: To stop bleeding, these words should be written on a piece of paper, which is then cast into the fire.

 ✦ *Barto, Buri.*
 📖 Espeland, no. 3.

B . 9 . ED . X . V . 1 . ¥ . X . T . W . O: To recover stolen property, a shaving or piece of something that was most closely in contact with the stolen item is cut off, and the above phrase is written on it in swallow's blood. This writing is then placed in the forest beneath a tree that is split in half. After this, the robber will know no rest during night or day until he returns what he stole.

 📖 Bak, no. 63.

This is as true a copie of the holie writing, that was brought downe from heauen by an angell to S. Leo pope of Rome; & he did bid him take it to king Charles, when he went to the battell at Ronceuall. And the angell said, that what man or woman beareth this writing about them with good deuotion, and saith euerie daie three Pater nosters, three Aues, and one Creede, shall not that daie be ouercome of his enimies, either bodilie or ghostlie; neither shalbe robbed or slaine of theeues, pestilence, thunder, or lightening; neither shall be hurt with fier or water, nor combred with spirits, neither shall haue displeasure of lords or ladies: he shall not be condemned with false witnesse, nor taken with fairies, or anie maner of axes, nor yet with the falling euill. Also, if a woman be in trauell, laie this writing vpõ hir bellie, she shall haue easie deliuerance, and the child right shape and christendome, and the mother purification of holy church, and all through vertue of these holie names of Jesus Christ following:

✠ Iesus ✠ Christus ✠ Messias ✠ Soter ✠ Emmanuel ✠ Sabbaoth ✠ Adonai ✠ Vnigenitus ✠ Maiestas ✠ Paracletus ✠ Saluator noster ✠ Agiros iskiros ✠ Agios ✠ Adanatos ✠ Gasper ✠ Melchior ✠ & Balthasar ✠ Matthæus ✠ Marcus ✠ Lucas ✠ Iohannes.

Pope Leo III's prayer addressed to Charlemagne,
from Reginald Scot, *Discoverie of Witchcraft*, 1584

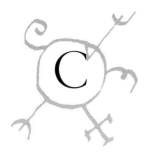

CA D I B V S I N R TER NA DUIS: To provide relief for a toothache that has lasted nine days, these letters should be written on a piece of paper on a Saturday evening. Although this step is not specified here, other spells indicate that this paper should then be pressed against the jaw or ailing tooth.

✦ *Athagon.*
📖 Bang, no. 1120.

CAIO LAIO QUAQUE UOAQUE OFER SÆLOFICIA SLEAH MANNA WYRM: This phrase must be chanted to heal a toothache. The Old English *sleah manna wyrm* can be translated as "strikes the worm of man." According to very ancient belief, it was thought this condition was caused by a worm gnawing on the tooth. This belief can be found in Babylon and in ancient Greece in Homer's *Hymn to Demeter,* and Shakespeare has his character Benedick say, "I have the tooth-ache," to which his friends respond, "What sigh for the tooth-ache? Where is but a humour or a worm?" (*Much Ado About Nothing* III, 2).

📖 Berthoin-Mathieu, 94, 473ff.; Storms. no. 65.

CALAMARIS: This is the word the Scandinavians use like *Abracadabra* to heal fever. This word is written down in a series,

```
Colameris+
Colameri+
Colamer+
Colame+
Colam+
Cola+
Col+
Co+
```

removing one letter each time (see Reductive Spell). The word has enjoyed enormous popularity, as shown by its numerous variants: *Kalamaris, Kalameres, Kalemeres, Kalemeris, Kalamarum, Kalminius, Karemerou, Kulumaris, Calæmarem, Halamitis.* The Norwegian Black Book of Jeløen version is shown on page 81.

 📖 Ohrt II, 110–12; Espeland, no. 28.

CANCKERA: This word is featured in a spell for getting rid of canker sores. All the different kinds are listed in the form of an alliterative phrase:

> *Canckera canckere canckere cankeri canckero canckero canckera canckerum.*

 📖 Braekman, 148.

VI CAPTOS, SADUCES: These words are written on a piece of barley bread as a cure for fever.

 📖 *Grimoires,* no. 48.

CARA CARICE: These words were used during the Middle Ages for protection against hemorrhages. The phrase took this following form during the sixteenth century: *In nomine Patris & filij & spiritus sancti, curat cara sarite confirma consana imaholite.*

 ✦ *Cato; chimrat.*
 📖 Franz II, 174; Braekman, 10; Weyer IV, 7.

CARADO: The first magical word from a spell against storms that dates from the thirteenth century: *Carado sancte Enoch sancta Fides me benedicat,* which means, "Carado, may Saint Enoch and Saint Foy grant me their blessing." It is reasonable to compare *carado* with the old French word *caraude,* "sorcery, spell, charm."

 📖 Franz II, 62.

CA ROI: For protection against daily fever, these two words must be written on an olive leaf that has been plucked before sunrise and then worn at the throat.

 📖 Thiers I, 417.

CATANOMARE: A word used in 1789, from which a letter must be subtracted, sometimes each day, that will, through sympathetic magic, cause a cold fever to vanish. This word is but one example of what is called a reductive phrase.
- ✦ *Cattatibusantrakus, Calamaris, Abracadabra.*
- 📖 Bang, no. 1047.

CA TA TIMUS: These words must be written three times in order to be effective against a toothache.
- 📖 Bang, no. 1102.

CATO CARUCE: These are magic words from a twelfth-century charm intended to heal snakebite: *Cato, caruce, sanum reduce, reduce sanum, Emmanuel Paraclitus.* Also present in this same time period is *Cara, caruce, senael, emmanuel, paraclitus,* and so on, whose meaning can be made clearer when compared with a spell for bleeding: *+ Caro + Cruce + fac restringere ysmahelite. famule tue N. Amen.* Senaël is the name of an angel, the Ismaelite is Hagar (Genesis 16:11), and the Paraclete and Emmanuel come from the Bible (John 14:16; Isaiah 7:14).
- ✦ *Cara carice.*
- 📖 Franz II, 175; Heim, 555; Thiers I, 357.

CATTATIBUSANTRAKUS: This is an example of a reductive phrase for fevers. It was used around 1780. By subtracting one letter each time you recopy the word, you cause the fever to fade away gradually.
- ✦ *Catanomare.*
- 📖 Bang, no. 1048.

CE: See *Consummatum est.*

CELAS CELIAR CELIAS: This is a phrase from a spell from the tenth or eleventh century for dispelling fevers.
- 📖 Franz II, 483.

† **CHAMACHA † AMACHA:** When they are written above the door of the house, these words make it possible to recover a piece of stolen property: † *Chamacha* † *Amacha* † *Amschala* † *Waystou* † *Alam* †† *Elast Lamach.*
 📖 *Egyptian Secrets* II, 157.

✱ **CHAVIT RAUTO †AD QUI BANY:** An obscure spell used in the ninth century to heal or prevent diseases affecting livestock.

 ✱ *chavit rauto* †*ad qui bany* †*de p̄ corte ut maxime rector* ✡

 📖 Saint Gall, codex 751; Heim, 564.

CHEILEI. CECCE: These are the opening words to an incantation intended to heal a toothache:

 Cheilei.cecce. becce. upseruicce. slamone. wuerm. naco. dicapron. s; noli. coli hyt an yerthe hates byrnet.

It is a variant of *Caio laio.*
 📖 Berthoin-Mathieu, 217.

✠ **CHIMRAT, CHARA:** To halt the blood flowing out of a wound, the following phrase would be recited:

 ✠ *Chimrat, chara, sarite, confirma, consona, Imohalite.*

It is a variation of *Cara carice.*
 📖 Scot, Book XII, chapter 18.

[CH] X : I : P : S : D : : This is the beginning of a coded phrase that closes a spell for healing fevers and dates from the beginning of the sixteenth century.

 $\chi : I : p : s : d : e : \sigma : d. \chi : rl : e : que : o. . \sigma. \sigma. p :q : d :n : y : \chi : \sigma : b : a. a. a. \chi : \sigma : d :$

It lists the seven sister fevers. For the three *a*'s, we should probably read *agios agios agios;* the χ is most likely the abbreviation of Christ.
 ✦ *Sicilia.*
 📖 Ohrt I, no. 1143.

CHOSTIA, SACRAN VEGO CAVRUM: These words are used to get a vehicle moving when a horse can't put it in motion.

Chostia, sacran vego cavrum. By placing the trouble on the Great Putiphar for the previously existing spell and character.

The corrupted Latin must have originally been: *Hostia sacra vera corrum,* which appears in a 1670 counterspell.

📖 *Le médecin des pauvres;* Honorius, 118.

CHRISME: This is a Christian symbol formed from the two Greek letters for *X* and *P* (*chi* and *rho*), used to designate Christ. It can be found on countless amulets. The letters *alpha* (A) and *omega* (Ω) express the notion of the whole and refer to his divinity.

CHRIST'S FIVE WOUNDS: Countless healing charms rely on this phrase: "May the five wounds of Christ/be a remedy for me/him" (*Vulnera quinque Dei / sint medicina mei / sui*), which it was said Saint Clare of Assisi recited frequently in the thirteenth century. We come across it in healing spells for fistulas, cankers, cuts, "all kinds of open wounds," and contagious diseases, and for providing protection against evil spirits and demons. Generally speaking, other references to the New Testament, like the cross and the Passion of Our Lord, come into play to reinforce this spell. The *Liber incantationum* provides an odd invocation in a session of onychomancy (fingernail divination): "By the 1006 wounds of our

Lord Jesus Christ, by the 106 wounds of our Lord Jesus Christ, by the 56 wounds of our Lord Jesus Christ."

The *Enchiridion Leonis Pape* has given us the following charm against "knives, swords, spears, arrows, and all kinds of weapons":

May the five wounds of Christ guard me! *Heli, heloy, hat, clavis, hegon, heth, hue. Proth, Ceteras, feros, homo.*

What we have here are essentially the names of God (*Heth, Heloy, Heth*) and some Latin words (key, others, man) that make no sense.

📖 *Liber incantationum,* folio 98 v°, Hunt, 266ff., 98. Other references: Ohrt I, no. 116, 263 (with *Ananzapta*), 265, 266 (with *Christus vincit*), 812 (to put a rifle out of commission); D. Gray, "The Five Wounds of Our Lord," *Notes and Queries* 208 (1963): 50–59, 82–89, 127–34, 163–68; Schulz, 313ff., 352ff. Camus 2002, 331.

CHRISTIAN SPELL: Medieval charms largely relied on the Holy Scriptures from which they lopped phrases they transformed into spells. These later are sometimes used alone and sometimes mixed with pagan elements; sometimes we have several.

✦ *Agla, Ananizapta, Abraham, Arcum, Christ's Five Wounds, Christus, Consummatum, Crux, Deus, Dismas, Dmvodm, Iesus/Jhesus, Ecce Crucem, Ecce Crucis, Effata, Ego Sum, Eleyson, Eli Lamma, Gaspar, Gospel, Hely, Holy Cross, Ibi Ceciderent, I.n.r.i., Iob/Job, Memento, Miserere, Omnis Spiritus, On, Os, Pax, Psalms, Sanguet, Sdiabiz, Tetragrammaton, Three Kings, Verbum, Vincit, V R S V S M V.*

† CHRISTUS BRUTUS ET DUTUS EST VANUM: By saying these words when you touch the lower jaw with a finger that has been dipped in holy water, you can heal godron [keratosis?].

📖 Honorius, 109.

CHRISTUS NATUS † CHRISTUS PASSUS EST: "Christ is born, Christ is dead" is a phrase that frees one of quotidian fever. It

is followed by the command, "Free X of fevers! Amen." To heal fever in fourteenth century Italy, this spell would be written on a sage leaf that was then given to the patient to eat († nato è Christo † morto è Christo † e risuscitato è Christo). In Sicily, a more developed spell was used, one written in Greek letters, for protection from fire: "Christ was born, baptized, and crucified; he resurrected and was buried. Flee far, fire, from this servant of Christ . . . " (Christû fu nnatu e fu baptizzatu e ffu crucificatu e rrisursitatu e fu sultirratu. Fui focu arestu di lu servu di Christu . . .). Appeal was then made to Saint Luke and the apostles Mark, John, and Matthew.
✦ *Jhesu.*
📖 Franz II, 105, 199; Braekman, no. 78; Amati, 105; Schneegans, 585.

CHRISTUS NATUS EST † CHRISTUS PASSUS EST † CHRISTUS CRUCIFIXUS EST † CHRISTUS LANCEA PERFORATUS EST: This extremely widespread spell was used for a variety of afflictions. It works for bleeding and for thorns.

When the crosses are replaced by *aaius* (meaning *agios,* "saint") and the last part is changed to *Christus resurrexit a mortuum,* it is used to fight erysipelas. By removing the verb *to be* (*est*) and replacing *lancea perforatus est* with *Christus venturus,* shivers and fevers can be banished. By keeping only the first two series and by adding "free X of fevers," a person can obtain an amulet against quotidian fever. Today this phrase is used to heal cuts and wounds and splinters and thorns.
📖 Hunt, 9, no. 67; *Grimoires,* no. 278, 284; Storms, no. 27; Berthoin-Mathieu, 62, 130; Braekman, no. 78; Camus 1990, no. 50, 52, 92, 93.

CHRISTUS TE VOCAT: "Christ summons you" is a prayer used during a birth.
📖 Braekman, no. 49.

CHRISTUS TONAT † ANGELUS NUNCIAT † JOHANNES PREDICAT †: To heal fever, one should write on a sage leaf for three days in a row: "Christ thunders" on the first day, "the angel announces" on the second, then "John preaches" on the third. At the same time the individual should recite one Our Father, one Hail Mary, and one Apostles' Creed on the first day, two of each of these prayers on the second, and three of each on the third. The individual should also have a mass said for the Holy Ghost, one for Saint Michael, and one for Saint John the Baptist.

 📖 Stockholm, Royal Library, ms. XIV in kl. 4°, folio 35; Braekman, 112.

CHRISTUS VAINCUS: To prevent wolves from entering the fields where the sheep are pastured, one turns to the east while saying a prayer that includes the conjuration, "Go far from here to seek your prey, wolf, she-wolf, and wolf cub," and closes with, "Begone O Satana! [*sic*]. The ritual is repeated toward the other cardinal points, and one casts salt while saying, "Vanus vanes Christus vaincus, to the attack Saint Sylvain in the name of Jesus." The errors in this spell bear the mark of an oral tradition.

 📖 Honorius, 94.

CHRISTUS VINCIT † CHRISTUS REGNAT † CHRISTUS IMPERAT †: "Christ triumphs, Christ rules, Christ commands" is a phrase that can be found in the tenth century in the *Laudes seu acclamationes* of the Special Liturgy of Reims, with a fourth proposition: May Christ protect us from all evil (*Christus ab omni malo nos defendat*).

 This was used by the army of Frederick I as a battle cry and was employed for a variety of ends: against fistulas, boils, cankers, glanders, and eye problems. For a birth, *Christus te vocat ut nascaris* would be added to help the pregnant woman. This phrase would be spoken to counter fever while drawing three crosses on the patient's right hand, then writing *Pater † on † Filius † on Spiritus sanctus* on the back of the hand. The phrase would finally be erased with water, which was then given to the patient to drink. On the second day the same procedure was followed, but writing the words *on aries † on . . . en agnus †* instead, and on the third the operation was repeated, but by writing *on leo † on vitulus † on vermis †*. This phrase has the value of an amulet and protects one from all evils. If one adds *Christus sanat* to it, the phrase stops bleeding, on condition that one dip one's thumb into the blood and write *consummatum est* with it. Otherwise it works against fevers, especially cold ones, and eye pains, and for uncovering the identity of a thief. Combined with divine names and names of the evangelists and the Three Kings, it allows one to be esteemed and be in favor with one's lord. Around 1815, it was reduced to the triple repetition of *Christus vincit* (Bang, no. 1074).

The same phrase can be found in a spell against mastitis, and it appears in the *Charm of Saint Suzanne* preceded by "and free your servant of this pain † in the name of the Father † and the Son † and the Holy Ghost † Amen." Against the plague, it would be written on a piece of virgin parchment that was long enough to encircle the neck. It would be tied shut with a linen thread after the Our Father and Apostles' Creed were recited.

Against meteors, the phrase is terminated with the addition of "to dissolve the clouds and tempests" (*Christus vincit, Christus regnat, Christus imperat vobis nubes et tempestates ut dissolvamini*). It is found abbreviated to *Christus Imperad* in Iceland.

In the Black Book from Vinje, Norway, the phrase appears in a charm intended to reveal in water the identity of a thief. The phrase is used as an epigraph in *Le médicin des pauvres, ou recueil de prières pour le soulagement des maux d'estomac, charbon, pustule, fièvres, plaie, &c* (*Doctor of the Poor, or Prayer Book for the Relief of Stomachache, Coal, Pustule, Fevers, Wound, etc.*). a hawked pamphlet from the Blue Library of Troyes.*

📖 Braekman, no. 148, no. 151ff.; Ohrt I, no. 1156; Hunt, 98; Braekman, no. 73; no. 148, 17; Ohrt I, no. 1144; Braekman, no. 164, no. 49, no. 90; Hunt, 84, 234; Ohrt I, no. 266, no. 269, no. 329–330, no. 974; Braekman, no. 234, no. 101; *Galdrakver*, 50; Vinje, no. 10; Bang, no. 1287. Other examples: Franz II, 87, 96, 106, 497, Ohrt I, no. 1087 (in the *Charm of Saint Agatha*); Van Haver, no. 549; Aymar, 325, 334.

† ch. u. r. k. X. σ. r. d. er. Y: These *caracteres* form the closing of the *Charm of Saint Elizabeth* in an Utrecht manuscript.

📖 Utrecht, Bibliotheek der Rijksuniversiteit, Ms 1355, 16°, folio 122 v°.

CHUCH BACHUCH BAKACHUCH: On a lead tablet discovered in Palestine and written in Greek, a long magic text can be read that was intended to bind a certain Samatian. It opens like this:

---

*[A famous collection of popular literature from the Middle Ages.—*Trans.*].

CHUCH BACHUCH BAKACHUCH BAKAXICH UCH BAZABACHUCH BENNEBECHUCH BADETOPHOTH BAINCHOOOCH

The body of the text also contains the words *Eulamô* (see that entry) and the spell *Maskelli Maskellô* (see that entry), and the names of various deities of the Middle East.

 📖 Gager, 108ff.; Lexa, 89.

CHUOCH EDAMINOPH (χυοχ εδαμινοφ): If you write these words on a frog tongue and then place it on the chest of a sleeping woman, she will immediately reveal everything she has done in her life.

 Variants: *χονοχ; cosoc; cuceh, cuchos; eola poφ edaminoph.*
 📖 *Cyranides*, II, B.

C. I. M. B. V. (meaning *Conceptio immaculata beatae Mariae virginis*): Formerly this phrase would be written either in its entirety or abbreviated, then placed in henhouses to ensure good egg laying.

CINIUM † CINIUM † GROSSIUM † STRASSUS † GOD † STRASSUS: When a dog has been bitten by a rabid dog, he should be given these words to drink after the words have been dissolved in water.

 📖 *Egyptian Secrets* II, 161.

CIOÉ SU MUGE DUÉ: For a woman in labor to give birth quickly, these words should be spoken over her.

 📖 *Libro de segretto e di magia*, 4.

C KORSMISE DEN I MAY: These words are recited three times over flour and salt in order to paralyze raptors who might otherwise harm the cattle. *Korsmise* means "mass of the Holy Cross."

 📖 Bang, no. 1169.

C.M.B. †† ABI MASSA DENTI LANTIEN J.J.J.: The purpose of this phrase is to provide protection to livestock from all sorcery.

 ✦ *Habi Massa.*
 📖 Spamer, 380.

CMB/KNB: These are the initials for the names of the Three Magi: Caspar, Melchoir, and Balthazar. They were inscribed over the doors of homes, barns, and stables with consecrated chalk, generally as a means of protecting the structures from fire and/or water. This is why

$$\dagger$$
$$C \dagger M \dagger B$$

is written on all the doors in Styria during King's Night.

In July 2012, in the town of Haslach in the Kinzig Valley (in the Black Forest), I noticed these types of inscriptions on numerous houses, accompanied by the millennial figure (see illustration below), which suggests that this protection spell needs to be renewed annually.

These initials have also been interpreted to mean *Christus mansionem benedicat* (may Christ bless this house). A document from 1566 recommends cutting an apple in half, writing or carving CMB on each half, then giving them to a pregnant woman to eat. This will prevent stillbirth. According to Pope John XXI (in 1276), whoever carries the names of the Three Kings on his person shall be protected from epilepsy.

The spell can also be found on protective notes, like the one shown on page 92, which combines it with I.N.R.I. and other Christian symbols.

The names of the Three Magi were also found on a *bref* that protected, or so it is claimed, a knight that Count Philipp of Flanders

wished to execute for his misdeeds. When it proved impossible to hurt this brigand, he was questioned, and he showed them the *bref,* on which was written:

> † *Iehus christus* † *deus fortis* † *Protege* † *Salva* † *Benedic* † *Sanctifica* † *Persignum sancte crucis de inimicis nostris Amen* † *Kaspar* † *Balthasar* † *Melchior* † *Jhus autem transiens permedium ibat* † *Vade inpace Amen* (Jesus Christ, strong God, protect, save, bless, sanctify [us] by the sign of the cross against our enemies † May Jesus pass among them † Go in peace, Amen.)

✦ *Three Kings, Jesus autem transiens.*
📖 Wackernagel, 611; T. Vernaleken, 342.

COHIZIARA OFFINA ALTA NETERA FUARA MENUET:
When repeated three times, this phrase was supposed to compel a spirit's obedience.

📖 *Verus Jesuitarvm Libellus.*

СOMПTA OCOΓMA CTYΓONTOEMA EKTYTOΠO † BERONICE: This phrase comes from a prayer that is used to halt bleeding; it is a mixture of Greek and Latin letters.

📖 Storms, no. 60.

CONSUMMATUM EST: These words that Christ spoke while on the cross (John 19:30) are used as the closing phrase in charms against worms. A cross is inserted between each syllable in these cases. The spell is used to stop hemorrhaging and must be written on the patient's forehead. The vein must be "fixed fast," as Jesus was fixed to the cross, so the blood will cease flowing. It is also used to arrest bleeding in horses and to stop nosebleeds. It is sometimes combined with *Agla*. When these words appear at the end of a spell or prayer, their semantic value is equivalent to that of *fiat*.

When combined with *caracteres* that are carved with a knife on the door to a room where a couple sleeps together, this spell prevents copulation. The spell was abbreviated to *CE* on Christian amulets, and it forms part of the *Orison of Seven Words,* attributed to Bede, which ensures protection against all evils and prevents an individual from dying without making his final confession.

In the form *ego mago et super magnum consummatum est,* which is repeated three times, the spell prevents a weapon from lasting a long time.

In Columbia, these words are part of a prayer intended to protect people from accidents.

Variants: *consummactum est, consumativi est, Kunsumantm mest, con sum actus,* † *Con* † *Su* † *Ma* † *Tuen* † *est.*

✦ *Christus vincit.*

📖 Scot, Book XII, chapter 18; Braekman, 12, 13, 18, 147, 164; Ohrt I, no. 173; *Dragon noir,* 165; *Enchiridion,* 1667, 104; Thiers I, 377, 413; Ohrt I, no. 267; Van Haver, no. 682 (against fire); *Secrets magiques pour l'amour,* no. LXI; Werner, no. 11, 199; *Libro de segretto e di magia,* 6.

CORIDAL NARDAC DEGON: These words are spoken aloud to prevent someone from eating at the table. It is necessary to stick a needle that was used to sew a dead man's shroud into the underside of this table as well as into the chair in which the targeted individual is sitting.

📖 Honorius, 68.

COVELTHO: If this word is spoken over an epileptic when he or she is suffering from a fit, while placing a hand on a live cat at the same time, the sufferer will instantly recover.

Variants: *covelcho, convertho, conveltho, condito;* κοβελθω.

📖 *Cyranides,* II, E.

CRÉON: A magic word from a Solomonic conjuration of the *Grimorium verum*. When repeated three times, it makes it possible for three women or three men to appear in your room after dinner!

CRON + CORON + CRON +: The start of a spell against rabies; one must take a mouthful of bread and, while drawing a rose from one's left hand, say:

> Cron + Coron + Cron + Laron + Korzon + Delphin + Dedelphin + Deus + Meus. +

📖 Vaitkevičienė, no. 1396 (spell from Lithuania).

CROSTES FURINOT KATIPA GARINOS: By placing a talisman bearing these words over the heart, one could recognize or stupefy people of ill intent. They could only recover the use of their limbs if the word Tonirut was spoken.

📖 *Trésor,* 183a.

CRUX CHRISTI REDUCAT: This phrase, which means "may the cross of Christ bring back," is commonly used to obtain the return of something that has disappeared, either by theft or some other means. When the missing things are livestock, it is necessary to speak the phrase aloud three times in the direction of each of the cardinal points. The reference is to the wood of the cross, which was hidden, then found. The same phrase is used when an animal has been stolen. When this spell has been completed it compels the intervention of the four directions.

> *Crux Christi ab oriente reducat*
> *Crux Christi ab occidente reducat*
> *Crux Christi ab meridie reducat*
> *Crux Christi ab aqvilone reducat.*

This is what it became in the fifteenth century:

> *Crux Christi rolucat te aberinte*
> *Crux Christi ruolucat te ab oe siolente*
> *Crux Christi reducat teameriolie*
> *Crux Christi reolucattem abaqvilone.*

It is obvious that the source manuscript of this charm was poorly deciphered, as witness the confusions between *d* and *ol, s* and *r,* and so forth.

 📖 Berthoin-Mathieu, 140, 162, 166, 178, 204, 218; Ohrt I, no. 924; Stevens, 23.

CRUX SACRA: Christ's cross is often invoked for protection against fevers. This is done by using the phrase: *Crux sacra* † *Crux splendida* †, followed by the request: "Cross, save and free this servant of God X from all fevers and ills, past, present, and future." It appears countless times in the manuscripts.

 The cross is combined with magic words and with *Sator Arepo* in a recipe for learning if an individual is a witch. The following spell is written on a piece of paper to which some Saint John's wort is added.

S A T O R †
Crux Jesu Christi mildepos
A R E P O †
Crux Jesu Christi mesepos
T E N E T †
Crux Jesu Christi Habenepos
O P E R A
R O T A S

 The paper and herb must be sewn together in a piece of leather. If you wish to identify the witch, you should carry this item on your person when the fourth quarter of the moon begins. No witch will be able to remain in the same room as you.

 ✦ *Holy Cross.*
 📖 London, British Library, Arundel 2558, in quart., folio 195, fifteenth century; *Egyptian Secrets* II, 69.

77 7 C T A N E A E G C X † X † C T H': To ensure that a woman have a good birth, hang these *caracteres* around her neck. If you wish to experiment to discover their virtues, attach them to a sterile fruit tree, and it will bear fruit.

 📖 Hunt, 31.

CUIGEU: On an opisthographic tablet from Hadrumetum (Roman Africa) we find a charm for causing the death of chariot drivers and their horses during a race in the arena. It includes a series of magic words arranged in a column next to the demon Antmoaraitto: *Cuigeu Censeu Cinbeu Perfleu Diarunco Deasta bescu berebescu anurara baζagra.*

The adjuration closes with Ιαω Ιασδαω οοριω αηια.

 Audollent, 396ff.

CURU CUS CO CAL: A Norwegian phrase from around 1800 for healing nosebleeds.

 Bang, no. 1103.

CUZO: If someone wishes to heal snakebite, this following phrase should be written on a paper that the afflicted individual then swallows: *Cuzo ouzuze sanum redire reputa sanum Emmanuël Paraclitus,* etc.

✦ *Cara carice, Cato caruce.*
 Thiers I, 411.

CYPRIANUS: The *Grimoire of Cyprianus* (*Cyprianus, Cyprianus kunstbok, Cyprianus frikonst*) is said to have been discovered at Wittemberg Academy in Germany around 1520, according to some, or 1722 according to others. It is a parchment manuscript kept in a marble chest. Copies of this grimoire of Danish origin later could be found throughout Scandinavia. It includes recipes for learning the future, fulfillment of wishes, healing spells, and so forth. The publishing dates are highly unreliable and range from 1516 to the nineteenth century, with a spike in production during the eighteenth century. The contents vary widely depending on the source manuscripts and publications.

This story was told in Schleswig around 1920:

Cyprianus was a Dane living on an island who was so evil that when he died the devil expelled him from Hell and sent him back home. There he wrote nine books in Old Danish, filled with spells and charms. Whoever reads them becomes the prey of the devil.

It is said that a monk made three or nine copies and spread them everywhere. The Count of Plön is said to have owned one, chained and buried beneath his castle, because he was so terrified after reading the first eight books he decided to hide them from eyes of the world. Another copy still exists in Flensburg. Several charms and prescriptions from these books are still known from old. Whoever wishes to be initiated into this knowledge must renounce his faith.

📖 Oslo, Norway, National Library: Ms. 8° 10, *Cyprianus,* copied around 1790; Ms. 4° 832; Ms. 8° 81, *Cyprianus-Formaning,* 29 pages, copied circa 1650–1700 by Tinn, in Telemark, discovered in 1868; Ms. 4° 279, *Extract aus dem Cypriano,* 18 pages, circa 1700; Ms. 8° 640a, *Cyprianus frikonst . . . ,* 1719, 10 + 1 pages, by Galgum, in the Romedal, around 1780; Ms. 8° 640e, *Cyprianus . . . ,* printed in Wittemburg in 1509, 34 pages, by Moland, in the Telemark; Ms. 4° 832, *Cyprianus, den over ald Verden viit berømte Sorte-Konstner . . . ,* Savanger anno 1699, 53 pages, circa 1750; Ms. 8° 2062b, *Den anden Del af Cyprianis skrifter . . . ,* 8 pages, 6–8, circa 1790–1800, discovered in Vingrom, Fåberg Parish; Ms. 8° 3136, *Cyprianus' Trekandt. Ret forklaring holdende inde formaninger og frie Konster Iligemaade Konste bog og Charactererne . . . ,* Copenhagen, November 2, 1760, 8 pages. Trondheim, Norway, Gunnerus Library: XA HA, Qv. 62, *Cyprianus eller Swart-Bogen-med Anmærkninger til Oplysning anførte og tilsatte af Chr. Hammer*; April 17, 1793, 55 pages LibR, oct. 5342, *Cyprianus eller Svartebogen. Forfattet av Cyprianus fra Antiokhia. Fortale av Willum Stephanson, Trondheim, 1798, 48 pages*; GO, Ky2f8 Cyp, *Mester Cyprianus eller Svartbogen. Forfattet av Cyprianus fra Antiokhia.* Bang, III, X–XIII, XVI–XXIII, XXVIII–XXVIIII, XXXIV–XXXV; Pio, *Cyprianus: Inde holder mange adskillige viddenschabe. . .*; Müllenhoff, *Sagen, Märchen und Lieder aus Schleswig, Holstein und Lauenburg,* 1921, 201 (no. 263); Amundsen, "A Genre in the Making: The First Study of Charms in Norway." For information on Cyprianus as a magician, see Thorndike, *A History of Magic and Experimental Science,* vol. 1, 428–33.

CYRANIDES: This is a Greek work written in the fourth century on the orders of the Persian king Kyranos. Its four books contain magical and medical recipes. The first book is divided into chapters under each letter of the alphabet in which the therapeutic or magical properties of a bird, fish, plant, and stone are described. The other three books examine the remedies that can be taken from quadrupeds, birds, and fish. It was translated into Latin in 1169 in Constantinople under the title of *Liber Kirannidarum,* of which eleven manuscripts survive. The Greek text is preserved in manuscripts dating from the fourteenth through the sixteenth centuries.

✦ *Aulu, Chuoch, Coveltho, Ioa, Nam, Piran, Tin.*

📖 Kaimakis; *Cyranides;* Maryse Waegeman, *Amulet and Alphabet: Magical Amulets in the First Book of Cyranides* (Amsterdam: 1987).

The *Cyprianus*, the most widespread grimoire
in the Scandinavian countries

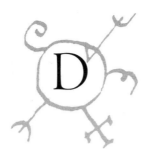

D

DABI: This term is featured in the creation of an amulet intended to protect its owner from bullets and sword blows. It is written on an object that is meant to be worn hung from the neck, over the chest, or beneath the left arm.

D. A. B. I. ✠
H. A. B. I. ✠
H. A. B. E. R. I. ✠
H. E. R. E. R. I. ✠
H. E. B. R. I. ✠

To heal epilepsy, one should say: *Dabit, habet debet*, or wear a silver ring on one's finger on which is inscribed: + *Dabi* + *habi* + *haber* + *hebr*.

In a love charm, the spell reads: *Daby* † *Daby* † *Daby* † *Huber* † *Huber*; a silver ring is made with this spell on the inside so it touches the skin of the person whose love is desired.

📖 Bang, no. 1117; Thiers I, 407; *Secrets magiques pour l'amour*, no. XIX.

DAIMON (δαιμων): In some Greek charms, the meaning of *daimon*, "god, deity, soul of a dead person, genie," does not correspond with *demon* so much as *spirit*. A silver ribbon, found in a tomb near Beirut, was worn around the neck as an amulet of protection against a wide variety of ills, spells, and *daimons*. It cites a plethora of names of the latter and includes their positions.

Marmariôth, Ouriêl, Aêl, Gabriêl, Chaêl, Moriath and Cachth each rule over one of the seven heavens; Riopha over the lightning, Zonchar over thunder, Tebriêl over the rain, Tobriêl over the snow, Thadama over the forests, Sioracha over the quakes, Souriêl over the sea, Eithabira over the serpents, Bêllia over the rivers, Phasousouêl over the roads, Eistochama over the towns, Nouchaël over the depths, and Apraphês over all forms of travel.

 Gager, 233ff.

DALET: To flush a stag when hunting and pursue it with your hounds, *Les vraies clavicules du roi Salomon* in the Lansdowne manuscript tells us that you must craft a copper ring in the third house of the moon, set in it lapis lazuli carved with the sign below, and place this word beneath the stone written in white dove's blood on virgin parchment perfumed with aloe.

 London, British Library, Lansdowne 1202, 4to, folio 172.

DAM PREIRE CLAUSES LA BOCA: This is the beginning of an Occitan phrase passed on by a thirteenth-century Provencal exemplum that means, "Lord priest, close thy mouth and bind thy feet, from this place you shall never take anything." While a large number of people were dying in Draguignan, France, a woman offered to show a neighbor whose husband was gravely ill what to do so that none would die in her home. Her neighbor accepted and was given a magical phrase to speak when the priest sought to give her spouse communion.

Dam preire clauses la boca e lias lo pe, de sains non traires mai ren.

 Rava-Cordier, 550.

DANATA, DARIES, DARDARIES, ASTARIES: This phrase allows dislocated limbs to be restored to their proper place. It was mentioned by Cato the Elder (234–149 BCE) in his treatise on agriculture in this form:

Motas Vaeta Daries Dardares Astataries Dissunapiter.

The spell is terminated by the following incantation:

Huat Haut Haut Istasis Tarsis Ardannabou Dannaustra.

In 1675 it was written as *Donatos, Daries, Dardaries, Astaries,* according to the *Treatise on Fascination* by J. C. Frommann, published in Nuremberg in 1675.

📖 Heim, 533ff.; Wessely, 34; Thiers I, 415; Van Haver, no. 492.

DANI ZUMECH AGALMATUROD: When using an iron object employed for engraving, such as a chisel or pin, to cast a spell, the object is suffumigated with smoke, sprinkled with holy water and this invocation is spoken over it:

Dani Zumech Agalmaturo Gadiel Pani Canelosas Merod Gamidoi Baldoi Metatror

This is done after Psalms 3, 9, 31, 42, 60, 61, and 130 have been recited.

📖 *Clavicules* II, 19.

† DANT † DANT † DANT † SANT † HELIOT ET VALIOT: To protect one's fields from the damage caused by rabbits, take the droppings of these animals and five pieces of tile collected from the passage of a funeral procession or in a cemetery, then bareheaded and on the eastern corner of the property, say these words, which are the introduction to a long conjuration.

📖 Honorius, 99.

DANUCOS, TENUS, AGIHE, AGIOS, AGIOTHET: To win a woman's love, draw a little blood from the little finger of your left hand and touch the hand or arm of the maiden while reciting a charm that closes with this spell.

📖 *Secrets magiques de l'amour,* no. XII, 8.

DAS, BAGUS † DE GLUTIN: The spell that contains this phrase says that these words must be ingested when one is suffering from fever. If the sufferer does so, he shall be cured.

📖 Aymar, 343.

DAYABEL: This word was used on an amulet housing a sign of the zodiac, in this instance Scorpio, that was described in texts attributed (probably falsely) to the doctor and astrologer Pseudo-Arnaldus de Villanova (1235–1311). This word resembles the name of an angel; the amulet protects its wearer from nerve disorders and diseases affecting the belly and bladder.

📖 Pseudo–Arnaldus de Villanova, *Opera*, folio 302 r°.

DAYADEBUÇ, HEYADIÇ: These words appear in a thirteenth-century magic treatise translated from Spanish and Arabic. They form the opening of an incantation of Mars when a person seeks to recover possession of an object that has been stolen from him: *Dayadebuç, Heaydiç, Mahydebiç, Haudabuç, Maharaç, Ardauç, Beydehydiç, Deheydemiç.*

The Arabic source, *Gâyat al-Hakîm*, informs us that these are spirits (*pneumata*) of Mars and offers this lesson: *Daġidûs, Hâġidis, Ġidijûs, Maġdâs, Ardaġûs, Hîdâġidis, Mahandâs, Dahîdamâs.*

✦ *Picatrix*.
📖 *Astromagia*, 266; *Gâyat al-Hakîm*, 249.

† DEALBAGNETH † DEBAGNETH † DEGLUTHUM: This is a charm against epilepsy found in the *The Coucher Book of the Cistercian Abbey of Kirkstall, in the West Riding of the County of York*. It indicates that the patient should wear a phylactery with these words.

📖 Lancaster and Baildon, 40.

DEBRA EBRA: In his *Book of All the Forbidden Arts, Miscreance, and Magic* (*Puch aller verpoten kunst, ungelaubens und der zaubrey*), written in 1455, the Bavarian physician Johannes Hartlieb (1410–1468) mentions this spell in the following context: "A man mounts a horse and in a short space of time travels vast distances; when he wants to get off, he takes off the bridle and when he wishes to remount, he shakes the bridle and the horse returns. This horse is none other than the Devil. These folk use bat's blood for this purpose, but they must still give themselves to the Devil with words that make no sense, like these: Debra Ebra."

📖 Heidelberg, Germany, University Library, Cpg 478, folio 38 v°.

DEDRA: This is the beginning of a charm intended to allow a horse to carry you in a night's time wherever you wish to go. Silently at dusk, you must enter a deserted house and write on the wall with bat's blood: *Dedra, syola dracon, draconco. Gramenkios. Kien. Belsebuuc. Astaroth, egipia, barrabas,* then conjure all the demons at the four cardinal points. You shall then see the desired animal appear.

📖 Braekman, no. 251.

DE. EL. X: According to the *Ars notoria* (thirteenth century) when one undertakes a magical operation at the time of the new moon, prayers are addressed to God asking him to purify the conscience and strengthen understanding so that one may remember what he has learned from an orison that contains God's "sacred names, that are unpronounceable and unintelligible to human understanding": *de. el. x p n k h t li g y y.*

✦ *Ars notoria.*
📖 *Ars notoria,* 117.

DEFFAUS DIFFAUS MAX PAX VUCAN MAX PAX VERAX: This spell is accompanied by "You are just, Lord, and your judgment is just." Nothing indicates what these words might have been used for.

📖 Ohrt I, no. 975.

DEFX: This is most likely an abbreviation of *defixio*, "enchantment;" it was found on a tablet discovered in Bath, England, that contained the inscription *ABCDEFX*. The use of the alphabet in proper or random order is a common practice in magic.

📖 Ogden, 48ff.

DE LATERE EIUS: To arrest bleeding, cite these words from the Gospel of John (19:34) while touching the wound: *De latere eius exivit sanguis et aqua* (Blood and water spurted out his side).

📖 Scot, Book XII, chapter 18.

DELEQUIS, GRELIIS, MALIIS, CONTEMPLIS: When one wishes a woman's love, one speaks this spell with her name.

📖 *Secrets magiques de l'amour*, no. VII.

DELIATUS-DEMERIATUS-AMORTITUS: To attract the desired individual—man, woman, young girl—and submit him or her to your will, a long recipe features a piece of white silver, a yellow brass pin, blood, and the demons Belzébud [*sic*] and Domon; the spell above makes it possible to send the person back once your desire has been satisfied.

Variant: *Taliy. Taliy. Taliy.*

📖 *Secrets magiques de l'amour*, no. XLI, no. LIX.

DELO X: OAGIATO X PANC HO X: To fight consumption, you must carve this spell on the obverse side of a seal forged from four cast metals under the new moon, surrounded by *Sepp ved arg* and other *caracteres*. On the other side: *Arzel ergimox salel* παχωσ.

📖 *Archidoxis magica*, I, 5.

DE SA LA MA RUKKA, FIKKA: To bind, or in other words, paralyze, a thief, one must, just before Saint John's Day, pull up the root of the black-spotted *Cirsium heterophyllum* (a plant of the Asteraceae family), while reciting these words three times. Afterward, put a silver schilling in the hole where the root had been and cover the hole. If this root is placed among things the owner fears are likely to be stolen, the would-be robber will be unable to move until the owner arrives and allows him to leave peacefully.

📖 Bang, no. 1166.

DEUS ABEAT PARTEN: This is the beginning of a prayer so that firearms cannot shoot, which must be recited with your left leg

crossed over your right: *Deus abeat parten et utecio a remone. Non tradus Dominum Nostrum Jehun Christum Matón. Amen.*
  📖 Werner, no. 13, 199.

DEUS MEUS: These words, meaning "my God" and taken from the Psalms (22:2ff., 40:18, 42:7, 71:12) or the Gospel of Mark (15:34), were standard additions to charms, blessings, and spells of the Middle Ages.
  ✦ *Psalms.*
  📖 Franz II, 264, 281.

DEYTUZ: This is the name of a magical composition in the *Picatrix* that is intended for the crafting of a *voult* (doll) that will win women's love. Gazelle marrow, mutton fat, camphor, and rabbit brain are blended together, then one makes a figure out of virgin wax, which is then pierced with a hole at the level of the belly, into which this mixture is poured. While the mixture is being placed in the doll, the caster says: "*Dahyeliz, Hanimidiz, Naffayz, Dabrayliz.*" Then a silver pin is stuck in the chest, and the caster adds: "*Hedurez, Tameruz, Hetaytoz, Femurez.*" The entire object is then wrapped in a piece of white linen that is tied shut with a silk thread bound with seven knots. Above each knot, the caster speaks these words: "*Hayranuz, Hedefiuz Faytamurez,*" then the entire object is buried in a pot beneath the house of the person who requested the operation. A suffumigation is then performed using these magic words: *Beheymerez, Aumaliz, Menemeyduz, Caynaires*. Here in order are the lessons from the Arabic source, the *Gâyat al-Hakîm* (eleventh century):

  1. *Dahjâjas, Ġanamawâdas, Nagarjâjas, Dîrûlâjas*
  2. *Hâdurâs, Timârûs, Hânîtûs, Wâmûrâs*
  3. *Arġûnâs, Hâdamijûs, Finûras, Armitâs*
  4. *Bahîmarâs, Ûrmaralîs, Qadâmîdus, Finûrâs*

  ✦ *Beheymeruz.*
  📖 *Picatrix* III, 10; *Gâyat al-Hakîm*, 260ff.

D F W S H H: This is the beginning of a long series of *caracteres* whose use is never specified. The title of the spell simply indicates it is "for an animal that has lost its usefulness.

D F W S H H D E S S Z Uz eo W V T V T D V I 1 7 F 9 W I X S V † † †

📖 *Egyptian Secrets* II, 284.

DIABOLO DIABOLICZO, SATANA SATHANICZOS: A fifteenth-century German manuscript provides this phrase in a conjuration of the devil, a part of which is encrypted with runes.

📖 Beckers, "Eine spätmittelalterliche deutsche Anleitung zur Teufelsbeschwörung mit Runenschriftverwendung," 113, 136–145.

DIC CUR HIC: When a father sent his son far away for an apprenticeship, he would write over the lintel of his chamber door this phrase, which means, "Say, why this?" Its purpose is to ensure his son's return, safe and sound.

📖 Schmidt I, 21.

DIDAY PATY ATON ESBREY: According to the orisons *Ecce Crucem* or *Crux Christi*, used as spells to counter storms, this would be the name of Jesus Christ. If carried on one's person, it earns the love of all and bestows success. *Esbrey* is most likely a corruption of *Eschereia* or *Eschereyeye* (אהיה אשר אהיה, Exodus 3:14), meaning "I am that I am." These words can also be found again in the *Enchiridion Leonis Pape*.

📖 Franz II, 92; *Enchiridion*, 74.

DIES MIES YES-CHET BENE DONE FET DONNIMA METAMAUZ: This phrase is used to help reveal the identity of a thief with the aid of a sieve suspended on a hanged man's rope. This is a variation found in the Lansdowne manuscript (1203): *Dies mies jeschet bene deafet dovvima énétémans.*

📖 *Clavicula* I, 9, 49.

DIS, BIZ, ON, DABULB, CHERIB: To heal pleurisy, one must write this inside a glass.

Variant: *Dia, Biz, On, Dabulh, Cherih.*

📖 Honorius, 65, 69.

DISMAS: The name of one of the two thieves crucified with Christ. For protection against robbers, the following phrase is spoken aloud:

Disparibus meritis pendent tria corpora ramis
Dismas and Gesmas medio divina potestas
Alta petit Dismas infelix infima Gesmas
Haec versus discas ne furto ne tua perdas

This is followed by *Jesus autem transiens* (Luke 4:30), *Irruat super eos formido* (Exodus 15:16), *Christus vincit . . .* , and the request.

According to Johann Weyer, sorcerers and witches can place themselves into a deep slumber that permits them to resist torture by saying:

Imparibus meritis tria pendent corpora ramis,
Dismas and Gestas, in media est divina potestas:
Dismas damnatur, Gestas ad astra levatur.

[Dissimilar in merit, three bodies hung from the branches (of the cross), Dismas and Gestas, and the divine potentate (Jesus) in the middle; Dismas was damned, Gestas was lifted up to heaven.]

It is interesting to note that the phrase can be found again in the *Petit Albert*, in the *Grimoire of Pope Honorious* ("To avoid suffering under the question: Swallow a note on which the followings words have been written in your own blood: *Aglas, Aglanos, Algadenas, Imperiequeritis, tria pendent corpora ramis dis meus et gesias in medio et divina potestas dimeas clamator, sed jestas ad astra levatur,* or else *Tel, Bel, Quel, Caro, Man, Aqua*"), and in a compilation known as the *Ritual of High Magic,* mistakenly attributed to Heinrich Cornelius Agrippa. These three verses are accompanied by magic words and make it possible not to feel the pain caused by the question [torture of the Inquisition—*Trans.*]:

Alas, Aglanas, Algadena
Imperubi es meritis, tria pendant corpora ramis
Dismeus et gestus in medio et divina potestas
Dimeas clamator, sed jestas ad astra levatur.

In passing, we can note the corruptions that have occurred to the original wording. During the sixteenth century, the doctor Richard

Anglo provided a longer spell, intended to provide protection from thieves and to ensure the safety of livestock.

> *Imparibus meritis pendent tria corpora ramis,*
> *dismas and gesmas, medio divina potestas,*
> *Alta petit dismas, infœlix infima gesmas,*
> *nos et res nostras, conferuet summa potestas,*
> *hos versus dicas, ne tu furto tua perdas.*

In the Italian *Grand Grimoire,* the phrase has been transformed into:

> *In paribus meritis, fria pendent corpora ramis.*
> *Dismas et gestas damnatur potestas.*
> *Disma et gestas damnatur.*
> *Ad astra levatur.*

📖 London, British Library, Arundel 36674, folio 89 r°; Arundel 2584, folio 73 v°; Scot, Book XII, chapter 17; Weyer IV, 10; Anglo, *De praestigiis et incantationibvs daemonum et necromanticorum,* chap. 17; *Gran Grimorio,* 53.

† DISTON † GRATON † BORSIBS ††: In the sixteenth century, when illness had made an individual insane, a piece of bread on which these words had been written would be given him to eat. Sometimes the phrase is extended as seen below:

"Diston" is perhaps from the Greek *dison* ("divide") and "graton" that of *craton* ("force").

📖 Heidelberg, Germany, University Library, Cpg 268, folio 24 r°.

DITAU RIDAS ATROSIS: A spell used on a talisman that gave its holder command over the elements. *Ditau* is used for thunder, *Hurandos* for hail, *Ridas Talimol* for quakes, *Atrosis Narpida* for waterspouts, *Unsur Itar* for tornados, *Hispen Tromador* for hurricanes, *Parenthes*

Istanos for inundations. To cancel the effects, put the talisman down and say *Finulem*.

📖 *Trésor*, 178 a–b.

† DITEM † PRISCOM † DRYXOM † PI ISCO † BRISUM † SIC GRECO REMANI: The bites from rabid dogs could be healed by eating bread on which this phrase had been written.

📖 *Grimoires*, no. 18.

DMVODM: Abbreviations of the words from the Gospel of Mark (15:34): *Deus meus, ut quid dereliquisti me?* ("My God, why have you forsaken me?"). It is used on Christian amulets like those at the Museum of Art and History in Geneva. These words are part of the *Orison of Seven Words*, attributed to Bede, which ensures protection against all evils and prevents death without confession.

DO. HEL, X. P. A. LI. O. F.: A thirteenth-century orison introduces these initials as being those of the names of angels who are so sacred their names cannot be spoken aloud and that the human mind cannot comprehend.

📖 *Ars notoria*, 20.

DOLEFECH: To heal eyesight, one must make a silver ring in the moon's ninth house and set in it a white stone carved with the figure below.

The word *Dolefech* is placed beneath it, written in white dove's blood on virgin parchment perfumed with henbane.

📖 London, British Library, Lansdowne 1202, 4to, folio 175.

DRAGNE DRAGNE: Part of the "secret of the hand of glory" (which permits its owner to obtain gold and silver) is the speaking of these words while tearing a hair out by the roots from a mare in heat. It is placed in a new clay pot that is filled with water, and nine days later, one will find there a small animal of serpentine shape with whom a pact will be concluded.

📖 *Honorius*, 49ff.

DRAS FIERNAL FLA YA CERMEL FLITZUEL FLEUTZUEL: These words should be spoken into the left ear of a horse if you would like it to gallop.

📖 Einsiedeln, Switzerland, Abbey Library, ms. 731, folio 64 v°.

DROCH: According to Johann Weyer (died 1588), this Kabbalistic wand or cudgel is used to enchant a hazel wand that has been cut in accordance with a specific ritual. This wand will strike a thief or other malefactor from a great distance. Its first confirmed use goes back to 1563.

> *Droch, Myr(r)roch, esanaroth + betu + baroch + ass maarot(h). Sancta trinitas puni hunc qui id mali designarit, utque hoc aufer per magnam iustitiam tuam + eson + elion + emaris rales ege.*

The magic words are greatly corrupted Hebrew terms, and the spell most likely means, "Strike well, be hard, branch, be confident! Praised by the word of the branch.... Be strong, all mighty. Say this three times in a low voice." The Holy Trinity is asked to punish the designated individual. *Elion* is the Hebrew עליון, meaning "supreme."

It can be found in Germanic regions in the eighteenth century in the booklet *Magia de furto* in this form:

> *Droch, Myrroch, Esenaroth † Betu † Baroch † Ars † Haaroth. It.*

It has even been abbreviated into *Esem, Eli, Eljon*.

📖 Weyer V, 5; Scot, Book XII, chapter 18; Spamer, 364.

† DUFA † FADIA † ABA † FRANEST † PENE † PLIATA: This is a phrase for an amulet. To prevent someone from shooting at you, it is necessary to write this and carry it on your person.

📖 Ohrt II, 98.

DURGOS: A word from the *Oración de los Siete Nudos* (*Orison of Seven Knots*). It is to be repeated three times while one is tying nine knots in a thread for magical purposes.

📖 Werner, no. 16, 200.

D. Y. I. T. OB. Y.: To compel an individual who is hostile toward you to treat you kindly, his name and these *caracteres* must be carved on lead or another support material.

📖 Heidelberg, Germany, University Library, Cpg 214, folio 43 v°.

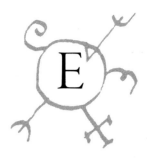

E + E: This abbreviation means Enoch + Elias, and holds the same virtues as CMB; it offers protection for property and for persons.

EAX, FILIAX, ARTIFEX, AMEN: The closing phrase of a spell intended to cure dysentery. It refers to the three individuals of the Trinity.

📖 Berthoin-Mathieu, 193.

EBAT † H CON: To "fight with anger as a weapon," an eighteenth-century Swiss grimoire says, it is necessary to be wearing this:

> *Ebat † h con † plion † en † sobot † Emmanuel Adonnay.*

Sobot represents *sabaoth* (to wage war), and *ebat* is probably *ibat* (he went).

📖 Hervé, 364.

EBER DIABER: This is a phrase that is formed from the initials of the words beginning each verse of a Latin orison against plague.

✦ *Heber; Habi.*
📖 King, 229.

† EBREA † EBREMON † EBRENAC †: The start of a phrase contained in a Provencal *bref* from the end of the fourteenth century, intended to protect the bearer from all kinds of fevers.

> † *Ebrea † Ebremon † Ebrenac † Christus natus est † Christus mortuus fuit † Christus ressuscitus est † Christus vincit † Christus imperat † Christus ab omni malo eum liberet.*

> [Christ is born † Christ is dead † Christ is resurrected † Christ triumphs † Christ governs † Christ frees him from all evil.]

After having written these words to be carried on your person, alms must be given to the souls trapped in purgatory and a candle lit for the Virgin.

✦ *Abremonte.*

📖 Scot, Book XII, chapter 18; Le Blevec, 127–31.

ECCE CRUCEM DOMINI: "Here is the cross of the Lord." This is the antiphon of the service of the Holy Cross (*Ecce crucem Dei/Domini, fugite partes aduerse*), which is frequently used in magic, especially in weather charms. It is spoken at each of the four cardinal points. It also figures prominently in exorcisms and tests, and on amulets, as well as in spells to heal the eyes and facilitate a birth. One can be freed of illness by repeating these words three times. Whether combined or not with other biblical extracts, the antiphon *Ecce crucem* was called the Blessing of Saint Anthony (of Padua) and used as a charm against evil spirits. It can be also seen in an exorcism of Pope Leo XIII (*Exorcismus in satanam et angelos apostaticos*), and even on the bell tower of the church of Corneilla-de-Conflent, as well as on a Byzantine reliquary given to one of Alexius Comnenus's daughters. It was used in the crafting of thirteenth-century Norwegian amulets and in healing charms. To cure a disease called *dysiaticum,* it is necessary to take a piece of lead, etch a small cross on it, and write this phrase on top and *Pax tibi Alleluia* at the end, then attach it to the patient. A Danish charm from around 1350 presents the lesson *Pax tibi Alleluia.* When combined with the names of the four evangelists and the Virgin, the spell is used to counter a cloudy eye.

A manuscript from the Dijon municipal library (448, folio 181) contains a recipe against tertian fever that combines *Ecce crucem* with other interesting Christian phrases.

> *Ecce crucem Domini triunius. Christus natus est. on. bon. jon. Christus passus, don. ron. con. Christe resurrexit, ton. son. yon.*
>
> [Here is the cross of the trinitarian Lord. Christ is born. on. bon. jon. Christ is dead. don. ron. con. Christ is resurrected. ton. son. yon.]

To give an idea of the corruptions due to a long transmission, here is what T. Kristensen found in a manuscript whose date he does not identify:

Kyhhe Christe domine, fuate patris adiva, sed bede trebed Suda, fon Davut, in nomina †††.

Behind the corrupted Latin we can recognize: *(ecce) crucem Christi Domini, fugite partes adverse, de tribu Iuda, son David.*

In a conjuration of cloud and wind spirits dating from the twelfth century that has been passed down by a ritual, we find the phrase *Ecce crucem* combined with these phrases: *Crux* † *Christi. Crux Chri*†*sti. Cr*†*ux Christi,* and ✦ *vicit Leo de tribu Iuda.*

📖 Franz II, 80, 87, 92, 94, 114; Hunt, 135; Bang, no. 1067, 1068; Heim, 552; Ohrt I, no. 1086; Braekman, 95; Ohrt I, no. 328, 332, Camus 2002, 297; Sankt Florian, Austria, Abbey Library, Codex Flor. XI 467, folio 161 r°. Braekman gives a list of manuscripts in which the phrase appears (119, note 241).

ECCE CRUCIS HOC SIGNUM: This is the beginning of a phrase that should be spoken three times over the water given to an individual stricken with boils to drink for three days in a row. The Latin text says, "The cross is the remedy of things; by this sign of the cross, all evil shall flee at once, and by the same sign, he who bears the cross of Jesus Christ shall be saved. Christ triumphs, rules, and commands."

📖 Braekman, no. 151; Franz II, 91, 97; *Enchiridion,* 60, 78, 95, 100, 138.

ECCE DOLGULA MEDIT DUDUM: This is the beginning of a magic spell passed down by a charm in Old English. It should be chanted nine times over what the man will drink; nine Our Fathers must also be recited.

Ecce dolgula medit dudum bedegunga bredegunda elecunda eleuahia mottem meerenum orþa fueþa letaues noeues terre dolge drore uhic alleluiah.

The purpose of the spell is not specified here, but a parallel operation provided by another manuscript suggests that the illness being fought is diarrhea.

📖 Berthoin-Mathieu, 152; Storms, no. 83.

ECCE LIGNUM CRUCEM: The beginning of a spell for making sheep become handsome and strong: *Ecce Lignum Crucem in que Salus Mundi Crucem.*

With mistakes and a word change at the end, it is borrowed from the Liturgy of Holy Friday, which says: *in quo salus mundi pepedit.*

📖 Werner, no. 17, 200.

† EDOAE † VEOAFP † BEOAEV †: To make cramps go away, these words should be attached to the patient until they stop.

📖 *Egyptian Secrets* III, 123.

EFFATA EFFATA EFFATA: *Effata (hephphatha)* is borrowed from the Gospel of Mark (7:34), in which Christ heals a deaf-mute by using this command, which means, "Open up!" By repeating this word three times, a person can open any door if he touches it with a milfoil leaf that has been collected before dawn on Friday and over which two masses have been said. The term is also used to heal illnesses affecting the mouth and eyes, to stop a thief, and to cure hernias, but the phrase varies this way: "*Hepheta ouvre-toi!* † † † *A. O. B. Tibas.*" To heal an animal of tetanus, the person places "the middle finger and the three index fingers [*sic*] in its mouth and says three times: *Hefeda, Hefeda, Hefeda ouvre, soit ouverte.* † † †.

📖 Braekman, no. 253; Ohrt I, no. 222; Franz II, 98, 492; *Egyptian Secrets* 1, 175.

E F T: This is the abbreviation of *ecce filius tuus* (here is your son), words from the Gospel of John (19:26), and it is used on Christian amulets. One like this is housed at the Museum of Art and History in Geneva. These words are part of the *Orison of Seven Words,* allegedly by Bede, that provided protection against all ills, including death without confession.

EGIPPIA BENOHAM: To uncover a thief, take the fingernail from a child's left hand, to which the following names are attached:

egippia. benoham. beanke ou beanre. reraresessym. alredessym. ebemidiri. fetolinie. dysi. medyrini. alhea. heresim.

egippia. benoham. haham. ezirohias. bohodi. hohada. aan. hohanna. ohereo. metaliceps. aragereo. agercho. aliberri. Halba.

Then a conjuration is spoken that features the names of God (Alpha and Omega, Messyas, Sother, and so on) and the two names—Joth and

Nabonoth—used by Solomon to imprison demons in glass jars (*in vase vitreo*).

 📖 *Liber incantationum,* folio 44 v°–45 r°.

EGO SUM ALPHA ET O † PRINCIPIUM ET FINIS †: "I am the Alpha and the Omega, the beginning and the end." These words, taken from Revelation (21:6), can be used to heal a sick woman in a Dutch charm. Nine sacred hosts must be taken and the preceding phrase written on the first three. On the next three it is necessary to write: † *Et fuit mortuus* † *Et ecce sum vivens* † (and he was dead † and here I am alive), then lastly: † *Et habeo claves mortis* † *Et miserui* † (and I hold the key to death and I had mercy), elements drawn from Revelation (1:18).

 📖 Braekman, no. 24.

EGYPTIAN SECRETS (ÄGYPTISCHE GEHEIMNISSE): This is the title of a grimoire that dates from the beginning of the nineteenth century (see illustration on page 119). It was first published in installments by publisher Ludwig Ensslin in Reutlingen, Germany; it was a leading seller at the time and was regularly reprinted into the twentieth century. It was erroneously attributed to Albertus Magnus (1193–1280) as were *Le petit Albert* and *Le grand Albert* of France. The standard editions included two hundred fifty recipes that aimed, among other things, to protect man and beast from evil spirits, to stop hemorrhages, to fight fevers, to counter Saint Anthony's fire (ergot poisoning, holy fire) and gall and kidney stones, to protect against slander, to reveal the identity of a thief, and even to make wine confer health.

E H T: A Swiss grimoire from the end of the eighteenth century that offers an odd phrase: "for fighting with anger as your weapon," and that includes the symbol for Venus. It should be worn or otherwise carried on one's person.

 Eht † ♀ 5e con † pnon † en † Serbort † Emmanuel Adonnay.

 📖 Hervé, 364.

EIS PNEUMATON: For individuals suffering from spleen problems, the following spell would be written, then placed on their naked skin while reciting three Our Fathers and three Hail Marys in honor of Saint Roch.

eis pneumaton archarton legetai en tô ôtis.

The entire prescription is written in Italian using Greek letters.

📖 Pradel, 31.

ELEC, OMSIDES, ABNEGOD: The closing words of a spell for wolves and ravens used in Norway in 1815. The conjuration must be read three times.

 📖 Bang, no. 1195.

† EL † ELOY †: To counter uterine pains, women were recommended to carry a virgin parchment on which the following spell was written:

> † *el* † *eloy* † *eloe* † *anxi* † *andriary* † *N. von* † *compunctary* † *ammenn.*

 📖 Zingerle, 176ff.

ELE. ERAPE. HEBE: This is the beginning of a long text for an amulet that needs to be worn to benefit from its protection against poisons and venoms.

> *Ele. erape. hebe. occentimos. ioth. hey. a. io. hoccayethos. ya. slay. amorona. asar. sycon. goyces. Beley. latem. sanctus. anon. raba. mefenecon. oncantia. tol. fa. tel. Ella. Sabira. Seda. Adonay. aaa. camsi. ayada. Maus. princeps. veni est. Emanuel. Adonay. Bethpha. Adonay. qm. hoy. hoy. aanai. Nanay. Sede Adonay. asamilias Ehur.*

Some divine names are recognizable in this spell—*Adonay, ioth,* meaning "beginning," and *princeps*—as is the triple repetition of *agios* (Trisagion), represented by "aaa."

 📖 Aymar, 345.

EL EV: These two words would be written on something that was then hung around the patient's neck to arrest bleeding. This spell is from around 1350.

 📖 Ohrt II, 118.

ELEYSON YMAS: This phrase means, "Have pity on me," and can be found in many charms and orisons, always in combination with other phrases of Christian origin, such as, for example, this Danish prescription from the beginning of the sixteenth century for winning someone's friendship:

Agnos otheos † *agnos yskios* † *agnos attannatos eleyson ymas. Amen.*

Eleyson ymas can be found in a ritual intended to remove an enchantment from milk.

Variant: *Ymon eleyson.* This phrase is the final part of the liturgical hymn "Trisagion": *Agios o Theos, Agios Ischyros, Agios Athanatos, eleison imas Aghios.*

 📖 Ohrt II, 871; Braekman, 375; Franz II, 111.

ELI, EL.I ÆM.6 AGIAN VRANATUN:

To make all the inhabitants inside a house start dancing, it is necessary to write this on an aspen leaf and place it beneath the doorsill. The 6 most likely stands for the letter *F*.

 ✦ *Ellon, Eras, L+.*
 📖 Espeland, no. 1.

ELIAON YOENA ADONAY CADAS EBREEL:

This is the beginning of the seventh *Semiphoras of Solomon*, which contains the names of God that should be spoken before any magical operation.

Eliaon yoena adonay cadas ebreel, eloy ela agiel, ayoni, Sachado, essuselas eloym, delion iau elynla, delia yazi Zazael, paliel man, umiel onela dilatan saday alma paneim alym, canal dens Usami yaras calipix calfas sasna saffa saday aglata panteomel auriel arion phaneton secare panerion ys emanuel Joth Jalaph amphia, than demisrael mu all le Leazyns ala phonar aglacyel qyol paeriteron theferoym, barimel, Jael haryon ya apiolell echet

 ✦ *Names of God.*

ELI, LAMMA SABACTHANI:

"Lord, why have you forsaken me?" These words by Jesus (Matthew 27:46; Mark 15:34) are widespread in exorcisms and weather spells, and although corrupted much of the time, they are always identifiable. For example: *heloi leba sabactani; lama asabatani.*

In two divination practices that were used in Norway between 1650 and 1880, these words can be found for revealing the identity of a thief.

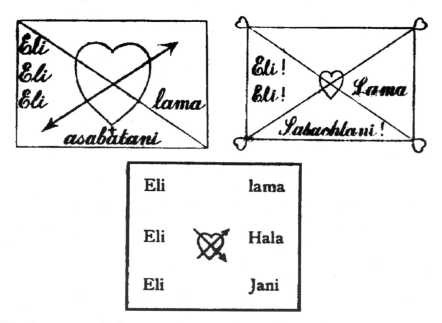

The first is inscribed across a heart in diagonal bars running left to right inside a square and transfixed by an arrow that is feathered at both ends. Inside the left triangle formed by this design *Eli* is written three times; in the right triangle we see *lama*, and below the triangle is *asabatani*, with the *a* of *ba* topped by a cross. In one variant the same procedure is used but with two large diagonals intersecting at the center of a heart. There are four hearts at the outside corners of the square, and there are only two *Eli*'s in the left rectangle. This variant is missing the cross above the *a* of *ba*.

In a variant from 1850, there are three *Eli*'s to the left of the square, one above the other, and they correspond to *lama Hala Jani* on the right. In the center is a heart pierced by two arrows whose points are pointed right.

✦ Hely, *S D S*.

📖 Franz II, 80; *Galdrakver*, 30; Bang, no. 1294 a–b.

ELIPHAMASAY, GELONUCOA, GEBECHE BANAI, GERABCAI, ELOMNIT:

This is a magical phrase from a Solomonic prayer that makes it possible to obtain a good memory. God is invoked, then the archangels, and then it ends, for good measure, with "the angels whose names are so sacred that we cannot speak them: *Do. Hel. X. P. A. Li. O. F.* Later in this same grimoire, the phrase reads: *Eliphamasay,*

Gelomiros, Gedo bonay, Saranana, Elomnia, and the sacred, unpronounceable names are: *de. el. x p n k h t li g y y.*

✦ *Ars notoria.*

📖 *Ars notoria,* 21, 117.

EL KOS: To gain a young woman's love, the following words are read over a pitcher or jug filled with beer. The speaker breathily says:

El Kos gui sen gued
Gvara lige ami

📖 Bang, no. 1168 d.

ELLIEUE X LU M: When a cow has calved, one must make her swallow the phrase below, and when the animal has fever, it should be attached around her neck on Friday between eleven o'clock and noon, then make her eat it before she ingests any other food in the morning at an odd hour for three days running. The spell will be repeated in a week's time.

Ellieue X Lu m Z u n d w v Meillum X
Lume Z im s v E v X eill im X Luie Z
un d v s r x.

📖 *Egyptian Secrets* II, 331.

ELLON AGRON GRAMATON: To set every guest dancing inside a house, it is necessary to write this phrase on an aspen leaf and place it beneath the threshold. *Agron Gramaton* represents Tetragrammaton.

Variant: *Elo Elleam Fagiam Grantem.*

✦ *Eli, Eras.*

📖 Ohrt II, 99; BBE, 61.

ELOHIM/ELOHYM (אלהים): This is one of the ten names of God. It is the plural of His Majesty Eloah (אלוה). It is much used in conjurations.

📖 Heim, 523; Isidore of Seville, *Etymologiae* VII, 1, 5; Agrippa III, 54ff.; Franz II, 92 passim; Thiers I, 355.

ELØN ELØNE ELONORUM: To make a young woman love you, you must write these words on an apple and give it to her to eat.

   Variant: *EZon EZone Ezonorum.*

   📖 Bang, no. 1154.

ELOY † ELOY † ELYON † ADONAY † SABAOTH † MESSIAS † PATIOR †: These words must be worn at one's throat to provide protection from quartan fever. They are strengthened by the *Sator* magic square.

   📖 Braekman, no. 83.

ELOY † TETRAGAMATHON † MESSIAS † OTHRES † YSKIROS †: These divine names, in which a corrupted Elohim and Sother are recognizable, are extremely frequent in spells and orisons. During the fifteenth century they were mainly used to uncover a thief who was forced to submit to the cheese test. A piece of cheese was enspelled by writing this phrase on it: "I conjure you, X, if you are guilty, by the one God, by the holy God, and by the preceding names, to not eat this cheese!"

   📖 Ohrt I, no. 949.

E † M N Z S: This is the opening of a *bref* offering protection against bullets that was commonly used in Denmark during the seventeenth century:

> *E † M N Z S † ✠ S A T A N T perire nvnqve potrit sagit lider B G K. † albra † grama † tamar † alion † plonsit † tamar † firar † s 6 † nay emander † transiens † yfy init Zalio † ibat † † levi † vieder † Meits † leits † olianti † ely † O Z † dales † plato Zator naty † mesias einarder † adochy † mei. mn.*

We can recognize some extremely corrupted divine names in this spell (Tetragrammaton, Ely, Elyon, Adonay), as well as a fragment of *Jesus autem transiens*, *Amen* (mn).

We can find this *bref* again in Norway around 1850, but with some changes:

> *L L m m 3 Z L X S A T A N G Rerive Nau Zwa Peitril suc git lederi D L X L obrat gevma Gj Kainor Juaret 2e6 flia auderli Fransius Gaepaud 3 Aletib Z L X Leva L Rumret mei gt Lecly*

Xv aliatili Lei X B 3 X dali ✠ *Paler audoi a y mei Z Z Z Z omp L L L m L L Vor3 X L P 5 R ip C + Rmo.*

We can recognize a request in Latin resembling "Hear me Father," followed by a proper name (Fransius Gaepaud). The comparison with the Danish text suggests that the *Z* represents Zator (meaning Sator), *m* represents *messias,* and *obrat gevma* represents Tetragrammaton, but the whole thing makes very little sense. Fortunately, some light is shed on part of this *bref* with the help of a grimoire dated 1789, which suggests:

L + M N 22 + X : S : I A N + peviro Nun qve peteit Sangit bidere Ed : G : X. + Abra + Grama + Famar Abion Plons stit lamar firar + 2 b + Nay.

This seems to be a phrase to stop bleeding.

📖 Bang. no. 1085, 1105.

E M T: This is the abbreviation for the Christian phrase *ecce mater tua,* taken from the Gospel of John (19:27) and used on amulets. There is an example of this on an amulet in the Museum of Art and History in Geneva. This phrase, which is included in the *Orison of Seven Words,* attributed to Bede, offers protection against all ills, including a death without confession.

EON EOTH RABBONS EC ORCISIOTH OPAGS: Spell used in Italy to summon spirits that will send fleeing any who are troubling you. It is written in Greek letters (εον εόδ ραββόνς εχ όρχίσιόδ όπάγς).

📖 Pradel, 31.

EONE GION ARGION TERRA GRAMATER: To stop a fire, these words would be written on a lead slab of the church (*kirkebly*) and the sign of the cross would be drawn over the fire. The remnants of the liturgical hymn "Trisagion" are visible here, accompanied by a corruption of Tetragrammaton.

📖 Grambo, "Guddommers navn. Magi og ordets makt," 18.

EPAS NEBAS EPIN NEBENNE TENDULA: See *Jhesus Christus qvi est.*

ERAS. NIRAS. PIRALLA: To make someone dance against his will, these words should be written on a piece of waxed canvas and placed beneath the threshold of his house, in the name of the Father, the Son, and the Holy Ghost.

📖 Bang, no. 1141.

ERERET JONER FORLIS SKDOMIN BON † ET TYLA † ET SPATBUS † KANT † AAUA: When inscribed on a note, this phrase provides protection against bullets if carried on one's person. *Forlis* should read *fortis, Skdomin* should read *Sanctus Dominus,* and *Spatbus* should read *Spiritus.* These errors speak in favor of a transcription from memory.

📖 Ohrt II, 100.

† ERI GERARI: A fourteenth-century English manuscript includes a recipe against epilepsy that says it is necessary to carve † *Eri Gerari* on the outside of a ring, and ON THEBAL GUTGUTHANI on the inside.

📖 Evans, 123.

† ERPA † AGALERPA: In the fifteenth century, these words: † *erpa † agalerpa † erpa † galerpa † diptoni † bristoni † bersis † rami †,* would be written on a piece of bread and given to the individual bitten by a rabid dog to cure him.

📖 Braekman, 104.

† EREX † AREX † RYMEX †: This is a phrase from a charm intended to facilitate a birth, and it relies on some well-known Christian expressions.

> *In nomine Lazarus et filij veni foras et speritus scantus Christus te vocat † Christus stonat † Iesus predicat † Christus regnat † Erex † Arex † Rymex † Christi eleyzon † EEEEEEEE.*

[In the name of the Father Lazarus and the Son, get out! And of the Holy Ghost, Jesus is calling you, Christ thunders, Jesus preaches, Jesus reigns.]

Several errors are readily noted (e.g., "stonat" for *tonat,* "speritus" for *spiritus*).

📖 London, British Library, Sloane 3160, folio 129 v°.

ERXELL † AMALL † ARTISELL: This is an amulet phrase that when written on parchment and carried on one's person, provides protection against bullets.

Variant: *Escell † amel † artisell.*

📖 Ohrt II, 100.

† ESA † HIS † MASMO † CALDI † MALE † AM † ES: To inspire the love of a person you are lusting after, write this on an egg laid on the night of the new moon, then cast it into the fire while saying, "May you burn as much for me as this egg in the fire; may you have no rest until you come to me and have done as I desire."

📖 Spamer, 266.

ESCHEREIA, ESCHEREYEE (אהיה אשר אהיה): According to Saint Jerome, this is one of the ten mystic names of God. The term comes from a phrase in the Old Testament (Exodus 3:14), "I am that I am," which is widely used in magic and on amulets. The word is often unrecognizable because it has been corrupted so thoroughly, as can be seen in the following phrase: *Gug Gug Baltebani Alpha et Omega Ezer ave Eger Ave Ezeam.*

E S P A S   F A C T U M: When a rifle has been enchanted, it is necessary to load it, then fire at a rock that is thoroughly lodged in the ground while saying these words at the same time. The author of the curse will have no rest and will come to you to beg forgiveness.

📖 Bang, no. 1165.

ETTIFIA NERUM INVIOLO: These words allegedly had the power to make one invisible with the ability to enter anywhere. *Ettifia* is most likely a corruption of *Effata* (see entry), and the spell's meaning must be, "I shall violate nothing—open up!"

📖 *Trésor,* 177a.

EULAMÔ (ευλαμω): Quite common in Greek charms, this word has been connected with the Egyptian god Amon. It has been thought it might be a reversed version of *sôma lue,* "destroy the body," while implying "of my enemy." Other researchers see it as being derived from the Assyrian *ullamu,* "eternal." *Eulamô* has been used as a reductive spell, either forward or backward (from *eulamô* to *ô,* or *sômalue* to *s*), and by changing the order of the letters: *Eulamô ulamoe lamoeu amoeul moeula oeulam,* as on a curse tablet found in Egypt.

📖 Gager, 55, 70, 74, 198, 212.

EULOGUMEN PATERA: These words, which form part of an exorcism spell and are remnants of a Greek prayer, can be found on an eighth- or ninth-century amulet intended for a possessed person. It is worth noting that the conjured devil is called "elf." In eleventh-century England, it read as follows:

> *Eulogumen patera cae yo. Cae agion. Pneuma. Cae nym. Cae ia. Cae iseonas nenonamini.*

📖 Franz II, 578; Storms, no. 61.

EXGVEDIA/EXQEIDAX: A magic word used in two spells intended to reveal the identity of a thief.

✦ *Neguba, Pax.*

EXI FORAS, SOL TE VOCAT: "Come out, the sun is calling you!" This phrase, intended to provide a good birth, can be found as early as the fourth century in the work of the Greek physician Oribasius, which was changed to the Pseudo-Priscian "Come out! Your brothers are calling you into the light." The phrase is a variant of the *veni fors* from John 11:43.

📖 Lecouteux, *Le livre des grimoires,* 87–90.

EXMAEL EXMAEL: To get a good sleep, these words must be written and placed on the insomniac's head. Exmael is none other than Abraham's son, Ishmael.

📖 Lecouteux, *Le livre des grimoires,* 87–90.

E X S: As a treatment for insomnia, a post-Byzantine charm recommends taking a piece of a church tile and using a consecrated stylus to write a prayer on it that recalls famous slumbers, those of Adam,

Abimelech in the vines of Heinrich Cornelius Agrippa, and the seven sleepers of Ephesus, then the fourth Psalm of David at the same time as the *caracteres* below, and finally, to place the entire thing beneath the house threshold while invoking "Diomides, Eugeneios, Symvatios, Stephanos, Provatios, and the god Sabaoth."

εξσχφσκθ

📖 Tselikas, 74ff.

EXTABOR HETABOR SITTACIBOR: When wax or earth is used for a magic spell, it must be sanctified and blessed to acquire the desired power. It should therefore be exorcised using the following phrases:

> *Extabor Hetabor Sittacibor Adonai Onzo Zomen Menor Asmodai Ascobai Comatos Erionas Profas Alkomas Conamas Papuendos Osiandos Espacient Damnath Eheres Golades Telantes Cophi Zades.*

Moreover, it is necessary to recite Psalms 121, 15, 102, 8, 84, 68, 72, 133, 113, 126, 46, 47, 22, 51, 130, 139, 49, 110 and 53, in this order. These are angels' names, according to the text.

📖 *Clavicules* II, 18.

+ EZERA EZERA ERAVERAGAN: The beginning of a magic inscription on a silver brooch now at the Collegio Romano of the Company of Jesus in Rome:

> *Ezera ezera eraveragan + gvgvralterani alpha et ω.*
> On the other side it reads: + *Aotvino oio mo ooio av.*

✦ *Thebal.*
📖 King, 229.

EZOMAMOS, HAZALAT, EZITYNE: This is the opening of a thirteenth-century orison intended to allow one to more easily learn theology, the fourth part of the liberal arts. It must be said before examining a certain geometrical figure called a "note" to obtain intellectual illumination.

Ezomamos, Hazalat, Ezityne, Hezemechel, Czemomechel, Zamay, Zaton, Ziamy Nayzaton, Hyzemogoy, Jeccomantha, Jaraphy, Phalezeton, Sacramphal, Sagamazaim, Secranale, Sacramathan; Jezennalaton Hacheriatos, Jetelemathon, Zaymazay, Zamaihay, Gigutheio Geurlagon, Garyos, Megalon Hera Cruhic, Crarihuc, Amen.

Because philosophy includes several figures, there are several orisons.

✦ *Ars notoria, Gezomelion, Lemogethom.*

📖 *Ars notoria*, 78.

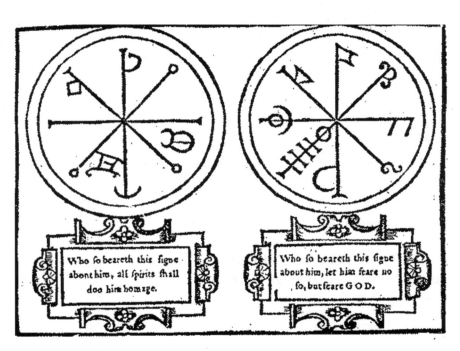

Amulets
from Reginald Scot, *Discoverie of Witchcraft*, 1584

†† F.A.P.H.P.Q: If you write these letters on a note that you carry in a piece of new linen, you can enchant a firearm to prevent it from firing.
  📖 Thiers I, 432.

FAUL: It was believed in tenth-century England that this magic word could protect an individual from snakebite.
  📖 Storms, no. 81.

F.C. †: If an enemy pulls you into court or into a duel, you must take a strip of lead and write these letters while your right foot is hovering over this series of letters: *g. e e o. e. d p a S N i, p o c i p s 9 e t c. c. o u s ai m p r i e pro inimico o.o.o.*
  📖 Aymar, 342.

FEBRIS FUBRIS FABERIS: The opening of a protection spell against fevers, which must be carried on one's person, written on paper after having stolen an object from a church. It continues with, "Go to Calabria, leave me in peace, in this way I will be content with myself." One will note the variation on the Latin word for "fever."
  📖 Abraham a Sancta Clara, 515.

FECANA, CAGETI, DAPHENES GEBARE: These are the opening words for a long phrase that heals fever.

Fecana, cageti, daphenes gebare, gedaco
Gebali stant, sed non stant phebas, hecas et hedas

It is necessary to write it on nine pieces of bread in the following manner. Each of the first six words on one piece, on the seventh piece *stant phebas, et hecas* on the eighth piece, and *hedas* on the ninth. Variants of the "dosage" indicate that the bread should also be buttered or that the phrase should be worn at the neck.

 📖 Ohrt II, 101.

FENUM—FICATUM—BÆLSEBUB: To put out a thief's eye, draw an eye in chalk and stick into it a needle made from the wood of a church that has been sharpened in the devil's name. Strike the needle three times with a hammer while saying these words.

 📖 Ohrt II, 101.

FESTELLE FESTELLA: To cure boils, all the different kinds are set down in a list in the form of an alliterative phrase: *festelle festela festelle festelle festelli festello festello festella festellum.*

 📖 Braekman, no. 148.

FETRA: First word of the phrase † *F E T R A /* † *gra* † *ma* † *lum* †, in which it is easy to recognize Tetragrammaton, "God's name in four letters." These letters would be written and then attached to the patient to cure him of fever or of the "evil disease," meaning syphilis.

 ✦ *Kariæ; Tetragrammaton.*
 📖 Bang, no. 1036; Ohrt II, 128.

FF † B † O † 2 † D: To win the love of an individual of the opposite sex, the individual would make a *voult*, meaning a wax effigy, that would then be plunged into running water for three days in succession. It would be given the name of the person who was the object of the *voult* maker's desire, and these *caracteres* would then be written or carved on it. It would then be cast into a fire.

 📖 Birlinger, vol. 1, 462.

FFF: Abbreviation of *(per filius) fecit, facit, fiat,* meaning "(by the son) He does, He has done, He did," sometimes preceded by *Jesus*. It appeared in the twelfth century in a Trevisan conjuration and was used up into the nineteenth century, primarily in Italy.

📖 Mondino, 29, 31.

FF LALE FF ALILA AYRATA B : B : U : F : ALIAS FFF: The text of an amulet that protected soldiers from being captured during a war.

📖 BBE, 15.

FILIAX: See *Eax*.

FILIBUM STRIT MASO FRANKO: It is necessary to write and carry these words on your person in order to draw the good slip, the "white slip," during a drawing for the fate of future conscripts. The white slip exempts the drawer from military service.

📖 Ohrt II, 101.

FIX FIX FIXON: To stop blood from pouring from the nose, this would be said in the patient's ear. The meaning is clear: "Stop!" with the underlying meaning: "flowing."

📖 Pseudo Theodore, 23, 276.

FODO, FERMA, FODO, FERME: Accompanied by essentially Christian *caracteres* (shown in the illustration on page 134), the following phrase, which dates from the eighteenth century, provides protection from bladed weapons and stones:

> *fodo, ferma, fodo, ferme, fodo Cadenard fogianra*

📖 Hervé, 361.

FONS ✠ ALPHA & OMEGA ✠ FIGA ✠ FIGALIS: There is a tradition stating that Joseph of Arimathea found a *bref* on the wounds delivered to Jesus's side when he was brought down from the cross. It said, "Whoever bears this text shall not die an evil death and will be spared from all perils."

Fons ✠ *alpha & omega* ✠ *figa* ✠ *figalis* ✠ *Sabbaoth* ✠ *Emmanuel* ✠ *Adonai* ✠ *o* ✠ *Neray* ✠ *Elay* ✠ *Ihr* ✠ *Rentone* ✠ *Neger* ✠ *Sahe* ✠ *Pangeton* ✠ *Commen* ✠ *a* ✠ *g* ✠ *l* ✠ *a* ✠ *Mattheus* ✠ *Marcus* ✠ *Lucas* ✠ *Iohannes* ✠✠✠ *titulus triumphalis* ✠ *Iesus Nazarenus rex Iudeorum* ✠ *ecce dominicæ crucis signum* ✠ *fugite partes aduersæ, vicit leo de tribu Iuæ, radix, Dauid, aleluijah, Kyrie eleeson, Christe eleeson, pater noster, aue Maria, & ne nos, & veniat super nos salutare tuum : Oremus, &*

📖 Scot, Book XII, chapter 9.

FOR FROE NOBALUTZ EST: These words are written on a piece of cheese to be given to someone suspected of theft. If he is guilty, he will spit it back out, as he will be unable to swallow it.

📖 Bang, no. 1145.

FRATTER, MATTER, ECRIGER: To win the love of a woman or girl, you should write these words, then take her by the hand. She will fall in love with you. The words for "brother" and "mother" are recognizable in this phrase.

📖 Bang, no. 1129.

FULGUR ARDIOS FILGOR SEMISSER FULGER MARITUDINEM EINDEN: This phrase was used in Mechelen, Belgium, in the nineteenth century to ensure that the best butter would be churned from milk.

📖 Van Haver, no. 1027.

FUTUS, EIORTUS FUL, KOUT, ERFRATUS: To protect one's pigs from death, the farmer would write this on as many notes as he had pigs, and place the notes in their slop.

📖 Bang, no. 1148.

GAA, SAGA, FASSAA: When a man or beast has been struck on the eye and a spot has formed over it, these words are hung around the neck to heal it.
   📖 *Egyptian Secrets* I, 227.

GABRIACH: For protection against all evil spirits, it is necessary to craft a silver ring in the moon's second house and set in it a crystalline stone on which ✡ is carved, then write *Gabriach* with white dove's blood on virgin parchment perfumed with aloe.
   📖 London, British Library, Lansdowne 1202, 4to, folio 175.

GABRIOT: To have a horse that will carry you easily wherever you wish to go, you must craft a tin ring in the fourth house of the moon and set in it a stone on which ♌ is carved, then write *Gabriot* with white dove's blood on virgin parchment perfumed with the caster's hair.
   📖 London, British Library, Lansdowne 1202, 4to, folio 173.

GAGNEYTANIA, GANEYTANIA: This phrase forms part of a complex ritual that takes place when the moon is in the sign of Libra.

It is accompanied by fire, suffumigations, and a sacrifice. These words must be drawn with the foot on the spot where the fire was built. Two effigies must be made with a blend of dirt and stagnant water. One must resemble the caster, and, if the purpose of the spell is love, both these effigies must be held so the two figures are embracing. In the Arabic source the spell is: *ġaniti ġaniti*.

📖 *Picatrix* IV, 8; *Gâyat al-Hakîm*, 314.

GALBES GALBAT GALDES GALDAT: These words must be recited to obtain protection from a toothache. They were handed down by Johann Weyer in the sixteenth century and Jean-Baptiste Thiers a century later. They also assume the form of *Gibel Got Gabel,* and in this case are also effective against illness.

📖 Scot, Book XII, chapter 14; Weyer V, 8; Thiers I, 361.

† GALGA † LEGA † LIGA: Spell used in Germany for protection from fires.

📖 Gotha, Germany, Ducal Library, ms. Chart., folio no. 566; folio no. 89b.

GAMILAREN AREN UXTOS BOHOT: Enchantment spell from popular Spanish-language books.

✦ *Turban.*

📖 Werner, no. 19, 200.

GASPAR (Caspar, Casber, Jasper): The Three Kings, Gaspar, Melchior, and Balthazar, were invoked for a wide variety of reasons, mainly in spells against the "falling sickness" (epilepsy), such as this one, for example:

> † *Jasper* † *fert* † *mirram* † *Melchior* † *thus* † *Baltasar* † *aurum* † *Hec* † *tria* † *qui* † *secum portaverit* † *nomina* † *regum* † *Solvitur* † *a morbo* † *ihesu* † *christ* † *pietate* † *caduco* † *Messias* † *sother* † *emmanuel* † *athanatos* † *alpha* † *et* † *Oo* † *principium et finis. Amen.*
>
> [Gaspas brought the myrrh, Melchior the incense, Balthazar the gold. Whoever bears on his person the names of the Three Kings will be healed of the falling sickness, by the grace of Christ . . .]

To walk without getting tired, the name of the Three Kings would be written this way on a note to be placed inside the individual's left shoe:

Gaspard   Balthazar   Melchior
†   †   †

Then while walking, the individual says: *Uriel, Jurinua, Badujet, Jaiel, Vianuel.*

✦ *Three Kings.*

📖 Braekman, no. 37; Hervé, 357.

G B O: To know in thirteenth-century Provence whether a patient would live, *G b o p o o S D* would be written on a laurel leaf and placed on the patient's foot; if he spoke he would be spared.

📖 Cambridge, ms. R. 14.30, folio 147 v°.

GEBAM, SUTH, SUTAM: Magic words that appear in *The Enchiridion Devoted to Jesus Christ* by Pope Leo XIII.

📖 *Enchiridion,* 66.

GEBARE GEDACE: To win someone's affections around 1650, these words would be written with bat's blood on an apple that was then given to the object of the individual's desire to eat at dusk. *Gebare* appears in another phrase: *Gebera Tibri Tridag,* which was used to blind a thief in one eye.

✦ *Fecana.*

📖 Ohrt II, 103.

G. E E O. E.: See F. C. †

GENEON GENETRON: The start of the phrase for a charm in Old English: *Geneon genetron genitul catalon carerist pabist etmic forrune nahtic forrune nequis annua maris santana nequetando,* which is good for a horse with a growth on its hoof.

📖 Berthoin-Mathieu, 144.

GEREL: The first word of a spell engraved on a ring found in England.

Gerel + got + gut + hai + dabir + haber + heber

✦ *Heber.*
📖 Evans, 122.

GERTRUDE'S BOOK (*Gertrudenbüchlein, Gertrudenbüch*): Title of a grimoire falsely attributed to Saint Gertrude of Nivelles (died 659) and published for the first time in 1536 by Johann von Lansperg. Particularly popular during the seventeenth and eighteenth centuries, it includes recipes for discovering hidden treasures and conjurations. During the nineteenth century, Tyrolean peasants carried it to ward off evil spells. It was said that *Saint Gertrude's Notes* drove away animals that harmed the fields and that *Saint Gertrude's Prayer* did the same for mice and rats. It is sometimes said that even if someone does not understand what one reads in this grimoire, the words still work. The various editions of this book are characterized by fanciful dates and a wide array of titles.

📖 *Die wahre und hohe Beschwörung der heiligen Jungfrau und Abtissin Gertrudis; Libellus St. Gertrudis*, 1401; *Heimliche Offenbarung St. Gertrudis von Nivel aus Brabant*, 1504; *Das Geheimnis der heiligen Gertrudis durch Sophia, das Gespons unsers Herrn und Heilandes Jesu Christi*, 1506; Heyl, 262–64; Schönwerth, 47–48; Baader, 400–401; Hörmann, 201–11.

GERUM, HEAIUM: This spell, *Gerum, Heaium Lada Frium, hide!*, is effective against rabies. It was written on the crust of a loaf of bread and given to humans or animals to eat.

📖 *Egyptian Secrets* II, 232.

GEZEMOTHON, OROMATHIAN: This is the opening phrase of a thirteenth-century orison that was used by those seeking an easy method to acquire philosophical knowledge. It had to be spoken before examining a certain geometrical figure called a "note" that provided intellectual illumination. It should be spoken aloud before the examination of the sixth figure of philosophy.

Gezemothon, Oromathian, Hayatha, Aygyay, Lethasihel, Lechizliel, Gegohay, Gerhonay, Samasatel, Samasathel, Gessiomo, Hatel, Segomasay, Azomathon, Helomathon, Gerochor, Hejazay,

Samin, Heliel, Sanihelyel, Siloth, Silerech, Garamathal, Gesemathal, Gecoromay, Gecorenay, Samyel, Samihahel, Hesemyhel, Sedolamax, Secothamay, Samya, Rabiathos, Avinosch, Annas, Amen.

✦ *Ars notoria, Gezomelion, Lemogethom.*
📖 *Ars notoria,* 82ff.

GEZOMELION SAMACH, SEMATH: This is the opening phrase of a thirteenth-century orison that gave the speaker the means to easily acquire the second part of philosophy, fourth part of the liberal arts. It had to be spoken before examining a certain geometrical figure called a "note" that provided intellectual illumination.

Gezomelion Samach, Semath, Cemon, Gezagam, Gezatrhin, Zheamoth, Zeze Hator Sezeator Samay Sarnanda, Gezyel, Iezel, Gaziety, Hel, Gazayethyhel, Amen.

Because philosophy includes several figures, there are several accompanying orisons.

✦ *Ars notoria, Gezemothon, Lemogethom.*
📖 *Ars notoria,* 79.

† GHEBAL: Initial word of an inscription of the ring of Saint Blaise, bishop of Sebastea in Armenia, preserved in the treasury of Vigogne Abbey. On the outside it reads: † *Ghebal gvt gvthensis gvthani,* and on the inside: † *Nai* † *gvba* † *vba* † *gota.* This is a variation of a phrase that included *Thebal* and so on that allegedly provided protection against gout.

GIGADE GIGADI: Spell used in the Upper Palatinate to make butter successfully.
📖 Schönwerth, vol. 1, 382, no. 14.

GILLCUM, PUNCTUM: When churning becomes difficult, this spell should be placed inside the churn: *Gillcum, Punctum, Satbot, Jesus* *of Nazareth king of the Jews* † † † *Satbot* represents the name Sabaoth.

📖 *Egyptian Secrets* II, 235.

GMIHID, GIHID, GHTR, GMHTR: Spell of Syrian phylactery for the house. It had to be written on a tree branch, which was then hung inside the house.

📖 Gollancz, § 17.

GOMET KAILOETH: When accompanied by *caracteres* and a ritual combining dust, walnut oil, and virgin parchment, these words make it possible to see aerial spirits.

📖 Honorius, 39.

GON † BON † RON † JON † CON †: This can be read inside a long spell dating from around 1450, in which the phrase about Christ's five wounds is accompanied by others that are all intended to cure all fevers and ills. This is simply a variation on *On,* one of the divine names. It includes a second part.

Febris depellant, qui me vexare laborant †
Wlnera quinque dej sunt medicina mej †
Piron † pupicon † diron † arcon † cardon † jadon † ason †

[May the fevers afflicting me depart! The five wounds of Christ are my remedy.]

The texts add, "I give you these names in the name of the Father, who is Alpha and o, of the Son, who is truth and way, of the Holy Ghost, who is the remission of sins." The addition of *on* as a suffix masks and alliterates a pagan phrase (*pir pupi dir arc card jad as*). The last two words give *Sadaj,* the Hebrew *Shaddaï* שדי, "Almighty."

📖 Ohrt I, no. 266.

GONOMIL ORGOMIL MARBUMIL: This is the start of a long phrase that should be sung into the right ear of a person who has swallowed an insect when drinking. If the person is a woman, it should be sung into her left ear, nine times in both cases and accompanied by an Our Father.

Gonomil orgomil marbumilmarbsai ramum tofeð tengo docuillo biran cuiðæ cæfmiil scuiht cuillo cuibduill marbsiramum.

The beginning is the Old Irish *Gono mil orgo mil marbu mil,* "I hurt the beast, I strike the beast, I kill the beast." *Cuillo biran* would mean "I destroy the thorn," the stinger.

📖 Berthoin-Mathieu, 477ff.; Storms, no. 73.

GOSPEL OF JOHN: The prologue to this gospel (1:1–14) has been ceaselessly employed in magic. It is worn as an amulet and, according to Saint Augustine, it was placed on the heads of individuals stricken with fever to cure them. Inscribed on virgin parchment, sealed in a pouch, and etched on a hazelnut or a gold or silver tablet, this gospel is effective against headaches, toothaches, demons, and witches. It protects wheat from fire, crops from storms, and even makes its bearer invulnerable. The Auvergne soldiers who mounted a surprise attack against Geneva in 1602 were equipped with charms bearing *In principio erat Verbum* accompanied by *caracteres*. Written on the bottom of the parchment was, "Whoever possesses this note cannot be killed today by either water or sword."

📖 Ohrt I, no. 1198; Bang, no. 1071; Franz II, 101 passim; Aymar, 300, 317, 340; Vinje, no. 49; Van Haver, no. 651–58, 1017. Le Blant, 9–13.

GÔTOUNE GÔTANE GÔBORRANNE: We find this spell written in Greek letters (γωτουνη γωτανη γωβωρραννη) in an Italian prayer that is intended to prevent the revealing of a secret. The words are attached like this: *perno maniphestari ounosigretou,* and the Greek letters reinforce their magical aspect.

📖 Pradel, 32.

GRABATON ULION ADONAI: This phrase used in hunting consists of three divine names, the first of which is a corrupted fragment of Tetragrammaton. The individual places a topaz in his mouth along with a southernwood leaf, then spits them into a silk cloth that is then firmly bound together before throwing it toward animals while saying these words three times. The animals will be frozen in place.

📖 Cardan, 1055ff.

GRIEL STATUEL ELAEL: By writing these words on an apple that you give a young woman to eat, you can win her love. The use of the suffix *el* gives the words the sense of an invocation to the angels.

📖 Braekman, no. 350.

GRIMOIRE: See the entries: *Ars notoria, Cyprianus, Gertrude's Book, Liber incatationum, Liber iuratus, Livre des esperitz.*

G T A D J C Q M C D E: These are the initials of the phrase that Saint Laurence allegedly spoke before being roasted alive: "I give you grace, Lord Jesus Christ, you who are worthy of giving me comfort" (*Gratias tibi ago Domine Iesu Christe, qui me confortare dignus es*). This phrase was inscribed this way on buildings as a protection from fires. By recalling the story of one who had been spared by fire, it was hoped that Lawrence's holiness would obtain the same result.

📖 *Acta sanctorum,* August II, 519.

GUARAC, COVDE, GIENNEM, BUNAS, COLATE: This phrase is used to take out the eye of a thief from a distance. It is necessary to draw, on a Sunday morning before sunrise, an eye, then strike it three times while invoking the devil to blind the thief's eye and to wear these words around your neck at the same time.

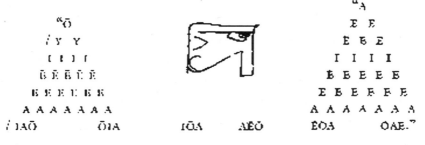

📖 Ohrt I, no. 964; Gager; PGM, 70–95.

GUGUL/GUGGUG: These words are found frequently inscribed on talismans and magic rings starting from the early fourteenth century on. The best example of one of these rings is the one preserved in the Bavarian Museum of Artistic Monuments and Antiquities in Donauwörth. The ring, from the fifteenth century, has this engraved on its inner surface: + *At.Ebel.Diabel* + *Gvgvl* + *Gugul*. As of the present, the meaning of these inscriptions has yet to be discovered.

📖 Oman, no. 72.

GURGUR: This word appears in a prayer intended to protect the doors of the house at night. It was collected in Iceland in the nineteenth century by Jón Árnason. *Gurgur,* or *Karkur,* seems to designate a demon. Here is the eviction spell:

> Outside Gurgur,
> Inside Jesus!
> Outside Gassagull,
> Inside angel of God!
> Outside Ragerist,
> Inside Jesus Christ!
> Outside Valedictus,
> Inside Benedictus!
> We entrust everything to the powers of God, and good night!

Valedictus can be corrected to *Maledictus,* and *Ragerist* probably hides "Antichrist." Another version collected by Konrad von Maurer from Sigrid Einarsdottir around 1855, says, "Get out Frugtus, come in angel of God! Get out Grasagull, come in Benedict(u)s. Amen."

📖 Jónsson, vol. 2, 383–84; Maurer, 208–10.

GUSTATE ET VIDETE: To prevent wine from turning sour, it is necessary to inscribe these words from Psalm 34:9 on the barrels. Johann Weyer says, "Aphricanus writes atop the barrel, for fear the wine might go bad during the year: *Gustate & videte quod bonus est Dominus:* in other words, 'Taste and see that the Lord is good.'"

📖 Scot, Book XII, chapter 18; Schmidt I, 64; Weyer III, 4.

GUTRIT: The lead-in of a phrase discovered on a thirteenth-century amulet in runic script: *Gutrit in nomine patris et fili et spiritu sancto Amen. Tomine Jesus Christus Amen.* We do not know what it was used for.

📖 Bang, no. 1066.

GUTUNE † GUTANE † GOBORRANI: These words were used in Sicily during the early Middle Ages to avoid betraying a secret. To be effective they were written in Greek letters (γωτονη + γωτανη + γωυωρραννη).
- 📖 Schneegans, 585.

GVG GVG: These words open a long magic inscription on a ring of the lords of Veltheim, intended to provide protection from the dangers incurred in military operations: *GVG GVG BALTEBANI ALPHA ET OMEGA EZER ave EGER ave EAGAM.*

Ezer ave Eger is a corruption of Eschereia, "I am that I am," one of the names of God (Exodus 3:14).
- ✦ *Gvgvaevgvbeavavaldera, Gvttani, Thebal.*
- 📖 Kronfeld, 59.

GVGVEAEVGVBEAVAVALDERA: This is the first word of a magic spell inscribed on a fifteenth-century gold ring in the British Museum: *Gvgveaevgvbeavavaldera + Vrvanialrra + Phaecarao.*
- 📖 Evans, 6.

GVTTANI: This term dating from the thirteenth century can be see in the phrase: *TEBAL GVT GVTTANI,* engraved on rings and on a Florentine silver broach as well as on the ring of Donauwörth (cf. *Gugul*). The word has resisted all attempts of clarification. It is assumed to transmit a magical charge to the object on which it is inscribed, transforming it into a talisman, probably against gout.

Variants: *Gudtani, Gutani, Guthani.*
- ✦ *Galabra, Thebal.*
- 📖 Dalton, no. 218; 872ff.

GYLLOY, MOTHROUS, AVYZOU: In a fifteenth-century Byzantine tale starring Saints Sisinnios, Sines, and Sinodorus, Gelloy/Gello (γελλω; plural Γελλουδες), an unclean spirit says, "I will not enter where there is a phylactery and there where it will be read [recited] I shall not enter that place; . . . and if someone can write my twelve names, I shall not harm that house, I will not take over that house, I will not harm its livestock, and I shall have no power over its members."

These twelve names are: Gylloy, Mothrous, Avyzous, Maramatotous, Marmanila, Selininous, Ariani, Salsaleutou, Egyptiani, Asvlitous, Aimavivon, Ktarkarischou.

This exorcism appears in manuscripts called the "Gylou Papers," (γιαλλονδοχαρτια/*Gialloudochartia*). It can be written by villagers or priests and can be used against the evil eye, magic, demons, or diseases, or inserted into phylacteries to be worn around the neck. The number of names varies from "12 and a half [*sic*] to 72 and a half" and many variants are known, such as the two below:

1. Amorphous, Abyzou, Karchous, Briané, Bardellous, Egyptiané, Barna, Charchanistréa, Adikia, [name missing], Myia, Petoméné.
2. Gyllou, Morra, Byzou, Marmaro, Petasia, Pelagia, Bordona, Apletou, Chamodrakaina, Anabardalaia, Psychanospastria, Paidopniktria, Strigla.

Paul Pendrizet revealed the following names:

Γυλλου	Μανλου	Γιλου	Γελου	Γυλου
Αμορφους	Αμορφους	Μωρρα	Μορφους	Αμορφου
Αβυζου	Καρανιχους	Βυζου	Καρανιχος	Καρχαριχρυ
Καρχους	Αβιζιου	Μαρμαρου	Αμιξους	Βυζου
Βριανη	Αβιδαζιου	Πετσια	Αμιδαζου	Αβυδαζου
Βαρδελλους	Μαρμαλατους	Πελαγια	Μαρμλατ	Μαρμαλετα
Αιγυπτιανη	Καριανη	Βορδονα	Καρανη	Σεληνου
Βαρνα	Ελληνους	Απλετου	Σεληνους	Αβηζατω
Χαρχανιστεα	Αριανη	Χαρμοδραχαινα	Αβιζα	Καρχανιτο
Αδιχια	Αδιχια	Αναβαρδαλαια	Αριανη	Κωρχανιτους
[lacune]	Χαρχανιστρια	Ψυχανοσπαστρια	Μαραν	Αιματοπινουσα
Μυια	Μυια	Παιδοπνιχτρια	Μαρμαλατ	Στριγλα
Πετομενη	Πετομενη	Στριγλα		

Abyzou is a female demon responsible for child mortality; Karchous is a corruption of Karko, a demon identified with Lamia; Empusa, Mormo, and Gello are devouring demons that slay children. Adikia means "injustice, the evil"; Myia, "the fly"; Pétoméné (flying) is sometimes read as Pseudomené (liar); Morra is the nightmare; Petasia refers to the ability to fly; Pelagia refers to the place where the demon arrives (the sea); Apletou means "boundless"; Paidopniktria, "smothers children"; and Strigla is the *strygoi,* the witch.

Abyzou

On the amulets of late antiquity or the proto-Byzantine period, Gyllou appears under the name of Abyzou. It is thought that the source would be *Solomon's Testament,* dating from the first century, in which Solomon defeats a female demon named Obyzouth.

In Bulgaria, a prophylactic incantation (*zagovor*) from the nineteenth century is constructed on the same basis, but the demons tormenting men are the Tresavice, "the twelve daughters of Tsar Herod." Their names are accompanied by their mode of action: Treseja, Ognieja, Lideja, Gnieteja, Ginousa, Gloukheja, Lomeja, Puchneja, Jelieja, Kerkoussa, Gledeja, Neveja.

The first three represent fevers, followed by oppression, coughs, deafness, broken bones, sprains, icterus, tears in the veins of the feet and hands, insomnia accompanied by the loss of reason, and the last, Neveja, "she who cuts off the head of Saint John," is therefore Salome, "the worst of all because when she got a hold of a man, he had to die." All these demons will flee at the sound of the Holy Apostle Sisini's name.

In Romania, Avestiţa, a demon akin to Gello/Gyl(l)ou, possesses nineteen names; he who writes them on a paper and carries them on his person shall protect his house as she will not be able "to approach within even seven miles of it."

According to a printed version, these are her names: Avestiţa, Navodar, Salomnia, Zurina, Nicara, Aveziha, Scarbola, Miha, Puha, Cripa, Zlia, Nevaţa, Pesia, Cilipina, Igra, Eosfor, Luţifer, Avie, Berzebuti. The following names appear in another text: Vestiţa, Avezuha, Valnomia, Navadaria, Scorcoila, Miha, Tiha, Grompa, Slalo, Nicozda, Sina, Necauza, Hatav, Hulila, Ghiana, Huva, Gluviana, Prava,

Samca. It should be noted that Samca, another female demon, is the equivalent of Gyl(l)ou in this country.

📖 Allatius, *De templis Graecorum recentioribus;* Patera, "Exorcismes et phylactères byzantins: 'Écrire, énoncer les noms du démon"; Ryan, 246; Perdrizet, 16–19; Léger, 33ff.; Oikonomidis, 246–78; Talos, *Petit dictionnaire de mythologie roumaine,* s.v. "Avetişţa"; Timotin, "*Irodia doamna zânelor. Notes sur les fées roumaines et leur cohorte fantastique,*" 179–94; Timotin, "Queen of the Fairies and Biblical Queen," 363–76; Greenfield, 83–142; Hasdeu, vol. II, 278, 719.

YωωBEVICI aIR: To counter sacred fire, this would be written on the ailing part, or else this: aOPOMalaω.

📖 Pseudo Theodore, 19ff., 282.

Obverse side of a Capricorn seal,
according to the *Archidoxis magica,* Basel, 1972

✠ HABAY ✠ HABAR ✠ HELIAR ✠: To heal oneself of a rabid dog bite, an individual would slip on a silver ring on which this phrase had been engraved and speak the charm *ad hoc*.
   📖 Scot, Book XII, chapter 14.

HABER ANDAVEX O VORT: For protection against curses, it is necessary to write these words and carry them on your person.
   Variant: *Haber Avavex Drei.*
   📖 Bang, no. 1101.

HABERE DABERE SACHERE: These words, when written on a crust of bread, will dispel fevers, epilepsy, and enchantments. They also permit thieves to be unmasked. These words have come down to the present day in countless variations. The phrase + *Mel* + *Gerel* + *Got* + *Gvt* + *Hai* + *Dabir* + *Haber* + *Heber* can be read on a magic ring discovered in Italy.
   Variant: *Hapora Fapora Sapora.*
   📖 Thiers I, 354–56; Ohrt II, 97, 104, 123.

H. A. B. I.: See *Dabi*.

HABI MASSA DENTI LANTIEN. J.J.J.: To overcome a man stronger than yourself, say, "I blow in your face; I take from you three drops of blood, the first from the heart, the second from the liver, the third from your vital force; I thereby strip you of your strength and courage." Then speak this phrase aloud. This spell gained great popularity in the eighteenth century by the *Livret de Romain* and has numerous variants depending on the editions, such as this example:

   H bbi Masra danti Santien. †††

   ◆ *C.M.B.*
   📖 Spamer, 379.

HABOR AHTLOGER ÆRATIN IN SOMISO PSTRES I : T : S : AMEN: For protection against the evil spells of sorcerers and witches, one should attach these words to his or her person.

✦ *Hafel.*
📖 Bang, no. 1093.

HACEDION: According to the *Semiphoras,* this is a name that God revealed to Moses on the Sinai. It has the power to banish sorrow.

📖 *Semiphoras,* Schäuble edition, 300.

HAFEL, AGELTOR, HAFEL: To recover what a thief has carried off, one must speak these words aloud five times while turning a mustard seed grinder, inside of which embers have been placed, counterclockwise with one's left hand. It is obviously a variant of *Habor.* Other variants:

††† *Hafel, Agel Iol, Hafel;*
Horel, Agel, Tarvel;
Safel, Agel, Tallafell, Seffel, Agel, Seffel, Egellugalet ell.

✦ *Habor.*
📖 BBE, 63; Bang, no. 1392.

HAEPHATHA: See *Effata.*

HAFIT SAGAL FASU: The beginning of a charm intended to compel a robber to return his loot. "Take a firebrand and place it on the eye of a coffee grinder, turn the handle backward and read these words three times: *Hafit Sagal Fasu.* Just as this mill is turning backward with this ember, just may this man also return to the same place. In the same way that this mill is turning backward with this ember, may it burn the soul of this man and never grow cold before he returns what he has stolen."

📖 Ohrt I, no. 934.

HALL. BIß ARTAMATI. ADONAY, ALEONO, FLORIT: This phrase is supposed to render the individual who wears it invulnerable.

📖 Schulz, 191, footnote 638.

HAMMANYEL: This is how the English wrote Emmanuel in tenth-century charms.

+ HANA + GINY HAT QUAL +: This spell is repeated three times to win at games. The last two German words mean "he suffers."
 📖 *Württembergisches Jahrbuch*, vol. 18, 198, no. 185.

HANAZAY, SAZHAON, HUBI: Opening of a Solomonic orison that should be recited before the caster begins magical workings in order to gain wisdom and the knowledge of what is being asked of him.

> *hanazay zarahoren hubisenaar ghu hirbaionay gynbar zanaile selchora zelmora hiramay iethohal yfaramel hamatha mathois iaboha gechors cozomerag zosomeraht hamy phodel denos gerot haoalos meliha tagahel sechamp salyhelethon monocogristes lemenron hachagnon hamyhon. Amen.*

The *Ars notoria* provided the following variation in the thirteenth century:

> *Hanazay, Sazhaon, Hubi, Sene, Hay, Ginbar, Ronail, Selmora, Hyramay, Lohal, Yzazamael, Amathomatois, Yaboageyors, Sozomcrat, Ampho, Delmedos, Geroch, Agalos, Meihatagiel, Secamai, Saheleton, Mechogrisces, Lerirencrhon.*

Omissions can be seen on the one hand, as can the different divisions of certain names.
 ✦ *Ars notoria.*
 📖 *Liber iuratus*, chap. 60; *Ars notoria*, 69ff.

HANCOR HANACOR HAMYLOS: These are the opening words for the *Liber iuratus* (Book of Consecrations), which is addressed to Jesus, "son of the incomprehensible God." It is in two parts, but its purpose remains unclear:

> 1. *hancor hanacor hamylos iehorna theodonos heliothos phagor corphandonos norizane corithico hanosae helsezope phagora.*
> 2. *Eleminator candones helos helee resphaga thephagayn thetendyn thahonos micemya hehortahonas nelos behebos belhores hacaphagan belehothol ortophagon corphandonos.*

Eleminator most likely represents *Illuminator,* a title of God. *Hancor* can be found in the form of *Acho'r* in the divine invocation of a Greek spell. *Heliothos* is the contraction of *helios* and *theos,* "sun god." The thirteenth-century grimoire *Ars notoria* offers the following reading of these phrases.

1. *Ancor, Anacor, Anylos, Zohorna, Theodonos, hely otes Phagor, Norizane, Corichito, Anosae, Helse Tonope, Phagora.*
2. *Elleminator, Candones helosi, Tephagain, Tecendum, Thaones, Behelos, Belhoros, Hocho Phagan, Corphandonos, Humanæ natus & vos Eloytus Phugora.*

✦ *Ars notoria.*
📖 *Liber iuratus,* chap. 57; PGM VII, 149ff.; *Ars notoria,* 24.

HANTARACERET, HANTARACERET: To make a man appear who will grant your wish, you must, when the moon is in Aquarius, follow a complicated ritual that brings into play three jar lids, fire, wine, and spices that are cooked, then crushed to be made into forty pills, and so on. These words are spoken in this working.

In the Arabic source the spell appears like this: *Hantar asrak hantar asrak.*

📖 *Picatrix* IV, 16; *Gâyat al-Hakîm,* 319.

HAPHOT HAPHOT: This phrase forms part of a complex ritual that takes place when the moon is in Virgo. It is accompanied by the sacrifice of thirty thrushes and suffumigations. A figure of the caster's choosing is carved on a lead blade with a gold needle and then buried. The request that has been made shall be granted.

In the Arabic source the spell appears like this: *'Afût 'fût.*

📖 *Picatrix* IV, 7; *Gâyat al-Hakîm,* 313.

HAPORA FAPORA SAPORA: See *Habere Dabere Sachere.*

HARMUM HARMUM: These words are used in a very long spell during which the caster must, while the moon is in Sagittarius, sacrifice a lamb in front of fifteen trees. These words are repeated five times before each of these trees. A man of fine and handsome

appearance shall come forth to take the caster where he wishes to go.
The corresponding chapter in the *Ġāyat al-Hakîm* does not offer this spell.

📖 *Picatrix* IV, 10.

HAROMEMYÇ: According to the *Libro de Mercurio* (Book of Mercury), a thirteenth-century treatise of astral magic, it is necessary to say this word three times when addressing Mercury. This planet must be in the sign of Pisces at this time.

📖 *Astromagia*, 285.

HARYM, HARYM, LAYAR, LAYAR: According to a thirteenth-century treatise of astral magic translated from the Arabic, it is necessary to use this phrase when one wishes to speak with Mars when this planet is in the sign of Scorpio.

📖 *Astromagia*, 281.

HASTA, HAVA, SHAVER: To cure fever, one should write these words on three almonds and eat one each day.

📖 *Egyptian Secrets* I, 181.

HAT × HEON × L. N × SABAOT × EMANUEL: By writing this in your own blood on a note that you will wear on your stomach, you will be protected from being hit.

📖 Hervé, 364.

HAX: This word enters into a preparation ritual for an amulet. It is necessary to take the hearts of a raven and a mole, carry them on your person, and say:

> *Hax Fax mensik asin lakom mano gievfe.*

📖 Bang, no. 1059.

HAX PAA SI MAX: To heal a patient, these words must be written on a piece of bread for him to eat. The exact phrase is: *Hax pax max Deus adimax.* Widespread since the sixteenth century, it is of much older provenance, as fragments have been found from two fourteenth-century spells: one is a blood-conjuring spell, and the other is a charm against fever. It is thought to be an extrapolation of the liturgical phrase *pax tecum* (peace be with you), enlarged through homophony. In the fourteenth century, *Pax max vax* was the accepted expression. Johann Weyer recorded the entire phrase.

> *O rex gloriae Jesus Christe, veni cum pace in nomine Patris + max in nomine Filii + in nomine spiritus sancti + pax Caspar Melchior Balthasar + prax + max + Deux ymax +.*

For protection against rabid dog bites, it was necessary to write these words on a note that one wore or otherwise carried on his or her person. When inscribed in whole or abbreviated form (*H.P.M. Deux adimax*) on a piece of bread or paper, or on an apple quarter, the phrase offers protection from rabies, fevers, and toothaches, on condition it is swallowed. During the restoration of Saint George's Basilica in Prague, a parchment strip was found beneath a coat of primer on a niche on which a certain Dobrozlava had written a request for the healing of trench fever. This prayer ended with, "May *Pax* † *nax vax* be the remedy of this servant of God, Amen."

✦ *Pax, Max.*

📖 Espeland, § 30; Schmidt I, 69, 396; Franz II, 202, 430, 469, 477; Heim, 537; Bang, no. 1058–64; Weyer V, 8; Delrio, 493; Thiers I, 355ff.; Espeland, no. 30; Ohrt I, 438; Ohrt II, 108, 116, 121 passim; Werner, no. 21, 201.

HAYA: A magic word that often appears in conjurations influenced by the *Semiphoras*. The *Liber incantationum,* for example, offers the following sequence in the *Conjuration of Tuesday.*

ya. ya. ya. A ; A. va. hy. hy. Haa. Haai. va. va. Han. Han. Hon. hy. Hyen. Haya. Haya. Hol. Hol. Hay. Hael. Hon. By the names of the Lord Adonai. haya. Hol. Plasmator seculorum. Cados. Cados. Cados. Ebel. el. ya. ya. Eloy. Arar. Eloym. Eloym.

Haya may be a name of God.

HAYRAHAB, HAYRAHAB: According to the *Libro de Mercurio* (Book of Mercury), a treatise of astral magic that was translated from Arabic into Spanish in the thirteenth century, the caster must repeat this four times when addressing Mercury when this planet is in the sign of Aries.

 📖 *Astromagia*, 273.

HAZARAM † HIHEL † HEHELILEM: Beginning of the thirty-first magic orison of the *Liber iuratus* (Book of Consecrations).

Hazaram † hihel † hehelilem † hethelilem † thelihem † hazagatha † agrnazcor † hizguor † hazaheimn † iesan † zezor † iesar † ysail † and you, holy angels whose names are written in the Book of Life, and are repeated here: iasym † horos † helsa † heremogos † myrecagil † resaym † lemay † lemar † rasamen † lemar † themamoht † irasim † iemamoht † themamoht † secray † sotthaht † sehan † hanathar † thansethay † helymaht † iosoihel † helymoht † saccamaht † helymyhot † iosey † theodony † iasamaht † pharene † panetheneos † phateneynehos † haramen † theos † hathanaym † hanataiphar † hatanazar † basiactor † iesenamay † iesamana † iesamanay † haziactor † hamynosia † zezamanay † hamos † hamynos † hiatregilos † cahegilihos † zaguhel † zatahel. Amen.

Contrary to what it says, this list only contains a few angel names, perhaps Myrecagil, Iosoihel, Zaguhel, and Zatahel. The addition of Greek suffixes to what are probably Hebrew words and those that are a mix of Greek and Hebrew makes very little sense.

H B R H C H T H B R H: When fighting fever, it is necessary to hang around the patient's neck, between eight and nine o'clock, a *bref* containing the reductive phrase shown on page 156.

H B R H C H T H B R H
H B R H C H T H B R
H B R H C H T H B
H B R H C H T H
H B R H C H T
H B R H C H
H B R H C
H B R H
H B R
H B
H

This word is in fact *Abracadabra,* which has been coded by the substitution of *A* by *H* and *D* by *T!* This means of doing things is quite revealing of the methods used to conceal a phrase or "to create" a new one out of an old one.

📖 *Egyptian Secrets* I, 222.

HEBER † NABI † ΘAVL † HASE: This phrase provides protection against epilepsy if written on a parchment that is worn on the person's arm, then burned.

📖 Ohrt II, 104.

HELL, BEFF, CLETEMATI, SOBATH, ADONAY, ELEONA, FLORIT: By wearing these words one makes oneself invulnerable to bullets. It is undoubtedly a variant of *Hall Biß Artamati* . . .

📖 *Egyptian Secrets* II, 51.

HELY AZELECHIAS: This is the beginning of an orison from the *Liber iuratus* that asks God to illuminate the heart and strengthen the spirit.

> *hely azelechias neloreos mohan zama sarnelohatehus saguaht adonay zoma lenezothos lithon ietemothon sabahot.*

The few identifiable words we find here let us know that what we are dealing with are names and titles of God.

📖 *Liber iuratus,* chap. 63.

HELY HELY LAMAZABATHANI: This phrase can be found inscribed on the rim of the seal of Libra, a zodiac amulet that protects from blood diseases, violent winds, maritime floods, kidney pains, and evil spells and curses when inside a house. This phrase is taken from the Bible and means, "My God, my God, why have you forsaken me?" accompanied by *Consummatum est* and Christ's triumphal title (I.N.R.I.). This information comes from the Pseudo–Arnaldus de Villanova.

In the Netherlands, this phrase is used to compel a witch to come forth, and the last word is written: *Lamasabatay*. In the lists of holy names, Hely is found by itself.

✦ *Hely, S D S.*

📖 Pseudo–Arnaldus de Villanova, *Opera*, folio 301 v°ff.; Van Haver, no. 1006.

HELY SCEMATH: The start of a magic orison that Solomon called "the first Revelation." We have two versions that differ in detail. Here is the fourteenth-century version:

> *Helysemath. hasaram. hemel. saduch. theou. heloy. zamaram. zoma. iecromaym. theos. deus pie et fortis hamathamal. iecronamayhala. zanay. hacronaaz. zay. colnaphan. salmazaiz. ayhal. gemelam. haymasa. ramay. genzi. zamath. helyemath. semay. selmar. ie crosamay. iachar. lemar. harnany. memothemath. hemelamp. And you, all-powerful holy father and God unknowable in all your works that are holy, just, and good. magalhamethor. semassaer. zamachamar. geogremay. megus. monorail. hamezeaza. hillebata. maraama. iehenas. iehemia. malamay. sephormay. zemonoma. melas. hemay. hemesna. iecormay. lemesey. senosecari. heltamay. calion. tharathos. vsyon. geysethon. semyna. themas. zezehas. thaman. helomany. hamel. Amen.*

The *Ars notoria* (thirteenth century) states that it comes "from the depths of the Greek, Hebrew, and Chaldean languages" and calls it "Orison of the Four Tongues" and presents it as follows:

> *Hely, Schemat, Azatan, honiel sichut, tam, imel, Iatatandema, Jetromiam, Theos: Ô God holy and strong, Hamacha, mal, Gottneman, Alazaman, Actuaar, Secheahal, Salmazan, zay, zojeracim, Lam hay, Masaraman, grensi zamach, heliamat, seman, selmar, yetrosaman muchaer, vesar, hasarian Azaniz, Azamet, Amathemach, hersomini. And you are holy and just, incomprehensible in all your works, which are holy, just, and good; Magol, Achelmetor, samalsace, yana, Eman, and cogige, maimegas, zemmail, Azanietan, illebatha sacraman, reonas, grome, zebaman, zeyhoman, zeonoma, melas, heman, hathoterma, yatarmam, semen, semetary, Amen.*

Variants of the lead-in: *HEly, Scemath, Amazaz, Hemel; Sathusteon hheli Tamazam.*

✦ *Ars notoria.*

📖 *Liber iuratus*, chap. 45; *Ars notoria*, 7, 115.

HENDEB HENDEB: This spell forms part of a complex ritual that takes place when the moon is in Leo, and it must be repeated four times. It is accompanied by the sacrifice of a rooster and suffumigations. The purpose is to cause the appearance of "a human form" who will grant the wish that has been asked of it.

In the Arabic source, the *Gâyat al-Hakîm*, the spell is "'Andab 'Andab."

📖 *Picatrix* IV, 6; *Gâyat al-Hakîm*, 313.

HEPHATA: See *Effata*.

HEREGO GO MET HUNC: In twentieth-century France, for the protection of one's animals, one says over them: *Herego go met hunc Gueridans Sesserant Deliberant Amen*. At the same time, one draws a cross in salt on each animal. The meaning of the whole thing is close to, "I am asking for [the misfortunes] to stop and that [the animals] shall be spared."

📖 Camus 1990, 107.

H. E. R. E. R. I: See *Dabi*.

HEURAXDAX: A magic word used in Middle Franconia during the fires of Saint John so that the hemp would grow well.
  📖 Panzer, 550.

HEYERIM HEYERIM: To compel the appearance of a man who will grant your wishes, you must, when the moon is in Capricorn, say: *Heyerim heyerim falsari tifrat tifrat,* then leave a house in which only two men can stand and circle it seventy times without stopping, make a suffumigation, and sacrifice a rooster. One will note the repetition of each word, which is common of grimoires translated from Arabic.

In the Arabic source text, the spell is: *Hajâwam hajâwam balgâr balgâr naqarâw naqarâw.*
  📖 *Picatrix* IV, 12; *Gâyat al-Hakîm,* 317.

† H. G. D. A. QQ. S. P. P. S. S. 9. F. G. A. S. S. N.: An encrypted spell allegedly written by Pope Leo III—a *bref* including *caracteres* protecting from plague, demons, poisons, snakes, and evil spells—that he is supposed to have sent to Charlemagne.
  📖 Aymar, 331, 339.

HIELMA † HELMA † HELIMAT: The beginning of the twenty-first orison of the *Liber iuratus*.

> *Hielma † helma † helimat † herina † hytanathas † hemyna † hitanathois † helsa † hebos † hiebros † helda † hagasa † hoccomegos † raitotagum † coictagon † myheragyn. Amen.*

Note the variants of *athanatos* ("immortal") in *hytanathas* and *hitanathois,* which give a good picture of how magic spells were "crafted."
  📖 *Liber iuratus,* chap. 32.

HINNITUS QUISITUS: Saying three Our Fathers and three Hail Marys combined with the spell below was believed in the fifteenth century to cure a horse of laminitis.

> *Hinnitus quisitus vena vacca vane barra*

  📖 London, British Library, Sloane 962, folio 136 v°.

HMEIF: This is the abbreviation of Christ's words, *Hodie mecum eris in paradiso* (Today, you shall be with me in paradise), with *F* for *P,* taken from the Gospel of Luke (23:43) and used on Christian amulets, such as one in the collection of the Museum of Art and History in Geneva. These words are also part of *Orison of Seven Words,* attributed to Bede, which grants protection against all ills and whose holder cannot die before making a final confession.

HOCATOS MARKILA ESTUPIT: These words will protect the bearer of the talisman on which they are carved from attack by ferocious animals and will drive away rabid beasts, which the bearer can kill by saying: *Tramantram Ricona Estupit.* If he finds himself surrounded by wild animals, he will say: *Hocatos Imorad Surater Markila,* while showing them the talisman.

 📖 *Trésor,* 182a.

HOCUS POCUS: This is one of the most famous Kabbalistic words, and it has been verified as a magical phrase since 1632. It was even used as the title for a film by Kenny Ortega that came out in 1993. The archbishop of Canterbury, Jon Tillotson (died 1694) believed it was the corruption of a term from the Mass, *Hoc est(enim) corpus (meum)*. Its first known appearance is in Giovanni Florio's *Giardino di Ricreatione,* published in London in 1501, then it was used by a number of authors in the form of a proverb: *Occus boccus, chi nazze pazzo, non guarisce mai* (Occus boccus, he who is born mad is incurable). It is also the title of a manual published in London in 1634, *Hocus Pocus Junior: The Anatomie of Legerdemain,* which was translated into German in 1667. In today's language, *hocus pocus* is used mainly to designate the tricks used by a magician, a prestidigitator, then secondarily as part of the pseudo-esoteric language of mages and sorcerers. In Scandinavia, *hocuspocus* is sometimes followed by *filiokus*. In Danish, Norwegian, and Swedish, *hocuspocus* always means "sleight of hand." In Holland, *Hoctus Boctus* is used, or a variation, *Oktus Barreboktus,* for protection against the spirits of the night that torment people. As a final historical note, we should note that a court magician for King James I of England was saddled with Hocus Pocus as a nickname.

 📖 Van Haver, no. 974; Wesselski, A. *Hokuspokus oder geborener Narr ist unheilbar.*

HOERBAE ETHO ORAS ERBE BO ABRAXAT BOETITE: To heal a migraine, this phrase is repeated three times while placing your hand on the patient's head. *Abraxat* is a corruption of *Abraxas*.
 📖 Önnerfors, 3.

HOL HAMA NEBANDAD: See *Minate*.

† HOL † HELO † JOEL †: A *bref* with these words would be written in the fourteenth century to prevent death by fire, water, or war, or following a test.

*† Hol † Helo † Joel † Hic † Adonay † Sabahot †
Tetanugiacon sive Migraton † Hely † Thoma*

If a pregnant woman carries this *bref*, she will give birth at once and incur no danger.
 📖 Le Blevec, 129.

HOLA NOA, MASSA: This phrase was used in 1920 to ensure that one's rifle would not miss. On rising in the morning, the weapon's owner would pick up his rifle and say, "Rifle, I, X, pick you up in the name of God the Father, God the Son, and God the Holy Ghost," then, passing his palm over the barrel, would say, "You must obey me, whatever happens, when lying in wait or slaying a game animal, so that you do not miss and squarely hit whatever I target, in the name of †††." This would be repeated five times, and the phrase would be written on the barrel. When someone wished to thrash someone from a distance, he would cut a hazel staff on Tuesday before sunrise and speak these three words.
 ✦ *Abia*.
 📖 Spamer, 369; *Egyptian Secrets* II, 85.

HOLOMAATI, BEKAHU AYALO INARE: These are the opening words of a magic phrase that people used when they had fallen out of favor with their Lord or sought to win someone's good graces.

Holomaati, bekahu ayalo inare asmia baene hieha yfale malieha arnya aramebolona queleye Lineno feyano, yoye malac babona nethee hycere.

📖 *Semiphoras* II, 3.

HOLY CROSS: The words *Christ's cross* are omnipresent in charms and orisons, and they were considered to be valuable on an amulet. For example, this spell to protect houses was popular at the beginning of the sixteenth century.

> *Nulla salus est in domo*
> *Nisi cruce munit homo*
> *Superliminaria.*
> *Neque sentit gladium,*
> *Nec amisit filium.*
> *Quisquis egit talia*

Another spell makes a good personal phylactery.

Signum crucis defendat me a malis præsentibus, præteritis & futuris, interioribus & exterioribus.

[May the sign of the cross protect me against all past, present, and future misfortunes, inside and outside.]

In sixteenth-century England, a *bref* known as *The Letter from the Holy Savior* said:

> Christ's cross is a wonderful protector ✠ may the cross of Christ be my constant companion ✠ it is the cross I shall always worship ✠ Christ's cross is the true health ✠ the cross of Christ dissolves the bonds of death ✠ the cross of Christ is the faith and the way ✠ I travel on the cross of the Lord ✠ Christ's cross strikes down all evil ✠ the cross of Christ gives us all that is good ✠ Christ's cross removes all cares ✠ may the cross of Christ save me ✠ I draw the cross of Christ over me, before me, behind me ✠ because the ancient enemy cannot stand sight of it ✠ Christ's cross saves me, keeps me, guides and directs me ✠

What we have here is an actual incantation that can be found in the Sloane manuscript 962 (folios 9v°–10 r°) of the British Library. Another sixteenth-century charm (from the Bavarian National Library) uses the Holy Cross against snakes.

† *crux* † *crux* † *crux* † *alma fulget, per quam salus reddita est mundo.*

The Latin phrase is the beginning of the antiphon:

> *Crux alma fulget,*
> *per quam salus reddita est mundo;*
> *crux vincit,*
> *crux regnat,*
> *crux repellit omne crimen.*
> (*Corpus antiphonalium officii,* no. 1960).

Christ's cross has been combined with other Christian spells, as in this protection charm:

> In the name of the Father, and of the Son, and of the Holy Ghost. Amen. They expel the demons in my name, speak new tongues, drive away the serpents, and if the poison they drink does not kill them, they will place their hands on the ill and heal them. ✠ *crux admirabilis* ✠ *euacatio doloris, restitutio sanitatis* ✠ *ecce crucem Domini, fugite partes adverse* ✠ *vicit leo de tribu Iuda radix Dauid allam* ✠ *Christus vincit* ✠ *Christus regnat* ✠ *Christus imperat* ✠ May Christ protect this servant of God N. from all the phantoms [*fantasia*], all the attacks of the Devil and from all the evils of every hour everywhere, may he be protected by the power of the holy cross ✠ Amen ✠ *agios* ✠ *hyskyros* ✠ *athnatos* ✠ *eleyson* ✠. (London, British Library, Sloane 962, folio 102 r°)

The Adoration of the Cross on the Friday of Holy Week includes a sequence in which the Greek and its Latin translation alternate. We find the sequence frequently in Latin charms that list the divine names.

> *Agios o Theos!*
> *Sanctus Deus*
> *Agios Ischyros!*
> *Sanctus fortis*
> *Agios athanatos*
> *Eleison imas.*

An orison of the Holy Cross was used by Savoyard soldiers as an amulet when they launched an attack on Geneva in 1602—an assault called the Escalade. The bulk of the orison has been found in the *Invocation to the Holy Cross,* published in the Vaugirard section of Paris by the printer Aubry in the nineteenth century.

It should be noted that some mission crosses or those at crossroads have an apotropaic function that is sometimes reinforced by the inclusion of I.N.R.I. and by instruments from the Passion of Christ, as I have observed in France, in Lautrec in the Tarn region (illustration, left) and in Saint-Véran in the Queyras region (photo, right).

✦ *Crux Christi, Crux sacra.*

📖 Many examples can be found in Scot, Book XII, chapter 9; XV, 9; and in Deonna, "À L'Escalade," 89ff.; Aubigné, *L'Escalade,* Appendix § II, 27; Schönbach, 36.

HORNER LARCI HABEK: The lead-in to an eleventh-century spell against epilepsy (*morbus comitialis*).

> *Horner Larci Habek Cisius elaoro hodier laciaon Virtus coeli libera pellet.*

📖 Heim, 226.

HOSALA DIESLA EUGA: These three words form part of a ritual intended to reveal the identity of the individual who bewitched your animals; the ritual should be repeated three times.
    📖 BBE, 13.

HOSCARAA RABRI MILAS: These are the opening words to a phrase that provides protection against evil spells, poisoned herbal potions, demons, snakes, and plague.

> *Hoscaraa Rabri milas filio. Aabonac. Baracha. Baracha abeba asar mesonor flotem bethel behon. Sethen. Teon. Yham. Tehos † an. All-powerful God, protect me, your servant.*

Teon and *tehos* are probably corruptions of *theos*, "God," and *an* is probably a corrupted version of *Amen*. *Bethel* (בית־אל) means "house of God," and *barach* means "dazzling."
    📖 Aymar, 336.

HOSTS: See *Ego sum, Recipe.*
    📖 Braekman, 63.

HUAT HAUAT ISTA PISTA SISTA DANNABO DANNAUSTRA: This phrase was used for treating fractures. Jean-Baptiste Thiers also claimed it was effective against afflictions of the thighs when written this way: *Sista Pista Rista Xista.*
    📖 Heim, 534; Thiers I, 361; Renou, *Œuvres pharmaceutiques.*

HUM, OTUM, UTUM †††: These words are spoken to make amends for prejudices; they are accompanied by the sign of the cross.
    📖 *Egyptian Secrets* II, 234.

HVTY: To enjoy good fortune in games of skill and chance, one must make a bracelet from dried eel skin, inside of which has been placed some bull manure and some vulture blood. It is bound shut using the rope from a hanging, then these *caracteres* are written on it in one's own blood.
    📖 *Petit Albert*, 31.

HYLA HYLARIA DULIA MALASINLA: This phrase is found in a tenth-century blessing of the eyes. In a fifteenth-century German charm, it takes these forms: *Nilaria dulcia filana* and *Nilaria del indena, dulta mila velena,* and the corruptions are evidence of how frequently this phrase was used.
 📖 Franz II, 496.

HYOF: In the fifth century, a cure for a migraine consisted of writing *hyof* on the right side of the head and *cela hhhc* on the other side.
 📖 Pseudo Theodore, 30ff., 314.

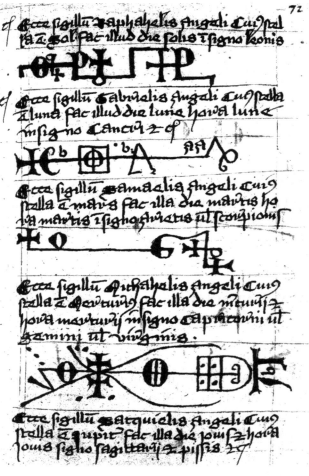

Seals of the days

I

IALDABRAE: To combat a cough, it is necessary to write this word on virgin parchment, then attach it to a cord made from sponge and wear it around your neck.

📖 Önnerfors, 13.

IAÔ: This is a Greek transliteration of Tetragrammaton YHWH (Yahwe) and the name of the supreme god of the Gnostics. It appears on Greek amulets discovered in Egypt, often accompanied by the depiction of Abraxas. On the reverse side of a piece of green jasper it is featured in the composition of an obscure phrase: *iaôanarabaranaôai sthombaolê baol sthombalakamoth ombalê.* It is associated with the names of Sabaoth and Michael. On a Greek papyrus holding a binding spell dating from the second to fourth centuries and discovered in Egypt, a long conjuration of various gods, demons, or spirits can be read, within which we find: *Iaô Sabaôth Iaeô pakenpsôth pakenbraôth sabarbatiaôth sabarbatianê sabarbaphai.*

Iaô and *Iaeô* can be found, for example, on a Greek tablet of

Egyptian origin that holds a charm for calming the wrath of a certain Paômis and provides the phrase: IAÔ ÊIÔ IAE OUIABOR.

✦ *Abraxas, Yao.*

📖 Bonner, no. 17, 173, 237 (*Iaô eulamô Abrasax*), 254, 299 and 309 (*Iaô Sabaôth Michael*), 361; Fauth, 65–103; Martinez, 757; Bernand, 342.

IAÔ AÏÔ AÏÔ PHNEÔS: This is the beginning of the closing phrase for a Greek conjuration of myrrh: the caster addresses Adonai with these words:

Iaô aïô aïô phneôs sphintes Arbathiao Iaô iae ioa ai
(Ιαω αιω φνεωσ σφιντεσ Αρβαθιαο Ιαω ιαε ιοα αι)

Another charm has a very similar sequence: *Iaô abriaô arbathiaô, adonaï sabaô,* in which variations on *Iaô* can be seen.

📖 PGM I, 122; Audollent, 9.

IBAT × THE OVAT: A late-eighteenth-century grimoire from the Swiss canton of Vaud provides instructions for crafting an amulet that prevents anyone from hitting you; it is necessary to carry this on your person.

Ibat × the ovat × poc × en ×
Sabaot e fro. ooo l. a. e. b. y.
Emanuel × Adonnay. L. u. b. b. b. b. b.

📖 Hervé, 364.

† IBEL † LABES † CHABEL † HABEL † RABEL: Twelfth-century soldiers would carry this spell on their persons to makes themselves invulnerable to bullets. According to a Swiss grimoire, it must be written on virgin parchment. It is also used to win at cards. According to the *Grimoire of Pope Honorius,* the phrase + *Ibel + Laber + Chabel + Habet + Rabel* written on virgin parchment and carried on one's person permits victory at cards, and if written on crosses, the phrase will break and destroy all evil spells.

Variants: † *Ibel* † *Laber* † *Chabel* † *Staber* † *Rabel;* † Ibel † Ebel † Abel.

📖 Thiers I, 356; Honorius, 64 (*Ibel, Ebel, Abel*), 72; *Enchiridion* 1633, 164. Hervé, 359; Werner, no. 23, 201.

IBI CECIDERUNT, EXPULSI SUNT INIMICI MEI: This phrase is taken from Psalm 35:13 and means, "They die there. My enemies are expelled." It should be written on slips of paper that are placed at the four corners of the granary holding wheat, or in the wheat itself, to drive away the weevils. The variant *Expulsi sunt quia non poterunt stare,* "They are driven out because they could not stay there," is used in the same way and for the same purpose.

📖 Thiers I, 410.

IBRIS, PALAMITIS, CAUDEBAT, SAUDEBAT, PAGAS ORBAT, ORBOT. AMEN: This is a phrase used to dismiss or send back a spirit.

📖 Thiers I, 190.

ICHTYOS/ICHTUS: This is one of the names given to God in benedictions and several spells.

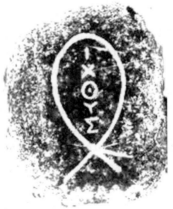

Originally this was an abbreviation of five Greek words (*Iesu Khristus, Theoú Uios Sôter;* ΙΗΣΟΥΣ ΧΡΙΣΤΟΣ ΘΕΟΥ ΥΙΟΣ ΣΩΤΗΡ), of which only the initial one remains, which means "Jesus Christ, Holy Savior." It was Clement of Alexandria who first requested Christians to carve a fish (*ichtyos*) on a seal (*Le pédagogue* III, 9).

📖 Dornseiff, 137.

ICUCUMA/SICYCUMA: According to the Bordeaux physician Marcellus (fourth century), this magic name should be borne as an amulet against hemorrhaging. He also said it could be written on virgin parchment, wrapped in a cloth, and girded on the patient, no matter what part of the body was involved. The term must be displayed in a reductive diagram.

Sicycuma
Cucuma
Ucuma
Cuma
Uma
Ma
A

The same physician added that a nosebleed could be stopped by whispering this word into the patient's ear. In the work of Jean-Baptiste Thiers, the term has been corrupted into *Su camy dur,* and it is intended to be whispered into the ear of a woman experiencing a difficult labor.

📖 Marcellus, chap. 10; Heim, 491; Thiers I, 417.

IEPPEL PAAIL IAIAS CHER: To compel a thief to turn himself in, one must draw four eyes behind a wall, take a small nail, place it on the third eye, and strike it with a hammer while saying the words above, and his identity will be revealed. This extremely corrupted spell goes like this: "Then [incomprehensible word: *Sorbup*] you wish that Saint Paul and Saint Goliath, you who let Adam be tempted to eat the fruit of the forbidden tree, you shall force this thief to confess. But God (†††) will not be present; then he shall make his confession. Read backward after *God* (†††), like this: *Dnaa gillih ned go nös redaf dug.* If the Danish closing phrase is restored, we get "God the Father, the Son, and the Holy Ghost."

Variants: *Ieppel lauischer gaar gaait; Jeppel, Jaliischer, gaar, gaail.*

📖 Ohrt I, no. 97; Ohrt II, 106; Bang, no. 1377.

I ERBUM DIE MANET ME TERUNEM: If these words are inscribed on the door of a burning house, it will stop burning. Thanks to other variations, we know that these words mean, "May the divine Logos remain for eternity."

✦ *Werbom.*

📖 BBE, 81.

† IGNARUM † IGNILUM ✠ JUGO DESERTATUM ✠: To heal a horse's sprain, place your thumbs on the ailing limb while saying these words and making the sign of the cross, then you must recite five Our Fathers and five Hail Marys.

   📖 Vinje, no. 26.

IHC + IHC + IHX + SOTER YNOS + ADONAI O.: At the beginning of the fifteenth century, this would be written on virgin parchment to bring down a fever; the patient had to carry it for nine days. It can be seen that this spell consists solely of names of God.

   📖 Cambridge, England, Cambridge University, Trinity College, ms. R 14.30, folio 145.

IHESUS FILI DOMINUS: The opening of a Solomonic prayer. The caster recites it in front of the patient, then asks him how he feels. If he responds positively, he will be healed; if not, he shall die.

> *IHesus fili Dominus Incomprehensibilis: Ancor, Anacor, Anylos, Zohorna, Theodonos, hely otes Phagor, Norizane, Corichito, Anosae, Helse Tonope, Phagora.*
>
> *Elleminator, Candones helosi, Tephagain, Tecendum, Thaones, Behelos, Belhoros, Hocho Phagan, Corphandonos, Humanæ natus & vos Eloytus Phugora. Holy angels, be present and inform me whether he shall recover or die from this illness.*

   ◆ *Ars notoria.*
   📖 *Ars notoria,* 24.

I H S: One of Christ's two monograms, which was much used on amulets, quite often in combination with other acronyms and *caracteres*. (See illustration on page 172.)

   ◆ *Three Kings,* for example (illustration).

I H V H: This tetragram represents Yahve. It was used extensively on amulets and in charms, benedictions, and spells. It figures this way on the first pentacle of the moon, which makes it possible to invoke the spirit of this astral body, and on the fourth, which is used to obtain

I H S, one of Christ's two monograms

an answer while asleep. It is found on the fourth and fifth pentacles of Mercury in *The Lesser Key of Solomon*. The fourth is used to acquire the knowledge of all created things, the fifth to open doors.

.II.R.ƎF.S.F.D.G.: To attract love, you must carry these letters written on a piece of virgin parchment.
 📖 *Secrets magiques pour l'amour,* no. XXX, 18.

ILAT GATOI ILLOY: These words would be written on the hand of a young woman around 1650 in order to determine whether she was a virgin. She would reveal the truth on the spot.
 📖 Ohrt II, 107.

ILLUSIABO: To obtain a favor from a powerful individual, you must craft a gold ring in the moon's first house and set in it a white stone carved with the sign below.

The word "Illusiabo" is set beneath the stone, written in white dove's blood on virgin parchment.
 📖 London, British Library, Lansdowne 1201 4to, folio 176ff.

I.M.L.K.I.B.: These *caracteres* would be written as shown, with the same mixture of uppercase and lowercase letters, on a slip of paper to stop bleeding: *I.mL.K.I.B.I.P.a.x.v.ss.St. vas I.P.O. unay. Lit.Dom.mper vobism.* If any doubts were expressed as to this spell's effectiveness, it would be written on a knife that was then stuck "into a dumb animal." The beast would not bleed. Furthermore, this spell allowed one to resist all enemies; it also relieved labor pains and nausea. The end section means, "May the Lord always be with you." *Unay* is probably put in for Adonay, and *I.P.O.* for Christo. This sequence provides a good illustration of what we could call "holding back information." The author abbreviated everything so that he alone can know what each series of letters is concealing.

📖 *Grimoires,* no. 257; Jaenecke-Nickel, 163-7.

IMOI SIMEON GIRICION: A spell that should be written on a dried pike bladder, then held up to the moon, at the same time petitioning it with a charm. Then the bladder is attached to the arm for winning at gaming.

📖 *Württembergisches Jahrbuch* 13 (1890), 216, no. 253.

I NAVSITUS DAUS PETRUS LEUS SILIS DEUS SPYRITUS KANALI †: This is the lead-in to a spell that is intended to provide protection from bullets. Once it has been written down, it should be buried in a fresh grave for three days and three nights, then worn. One should be able to say it *in petto* (in secret) when facing danger. An extremely corrupted version of the common phrase "in the name of God the Father, God the Son, and God the Holy Ghost" can be recognized here. *Navsitus* was probably coined out of the Norwegian *navn,* "name," to thereby appear like a Latin word. We should note that the *In nomine* has been so deformed as to be unrecognizable: *in Noralni Patri.*

📖 Ohrt I, no. 815; Bang, no. 1376d.

IN CARO JN CARNE IN CARICIE IN CARSTIRA INFIRMO ANANIZAPTA: To heal someone who was bitten by a snake, this phrase would be written on the victim's hand, then the writing would be dissolved in holy water, which was then given to this individual to drink. A variation on the word *flesh* can be recognized here, as well as the *Antidote of Nicolas*.

✦ *Ananizapta.*

📖 Ohrt II, 108.

INDOMO: The first word of the phrase *Indomo mamosin inchorna meoti. Otimeoti quoddealde otuvotiva elmarethin,* which must be chanted nine times at morning and night while in a body of running water to cure erysipelas. If a horse is sick, the spell is chanted into its left ear, if a man, it is chanted over his head. The phrase is a blend of Greek and Latin.

📖 Berthoin-Mathieu, 152; Storms, no. 67.

INFERIOR SPIRITS: The *Grimorium Verum,* which is said to have been published in Memphis in 1517, provides a list of inferior spirits: Bechaud, Bucon, Clisthert, Frucissiere, Guland, Morail, Hicpacth, Frutimiere, Huictiigaras, Humots, Khil, Klepoth, Mersilde, Minoson, Musisin, Segal, Sirchade, Surgat. They are all subordinate "to Duke Sirach," They can be summoned with the help of the following conjuration:

Osurmy + Delmusan + Atalsloym + Charusihoa + Melany + Liamintho + Colehon + Paron + Madoin + Merloy + Bulerator + Donmedo + Hone + Peloym + Ibasil + Meon + Alymdrictels + Person + Crisolsay + Lemon Sessle Nidar Horiel Peunt + Halmon + Asophiel + Ilnostreon + Baniel + Vermias + Slevor + Noelma + Dorsamot + Lhavala + Omor + Framgam + Beldor + Dragin + Viens, N . . .

Guland, Surgat, and Morail help to "nail," in other words, to paralyze an enemy, by "nailing him to the spot." The sign (symbol) of Frutimiere drawn on virgin parchment with bat's blood allows the caster to compel a young woman to dance naked.

"To make a young woman dance naked" can also be found in the *Trésor des émerveillables secrets du Petit Albert* (Geneva, 1675), but there plants are used: marjoram, wild thyme, verbena, myrtle leaves, three walnut leaves, and three little sprigs of fennel, harvested on Saint John's Eve, before dawn.

✦ *Names of demons.*

I. N. G. D. V. D. S. U. D. HL. G.: A German abbreviation for "in the name of God the Father, God the Son, and God the Holy Ghost," which is often the closing line of a spell.

INGODUM ENGLABIS PROMODIUM: The invocation of Lucifer according to the *Gran Grimorio*. It should be spoken aloud between eleven o'clock and midnight after a magic circle has been drawn with consecrated charcoal.

I N G T G OG H. A.: An incorrect Danish abbreviation for "in the name of God the Father, God the Son, and the Holy Ghost." The *T* in fact represents *F*.

📖 Ohrt I, no. 433.

I.N. I. P. S. O. I.: When it seems that butter or cheese cannot be made properly, to know whether the milk of a cow has been bewitched, take a round of cheese and draw a cross on it. Then write *I.N.I.P.S.O.* on its first quarter, *C. U. M. I. P. S. O.* on its second quarter, *P. E. R. I. P. S. U. M.* on its third, and in a circle surrounding the cross, write *S. U. M. O. M. N. I. A.* Despite its depiction in a way similar to that of texts on amulets, we can recognize the Latin phrase: *in ipso, cum ipso, per ispum* and *sum Omnia*, "in him, with him, by him, I am all things."

📖 Bang. no. 1296.

INOMINE: This corruption of *In nomine* ("in the name of") is quite frequent in charms. In January 1955, an inhabitant of Bâtie-Neuve (in the Upper Alps) gave Charles Joisten the following spell for healing a horse's eye:

> *Please heal, Virgin, the eye of our mare, and make the sign of the cross; and speak the following words three times: Inomine Jesus, haec sanguis ob haec formula veli pace formili. Let it be; do it well. Whoever scorns you shall have cause to repent it later. And say five Pater and five Ave.*

The informant, around sixty-five years old, said she had copied it into *The Book of the Good Lord* that someone lent her.

📖 Joisten, 210, sent by Alice Joisten.

INQUINSINTAS, INIHSINTAS: When a horse is suffering from a sprained limb, one should place his thumbs over the ailing leg and say these word to make it better: *Inquinsintas, inihsintas, sorubas, cnitas.*

📖 Braekman, no. 159.

I.N.R.I.: These four letters mean "Jesus of Nazareth, King of the Jews." In Latin this is the triumphal title of Christ (*titulus triumphalis*), which can also be written as *J.R.N.R.J.,* "Jesus Roi [king], Nazarean, Roi of the Jews." They are frequently found in benedictions, namely in the *Bref of Saint Luke,* a Christian amulet once used in Bavaria to combat fever. The slip of paper with these words on it was given to the patient to eat:

*J + N + R + J
et verbum ca
ro factum est
et habitavit
in nobis.*

In other words Christ's *titulus triumphalis* and the words of the Gospel of John (1:14). In the Tyrolean valley of Inn, this spell, written in a cross on the door to the house, offers protection against ghosts and witches:

*J
N J R
J*

The inquisitors James Sprenger and Heinrich Institoris (or Henry Kramer), who were active in the Rhine region during the fifteenth century, wrote this in *The Hammer of the Witches:* "But the surest protection for places, men, or animals are the words of the triumphal title of our Savior, if they be written in four places in the form of a cross: Jesus † Nazarenus † Rex † Judaeorum †. There may also be added the names of Mary and of the evangelists, or the words of Saint

John: The word was made flesh." People wore these letters to obtain justice in court or to avert misfortune or peril to the house, combined with *Ita* and *alo*. To stop blood loss, *I.N.R.I.* would be written in blood on a piece of paper that was then pressed to the forehead, but Christ's triumphal title was replaced by *consummatum est* in this case. Marked with a branding iron on stable doors in the Tyrol, *J.N.R.J* protects from the evil eye and, when put on the churn, helps with the making of butter.

When combined with *Sator*, the names of the Three Kings, and so forth, *I.N.R.I.* is effective against all kinds of evil spells targeting both humans and animals. The spell would be hung like a necklace at an odd hour on those who were believed to have been bewitched. A recipe for forcing the sorcerer or witch to come forth follows:

† *I N* † *R I* †
S A T O R
A R E P O
T E N E T
O P E R A
R O T A S
C † *M* † *B* †

📖 Franz II, 12, 64, 107; Sprenger and Institotis, II, 1; *Grimoires*, no. 253, no. 231; Honorius, 66; *Egyptian Secrets* II, 349; Ohrt I, no. 269, 1089; Werner, no. 24, 201; Zingerle, 39, no. 323, no. 326.

IN TES DALAME BOUIS, VINS DIVERNAS SATHAN: To heal a beast suffering from hemorrhaging, speak these words aloud three times over its head.

📖 Honorius, 109.

Iω: This fifth-century spell was used to put a woman to sleep. The spell below had to be written on virgin parchment and in complete silence:

IωIωKONNIaa C. NNOYε to the one who birthed this woman

And then place it under her head.

📖 Pseudo Theodore, 23ff. 307.

IOA OIA RAUIO UOI CHOOX (Ιωα ωαι ραυιω υοι χοοξ): To prevent conception from occurring during sexual relations, these words are written on mule skin that has been wrapped around a weasel's left testicle. The scribe placed the Latin word after the Greek word, but the Greek manuscripts in the latter part of the third century contained the lesson: ΙΩΑ ΩΙΑ ΡΑΓΙΩ ΟΓ ΟΙ ΚΟΟΧΡ.

📖 *Cyranides,* II, G.

† IOB † VEMES † SICHAVI: On a *bref* intended to protect children from worms we can read:

> † *Iob* † *ve(r)mes* † *sichavi*
> † *mortui* † *sunt* † *per manum*
> † *domini nostri* † *Iesus*
> † *Christi* † *si sunt* † *in massa*
> † *deficiant* † *et* † *in aqua*
> † *revertetur* † *ame* †

The text would be hung around their necks and an Our Father and a Hail Mary recited. *Vemes* is used for *vermes* and *ame* for *Amen.*

📖 Astori, 113.

IPA : PIPA : EDŬLA : VEL : EDULA: These words will cause your guests to fall asleep, but the spell does not say for what purpose.

📖 BaK, no. 68.

IRAM, QUIRAM FRAN FRATEM FRATRESQUE: This thirteenth-century spell was used to ward off sword blows, mainly in Switzerland. In Germany, the variation *Iria Kiria Critha X Katfer Furias Drach X* was effective against the bite of rabid dogs. It would be written on a piece of bread and eaten. In Saxony, it took the form *Uram Eviram Cafram, Cafratem Cafratosque* and seems to have sometimes been abbreviated as *Ira bira lira pira.* An eighteenth-century Swiss grimoire cites this spell under the heading "For beating," and specifies it should be spoken aloud when drawing a sword from its sheath.

📖 Thiers I, 376; Hervé, 362.

IRAN + TIRAN + CASTAN: In both West and East Prussia and in Lithuania a specific spell of protection against all kinds of disease has been noted:

> *Jran + Tiran + castan*
> *+ cacasten + Eremiton*
> *+ in + nomine + Patris*
> *+ et + Filii et + spiri.*
> *+ sanct. + Amen +*

It is undoubtedly a short form of the following spell, which is found in the same region:

> *Aron + y aran +*
> *Syran + cyron +*
> *Ceraston + crisan*
> *Castan + Bastan +*
> *Syran + castan +*
> *Operam + catha +*
> *Eron + et stacyden +*
> *Tetragramatan + et ay +*
> *Ab onay + ostanum +*
> *Ab unos + avit + militia +*
> *Et + lingua + continuab +*
> *+ davin + et + verbum +*
> *curo + factum + et XXXXXX*
> *et habitavi + + et XXXXXX*

The names of God (*Ab onay* = Adonai; *Ab unos* = Athanatos, most likely; Tetragrammaton) are recognizable, with *agios* shortened to *ay* and the beginning of the Gospel of John. *Ostanum Ab unos . . . continuab* is the corruption of Psalm 49:19 (*Os tuum abundavit malitia et lingua tua concinnabat dolos;* "Thou giveth thy mouth to evil and your tongue frames deceit").

📖 Tettau and Temme, 270ff.

IRE † AREX † XRE † RAUEX † FILIAX † ARAFAX: A phrase from a spell providing protection against fevers in eleventh- and twelfth-century England. It had to be worn or otherwise carried on one's person to be effective. Other manuscripts offer these variations:

1. † *Christus* † *rex* † *yre* † *artifex* † *ranx* † *yriorum*
2. + *Ire.* + *arex.* + *xpe.* + *ravex.* + *filiax* +

Comparison of the various written forms indicates that *xpe* is the abbreviation of Christ(e), *arafax* is a corruption of *artifex* (artisan), *filiax* represents *filius* (son), and *arex* is something like *o rex* (o king). The *Ire* that begins the second variant could be Jesus Rex. In the *Rituel de Haute Magie* (Ritual of High Magic), attributed to Heinrich Cornelius Agrippa, we find the phrase *Omax Opax Olifax,* which should be written on a pancake to reveal a thief's identity.

📖 Storms, no. 80; Ghent, Belgium, University Library, ms. 697, folio 6 r°; London, British Library, Cotton Caligula A.XV, folio 129 r°; Cambridge, Corpus Christi College ms. 367, folio 52.

IRE VRE ARE WIRE CHRISTUS FILANX ARTIFEX. AMEN: The caption of an amulet against quartan fever. This is in fact the merging of two distinct phrases, *ire arex xre* and *eax filiax artifex.*

📖 Braekman, no. 81.

IRIJON + SIRIJON + KARBON: This would be used in Lithuania to fight rabies; this spell was written on three pieces of bread that were given to the patient to eat in the morning, evening, and following morning.

Irijon + Sirijon + Karbon + Karfun + Stilida + Stalitara + Kakara + Idata + Stridata + Sijan + Brijan + Ad deus + Meus +

📖 Vaitkevičienė, no. 1395.

IRIONI KHIRIONI ESER KHUDER FERES: This spell was used in the sixteenth century to heal the bite of rabid dogs. Jean-Baptiste Thiers notes it as *Izioni Khirioni esseza kuder feze,* which can be traced back to a manuscript reading error. In fact one of the *r* shapes does resemble a *z*, and anyone who is not a paleographer could be easily fooled.

📖 Scot, Book XII, chapter 14; Thiers I, 376.

IRLY, TERLY, ERLY, BALTHAZARD, MELCHIOR, GASPARD, MARCHONS!: This phrase is part of a ritual for manufacturing a garter that allows the wearer to travel without becoming exhausted. It is accompanied by a sacrifice of bread dipped in wine to the three spirits named at the beginning of the spell. *Erly* is also called *Firly*.

✦ *Gaspard*.
📖 Dragon noir, 163.

ISEÊ IAÔ: A fourth-century Greek charm that calls for winning a woman's love by crafting a wax effigy of the desired individual and writing certain words on the body.

ISEÊ IAÔ ITHI BRIDO LOTHION
   NEBOUTOSOUALETH on the head;
OUER MECHAN on the right ear;
LIBABA OIMATHOTHO on the left ear;
AMOUNABREO on the forehead;
OROMOUTHIO AETH on the right eye;
CHOBOUE on the left eye;
ADETA MEROU on the right shoulder;
ENE PSA ENESGAPH on the right arm;
MELCHIOU MELCHIEDIA on the left arm;
MELCHAMELCHOU on the hands;
BALAMINTHOOUTH on the heart;
AOBES AOBAR on the stomach;
BLICHIANEOI OUEIA on the sex organ;
PISSADARA on the buttocks;
ELO on the sole of the right foot;
ALOAIOE on the sole of the left foot.

The name of the desired woman is written on the chest. Then one takes thirteen copper needles that are placed in the head, mouth, hands, and sex organ, two in the stomach, and two in the soles of the feet, while saying, "I pierce these various parts so they will think of no one but me." The doll is finally placed at sunset in the grave of someone who died prematurely, with some seasonal flowers. This very long love magic spell features deities like Abrasax, Adônai, and Sabaôth.

📖 Gager, 94ff.

ISUS HRISTOS NIKA: The inscription "Jesus Christ victorious" appears frequently on the amulets of southeastern Europe. It was used for protection from or the healing of diseases. The spell is written like this: Iis. Chr. Na. Vi., and IS HS NI KA.

📖 Timotin, 237.

ISVOLE, IO: In Romania, according to a manuscript dated 1784, the following spell was written on an apple that would be given to a feverish person to eat:

> *isvole, io, naculte, iavoleiog, să şezi, isvoleio, vogronai, tolejea, itrize nevşico, voscrişenia ianco sileschi, iar trisavita procleora, orarabo, boţueo, inumele vreime, otgaisima isfetago duha, amin.*

Să şezi means "sit down" in Romanian, and *isfetago duha* means "(in the name) of the Holy Ghost" in the Slavonic liturgical language.

📖 Bucharest, Romanian Academy Library, ms. 4458, folio 94 r°.

ITE NERON (ITE NEPΩN): To heal a liver disease, this would be carved on a tin strip with the patient's name below it.

📖 Marcellus XXII, 10.

ITO, ALOS MASS DANDI BANDO. III. AMEN I.N.R.I.: This is the opening phrase of the *Tobias Charm,* whose purpose is the protection of home and farm from theft. It was extremely popular and has been passed down by the *Livret de Romain* and has engendered many variations. Here is one: *Ito, alo Maffa Dandi Bando Amen.*

📖 Spamer, 158; *Grimoires,* 223–47; Zingerle, 459, no. 1041.

IWORXIS CARO PER: These words heal leprosy when carved on the obverse side of a gold seal during the hour ruled by the sun when the moon is in Leo.

📖 *Archidoxis magica* I, 16.

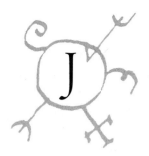

J

JAGERON, AGERON, NAGERON, VAGERON, SEPIO: These words are written on a piece of bread to be eaten every day to combat a toothache. The last word must be tossed into the woods on the fifth day. This is a variation of *Agerin-Nagerin* and *Agerani † Jegerini*.

📖 Bang, no. 1022.

JAKEPTA VIRTUTOS SPIRITUS INVISIBILIS: The magician must speak this phrase aloud when he wishes to erase the magic circle he used to summon spirits, then follow the words with:

Horepta Kaminecka priosa labiratam Imperite band solventi.

It is evident that the caster is commanding (*imperare*) the dissolution (*solvere*) of the bond (*band*) that was created. The three magic words are followed by the erasure of the bond represented by the circle and thus the liberation of the spirits summoned into it.

📖 Herpentil, *Grimoires*, 285.

JAMPELUCH: To catch wild birds, you must make a tin ring in the fifth house of the moon and set in it a crystal stone on which the sign below has been carved. Place under the stone, the word *Jampeluch*, written with dove's blood on virgin parchment perfumed with amber.

📖 London, British Library, Lansdowne 1202, 4to, folio 176.

† JANNA † SARULT † DUTTER † JER † OR: To drive away the sprites that steal the cows' milk, it is necessary to write this phrase three times on a piece of paper, then nail it to a secure spot in the barn.

📖 *Egyptian Secrets* I, 226.

JAWEL JOEL † SALUATOR AGEA: One who carries these names on his person shall be protected from weapons, drowning, and so forth, according to a charm from around 1450. It is explicitly stated that *Agea* represents human life and the true faith. *Jawel* could represent God—Jaweh/Yaveh + el—and Joel is a minor prophet. This is therefore a prayer to the Savior to spare our lives.

 📖 Ohrt I, no. 1089.

JEBELA: This is a magic word formed by the contraction of the beginning of a phrase from a fourteenth-century German spell that says, "Job lay in the dung pile" (*Job der lak in dem miste*). It was used to get rid of round worm (*Trichocephalus trichiuris*), a parasite that infects humans and other mammals.

 📖 Mone, "Beschwörung und Segen," 279, no. 3; Heidelberg, Germany, University Library, Cpg. 367, folio 173 v° (for the entire spell).

JESU BRASIN: This is a zodiac amulet in the sign of Capricorn, described in a text attributed (probably falsely) to the physician and astrologer Pseudo-Arnaldus de Villanova (1235–1311). It bears these words encircled by "Glory to God of the highest heaven and peace on earth to all men of good will" in Latin. It protects the bearer from the bites of venomous beasts, rabid dogs, and gout of the knees.

 📖 Pseudo–Arnaldus de Villanova, *Opera*, 1509, folio 302 r°.

JESUS AUTEM TRANSIENS: These words mean, "But Jesus passed on." They were borrowed from the Gospel of Luke (4:30) and are used in a number of charms, mainly spells for traveling, as well as those for protection against bladed weapons, enemies, and murderers, thieves, and other folk of dubious reputation likely to end up on the gallows. Against the falling sickness (epilepsy), these words are combined with the names of the Three Magi in a phrase of noteworthy corruptions.

> *Cas Ber* † *Balcer* † *Milcorium. Jesus antrocius* † per *medium* † *senum.*

Johann Weyer tells of his surprise, when participating in the questioning of a "cunning rogue guilty of two crimes," to see that the man acted as if he was asleep and felt no pain.

Ce qui me feit douter incontinent que par auanture il auoit sus soy quelques sorcelleries ou charme: ou bien que par ces paroles il receuoit quelque aide. Ie cherchay doncques diligemment par toutes les parties de son corps, & trouuay en la fin vn petit billet dedans ses cheueux, soubz sa coiffe, dedans lequel il y auoit escrit † Iesus autem † transiens † per medium illorum ibat † os non comminuetis ex eo †. Il estoit ainsi marqué de croix. Ie lui ostay incontinent ce billet, & encores qu'il s'en pleignit fort: toutesfois estant remis sur la torture & de rechef esleué, il ne laissa pas de faire comme deuant, ayant des le commencement dit quelques parolles si bas que ie ne peux oncques les entendre, & de faict il ne confessa rien.

A sixteenth-century author recommends this for those who wish to travel in complete safety:

Irruat super eos pauor & formido in magnitudine brachy tui. Fiant immobiles quasi lapis, donec pertranseat populus tuus domine, donec pertranseat populus tuus quem formasti. Iesus autem transiens per medium illorum ibat, Obscurentur oculi eorum ne videant, & corda eorum ne mala cogitent, & dorsa eorum semper incurua, in quibus & similibus sapiens discutit quod audit & probat quod credat.

The first phrase is taken from Exodus (15:16), with a modification of the end: *populus tuus quem formasti* instead of *populus tuus iste quem possedisti*. Then *Obscurentur . . . incurua* comes from Psalm 68:24, but with an odd element (*& . . . cogitent*).

In the Spanish *Enchiridion Leonis Pape*, *Jesus autem transiens* appears in an orison for protection from all danger and is connected with the names of angels and God.

† *Y Jesús, pasando por en medio de ellos, se fue.* † *Vehuiah,* † *Jeliel,* † *Sitael,* † *ElemIah,* † *Mahasiah,* † *Selahel,* † *Jehová.*

Vehuiah, Jeliel, Sitael, Elemiah, and Mahasiah are the names of seraphim, and Selhel is the incorrectly written form of Lelahel, another seraphim.

A zodiac amulet of Sagittarius, described by the Pseudo–Arnaldus de Villanova, bears *Jesus autem transiens* encircling the name Sabaoth. *Acathiatos* (meaning Athanatos) provides protection against sciatica, hot-tempered fevers, epilepsy, possession, and madness.

📖 Braekman, no. 267, 272, 277; Hunt, 94; Ohrt I, no. 230; Johann Weyer III, 10; Argentine, *De praestigiis et incantationibvs daemonvm et necromanticorvm*, chap. 17; Pseudo–Arnaldus de Villanova, *Opera*, 1509, folio 302 r°; *Libro di segretto e di magia*, 6.

JESUS NATUS, CHRISTUS MORTUUS, RESURREXIT: Each sequence of this phrase summing up the life of Jesus must be written on a sage leaf that is given to the patient to eat every day in order to cure his fever. In the sixteenth century, the phrase was used for cold fever and was written † *ortus* † *mortuus* † *Cristus* † *surrexit* on each sage leaf in this instance, and the patient had to ingest three of them at a time. A Latin spell used the phrase against all fevers: daily, tertian, quartan, night, and day.

The phrase is most likely of Byzantine origin. In fact we can read on a sixth-century amulet for fighting fever, "CS [Christ] has come/CS has suffered/CS has died/CS has resurrected/CS has risen [to heaven]," all of which is part of the Apostles' Creed.

✦ *Christus natus, Ortus* †.

📖 Braekman, 64; London, British Library, Harley 273, folio 213 r°, Sloane 2457, folio 29 v°.; Boswinkel et al., eds., 98.

JHESUS CHRISTUS QVI EST ET QVI ERAT ET QVI VENTURUS EST: These words, which sum up the whole of Jesus's life in three stages—past, present, and future—are commonly combined with other phrases, both Christian and pagan, as in this spell for removing dental pains dating from the fifteenth century:

> *Jhesus Christus qvi est et qvi erat et qvi venturus est, libère N. de ses maux de dent! Epas nebas Epin nebenne tendula dragons et vers, au nom du père* † *pax et du fils et de l'esprit saint, sauveur et remède* † *au nom* †††.

📖 Ohrt I, no. 389.

J. H. R.: Three notes would be created on the second day of the moon before sunrise for protection against bullets. Inscribed on these notes was *J. H. R. In nomine Patris.* When the individual wanted to make use of them, he had to eat them! *J. H. R.* means "Christus."

📖 Hervé, 359.

JMPINDIA † PROPENDIA † JMPEDIAS † PROPENDIAS: If a thief is reluctant to return what he stole or does not wish to confess his crime, this phrase should be written on a piece of lead in the name of the devil Lucifer (*Jnomine Diaboli Luciferi*) and then placed under the threshold of his house in such a way that he will walk over it. The words are derived from the verbs *impedio* and *prepedio*, "to shackle or hinder," and the word *compedus*, "what binds the feet together." The fugitive's limbs are bound from a distance. The same phrase can be found in fifteenth-century Germany.

 📖 Ohrt II, 108.

JNFANS DIVANS EVAX PAX MAX VIVAX: To summon forth and to reveal what has been lost or hidden, a circle is drawn next to each of these words. Two diametrical lines forming a cross are in each circle. The first two words mean "child, living God."

 📖 Ohrt II, 108.

JOB GRAX SON MAGULA: This is the beginning of a spell that is known as the *Charm of Job,* which is used for getting rid of worms, but more broadly as a means of ridding oneself of certain afflictions and pains. The whole thing goes as follows:

> *Job grax son magula, Job guilia † Job sorokamijs Job trahu † gon anacula † conubia macula gula † Job sarobant † In nomine Patris alaia agla † et Filij messyas † et Spiritus sancti † sorchistin † Amen.*

The Danish variant *Iab † crason † crabson † Corpanisis † Cornobion † Iab* was used for a toothache, and as it obviously was a smashing success, engendered the following variations:

Job trayson magulus †	*† Job adrasson †*	*Job tridanson †*
Job tormulus malgulus †	*Job zarobabatos †*	*Gruba †*
Job zentobarbarus †	*Job Thanobratos*	*zerobantis*

According to the Bible of the Septante (Job 2:9), Job was covered with abscesses and crawling with worms. *Zentobarbarus,* which could be translated as "one hundred times wild," might be an allusion to this.

 ✦ *Magula.*

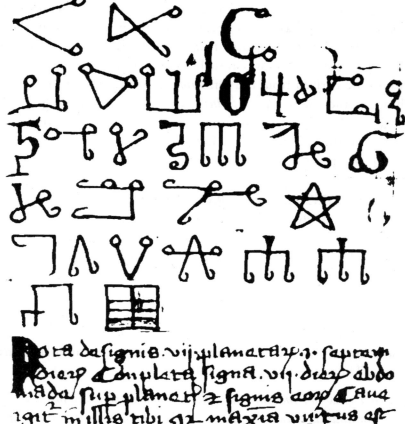

From the *Liber incantationum*, fifteenth century

📖 Braekman, no. 145; Ohrt II, 106; Vinje no. 40; Gallée, 454; Utrecht, the Netherlands, University Library, ms. 1355, folio 47 r°.

† JOB † TRAYZON † CONOBIA † ZATRAYA † ZOROBANTIZ † JOB †: Another variant of the preceding spell is used to expel worms. It must be written on paper with the patient's name and attached around his neck.

📖 Utrecht, the Netherlands, University Library, ms. 1355, 16 folio 47 v°–48 r°.

JON KLINGELMANN: This is a name give to a serpent in Norwegian spells. It may take its name from the verb *klingra,* "to circle, to coil."

📖 BBE, 17. For more on magical phrases used to drive away or paralyze snakes, see Ritwa Herjulfsdottir, *Jungfru Maria möter ormen—om formlers tolkningar.*

JORSA, MORSA, DORSA: To win the love of a woman or girl, one would write these words on a cup or goblet with his own blood and have her drink what it contains. She would then do whatever one wishes. One could also write on a ribbon in this order: *Morsa Jorsa Dorsa,* then touch her hand with one's right hand.

📖 Bang, no. 1129.

JOVE: The first *Semiphoras of Solomon,* which Adam learned while he was still in Eden. It should not be spoken except in situations of extreme distress and with the utmost of devotion toward the Creator.

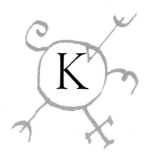

KA: This is the first word of a long, incomprehensible spell that is intended to stop bleeding. Among other things it includes divine names and the *Charm of Longinus*. The identification of some words from its final two lines indicates that the caster is commanding the blood to stop flowing and to dry.

> *ka † ay † vinga † adonay † satheos † o theos † emanuel † ineffabile † ominigan † onaan † iman † misane † dias † modo † undi † nemar † gamasten † orcamin † signimie † berusor † irritas † venas † causidulis † fervor † fixantis † sangnens † siccatur † fla † fla † graza † frigula † mugon † et sidon † benedicite dominus †*

The same phrase, with slight variations, can be used to cure plague if written on virgin parchment—a piece long enough to go around the patient's neck.

> *† kaey vinghan adonay satheos mirre ineffabile ominigan ona animam misane dyas mode unde nemat gemastem orcamin sanguine berenisone irritas venas cansi dulis fervor fixiantis sanguinis siccatur. Fla fla gra gra frigela virgum et siden benedicite dominus.*

The presence of *irritas venas . . . siccatur* indicates that the original hemostatic spell was diverted from its purpose. *Misane* is most likely "heal me!" and *berenisone* conceals the name of Veronica/Beronix, which is confirmed in an Old English charm against diarrhea.

✦ *Ranmigan.*
📖 Braekman, no. 5, no. 101; Berthoin-Mathieu, 146.

KACOCHILLA/KAKUKAKILLA: This word appears in a fifteenth-century charm that was collected in the Tyrol. It is recommended for use as protection against rats. To achieve this, it is necessary to write *Sanctus Kakukakilla* on the four corners of the house. In Denmark, as orison to Saint Kakochilla that protects homes from rats and mice is confirmed for that same time period. It is thought that this word is a corruption of Columcille, which appears in some blessings.

📖 Ohrt I, no. 663; Franz II, 94.

KADOS/CADOS: This is most likely derived from the Hebrew *qadosh*, "holy," (קדוש), which was much used in magic orisons and the exorcism of objects. In a long spell intended to prevent the individual from being wounded by weapons, which are listed, we read:

> † *Hel*, † *Yah*, †*Hye*, † *Joe*, † *Va*, † *Azel*, † *Adonay*, † *Kados*, † *Oborel*, † *Agla*, † *Agiel*, † *Sadon*, † *Esul*, † *Delis*, † *Heloim*, † *Jeni*, † *Jaser*, † *Del*, †*j4 Josi*, † *Helim*, † *Il Rosael*, † *Phaliel*, † *Mamiel*, † *Onka*, † *Ii Dilaton*, † *Xiday*, † † *Pavix*, † *Alma*, † *Aiim*, † *Catival*, † *Utanzanaph*, † *Zuiphi*, † *Eala*, † *Carsaly*, † *Jauftha*, † *Hictimi*, † *Seth*, † *Der*, † *Aglaia*, † *Pamiel-Pamon*, † *Oniel*, † *On*, † *Homon*, † *Aüm*, † *Oneon*, † *Il Lestram*, † *Pantheo*, † *Bamboi*, † *Emmanuel*, † *Joth*, † *Lucaph*, † *Via*, † *Calip* † *Lon*, † *Israel*, † *Miel*, † *Cyel*, † *Pieel*, † *Patriteron*, † *Jafanon*, † *Lenyon*, † *Jael*, †† *j4*

A part of this conjuration from *The Lesser Key of Solomon* can be also seen in the *Enchiridion Leonis Pape*, in the enumeration of the seventy-two sacred names that are borrowed—and corrupted—in *Pope Leo III's Letter* to King Charlemagne:

> *ADONAY*, † *Agiel*, † *Agios*, † *Agia*, † *Aydy*, † *Alla*, †*j4 Agzi*, † *Anod*, † *Aded*, † *Anub*, † *Athanatos*, † *AglaIa*, † *Alfa y Omega*, †*Ariel*, † *Bamboi*, † *Binah, Bit.id*, † *Boog*, † *Cados*, † *Chocmah*, † *Dominus*, † *Deli*, † *Deus*, † *Eleyson*, † *Eloy*, † *Eloim*, † *Ely*, † *Esar*, † *Ella*, † *Hana*, † *Hey*, † *Heth*, † *Hobo*, † *Hommon*, † *Iddio*, † *Jay*, † *Jafaron*, † *Jehová*, † *Jesus*, † *Josy*, † *Jot*, † *Jother*, † *Kether*, † *Kalo* †*il Lenyon*, † *Maniel* † *MesIas*, † *j4 Oborel*, † *Omiel*, † *Oreon*, † *Oxio*, † *Orsy*, † *Paracletus*, † *Polyel*, † *Pora*, † *Pino*, † *Rosael*, † *Saday*, † *Sabahot, Tara*, † *Tetragrámmaton*, † *Theos*, † *Teuth*, † *Uriel*, † *Venaliah*, † *Umabel*, † *Yael*, † *Yschyros*, † *Zamary*, † *Zeut*, † *Zimi*, † *Zulphi*.

We can recognize the names of God, such as *Heth*, glossed as *vita*, the sephiroth (*Binah, Chochma*, and so on), the seraphim (*Venaliah* for *Vehuiah*), and angels (*Polyel* for *Poyel*).

Cados can also be found in an orison from the *Claviculas* also known as the *Lesser Key of Solomon* that is recited while preparing a knife to be used in magical workings.

Hel, ya, yac, va, adonai, cados, cados, Aborel, Eloïm, yeny, del, agios, agios, agios, Rararel, Rararel, Rararel.

Variant: *hel, ya, yac, va adonay, Cados, Cados, Cados, oborel, Elohim, agla, hagiel, asel, Sadon, Esul, Elhoy, heloim, delis, yeuy, del, Agios, Agios, Agios, Rafael, Rafael, Rafael.*

This orison is called *"exorcisme du stilet"* [exorcism of the dagger—Trans.] in the Old French translation of *Les véritable clavicules de Salomon*.

✦ *Adhuma, Adonai, Haya.*

📖 *Enchiridion.* (Spanish), "Tabla de los setenta y dos nombres sagrados de Dios."

KAFE, KASITA, NON KAGETA ET PUBLIA FILII OMNIBUS SUIS: If you pretend to be casting a woman's horoscope and you oblige her to look into your eyes while saying this spell, she will obey you and do all that you ask of her.

📖 *Secrets magiques pour l'amour,* no. VIII.

KAIJDA: The lead-in to a long spell whose purpose is to deworm a horse.

*Kaijda † kaijdaria † densaria † panaria †
gomson † efrison † abachasis † gerobancon*

It should be written on a *bref,* then attached to the animal.

✦ *Pergama.*

📖 Braekman, no. 207; *Grimoires,* no. 35.

KAILOS: This word is repeated several times in the invocations of spirits in the *Gran Grimorio,* which are accompanied by the sacrifice of a chicken—sometimes black—inside the circle in which the caster is standing. It is written with the blood of this same chicken on virgin parchment and accompanied by these *caracteres:*

Gomeret kailos oxo, to Surgat, spirit of Sunday;

Gomer et kailos anglobis, to Frimost, spirit of Tuesday;

Curkum kailos teremog, to Astaroth, spirit of Wednesday;

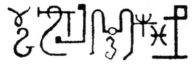

Carabax kailos anglobis, to Silchart, spirit of Thursday;

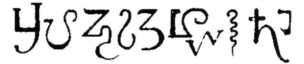

Sorebex kailos anglabis, to Béchart, spirit of Friday;

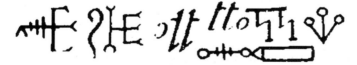

Sorebex kailos englabis, to Guland, spirit of Saturday.

Although the spirits of the days of the week are cited in *Le Véritable Dragon noir* and *La Poule noire,* these phrases are not present.

✦ *Musso, Sumus oxo, Oxila.*

† KALEPIIS † AVALAPIIS: If you wish to prevent thefts, it is necessary to write the following spell with the blood of a black chicken and carry it on your person:

† *Kalepiis* † *Avalapiis* † *Jette* † *Mage* † *Gimum* † *Simma* † *Malmort* † *Vej seratamier*

Even though several Norwegian words, and possibly French words (*malemort*), have been identified (*vej*, "path"; *mage*, "relative"; *jette*, perhaps "giant"), the whole phrase is meaningless.

📖 Ohrt II, 112.

† K A O R K S S O R E Z O N R H: When an animal is suffering from erysipelas, the following spell should be written on a chicken egg that is then given to the affected animal to eat:

† *K a o r K S S O r E z o n r h*
a r K O C tz tz a h u r o x K a o tz a
E a E S x i i x a r o t t t o x

It should be noted that this feat appears almost impossible to achieve successfully!

📖 *Egyptian Secrets* I, 224.

KAPHE KARITA: To win the love of the person with whom you are conversing, you must speak this aloud: *Kaphe Karita non Paphete et publica filii omnibus suis.*

📖 Werner, no. 25, 201ff.

KARDÎLÂS: To inspire disfavor, anger, and vengeance, a wax figurine is crafted whose chest is then pierced while its maker says: *Kardîlâs, Dîqâjûs, Bâhûlîs, Ba'rûmâs,* then it is suffumigated while he requests aid from four spirits. The request opens with: *Mâtîrâs, Ġidûris, Mâmûlâs, Farhinûs.* This spell is not found in the *Picatrix,* the Latin version of the *Gâyat al-Hakîm.*

📖 *Gâyat al-Hakîm,* 267.

KARIÆ FETRAGRAMATON: To win the love of a young woman, you must write this phrase on an apple along with her name and give it to her to eat. The first word is a corruption of *kjaere,* "dear," and the second a corruption of Tetragrammaton, "God in four letters."

📖 Ohrt II, 113.

KARIPATA OSSY KILIM KARIJA: This phrase is inscribed within a magic circle when summoning the spirits. The phrase has been passed down in the *Herpentils,* a book dating from the end of the seventeenth century or the beginning of the eighteenth century, and it is akin to one in the treatise by Johannes Kornreuther titled *Magia ordinis artium et scientiarum abtrusarum* (1515), which was inspired, according to its author, by his meeting with Thagi-Alfagi in 1495 during a trip to the Middle East. Kornreuther's grimoire is quite similar to the *Compendium magicae nigrae* and *The Secret of Secrets,* both by Reginald Scot (1570) and to Faust's *Magia naturalis et innaturalis.*

📖 Herpentil, *Grimoires,* 283.

KASTELYA ELOGO YETAS: In an operation intended to procure its caster a horse, these three words form the conjuration that allows him to ride it. For more detail see: *Tudicha Stelpha.*

📖 *Liber incantationum,* folio 36 r°–v°.

KEFI DHAZEVOM DECHWONT: When the caster enters the magic circle, he must say:

> *Kefi Dhazevom dechwont Cedholum Durit Simirt, Fedelwamdalge. Kemsed Cahim. Ze Wasegel. Sege.*

📖 Kornreuther, ms. 253.

KESHERUL NEG PINEG: Beginning of the summoning spell (citation) of Prince Mezaphar, which must be repeated three times:

> *Kesherul neg Pineg Kegiteah Cifi Sed Kaki des ses nules nedh Si die Sedh Legim wowo habals rulem bamgulaki furihesti kesemidam Heliman Narledh Hefegh Sechono Hedano Heliman Narledh*

📖 Kornreuther (ed. Eberstein), p. 22.

KKK ΛΛΛ ΛΛΛ: Seven rival coachmen are named on a curse tablet from Hadrumetum (Roman Africa) and singled out to be the target of the wrath of demons, as are their horses (who are also named). One line that is repeated seven times, composed of *Ephesian grammata* grouped three by three, gives the object its magic power. At the end a variation of ιαω can be seen.

ΚΚΚΛΛΛΛΛΛ ᴄᴏ ѡ ʓ ΘΦΙΟΙΙΛΙΛΙΛΟ

📖 Audollent, 382–85.

K. M. G. C. T. O. P. O. A. Q. P. P. Q. J.: By writing these *caracteres* on something and then attaching it to the side of a woman in labor, she will give birth and experience no pain.

Variant: k. m. g. r. t. t. r. o. x. a. n. g. q. p. m. q.
📖 Braekman, no. 47; Kornreuther, ms. 253.

KOTA, ROTA, DOTA: In Lithuania, these meaningless words are supposed to provide protection against the venom of a snakebite.
📖 Vaitkevičienė. no. 1371.

KRISTUS, BERTUS, ZEBUS: The following spell is used in Lithuania to halt a hemorrhage:

Kristus. Bertus. Zebus. Marinet. Marija. Juozapas. Amen, amen, amen.

Variant: *Bim Kristus Bertus Nomen Sebuska Monet Jēzus Marija Jāzeps.*
📖 Vaitkevičienė, no. 1394.

K R S U: These *caracteres* were used to heal the bite of rabid dogs; they would be written on a piece of bread and then eaten.
📖 Ohrt II, 92.

K S L S 2 6 4 9 β: In the middle of the seventeenth century, people would draw these *caracteres* on an apple or a piece of bread before ingesting them to cure a fever.
📖 Ohrt II, 113.

KTO ENOY: To discover whom they will marry, young girls and widows speak the following phrase: *Kto enoy sonnjoy, kto moy, viajanov, tot pakajetsia ninie.*

Reinhold Werner believes the spell is of Russian origin and suggests the following reading: кто, сомой въявь, тот покйтся ныне, which means, "He who is mine, he who is with me, is truly mine, and so he shall remain henceforth." Here is another example of an idiom foreign to the local tongue being viewed as magical in nature.

📖 Werner, no. 27, 202.

KULOMETOW PINECH RELASWECH: The opening of a long spell for convoking Ascharoth (or perhaps Astaroth).

Kulometow Pinech Relaswech wordigasi Kidchimgas chilidum Wachaii Welebhe Permech Ketholud Kedtzahe Sekhered Wanna tegier Kamseck

📖 Kornreuther, ms. 253.

KY CYGMOPUM: To win the love of a young woman, you must write these letters in your own blood on her hand before sunrise, place her hand in yours, and say to her, "Follow me!"

📖 Bang, no. 1132.

Circle used for oneiromancy
(*Liber incantationum*)

L. BIAN † PUNCTUM † SOBAT †: When a cow stopped giving milk, this phrase would be written three times on three pieces of paper. One piece of paper would be nailed to the outside of the barn door, one would be placed in the manger, and the last would be hung from the animal's left horn. Then it was necessary to say the phrase out loud.

 📖 *Egyptian Secrets* I, 219.

L. † 2. 7, D. 1. A. †: This is the beginning of a text for an amulet that should be written above the door on one's home for protection against the plague.

L. † 2. 7, D. 1. A. † B I 2. S. A. V. † 2
†, H. 6 f. †. B. F. 2. S. † † †

 📖 *Egyptian Secrets* II, 258.

† LABON † DOLON † ACUS LUCIFER † LUCIS † LUCTANS: To make a woman lift up her dress, all one need do is write "these names" on virgin parchment. The power of this spell comes from its alliterations and prosody.

 📖 Braekman, no. 338.

LACEYLEÇUN, CELYM, CAYHAEÇAR: This is from a work of astral magic that was translated from Arabic to Spanish in the thirteenth century. It is part of an orison to Mercury in which that planet is conjured by this spell: *Laceyleçun, Celym, Cayharzar, Celhym, Celheyuth, Celquemuth,* while asking the planetary spirit to listen to one's request.

 📖 *Astromagia,* 273.

LAEBE: This is a magic word from the "orison to make a woman remain faithful to her husband and for the husband to remain faithful to his spouse."

> *Emmanuel, Sathor, Jesse, Tetragrammaton* † *Heli, Heli, Hell! Laebe, Hey, Hamy.*

📖 *Enchiridion.* (Spanish), Oracion para que una mujer sea fiel a su marido, o para que un esposo sea fiel a su mujer.

LAGUMEN, IAVA, FIRIN: According to the fourth *Semiphoras of Solomon,* God bound and unbound all the animals with the following names:

> *Lagumen Iava, firin, Iavagellayn Lavaquiri, Lavagola, Lavatosorin, Layfialafin, Lyafaran.*

> **Variant:** *Layumen lava, firin, lavagellayn Lavaquiri, Lavagola, Lavatosorin, Layfialafin, Lyafaran.*

LAILAM (λαιλαμ): This word appears in many Greek charms and has been likened to *lailaps,* "storm" or "hurricane," because, on a lead tablet discovered near Carthage, *Lailam* is called "god of winds and spirits." This word has also been viewed as a variation of the Hebrew *leolam,* "forever." *Lailam* is often associated with *Semeseilam* and *Eulamô* (see their respective entries).

On a fourth-century Roman lead tablet created to spare a slave named Polidora from the fate awaiting her, the reverse side reads:

> *ARTHU LAILAM SEMISILAM BACHUCH BACHAXICHUCH MENEBAICHUCH ABRASAX.*

📖 Wünsch, *Antike Fluchtafeln* no. 3–4, 248ff.; Wünsch, "Deisidaimoniaka," 37–41.

LAMED, ROGUM, RAGIA, RAGIUM: This is the opening phrase of an orison from the *Ars notoria* (thirteenth century), attributed to Solomon. It is recited when an individual wishes to gain full understanding of all the mystery sciences.

> *Lamed, Rogum, Ragia, Ragium, Ragiomal, Agaled, Eradioch, Anchovionos, Lochen, Saza, Ya, Manichel, Mamacuo, Lephoa,*

Bozaco, Cogemal, Salayel, Ytsunanu, Azaroch, Beyestar, Amak.

The *Liber iuratus* provides this variation in its eighteenth orison:

Lameth. ragna. ragahel. ragia. ragiomab. hagnaht. hagnolam. exaccodan. hanthonomos. hethaeneho. hemones. iothe. lothesezatha. sazaratha. hensazatha. serail. marab. minathil. marathal. mairathal. brihamocon. thahamathon. leprodoz. lephoris. leprehoc. lephons. hesacro. hesacrohen. corquenal. choremal. gnoyoemel. validiol. salail. salaiz. salaior. halaiz. salquihel. gessydomy. gessenazi. iessona. hazoroz. hazarob. tharhal. bostyhal. hamol. hamalamyn. Amen.

The Greek word *(h)anthonomos,* meaning "that which feeds on flowers," is recognizable here.

✦ *Ars notoria.*
📖 *Liber iuratus,* chap. 28; *Ars notoria,* 30.

LAMETH, LEYNACH: This is the lead-in for a Solomonic orison that invokes the angels for the purpose of acquiring eloquence. It must be recited at the beginning of the month when one is writing the grimoire. The speaker must also be chaste and pure in mind.

Lameth, Leynach, Semach, Belmay, Azzailement, Gesegon, Lothamasim, Ozetogomaglial, Zeziphier, Josanum, Solatar, Bozefama, Defarciamar, Zemait, Lemaio, Pheralon, Anuc, Philosophi, Gregoon, Letos, Anum, Anum, Anum.

There are two recognizable Greek words; *anum* could be *Amen.*

✦ *Ars notoria.*
📖 *Ars notoria,* 20.

LANDA ZAZAR: See *Adibaga.*

LASGAROTH, APHONIDOS, PALATIA: This is the start of the orison that is known as the orison of Pope Leo III. It dispels all kinds of spells and enchantments.

Lasgaroth, Aphonidos, Palatia, Urat, Condion, Lamacron, Fondon, Arpagon, Alamar, Bourgasis veniat Serbani.

LEA LEO TAURUS TIGRI URSUS PANTERA PARDUS: This enumeration of wild animal names is written on papyrus and tied around the neck of a person suffering from headache. It is supposed to heal this ailment.

 📖 Önnerfors, 1.

L + LE L + LEM : FAGIAM GRANTAN +: If one wishes to force all the inhabitants of a house to start dancing, one must take an aspen leaf, write these words on it, and place it beneath their doorsill. The frequency with which this action of "making people dance" comes up in Nordic charms prompts me to think that it does not mean dancing literally.

 ✦ *Eli, Elo, Eras.*
 📖 Bang, no. 1098.

✠ LEMAAC ✠ SOLMAAC ✠ ELMAY: This is the lead-in to a magic orison called *Regina linguæ*, whose purpose, alas, is not indicated. It must be spoken aloud when fasting.

> ✠ *Lemaac* ✠ ✠*olmaac* ✠ *elmay* ✠ *gezagra* ✠ *raamaa* ✠ *in* ✠ *eziergo* ✠ *mial* ✠ *egziephiaz* ✠ *Io*✠*amin* ✠ ✠*abach* ✠ *ha*✠*aael* ✠ *re* ✠*b* ✠*e* ✠*epha* ✠ ✠*ephar* ✠ *ramar*✠ ✠*emoit* ✠ *lemaio* ✠ *pheralon* ✠ *amic* ✠ *phin* ✠ *gergoin* ✠ *lesos* ✠ *Amin* ✠ *amin*.

 📖 Scot, Book XV, chapter 11.

LEMOGETHOM, HEGEMOCHOM: This is the beginning of a spell that is intended to facilitate the acquisition of philosophical instruction on the liberal arts. It is necessary to speak this orison before examining the geometrical design known as a "note" for obtaining intellectual illumination.

> *Lemogethom, Hegemochom, Hazachay Hazatha, Azamachar, Azacham, Cohathay. Geomothay Logomothay, Zathana, Lachanma, Legomezon, Legornozon, Lembdemachon, Zegomaday, Hathanayos, Hatamam, Helesymom, Vagedaren, Vadeyabar, Lamnanath, Lamadai, Gomongchor, Gemecher, Ellemay, Gecromal, Gecrohahi, Colomanos, Colomaythos, Amen.*

Because philosophy has several of these geometrical figures, there is a different orison for each. The Yale manuscript, copied from a manuscript from circa 1225, greatly abbreviates this orison.

✦ *Ars notoria, Ezomamos, Gezomelion.*
📖 *Ars notoria,* 79ff.

LEMPEDRIAS LEMPEDIAS: This spell comes from the period around 1650. These words would be written on a playing card that was then placed beneath the doorsill to compel a suspected robber to return his loot. However, we do not know whether it is the threshold of the thief's house or that of his victim.

Variants: *Lem nedria, Lemnedria.*
📖 Ohrt II, 113.

LETAMNIN, LETAGLOGO: This is the opening phrase of the sixth *Semiphoras of Solomon,* "which possesses great powers and virtue." The caster uses these names when he wishes to bend the elements or winds to his will.

Letamnin, Letaglogo, Letasynin, Lebaganaritin, Letarminin, Letagelogin, Lotafalosin.

LETHOMIUS: To make a woman love, you must craft a gold and silver ring before dawn, speak this word over it, then carve the following *caractere* on it:

📖 *Secrets magiques pour l'amour,* no. II, 2.

LIBER INCANTATIONUM (**Book of Incantations**): Held by the Bavarian National Library in Munich (ms. Clm 849) this grimoire, which has been given the name of *Liber incantationum, exorcismorum et fascinationum varium,* is a compilation of various recipes that notably includes a copy of *The Book of Consecrations,* an explanation of the name "Semiphoras," a manual of astral magic with the conjurations of the days of the week, the preparation of magic mirrors, the "key of Pluto" that will open any lock, and a list of spirits. The operations are intended to obtain things (boat, horse, castle, flying throne), to make oneself invisible, to uncover the identity of a murderer, to inspire hatred or love, to make someone insane, to win honors and titles, to discover hidden treasures, and so on.

📖 Kieckhefer.

LIBER IURATUS (**Book of Consecrations**): This book is also called the *Sacred* or *Consecrated Book* (*Liber sacer, sacratus*). It is a Solomonic grimoire dating from the fourteenth century, attributed fictitiously to Honorius of Thebes. There are eight known manuscripts. It consists of ninety-two chapters that are divided into four "tasks." The first one includes the *Semiphoras* (the seventy-two letters of the name of God), a treatise on God's vision, knowledge of divine power, and the forgetting of sins. The second offers knowledge of heaven and angels, with their names and seals, instructions on how to interrogate them, and information on what they can give to one. The third part deals with how to constrain spirits with words, seals, and tables, and it contains many magical spells. For example, a spell shows how to enchant a glass so it will let one destroy a building or to see the whole world. Other spells included are those for causing discord, becoming wealthy, or compelling the return of stolen property. The fourth "task" offers means of freeing a prisoner, opening the gates of a castle, discovering a hidden treasure, and so forth. This book's distinguishing feature is the large number of magic orisons.

These orisons are composed of words that sound like they are Greek, Latin, and Hebrew; few are identifiable. Some words can be likened to verbs, although this does not mean they are grammatically correct: *crememon* (to suspend), *hymon* (we), *nathanothay* (Nathaniel), and so on. Some have an obvious meaning and possess correct grammatical form: *arethon* (virility, strength), *decaponde* (fifteen), *hysichon* (tranquil), and so forth. Others are Greek or Latin compounds but remain obscure: *iethonomos* (*nomos* means "law, custom"), *stimulamathon* (*stimular* + *mantano* means "to teach"), and so on. No meaning comes out of these orisons, which appear to be compilations of words chosen for their consonance.

✣ *Abba, Agloros, Hanazay, Hancor, Hely, Hielma, Lamed, Megal, Seme(h)t, Stoexhor, Theon, Theos.*

📖 Hedegård; Waite; Peterson, *Twilit Grotto, Esoteric Archives*; Fanger; Boudet, "Magie théurgique." For more on the formation of words and names, cf. Daniel and Maltomini, 4–6; and Dornseiff, 63–67.

LIBRO DE SEGRETTO E DI MAGIA NERA I BIANCHA: Manuscript copy of an ancient grimoire (from perhaps the nineteenth century), owned by an inhabitant of Cantoira, in the Val Grande di Lanzo, Turin Province, Italy, and used as a sorcerous medical book.

It has three parts: (1) Twenty-three charms, prayers, and remedies (pp. 1–5), (2) *Libro di Maggio,* inspired by the tradition of *The Black Pearl,* mainly with regard to the crafting of the thunderous ring (pp. 6–10), and (3) *Centum regnum chiamatta di Lucifero,* which explains how to address the spirits so they will grant a wish (pp. 11–14). The whole book contains charms against the evil eye, bloodlettings, and

snakes, and for winning at gambling, catching fish, a good birth, winning the love of an individual, and more. To the best of my knowledge this text has never been published or studied.

LIE TYRO SYDOME: A text on a Norwegian Christian amulet that opens with a triple invocation to the Holy Trinity and closes with this magic spell:

Lie-Tyro-Sydome-Aig-Tonit-Amnind
9.8.7.6.5.4.3.2.1. Intet

📖 Bang, no. 1077.

LIVRE DES ESPERITZ **(Book of Spirits):** Copied in the middle of the sixteenth century, this grimoire smacks of the kind of magic that goes back to the thirteenth century. Jean-Patrice Boudet regards it as a demonological Who's Who because it includes a list of of forty-six demons with their titles, physical appearance, duties, and the number of their troops. It is part of a Cambridge University manuscript (Trinity College, ms. O. 8. 29, folios 179 v°–182 v°) that also contains *Le Livre des conjuracions* (folios 183–186 v°), which serves as a kind of instruction manual as it shows how to constrain the spirits to obedience.

📖 Boudet, "Le *who's who* démonologiques de la Renaissance et leur ancêtres médiévaux."

L † M N 22 †: This is the start of a long encrypted phrase against evil spells and attack from all kinds of spirits. It must be worn or otherwise carried on one's person to enjoy the protection it affords. Used in Norway in 1789, it in fact consists of two different phrases with the same purpose—something the scribe did not realize. The second phrase is introduced by the German *"ein Ander."* Other words from this language (*mit Zalln*, "with numbers"; *vider* (*wieder*), "again") speak in favor of a foreign origin to this spell.

Here is the first one:

L † M N 22 † † X : S : I A N †
Peviro Nun qve peteit Sangit bidere
Ed: G: X. † Abra † Grama †
Famar Abion Plons stit † lamar
Firar † 2 b † Nay

The second line here could be interpreted this way: "May he who wishes to drink blood perish now."

The second spell:

Ein Ander
† transsius Yfy Mit Zalln †
▭ *† levi † vider † Mertz †*
Leit Ollianti Elly † b z †
Dalle † poeto Zater Naty † mers
Sias ener dev † doct ymy
2 2 2 2 2 2 / om

PL†h ᚠ1111P D C
† PT † RPᚴ † R

By transliterating the last two lines, we read: *PL † n uttttþ D C † þT † RKc † R;* an earlier instance of *uttt* with three *t*'s can be seen on the Lindholm amulet (sixth century).

📖 Bang, no. 1085.

LOLE: The beginning of a spell that permits one to avoid ever being taken prisoner. The following words must be written down, then carried on one's person: + + *lole* + + *alila ay yg b b de ali as* + + +

📖 Bang, no. 1100.

LOLISMUS LOLISTUS: These two words are written on any kind of support medium that will allow itself to be attached to the navel of a human or animal suffering from stomach disorders. It will heal them.

📖 Önnerfors, 26.

† LOY † LOYE † NAZIR † OY † ELOY †: Whoever carries these words shall be free from toothaches.

📖 Braekman, no. 122.

✠LUEPORATOR: A magic word that is carved on the obverse of a round, lead seal on the hour ruled by Venus when the moon is in the sign of Aries. This seal, accompanied by *caracteres*, provides protection for the eyes and makes it possible for old men to see with the eyesight of young men.

📖 *Archidoxis magica*, I, 4.

LUPUS IBAT: The fourth-century physician Marcellus of Bordeaux left us a curious spell in his *Marcelli de medicamentis liber* (XX, 78). Its use permits one to enjoy good digestion.

> *Lupus ibat per viam, per semitam, cruda vorabat, liquida bibebat.* (The wolf followed the way, went on the path, ate things raw, and drank liquid.)

LYACHAM, LYALGEMA: The start of the fifth *Semiphoras of Solomon,* which can be used to bind, meaning to sterilize, all plants, trees, and seeds.

> *Lyacham, Lyalgema, Lyafaran, Lialfarab, Lebara, Lebarosin, Layararalus.*

LYMOKIA: To heal neck pains, in the fourth century it was believed efficacious to write these *caracteres* three times on a gold strip that was then wrapped in goat skin and attached to the foot—the right one of the pain was on the right, and the left if it was on that side.

📖 Marcellus XXVIII, 26.

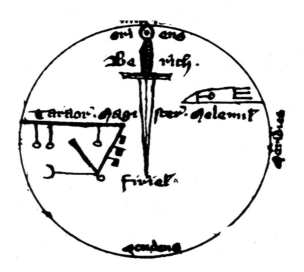

Pentacle, fifteenth century

† MA † CHABE † O † SUNT † RECITANDO † TE † TRAGA † MA † TON: In fifteenth-century England, these words would be written on a hazel wand as a cure for a toothache. The ailing tooth has to be touched by this wand. Another manuscript suggested this spell:

† *m* † *a* † *k* † *a* † *b* † *b* † *e* † *o* † *s* † *o* † *i* † *n* † *y* † *t* † *h*

The name *Makabe* becomes almost illegible because it has been divided up so severely, and the final part can be read as *sto in yth,* which means "stop!" In the Middle Ages it designated both death and the devil. It was common on charms for teeth in both Holland and England.

📖 London, British Library, Sloane 121, folio 108 v°; Braekman, no. 117, 165ff.

MAGIC RUNES: The common interpretation of nonspecialists is that runes are primarily a magical writing, whereas in reality they are letters of a particular kind. While Futhark, the runic alphabet for magic inscriptions, was used mainly on bracteates, examination of Scandinavian grimoires shows that magic possesses its own runes that are equivalents to the *caracteres* of Greek and Latin charms. They are signs to which a virtue has been attributed because of the esoteric and abstruse character they hold for the average person. Many examples can be found in the appendices of this book.

These particular runes permit all kinds of actions—defensive and

209

offensive, beneficial and malefic. With them people sought to induce love, sleep, suicide, the death of animals or individuals, and storms. They made it possible to know the future, blunt swords, gather animals together, obtain wind for sailings, and so forth. In short, nothing was impossible for them.

📖 Olsen, 6–29; Bæksted, *Målruner og Troldruner;* Nielsen, "Runen und Magie" 75–97; Flowers, 53; Page, 14–31; Elliott, "Runic Mythology: The Legacy of the Futhark" 37–50; Elliott, "Runes, Yews, and Magic" 250ff; Düwel, "Buchstabenmagie und Alphabetzauber" 70–110.

General works: Bæksted, *Runerne. Deres historie og brug;* Musset, *Introduction à la runologie;* Düwel, *Runen,* 72; Elliott, *Runes: An Introduction;* Derolez, *Runica manuscripta: The English Traditions.*

MAGULA/MAGULUS: This is a magic word that recurs frequently in spells against worms, and it associates Job with the cure: † *Magula* † *malagula* † *Job* † *magula* † *malagula.* It reinforces *Kaijda* (see entry) and so forth.

When a horse fights against being shod, the words "Magula Magula, hold still!" would be written on a note and slipped into its right ear.

✦ *Job grax.*
📖 Braekman, no. 207; Ohrt II, 114.

MAGULUS: See *Job, Magula.*

MaJNꟼN. MaJNꟼal. MaJNꟼN.: According to the Pseudo Theodore (fifth century), this spell cures nosebleed.
📖 Pseudo Theodore, 276, 31ff.

MALA MAGUBULA MALA MAGUBULA: This phrase was supposed to cure glanders in horses if whispered in their ear.
📖 Hunt, 96.

MALATON, MALATAS, DINOR: These three words can be used to divert a bullet, rendering it harmless. *Malaton* can also be found in a Swiss spell that was recorded at the end of the eighteenth century.

✦ *Milata.*
📖 Thiers I, 379; Deonna, "À L'Escalade," 124.

MANATA, MANATANT, MANANTIT, D'OR CE: This charm against weapons and wounds can be found in a book of voodoo superstitions dating from the beginning of the nineteenth century. The person speaking it should cross his left leg over his right and look over the left shoulder of the person shooting at him.

📖 Deonna, *Revue d'histoire vaudoise*, 231, no. 23.

MANAY: A magic word found in a prayer intended to consecrate water before using it to treat snakebite. It comes from the Aramaic language (see Daniel 5:2 and 5:23) and would designate God, a supernatural entity, or an idol.

📖 Franz II, 174.

MANET LARGUS LUPUS EST MEDI BESELBU: This magic spell allows the caster to acquire a flying *pistole* (doubloon), in other words a coin that would always come back to its owner, even when it has been given away as payment. To get it, one must take a black cat to church on a Thursday night and walk around the building three times with the animal while saying these words. Largus, a demon personifying wealth, will then appear bearing this coin. Word for word, the phrase means, "May the generous wolf remain with Belsebuth!" The flying doubloon was called *pasetis obolus* in Latin because the magician Pasès was believed to owe his money to this coin.

📖 Bang, no. 1434.

MARIA PEPERIT JESUM CHRISTUM, ANNA MARIAM, ELIZABETH JOHANNEM BAPTISTAM, CILINIA REMIGIUM (Mary gave birth to Christ, Anne of Mary, Elizabeth of John the Baptist, Cécile de Rémy): This is a variant of a spell known as *Saint Anne's Charm,* used frequently to facilitate a birth and sometimes reinforced with the magic square *Sator,* and so on. It was placed on the woman in labor or otherwise tied to her.

📖 Braekman, no. 48, 49 (abbreviated), 50.

MARTIFICION HONDENDION REQVICION: To put out a thief's eye at a distance, these words should be written on a piece of paper, then a hammer should be struck three times while saying, "May the hand of Saint Rubbin tear it out/or the bond of Saint John, or God the father, the son, and the holy spirit, Amen." Rubbin is probably Reuben, the youngest child of Jacob in the Bible (Genesis 29:32). There are clearly some gaps in this recipe because similar spells indicate that one or more nails should be hit with the hammer.

✦ *Fenum, Ieppel.*
📖 Ohrt I, no. 970.

MASKELLI MASKELLÔ: This is the opening of one of the most common spells in Greek magic.

MASKELLI MASKELLÔ PHNOUKENTABO
OROBAZAGRA REXICHTHON HIPPOCHTHON
PURIPEGANUX

Researchers believe its origin would be the Aramaic phrase "God of gods." Several words in this spell have been identified: the Greek *rêichthôn*, "springing from the earth," *hippochthôn*, coined from "horse" and "earth," and *puripêgenaux*, "god of the source of fire."

This spell is also found in an incomplete or abbreviated form (*MASKELLI . . . OREOBARZA*), as seen on a lead tablet found in Syria and intended to prevent rival chariots and horses from winning during a race. On the other hand, on a papyrus in which two embracing figures have been wrapped, it reads: *LEPETAN LEPETAN MANTOUNOBOËL.*

A recipe from a demotic grimoire for compelling a thief to come forward mentions the spell for the names of the gods that will allow the thief to be questioned: *Maskelli, Maskello, Phnouguentabao, Hregssigtho, Perigtheon, Peripeganeks, Areobasagra.*

📖 Gager, 55, 105, 169, 268.

MASSA: The first word of a witch's conjuration passed on by a manuscript of Saint Gall.

+ *Massa* + *ma* + *on* + *inchamo freno maxil*
las eorum constringe + *nax* + *max* + *pax* +
Pax.drax + *gagar* + *flax*

The first line dates from the eleventh century, then a more recent

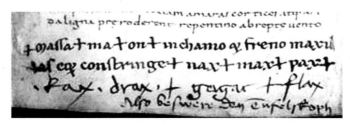

hand finished it with the closing of, "Witch, I conjure you!" Part of the text could be deciphered as meaning, "By the serrated bit their jaws are bound!" It comes from Psalm 31:9 [in the Vulgate Latin translation; this is Psalm 32 in the King James Version—*Trans.*]

📖 Saint Gall, ms. 878, folio 390 v°.

MATHREBETON KEFER BRATH BOSEB XFOL: This is an inscription on a paper amulet dating from the sixteenth or seventeenth century.

MATTHEW: To counter demons, Greeks of the post-Byzantium period would use an amulet carved on a Saturday that bore the phrase:

Ματθαιου φεισον Ιωαννη εφραζον δσμμψη. Λουκα γινα μαρκου τιγρις η β β β β.

These are the names of the four apostles, each followed by the names of one of paradise's rivers, *phison* (Pishon), *ephraxos* (Euphrates), *gina* (Gihon), *tigris* (Tigris). The amulet displays two obvious series, each with two evangelists, and ends with this series of letters,

δσμμψη
ηββββ

which give it its magical powers. It is likely that the four β's represent the abbreviation of *agios* encrypted by substitution. In other charms, we more often find a series of three *caracteres* corresponding to the liturgical hymn "Trisagion." Oddly enough, we can also find the four rivers of Eden in a Latin spell against cataracts, combined with other very common Christian spells: *Syon, Physon, Eufrates, Tygris* † *Xristus vincit* † *Xristus adjuvet te* † *agal per hoc nomen audet nominare.*

📖 Tselikas, 79; Gallée, 456.

MAUDITION PERDITION: To cause harm to a flock of sheep, cut up a ball of wool that is then scattered in a variety of ways; the pieces are placed in an anthill while speaking these words and then left for nine days. The spell is repeated and the pieces crushed into powder to be cast on the area where the flock grazes.

📖 Honorius, 87.

MAX: This word is an element in many spells ending in *–ax*. When someone is bewitched, the following words would be written in cat's blood and tied beneath the person's left foot: *Vax max cax*, with the *m* written in runic script. To win at cards, an individual would tie to his right arm a piece of paper bearing: *Max. A. E. Mix. I. A. Røt torbul. Max max pax pater noster* is featured in an English charm to halt bleeding.

✦ *Deffaus, Hax, Jnfans, Massa.*
📖 Bang, no. 1121; London, British Library, Sloane 122, folio 48 r°.

MAXIS, AMAXIS, ORBL: To win at dice, take bat's blood and use it to write these words on your hands. Variants are:

   1. *Nexis, Amxis, Oletal*
   2. *Nesis Alox + Montra + Anifis Oim +*

📖 Bang, no. 1140.

† MAX † MOX † MARLA: Thanks to Sandra Schlegel (from Strasbourg, France), I learned of an article by Anne Sophie Stockbauer that appeared in the *Bulletin de la société de la Hardt et du Ried* (no. 25, 2013) about an interesting discovery. In May 1981, when a barn was being torn down in Mussig (Alsace, France), inside a beam someone found a small sack containing millet seed as well as a scroll of paper on which this spell was written. It was obviously intended to protect the barn, which—by mere coincidence—had been spared by the 1891 fire that destroyed the house where the farmer lived.

MAX † NAX † PAX †: In the fifteenth century, if someone had a nosebleed, this phrase would be said three times, and he or she was healed!
  📖 Aymar, 346.

MAX PAX FIRAX: To uncover the identity of a thief, this would be written on a cheese over which the Our Father had been said for three Sundays in a row while fasting and without saying "Amen." It would then be given to the suspected individual to eat.
  ◆ *Neguba.*
  📖 BBE, 63.

MAX PHAX UMAX PARTIS FILIUS SPIRITUS SANTE: These words, written with the blood of a black dog on paper, allowed the individual to get free of a thoughtless promise. *Partis . . . Sante* is the remnant of the common closing phrase "in the name of the Father, the Son, and the Holy Ghost."
  📖 BBE, 17.

MAY NAY PAX: This variation of *max nax pax* consists of the final words in a list of the seventy-two names of God in an Occitan manuscript housed in Florence, Italy.
  📖 Meyer, 528.

MAYA, AFFABY, ZIEN: The first words allegedly spoken by Moses when he addressed the burning bush.

> *Maya, Affaby, Zien, Jaramye, yne Latebni damaa yrsano, noy Iyloo Lhay yiy yre Eylvi Zya Lyelee, Loate, lideloy eyloy, mecha ramethy rybifassa fu aziry scihiu rite Zelohabe vete hebe ede neyo ramy rahabe (conoc anuhec).*

When a prayer with these words is reverently addressed to God, one can be sure that the project one has in mind will be realized.
  📖 *Semiphoras* II, 1.

MEGAL † AGAL † IEGAL: The opening of the thirty-fifth magic orison from the *Liber iuratus*.

Megal † agal † iegal † hariothos † handos † hanathos † hanothos † lemozay † semezai † lamezai † lethonas † iethonap † zemazphar † zeomasphar † zeomaphar † tetragramos † thethagranys † hatamar † haziamahar † Zahamir † iechoiaphor † zethesaphir † gethor † saphor † halaguha † hasacapria † hasamypa † haragaia † hazagny † phasamar † samar † saleht † salym † salmeht † sameht † saloht † sillezaleht † sadayne † neothatir † neodamy † hadozamyr † zozena † belymoht † hazat † helyot

Despite the corruptions, several names of God can be recognized (Athanatos, Tetragrammaton), and the reader will note the use of *homeoteleuton* in this spell. Also recognizable is the Greek word *(h)anothos,* meaning "legitimate, open, candid."

📖 *Liber iuratus,* chap. 35.

MELCHECEDICH: This word, in which it is easy to recognize Melchizedek (which the medieval lexicons glossed as "just king"), is the first one in a spell intended to win a woman's love. The wooer would say, "*Melchecedich, Vol, fregum, qvarti, qvame,*" over a mug of beer, then blow over it through both his nose and mouth. He would next give it to the object of his fancy to drink.

Variant: *Melchisedech qvi Siiguet gros Religani.*

📖 Bang, no. 1168c.

MEL + GEREL: This long spell can be read on an Italian talismanic ring: *MEL + GEREL + GOT + GVT + HAI + DABIR + HABER + HEBER*

It is akin to *Thebal Gutani* and to *Heber,* with the word *Eberdiaber* being a memory aid made from the first letter of each verse of a Latin prayer against plague.

✦ *Habere.*

📖 King, 29.

MEMBRA FIAT TASIT NAM CUM TEMPUS ALLIQVO SUNT: This spell from around 1650 was used to reveal the identity of a thief with the help of water (hydromancy). These words would be written on a piece of paper, the back of which would be rubbed with white lead. It would then be placed underneath a stone that was solidly anchored in the ground for three Thursday nights, after which it was removed and placed in a dish filled with water. This dish would then be placed in a darkened house until morning. The caster would return at an early hour and see the thief's face in the water.

A variant from around 1800, somewhat simplified the procedure:

"Write these words on a paper:

Sembra te at Foul Nalneum olix vium tiomrn.

Place it beneath a stone fixed to the ground for three Thursday nights. Then take it once and coat the back side with white lead, turn the writing side over, and place it in a dish filled with water, and fix it with the four corners. After you shall see the face of the thief during three hours."

It is hard to figure out what "fix it with the four corners" means. Perhaps it had to do with attachments coming from the four corners of the house.

✦ *Neguba.*

📖 Bang, no. 1396.

MEMEND OMEND: In these words we can recognize the word *memento*, "I remember." It is the introduction to a prayer intended to cause the cessation of a pain, "like God delivered Daniel from the lion's den." The expanded phrase introduces a request for the healing of a skin disease that is addressed to Saint John, or even a benediction of flowers.

Memend Omend Nemen Noemen

📖 Van Haver, no. 310, no. 63, no. 299.

MEMENTO HOMO: If these words from Genesis 3:19 were worn inscribed inside a ring, the wearer would be cured of epilepsy. Literally, but with incorrect syntax, the phrase means "Remember, man."

📖 Thiers I, 410.

MEPHENAIJ PHATON: According to the *Schemhamphoras,* the bearer of this phrase is invincible.

📖 *Schemhamphoras,,* Schäuble edition, 300.

MERCURION † P. 2, BELZEBON † P., SMARTHAGON † P.: These words would be used in the seventeenth century to summon whatever food or drink the individual desired. They would be written on a slip of paper inside of which would be wrapped a small coin marked by a cross. This packet would then be placed beneath the threshold of a cemetery, and the individual would then enter a church to recite Psalm 13:9 and so on. These three words are the names of demons.

📖 Braekman, no. 256.

MERGASTOR CHERIPAS BURGUM: This is the opening of the incantation of Aschirikas, a spirit mentioned in the seventeenth-century grimoire the *Herpentils*. This book recommends, "When you enter the circle, call the spirit by his name and command him, in the name of the ruling planet and in the four signs of the archangels, to quickly grant your wish. He will ask you, 'What do you wish?' and reveal to you the full secret."

Mergastor Cheripas burgum Zephar brui siat aliorsar. Sorikam abdizoth Mususim Ferozim Thittersa Alymelion Hamach morgoseos Nomirim aristos Etagas.

📖 Herpentil, *Grimoires*, 285.

MERIDA, MERON, MIONDA, RAGON: For protection against spells, these words must be written in large letters on paper on a Thursday before sunrise. The paper should then be worn secretly beneath one's left armpit.

📖 Bang, no. 1094.

MERMEUT: Several eleventh- and twelfth-century weather spells of German origin and some Latin prayers give this name to a demon of the air. Mermeut is thought to be a master of storms, and this demon is also believed to be none other than Meremoth, who is invoked for rain. The name seems to have been transmitted by the tradition of apocryphal literature, as it appears in the magic papyri, in the apocryphal acts of the martyrdom of Saint Matthew, and in Ezra 1:73. The name Marmaraouth can be read on a carnelian in the Froehner collection (no. 460). Scholars believe that this name, common in Greek charms, where it often appears in the company of Iao and Sabaoth, comes from an Aramaic phrase meaning "God of the gods."

Variant: *Mermeunt.*

📖 Franz I, 56ff.,; II, 56, 77, 80; Munich, Germany, Bavarian National Library, ms. Clm 6426, folio 60. In addition, Greek magic texts show *Marmaraouth and Marmaraôth:* see PGM IV, 296ff.; VII, 302; Gager, 63, 100, 235, 268.

MERSUS STALON, METORO TEXTO: To be in favor with everyone, it is recommended to write these words on a piece of paper with your own blood.

📖 Bang, no. 1131.

METATRON, MELEKH, BEROTH, NOTH, VENIBBETH, MACH: After a *voult* (wax effigy) has been created in January on the day and hour of Saturn, and *caracteres* have been drawn on its head, and it has been suffumigated, the *voult* is conjured for the power to become invisible. The sixth pentacle of the sun allows the same result to be achieved. The Hebrew *melekh* means "king."

📖 *Clavicules* 1, 10.

MEUNTIEN MEUNTIEN: To cause warts to go away, you must stick your hands under flowing water during a full moon and speak these words aloud.

📖 Van Haver, no. 541.

M 27 I H N O M F H N: To protect houses from witches and spirits, this spell would be written on homes in southern Sweden, along with other symbols such as a magic square.

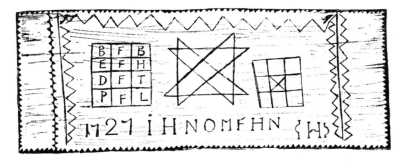

MICRATO, RAEPY SATHONICH: This is the beginning of the spell Moses spoke when changing his staff into a serpent. The following words are spoken to see one's wish come true:

> *Micrato, raepy sathonich petanith pistan yttn yer hygarin ygnition temgaron ayeon dunsnas castas Lacias astas yecon cyna calbera nater facas.*
>
> 📖 *Semiphoras* II, 4.

MIERTR: This word is spoken aloud prior to leaving one's house by walking backward. Once one has reached the forest, one should take three clumps of dirt from beneath one's left foot and throw them over one's head without looking. This will allow an individual to advance without making any noise and capture birds and animals.

> 📖 Bang, no. 1170.

MILANT VATT VITALOT: These words are found in a charm against headaches in Denmark and Colombia, as well as in contemporary French spells against the same ailment. Three Our Fathers are added to it for a man, and three Hail Marys for a woman.

> 📖 Ohrt II, 115; Camus 1990, no. 126; Werner, no. 29, 202.

MILATA, MALATON DIT CORPS FIN: A family grimoire found in the Swiss canton of Vaud at the end of the eighteenth century provides an odd recipe for "drawing the sabre." I have respected the spelling.

> *Milata, Malaton dit corps fin—Corps auricé du Diable, soit tu aussi vite serré comme le Diable a été habile pour prendre l'hôtesse qui avait mis l'eau dans le vin.*
>
> [Milata, Malaton says thin body.—Auricé body of the Devil, may you as quickly gripped as the Devil was deft at taking the hostess who put water into the wine.]
>
> 📖 Hervé, 362.

MILKEFE QUISEN GUND QVARA LIGEAMI: To make oneself loved, it is necessary to speak these words over a pitcher of beer and blow over it. The first term is a corruption of Melchizedek.

✦ *Melchecedich.*
📖 Bang, no. 1168b.

MINATE: To fix, in other words, paralyze the birds and animals one hunts, the individual should say *Minate* before leaving his house by walking out backward. Once he reaches the woods or field, he should throw himself on the ground atop his rifle and say, *"Hol hamá nebandad"* ("Go find and bind them"), then circle three times saying, "As Lucifer wishes, as Astarot wishes, as Belsebub wishes." When birds or animals come into view, the individual says, *"Tax. Moax. Voax."* When an animal has been slain, a little flesh should be taken from its left fore paw and cast toward the north while saying, *"Habe nihil ampt."* If the prey is a bird, tear off the left claw and cast it toward the north while saying, *"Sela malatua."* The names Lucifer and Astarot are written in Greek letters with errors (λψϹφρ, ασροτ). *"Habe nihil ampt"* is a blend of Latin and German, and might mean, "Stop working!"
📖 Ohrt I, no. 821.

MISERERE MEI DEUS SECUNDUM ETC.: When recited seven times over a person suffering from blood loss and over a glass of wine given the patient to drink, Psalm 50 will halt bleeding. *Caracteres* and other words of the same psalm can be drawn on a piece of virgin parchment and bound to the patient's navel for the same purpose.
📖 Braekman, no. 23.

MOLATUM: To enchant a weapon, this word is spoken over it, followed by *Molatus, dives, regina.*
📖 Thiers I, 377; Deonna, "À L'Escalade", 124.

MORSAT, FORSAT, MORSAT: To win the love of a young woman, these words must be written on an apple that is then given to her to eat.
📖 Bang, no. 1155.

MOT, TOT, FOT: To counter toothaches and neuralgia, these words should be written on the patient's jaw with a goose quill. The quill should then be burned in the fireplace with a candle flame.
📖 *Egyptian Secrets* I, 78.

MOUTHABAR BARNACHOCHA: This is the beginning of a Greek spell that is spoken aloud when harvesting simples, before sunrise.

Mouthabar barnachocha braeo menda laubraasse phaspha bendeo.

[μουδαβαρ ναχ βαρναχωχα βραεω μενδα λαυβρaασσε φασφ βενδεω]

📖 PGM I, 82.

M S D H D E P L: The record of the life of Saint Agatha of Catania says that an angel placed a marble tablet in her grave close to her head. Written on it was: *Mens sancta, spontaneus honor Dei et patria liberatio* (Holy and generous soul who gave honor to God and was the deliverer of her country). This extremely popular phrase can be seen in Jacobus

de Voragine's book *Legenda aurea* (The Golden Legend) and is commonly known as the *Charm of Saint Agatha*. It can also be written in abbreviated form—MSDHDEPL—or with an addition: *Ignis a laesura protege nos, o Agatha pia* (Protect us from the wounds of fires, o pious Agatha). This spell is also used against storms.

📖 Jacobus de Voragine, chap. 39; Franz I, 113, 199, 272.

MURA, MARTHA, MARSCHA, T. X. T.: When a cow is ceasing to give milk, this phrase is inscribed on an iron spade that is then heated red hot and plunged into her milk for three Fridays in succession.

📖 *Egyptian Secrets* I, 183.

MUSSO: This word is part of a spell from the *Gran Grimorio* commanding the spirits of the week to obey the caster.

Oxila Musso Oxo, for Astaroth, spirit of Wednesday;
Musso Kailos Somux, for Silchart, spirit of Thursday;
Musso Kailo oxila, for Béchart, spirit of Friday.

Musso is most likely the anagram of *somus,* which appears in other incantations. Although the spirits of the week are found in *Le veritable dragon noir et la poule noire,* these spells are absent.

✦ *Kailos, Sumus oxo.*

M W ST O E V: Before starting a fairly long magic working intended to remove the evil spell of a *callebotière* [witch specializing in hexing milk—*Trans.*] that has stopped a cow's milk, the cow must be made to eat this phrase written on a piece of paper that has three crosses drawn on one side with black cumin and holy water sprinkled on the other.

*M W st O E V F E L S D K E C K 34 W E † R A U E X X. A.
M. E. R. A.
Sator Arepo Tenet Opera Rotas Hagobeas
Agablet gricherma alle maas nastia Helenfasz Marablium.*

We can recognize the German word *Teufelsdrek,* with two, perhaps intentional, errors. This is the name for asafoetida, a strongly odorous plant with a reputation for repelling witches. It was used to suffumigate barns, stables, living quarters, and the possessed. In nineteenth-century Prussia, it was given to people who had been bewitched, written on bread to eat, along with the *Sator* spell. It was necessary to eat this bread for nine days in a row.

📖 *Egyptian Secrets* II, 366; Frischbier, 23.

1 N: A: Polish charm recommends that the following figure be drawn on paper (*Noś przy sobie następującą figurę napisaną na papierz*), but does not indicate what for.

1

N 1 R

1

Sanctus spiritus

1

N 1 R

1

The same figure is found in the *Romanusbüchlein* (Booklet of Romania), where it is used for protection "against ghosts and all kinds of evil spells." The sole difference, if this is indeed a variation, is that "1" is replaced by "*i*."

📖 Vaitkevičienė, no. 1623; *Grimoires*, no. 230.

NABI, RABI, HABI: To fight "intermittent fever" these three words should be written on three almonds or bread crusts and given to the patient to eat three days in a row.

📖 Spamer, 380.

NABOR: This word needs to be spoken three times in the command, "Nabor, return from whence you came!" when a horse has sprained its leg. This could be the demonic personification of twisted limb.

📖 Berthoin-Mathieu, 142.

NADÈS, PROSTAS, LABER: To win the love of another, you must wear a talismanic ring carved with these words on the second finger of your left hand and press it to your mouth while saying: *O Nadès,*

Suradis, Maniner. A genie will appear to take your commands, which he will execute once you have said: *Sader, Prostas, Solaster.* To end this spell, you must say: *Mammes, Laher.*

📖 *Trésor,* 176.

NÆSI AXUS PORUS: By writing these words on your hand with your own blood, you shall win at cards.

Variant: Nesi Axus Prosus.

📖 BBE, 19; Bang, no. 1135.

NAM AAAAM: According to the Latin translation of the *Cyranides* (twelfth century), these words should be carved on a hierachite along with a sparrow hawk and a frog. By wearing this stone in such a way that it hangs over the middle of the stomach and the heart, it gives the bearer prescience in all things. The translator notes that "found in another manuscript" is: † ζες vb pblie aazia isocira. Then one carves on a magnet: † *xiam* or † *valata.* The rest of the prescription describes everything necessary to create the phylactery.

The Greek texts of the *Cyranides,* which date from the fourteenth to sixteenth centuries, offer another teaching.

1. ΜΑΛΛΕΝΕΚΑΑ   2. ΜΑΛΘΑΛΑ   3. ΜΑΜΑΛΛΑΙΝΑ
4. ΜΑΛΑΛΛΑ   5. μλλλλλ   6. ναλατα

📖 *Cyranides,* I, F.

NAMEIT RARIE ALOSCORA MEMATUS: To win the love of a young woman, this phrase is written on an apple that she is then given to eat.

Variant: *Nave Jameth. Raris Atocora Mematus.*

📖 Ohrt II, 117; Bang, no. 1156.

NARCADOS FOKORAM: The beginning of a phrase of greeting for the summoned spirits by the magician standing inside his magic circle (from the *Herpentils*).

Narcados fokoram Anafiren
Amosan Zezyphulos Aspairat Anthyras zyriffen

📖 Herpentil, *Grimoires,* 258.

† NAX † PAX MOX: One of the countless variations of *Hax pax max*. These words must be written on one of three hosts and is used to heal fever.

📖 Heidelberg, Germany, University Library, Cpg 267, folio 16 r°.

†† N. dan gut. t. N.: For protection from epilepsy, a prescription in Middle Dutch recommends writing this encrypted spell and carrying it on your person.

> †† *N. dan gut. t. N. Amen. rex. aax. vax. t. s. s. u. a. m. t. m. t. m. x. y. azit. y. ago. o. h. e. y. a. f. m. Xristus. x. t. g. l. g. ut Xristus. t. ham.*

One must also say: *Deus in nomine tuo salvum me fac et in virtute tua iudica me,* which is from Psalm 54:3 in the Vulgate Latin translation.

📖 Gallée, 458.

NEFORUZ, HEMIRULIZ: In a casting for winning a woman's favors, a wax figurine is made that is then suffumigated while the caster says a spell that opens with:

> *Heydinez, Beyduriz, Affihuz, Deriyenuz*

Then a simple suffumigation is made, without the figurine, accompanied by a request that begins with:

> *Neforuz, Hemiruliz, Armulez Feymeriz*

The Arabic source of the *Picatrix* offers these corresponding spells:

> 1. *Îdîidâs, Bidûris, Afi'ûs, Darjânûs*
> 2. *O Nûrûs, 'Andûlis, Armûlâs, Fimâris*

📖 *Picatrix* III, 10, 12; *Gâyat al-Hakîm*, 265.

NEGUBA EXGVEDIA ARRARO FINTE AM TUAM TASIE DOLLORE:

To uncover a thief, these words need to be written on a cheese over which the Our Father is recited for three Sundays in succession while fasting and without saying "Amen." The cheese is then given to the suspected individual to eat. In the Norwegian Black Book of Jeløen, the phrase is presented like this:

[handwritten manuscript text]

◆ Max † nax, Membra fiat, Pax.
📖 BBE, 63.

NEON. SINEFOR:
The opening of a twelfth-century spell intended to expel worms from a horse.

Neon. Sinefor. Sinetu. Corantrix. Convallis. Morbor. Nordor. Redde unde venisti.
Arbor. + narbor. + vade redde und venisti †

In this spell we have the names of the worms (*Sinefor . . . Nordor*) that are being asked to leave and go away (*vade redde*).

📖 Oxford, England, Oxford University, Bodleain Library, Auctarium Manuscript T.2.23, folio 126 v°.

NEPTALNABUS:
This word appears in a ritual intended to make the practitioner invisible. Among other steps, it is necessary to write the following phrase on a piece of paper that is weighted down with a pound of silver before it is stuck inside an oil lamp.

Neptalnabus echecar milon horti samuel saphai ghardam farcheijs bore brorithire †

The word is a corrupted form of *Neptanebus/Nectanebus,* the name of Alexander the Great's sorcerer father in medieval romances.

📖 Braekman, no. 242.

NEUŽMUŠ: This Lithuanian word means "that will not kill you," and it refers to lightning. If you are scared of lightning, when you hear the first roll of thunder, you must write this word on your forehead with a piece of consecrated charcoal.

 📖 Vaitkevičienė, no. 1397.

NITRAC RADOU SUNANDAM: To unearth the deepest secrets, these words are carved on a ring with an oval bezel. If you speak these words aloud while holding this ring close to your ear, invisible beings will give you information.

 📖 *Trésor*, 177a.

NλατψιHαSOSαλυτις: Written on a piece of parchment, then carried on one's person, these *caracteres* afforded its bearer protection from bullets in the seventeenth century. The last seven letters form the word *salutis*, "salvation," and letters four to six spell the word *tui*.

 📖 Ohrt II, 117.

NAMES OF DEMONS: The names of demons appearing in charms and spells form an incongruous group in which we can find devils from the scriptures like Belzebuth and Astarot alongside figures from mythology. The list I am providing cannot help but be incomplete as, if we place our faith in certain treatises of Byzantine magic, there would be anywhere from 10,969 to 60,000 demons! For his part, Johann Weyer counts some 111 legions of 6,666 demons each, coming to more than seven hundred thousand! They appear in a variety of shapes and sizes, both male and female, of which some are monstrous: Belzebuth appears as a hairy, winged demon with claws. Sathan is depicted with a lion's head, human's head, goat's head, and a snake's tail; he also spits flames. Lucifer has seven heads, and Volac has angel wings, but descriptions appear rarely before the fifteenth century. Jean-Patrice Boudet has noted that out of the sixty-nine demons described by Weyer, thirty-six are monsters.

Grimoires are happy to list demon names, like this manuscript from the Laurentian Library in Florence, Italy, in which we read:

> *Aveche, Boab, Bille, Fameis alias Fronam, Beduech alias Banone, Astaroth, Forches, who is also called Fortas and Sartii, Furfur, Margoas (Margodas, Margutas), Malphas (Malapas), Gorsor*

(*Gorson*), *Simias (Sitmas) [which reflects the depiction of devils as apes], Volach, Cambra, Gudiffligei, Andrialfis, Vuduch, Andras (Vandras), Saymon (Zamon), Azo (Oze), Bachimy, Albernis, Cabeym, Arabas (Accabas, Irabas), Lanima, Primam, Paimon, Belial, Egym, Ras, Torcha, Ara, Acar, Paragalla, Ponicarpo, Lambes, Triplex, Complex* (ms. Plut. 89, suppl. 38, folios 459 v°–467 v°).

The *Liber incantationum* (fifteenth century, 156 folios, in-4°) provides 219 names of demons or spirits.

The human imagination knows no bounds in this domain, and Johannes Weyer (1515–1588) added an appendix with the title "Pseudomonarchia daemonum" to his *De Praestigiis Daemonum* (1563), in which he compiled a long list of demons.

Baël, Agares, Marbas alias Barbas/Barbatos, Pruflas alias Bufas, Amon or Aamon, Buer, Gusoyn, Botis alias Otis, Bathym (Bathin), alias Marthim, Pursan alias Curson, Eligor alias Abigor, Loray alias Oray, Valefar alias Malaphar, Morax alias Foraii, Ipes alias Aypeos, Naberus (Naberius) alias Cerberus, Glasyalabolas alias Caacrinolaas or Caassimolar, Zepar, Byleth, Sytry alias Bitru, Paymon, Belial, Bune, Forneus, Roneve, Berith, Astaroth, Forras or Forcas, Furfur, Marchocias, Malphas, Vepar alias Separ, Sabnac alias Salmac, Sydonay alias Asmoday, Gaap alias Tap, Chax alias Scox, Pucel, Furcas, Murmur, Caym, Raum or Raym, Halphas, Focalor, Vine, Bifrons, Gamygyn, Zagam (Zagan), Orias, Volac (Valac), Gomory, Descarabia or Carabia, Amduscias, Andras, Androalphus (Andrealphus), Oze, Aym or Haborym, Orobas, Vapula, Cimeries, Amy, Flauros, Balam, Alocer, Zaleos, Wal (Vual), Haagenti, Phœnix, Stolas.

We encounter diabolical imitations of the names of God in nineteenth-century grimoires such as in this list: Moloch, Lucifer, Asterroth, Pemroth, Forni galor [fornicator?], Ancetor, Somiator [Somniator?], and in *The Lesser Key of Solomon* we find, for example, Somniator, Vsor, Dilapidator, Tentator, Divorator [*sic*], Concisor, and Seductor.

Demon names appear in some magic operations. In a spell intended to cause an individual to lose his sanity, the caster conjures Oreoth,

Pinen, Ocel, Tryboy, Noryoth, Belferith, Camoy, Astaroth, Sobronoy, and Sismael (Liber incantationum, folio 6 v°).

Charms mention the following demons:

Aasmedeus (Asmodum), Abadamon, Abadon, Ædebus, Africo, Agel, Agnagod, Agrabor, Apylon, Araben, Astorat (Astrat, Astrod, Astært), Baal, Babell, Babou, Ballas, Bambale, Bamola (Bomale), Bana, Bark, Beatrix, Beezebul (Balsebud, Beelsebu, Bellzebu, Belsebub), Behal, Belial, Bellas, Benocha, Bibalde, Bilathe, Bua, Bufo, Buken, Bul, Bumota, Buse, Busel, Carvel, Chordi (Corde, Cordi), Cizitio, Collo, Corduomen, Deis, Disael, Dracus Bilial, Egel, Egellugalet Ell, Egin, Eliatil, Erebi, Fulus, Grogon, Gudius, Gulex, Heseky, Isophim, Jachel (Janel, Jarel), Janus, Jekely, Jeng, Kajoth, Karmatia, Kobi, Kurg, Laban, Largus, Leibi (Lerbi), Lucifer (Lucifær), Lupus, Malachim, Mermeut, Mestort (Meæsto,) Norman, Ophanim, Oralim, Pior, Pluto, Ragirist (Rist, Ragi), Raphel, Rebos, Reichel (Richel), Reor, Sabat, Sabul, Sadnit, Sadrat, Safel Agel, Saffel, Saraben, Satan (Satanos, Saran), Seffel, Sessec, Sextral, Sixbrat, Sosten, Stubis, Tallafell, Totafell, Tartaruchus, Troffel, Ugalesfell, Ugartilok, Vulchanus, Wabgract, Witz, Zetzott, Zizilo.

It will be noted that many of the names use alliteration: Bella Ballas, Araben Saraben. Wordplay can also be cited as instrumental in their creation, especially when they are present in the same spell, as is the case with these two examples. Others are grouped together under the heading "princes of the abyss," and their list is subject to variation.

Bang, no. 1371: Aasmedeus, Norman, Satan, Belsebub, Kobi, Buse, Jeng, Busel

Bang, no. 1381g: Corduomen, Richel, Janel, Behal, Belsebud, Kurg, Benneha

Bang, no. 1387a: Asmodum, Corde, Norman, Reichel, Jachel, Belial, Beelsebu, Disael, Buse

Bang, no. 1387b: Asmedæus, Ivedil, Normod, Belsebub, Jakkel, Billecu, Wuung, Bikkel, Duboel

Clarifications are sometimes provided; for example Grogon, Sosten, Lupus, Largus, Heseky, and Beatrix are called the "six fatherless devils." On the other hand, we have no idea if Hafel (Hasel, Nasel) or Agel and Iol (Toe) are angels or devils.

Demons are organized into hierarchies and hold the titles of king, duke, count, and so on. They all seem to have a specialty, if not several, for which I will give some examples. Some can make an individual invisible (Beal, Carmolas, Parcas, Furfur); others transport you wherever you wish to go (Machin, Bune, Parcas, Distolas, Malpharas), sometimes by procuring a mount that "will carry you one hundred, two hundred, three hundred leagues or more in an hour." Others allow you to understand the languages of animals (Barba, that of birds and dogs; Ducay, all languages), or teach you languages (Agarat), or permit you to transmute metals (Berteth, into gold; Lucubar changes lead into gold or tin); Bugan changes water into wine or oil. They can reveal the past or future (Amon and Gazon), or the virtues of plants and precious stones (Machin and Forcas); procure you the love of women or of everyone (Ducay, Furfur, Bitur, Amon, and Artis); and change your appearance or permit you to shift shape (Oze, Tudiras Hoho, Parcas, Salmatis, Barthes, and Sathan). They are able to heal or cause disease (Gemer), cause discord and battles (Bulfas), build towns and fortresses (Salamtis), or destroy them (Bitur), and with their help, you can learn the secrets of women and make them dance naked (Dam). As a general rule, demons have several duties. Let's look at Parcas:

> Parcas is a great prince who confers subtlety on a man. He appears in a handsome guise. He knows the virtues of herbs and precious stones, and brings them when commanded to do so. He makes man invisible and learned in all sciences, can give youth or age to whoever desires it, and can restore sight to those who have lost it. He brings gold and silver hidden in the earth

and many other things, bears the master across the world if so ordered, or any other person if his master commands it. (*Livre des esperitz*)

In the *Secrets magiques pour l'amour en nombre de octante et trois*, two series of demons come into play: Balibeth, Assaïbi, Abumalith, and Palavoth, Minkenphani, Elkuros (no. XXXIII, no. XXXIX).

This overview would be incomplete if I did not mention the demons that embody diseases and assaults on the integrity of humans, animals, and even property. In Eastern Europe there are several traditions about demons that kidnap, kill, and devour children. They can either form a group or possess several names.

In Romania we have Avestiţa, the counterpart of Gylloy/Gyl(l)ou.

Avestiţa/Vestiţa, Nardarca, Salomnia, Nacara, Avezuha, Nadarica, Salmona, Paha, Puha, Grapa, Zliha, Nervuza, Habma, Glipina, Humba, Gara, Glapeca, Tisavia, Pliasta.

It should be noted that Avestiţa is called Satan's Wing (*aripa satanei*) and Samca. It is said she gave Saint Sisin a book, "the book protecting from Samca," that every child and pregnant woman should wear an amulet to avoid being sacrificed to Avestiţa. It includes several prayers against "Samca's disease." Elderly priests or monks must copy this book in a monastery over a period of three nights in a row. Avestiţa will spare the women who have written her numerous names on the wall of their room.

In Bulgaria: Treseja, Ognieja, Lideja, Gnieteja, Ginousa, Gloukheja, Lomeja, Puchneja, Jelieja, Kerkoussa, Gledeja, Neveja.

In Greece: Gylloy, Mothrous, Avyzous, Maramatotous, Marmanila, Selininous, Ariana, Salsaleutou, Egyptiani, Asvlitous, Aimavivon, Ktarkarischou. There are also these numerous variations:

1. Amorphous, Abyzou, Karchous, Briané, Bardellous, Egyptiané, Barna, Charchanistréa, Adikia, [missing], Myia, Petoméné.
2. Gyllou, Morra, Byzou, Marmaro, Petasia, Pelagia, Bordona, Apletou, Chamodrakaina, Anabardalaia, Psychanospastria, Paidopniktria, Strigla.

Phylacteries are crafted with the demons' names inscribed on papers that in Greece are called gialloudocartia or *gialloudochartia,* "Gyllou papers," and in Romania, charms or prayers against Samca's disease.

+ *Gylloy, Inferior Spirits.*
📖 Bang, no. 1456, 1394; Spamer, 249; *Clavicules de Salomon,* chap. 15; Peterson, 393–481; Ryan, 246; Perdrizet, 16–19; Léger, 33ff.; Oikonomidis, 266ff.; Talos, *Petit dictionnaire de mythologie roumaine,* , s.v. " Avestiţa"; Talos, *Gândirea magico-religioasa la Romani, dictionar* 13ff.; Herter, 112–43.

NAMES OF GOD: Such names are much used in charms and spells. There are seventy-two ways of naming God in Exodus. Lists of names that form orisons were created using this as a model. They were sometimes attributed to an angel who allegedly gave a *bref* to Charlemagne. It was said that wearing the seventy-two names would protect the bearer from all ills and perils. The lists vary from one manuscript to the next, and we find there names taken from the Hebrew, Arabic, and Greek languages, sometimes blended with denominations drawn from the vernacular tongue. A fourteenth-century charm against epilepsy expressly says, "The best remedy is to write the sacred names . . . first in Hebrew, then in Greek, then in Latin." The *Picatrix* (IV, 4, 61) notes, "There are words in the names of God that cause the spirits of heaven to come down to earth." It will be noted that a number of names also apply to the Holy Trinity. Here is the list of the most noteworthy variants I have encountered:

> Abac, Abba, Abba Pater (father), Abraca, Adonai (Adonay), Agango, Agios (Agyos, Hagios, Agies; saint), Agla, Aglotas, Agnus (Angnus; lamb), Aleth, Alpha, Alpha and Ω (Omega) (*Apocalypse* XXI, 6), Amara, Amioram, Anaphaxeton, Anet, Angelus, Ararita (seat of all unity), Arathon, Archima, Aries, Artifex, Artor, Athanatos (Atanatos, Attannatos, Altinatos; immortal), Autacros, Binamon, Boberi, Caput (head), Caritas (charity), Celyon, Christus, Codar (from the Arabic *kader,* "powerful"; Potens), Codus, Conteraton, Contines, Corifao, Craton (powerful, potent), Creator, Custodictis (guardian), Custos (guardian), Deus Dominus, Dinotor, Ego Sum Qui Sum (I am that I am; *Apocalypse* XXI, 6), Eio, El (king), Eleison (have pity), Eley, Elyas (Elias), Elyon (most high), Emmanuel (Emanuel, Hemanuel), Ens (to be), Eternus, Falax Proanabonac,

✠ Helie ✠ helyon ✠ esse-
iere ✠ Deus æternus ✠ eloy ✠ clemens ✠ heloye ✠ Deus sanctus ✠ sabaoth ✠ Deus exercituum ✠ adonay ✠ Deus mirabilis ✠ iao ✠ verax ✠
anepheneton ✠ Deus ineffabilis ✠ sodoy ✠ dominator dominus ✠ on for-
tissimus ✠ Deus ✠ qui,

Fenahton, Fib, Filius, Finis, Flos (Floxs), Flos Vite, Fons (source), Fortis, Fortitudo (force), Frenecon, Ful, Gloria, Haly Conscius, Hebreel, Hel, Heloe (Heloy, Heloi, Hely), Hemon, Henrainarti, Hension, Hesererie, Heto, Hieritos, Hischiros (Ischiros, Yschiros, Ysros, Schyros), Hyluch, Ia, Ihozath, Imago (Ymago), Imago Patris (image of the Father), Immortalis, Inicium, Ioth (Jothe, Iyothe, Iotha, Iothey), Ixion, Janua, Jhesu Fortis Jhesu, Kyrios (master), Lali, Lapis (stone), Laus, Leo, Lex (law), Lien, Loypth, Lux (Luxs; light), Magnus (great), Manus (hand), Mediator, Messias (Mosias), Milator Misericors, Mons (mount), Naabnoth, Nesimen Novissimus, Novus, Oliva (olive), Omnipotens (all powerful), On (Hon), Onelech, Onohith, Orc, Origo Bonis (source of good), Os (mouth), Ovis, Oziam, Panis, Panstraton, Pantateon, Pantogramaton, Panton, Panton Craton (all-powerful; Pantorator = Pancrator), Pantur, Paraclitus (Paroclitus, Paraclete), Pastor, Pater Filius, Pater Pentager (to write in a cross), Pax, Pentagna, Pentaton, Permocraten, Petra Angularis (Petra Anglis; cornerstone), Petra Lapisque (rock and stone), Potentia (power), Potestas (power), Primogenitus (firstborn), Primus (premier), Principium, Propheta, Rabur, Rachim Redemptor (Redeemer), Rex, Rion, Rubb, Sabaoth (Sabahot, Seba Oth, Zeboath; God of the armies), Sacerdos, Sadai (*Shaddaï* [שדי]; the all-powerful), Sadar, Salus, Salvator, Sanctus, Sanctus Immortalis, Sapientia, Sator (Satod, Satos), Serpens, Sol, Soter (Sothes, Sotir, Sotha, Sater, Sadar, Othres, Solhoer [Greek *Sother,* "savior"]), Spiritus, Spiritus Sanctus, Splendor, Studia Sumum, Summum Bonum, Tetragrammaton (God in four letters), Theluch, Then, Theophebus, Theos (Thos, Heot, Otheos; "God"), Tinesi, Ton Unus, Trinitas, Trinus, Unigenitus, Unitas, Usyon (Usion, Ysion; essence, substance), Venas, Verbum, Vergiton, Veritas, Vermis (Vermius), Verth, Via, Virtus, Vita,

NAMES OF GOD

Vitis, Vitulus, Vox, Yephaton, Yeseraye (infinite God), Yrus. We also find Ye, Ya, or Y for Yehova and Yahve.

In a charm that belongs to a model of the Letter from Christ that provides protection from all danger, we have the following list:

† *Messias* † *Sother* † *Emanuel* † *Sabaoth* † *Adonay* † *Otheos* † *Panton* † *Craton* † *et Ysus* † *Kyros* † *Mediator* † *Salvator* † *Alpha et O* † *Primogenitus* † *Vita* † *Ueritas* † *Sapiencia* † *Virtus* † *Ego sum qui sum* † *Agnus* † *Omnis* † *Uitulis* † *Serpens* † *Avis* † *Leo* † *Vermis* † *Ymago* † *Lux* † *Splendor* † *Panis* † *Flos* † *Misercors* † *Creator* † *Eternus* † *Redemptor* † *Trinitas* † *Vnitas* † *Amen* † *Adhonay* † *Flos* † *Sabaoth* † *Leo* † *Loth* † *Tav* †

(London, British Library, Sloane 2584, folio 45 v°)

In manuscript Libri 105a (fourteenth or fifteenth century) from the Laurentian Library of Florence, Italy, one of the seventy-two name prayers includes *Iaf – hic geren – hic geronay – gey – iamo – zachias – cazarny – ydonai – conditor,* as well as the phrase *may – nay – pax.* In this phrase the *y* is only a manuscript *x* that would resemble a *y* to a nonpaleographer.

One of the manuscripts of the *Liber iuratus* (London, British Library, Royal 17 A xlii, folio 6 r°–v°, dating from the middle of the fourteenth century, provides a list of one hundred names.

1. Aglai, 2. Monhon, 3. Tetragramaton, 4. Olydeus, 5. Ocleiste, 6. Aniphinethon, 7. Lamiara, 8. Ianemyer, 9. Saday, 10. Hely, 11. Horlon, 12. Portenthymon, 13. Ihelur, 14. GofGamep, 15. Emanvel, 16. On, 17. Admyhel, 18. Honzmorp, 19. Ioht, 20. Hofob, 21. Rasamarathon, 22. Anethi, 23. Erihona, 24. Iuestre, 25. Saday, 26. Maloht, 27. Sethee, 28. Elscha, 29. Abbadia, 30. Alpha and Omega, 31. Leiste, 32. Oryistyon, 33. Iremon, 34. Hosb, 35. Merkerpon, 36. Elzephares, 37. Egyryon, 38. Betha, 39. Ombonar, 40. Stymulamathon, 41. Orion, 42. Eryon, 43. Noymos, 44. Peb, 45. Nathanothay, 46. Theon, 47. Ysyton, 48. Porho, 49. Rothon, 50. Lethellete, 51. Ysmas, 52. Adonay, 53. Athionadabir, 54. Onoytheon, 55. Hosga, 56. Leyndra, 57. Nosulaceps, 58. Tutheon, 59. Gelemoht, 60. Paraclitus, 61. Occymomyon, 62. Ecchothas, 63. Abracio, 64. Anepheneton,

65. Abdon, 66. Melche, 67. Sother, 68. Vsiryon, 69. Baruch, 70. Sporgongo, 71. Genonem, 72. Messyas, 73. Pantheon, 74. Zabuather, 75. Rabarmas, 76. Yskyros, 77. Kyryos, 78. Gelon, 79. Hel, 80. Rethel, 81. Nathi, 82. Ymeynlethon, 83. Karer, 84. Sabaoth, 85. Sellaht, 86. Cirhos, 87. Opyron, 88. Nomygon, 89. Oryhel, 90. Theos, 91. Ya, 92. Horha, 93. Christus, 94. Hosbeke, 95. Tosgar, 96. Occymomos, 97. Elyorem, 98. Heloy, 99. Archyna, 100. Rabur.

Only some of these correspond with those of other lists.

The *Enchiridion Leonis Pape* offers a "Table of Seventy-two Sacred Names of God," reputed to afford protection from enemies and dangers encountered when traveling by land or sea.

ADONAY + Agiel + Agios + Agia + Aydy + Alla + j4 Agzi + Anod + Aded + Anub + Athanatos + AglaIa + Alfa y Omega + Ariel + Bamboi + Binah, Bit.id + Boog + Cados + Chocmah + Dominus + Deli + Deus + Eleyson + Eloy + Eloim + Ely + Esar + Ella + Hana + Hey + Heth + Hobo + Hommon + Iddio + Jay + Jafaron + Jehová + Jesus + Josy + Jot + Jother + Kether + Kalo +il Lenyon + Maniel + Meslas + +j4 Oborel + Omiel + Oreon + Orsy + Oxio + Paracletus + Polyel + Pora + Pino + Rosael + Saday + Sabahot, Tara + Tetragrammaton + Theos + Teuth + Umabel + Uriel + Vernaliah + Yael + Yschyros + Zamary + Zeut + Zimi + Zulphi.

The sheer accumulation of names has produced amulets like the one of Borgund, Norway (dating from the thirteenth century), that opens with: *Mæssiassother imanuel sabaoth,* and mentions *athonai usion agios othan nathos* (*athanatos*), and so forth.

The names have sometimes been provided with an explanation, mainly in the *Heptameron* of Peter D'Abano and *The Lesser Key of Solomon*. It was said that Aaron heard *Anaphaxeton* and become wise and eloquent, and that when Moses said *Sabaoth,* the rivers and marshes of Egypt were changed to blood, and that Moses caused hail to fall by saying *Elion* (most high, supreme), caused the birth of grasshoppers with *Adonay,* and that, thanks to *Primeumaton,* he caused Dathan, Core, and Abiro to be swallowed by the abyss. It was also said that Joshua stopped the sun with *Schemes amatia*. With *Alpha and Omega,* Daniel destroyed

Bel and slew the dragon. *Iod,* which Jacob heard from the angel's mouth, freed him from the clutches of Esau, and the name of *Emmanuel* freed the three children from the fiery furnace. Another interpretation of the names can be found in the *Semiphoras,* which was printed in 1686.

In invocations and conjurations it is hard to clearly distinguish the divine names from pure and simple exclamations. For example, the *Enchridion Leonis Pape* provides this: *Hel, Ya, Haye, Yac, Va, Cados, Ebrore, Heloina, Yael, Eyel, Pyel, Lulapti, Casali, Calafafli, Zaphi, Hictimi, Oreon, Dilaron, Panuion, Patriteron, Sazaron, Lenion, Sed, Dar.*

Here is an example of the use of the names of God with which any spirit can be summoned according to the *Herpentils* (seventeenth century):

> I, N. conjure, summon, and command you, by the power of the Word made flesh, by the power of the Holy Father, and by the force of these words: Messias, Sother, Emmanuël, Sabbaoth, Adonai, Athanatos, Tetragrammaton, Heloim, Heloi, El, Sadai, Rugia, Jehova, Jesus Alpha and Omega, to obey all my orders and to respond to all questions I give you.
>
> I conjure, summon, and command you, by the one and Trinitarian God, the Eternal One, Jehovah, the Holy and Immortal, by His Supreme Majesty, Ohel, Hecti, Agla, Adonai, and by the omnipotence, strength, and power of God, that the Lord bestowed the night of his birth, to be obedient to my will down to the slightest detail. ††† Amen!

Many of these names are still used in contemporary magic. Dominique Camus has come across them in many of his studies in the field.

In the sixteenth-century manuscripts of *The Lesser Key of Solomon,* the following names, which are used in the orisons, summonings, and spells cited above, appear. Italics indicate that they are the names of the ten sephiroth, or spheres, that form the attributes of God according to the Kabbalah.

Abbaton, Abelech (or Helech), Adonai Melekh, Æchhad, Albamachi, Alcheeghel, Amator, Anabona, Anai, Anaphoditon, Aquachai, Araritha, Arpheton (Hipeton), Aven, Axineton (was inscribed on Aaron's chest), Bacurabon, Baruh, Ben Ani, *Binah* (בינה, intelligence), Briah, Cebon, Chai, Chaia, *Chesed* (חסד, mercy), Chevon, *Chokmah* (חכמה, wisdom), Creator,

Eheieh, El Chai, Eloah Va-Daath, Eloha (אלוה), Elohim Gibor (אלהים גבור, God the powerful), Elohinu, Emeth (truth), EmethHoa, Erel, Esch, *Geburah* (גבורה, strength), Gedulah, Ha-Kabir, Hazor, *Hod* (הוד, majesty), Homorion, Iaht, Innon, Iona, Ionah, Kaphu, *Kether* (כתר, crown), Kuzu, Mal-Ka, *Malkuth* (מלכות, royalty), Maron, Matzpatz, Messaich, Nale, ✲*Netzach* (נצח, eternity), Oneipheton (multiple variants, such as Docecepheron), Oratgu, Oyzroymas, Patacel, Profa, Qadosch, Ruachiah, Shaddai (שדי), Spazor, Theit, Tifache, *Tiphereth* (תפארת, beauty), Transin, Yah, Yaii, *Yesod* (יסוד, the foundation [of the world]), Yeze (or Scheze), Yova, Zedereza, Zio, Zucor.

It is necessary to add the sacred name, each of whose twelve letters is an angel's name: *Aleph, Beth, Beth, Nun, Vau, Resh, Vau, Cheth, He, Qoph, Daleth, Shin.* The Spanish version the *Enchiridion Leonis Pape*, printed in Rome in 1740, includes the following names in an orison for seducing a woman:

+ *Jahel + Patriteron + Israel + Aglala + Xiday + Rosael + Helim + Agla + Tetragrammaton.*

Another orison that offers protection against all manner of perils closes with these names:

+ *Vehuiah + Jeliel + Sitael + ElemIah + Mahasiah + Selahel + Jehová.*

Stories that deal with magic and esoteric subject matter, like those of H. P. Lovecraft (for example, "The Horror at Red Hook"), take full advantage of names like this. Lovecraft cites:

Hel, Heloym, Sother, Emmanvel, Saboth, Agla, Tetragrammaton, Agyros, Otheos, Ischyros, Athanatos, Iehova, Adonai, Sasay, Homonion, Messias, Eschereheye.

And in his recent book *The Lost Symbol* (2009, chap. 77), Dan Brown mentions "Emmanuel, Massiach, Yod, El, Va . . ."

✦ *Eliaon.*

📖 Vienna, Austrian National Library, Codex 3071, folio 102 v°; *Liber incantationum*, folio 99 v°ff.; Bang, no. 1069; Camus 2002, 270; Agrippa, 11; Cartojan, 104–6.

NAMES OF THE PATRIARCHS: As everything is grist for magic's mill, it offers twenty-three names of patriarchs, the majority of which do not correspond with the scriptures. Those who invoke them each day and carry their names on their person will receive their assistance.

> † *yarebidera balea mariea chorel. Sereb. Hyba. Abya onte. Banney. clinor. Jhesu. Seichemmy ececihiel. Samuhel. afesorcherin. chobia. theos. Benjamin anacibi. Marin sanctus Deus. Sanctus Fortis.*

This list contains a barely recognizable Ezekiel (*ececihiel*), and Tobias (*chobia*) is no easier to identify.

📖 Aymar, 336.

NAMES OF THE PLANETARY SPIRITS: When beginning a magical working, it is necessary to respect the appropriate day and hour, in other words, to know the name of the ruling planet at these times and its spirits' names. In a chapter titled "Method for Attracting the Forces of Each Planet, Naming the Spirits of These Forces According to Their Parts and Operating on the Names So Listed," the *Picatrix* provides the following lists:

> Saturn: Redimez, Toz, Corez, Deytiz, Deriuz, Talyz, Daruz, Tahaytuc.
> Jupiter: Demehuz, Dermez, Matiz, Maz, Deriz, Tamiz, Foruz, Dehydez.
> Mars: Deharayuz, Heheydiz, Heydeyuz, Maharaz, Ardauz, Hondehoyuz, Meheyediz, Dehydemez.
> Sun: Beydeluz, Dehymez, Eydulez, Deheyfez, Azuhafez, Mahabeyuz, Hadyz, Letahaymeriz.
> Venus: Deydez, Heyluz, Cahyluz, Diruez, Ableymez, Teyluz, Arzuz, Dehataryz.
> Mercury: Merhuye, Amirez, Hytyz, Cehuz, Deriz, Maylez, Dehedyz, Mehendiz.
> Moon: Harnuz, Hediz, Marayuz, Meletaz, Timez, Hueyz, Meyneluz Dahanuz.

A spell then corresponds to each planet with a new list of the names of the spirits, as shown in the example that follows on page 240.

Saturn: Bedimez, Toz, Eduz, Hayz, Derniz, Tayuz, Huaruyz, Talhit, Naycahua, Huenadul.

Another manuscript gives us:

Berdinem, Tom, Edum, Haym, Dernym, Taym, Huaruym, Talit, Neycahria, Huenaldul.

Jupiter: Demeuz, Armez, Ceylez, Mahaz, Erdaz, Tamyz, Feruz, Dyndez, Afrayuz, Tayhaciedez. (*Variants:* Demum, Armem, Coylem, Maham, Erdam, Tamyn, Fereum, Dinden, Afrayum, Tayhanedem.)

Mars: Dahaydanuz, Hahhayduz, Haydayuz, Mihyraz, Ardehuz, Heudaheydez, Mehedeniz, Dehydemez. (*Variants:* Dahaydamuz, Haehaidam, Haydayum, Myhyray, Ardauz, Hoydaheydem, Mehenedim, Achymen.)

Sun: Tebdeluz, Dihymez, Andulez, Dehycayz Aginafez, Mahagnuz, Ahadyz, Tuymeryz.

Venus: Hueydez, Helyuz, Hemyluz, Deneriz, Temeyz, Cemluz, Arhuz, Meytaryz.

Mercury: Barhurez, Emirez, Haytiz, Cociz, Deriz, Heniz, Deheriz, Zahudaz.

Moon: Heydyuz, Denediz, Mubrynayz, Miltaz, Tymez, Rabyz, Celuz, Deheniz, Merniz.

Each operation is accompanied by a sacrifice and a suffumigation. About this, an ancient anonymous author said, "Suffumigations create forces that attract the spirits toward the images."

The *Liber incantationum* (Book of Incantations, fifteenth century) cites spirits in whom we can recognize paranatellons, symbolic representations of the decans of the zodiac or planets.

Otius: A man with large teeth and three horns who is holding a sword in his hand.

Curson: A crowned man with the face of a lion who is mounted on a horse, holding a viper in his hand.

Alagor: A handsome knight, holding a lance with a gonfalon and a scepter.

Volach: A boy with angel wings riding a two-headed dragon.

Gaeneron: A beautiful crowned woman (who must represent Venus) riding a camel.

Tvueries: A knight on a black charger.
Sucax: A man with a woman's head.

The *Liber incantationum* includes a passage naming the spirits of the sun (folio 86 r°–v°): Abrayn, Acamon, Abragon, Risar.

📖 *Picatrix* III, 9.

NAMES OF THE SPIRITS: A plethora of individuals called "spirits" (*spiritus*) appear in the Grimoires. This is a vague term that obviously covers very different elements, sometimes demons and sometimes *daimons*. The *Liber incantationum* mentions some seventy-two spirits whose names are accompanied with one detail, either a hierarchical ranking (seven are princes, two are of hell, and so on) or an adjective descriptive of their nature. Forty are armed, fourteen are very joyous, twelve quite benevolent, seven live in the water.

They are cited in various operations. For example, in a casting for discovering information about a thief using onychomancy (fingernail divination), the caster appeals to Umon, Progemon, Mithiomo, Pist, Uralchum, Althes, Panite, Fabar, Thobar, Cormes, Felsmes, Diles, and Dilia as well as the demons Berith, Belzebub, and Astaroth, who is described as "fornicator, temptator, seductor, and possessor" (*Liber incantationum*, folio 97 r°–v°).

NAMES OF THE SPIRITS OF THE CARDINAL POINTS: The *Livre des esperitz* names Orient, Poymon, Amoymon, and Equi. The *Liber iuratus* gives us different names: Corniger, who rules over Drocornifer (east), Malifer (west), Evifaber (south), and Mulcifer (north). The *Semiphoras* (see entry) provides the same names in a different order. Johann Weyer names Amoymon, Gorson Zymymar, Goap (Gap, Tap), which is also another name for Belzebuth, who rules over the east while Sathan rules over the north. Some spells have as many as thirty-three names of demons! Cecco d'Ascoli, who was burned at the stake on September 16, 1327, left us a commentary on the *Sphaera mundi noviter recognita cum commentariis* by Johannes de Sacrobosco (circa 1232–1235) in which fragments from an apocryphal treatise by Hipparchus on the hierarchy of the spirits have been inserted. In it we read:

Oriens, Amaymon, Paymon et Egin, qui spiritus sunt de maiori hierarchia et habet unusquisque sub se xxv legione spirituum (Sacrobosco, folio 37).

Egin would therefore be the demon of the north. The *Liber incantationum* cites Discobermath, Archidemath, Fritath, Altramat, Pestiferat, Helyberp, Hergibet, and Sathan (folio 45 v°), who are considered rulers over the cardinal points. The *Livre des espiritz* indicates that Poymon, demon of the south, "appeared in the form of a crowned woman riding a dromedary," which corresponds to Gaeneron.

Scandinavian spells include: Veris/Wiiris (West), Prius/Prias (East), Trilli/Trille (North), and Harpus/Farpas (South), or else Sarael (West), Sexal (East), Allitarius (North) and Caral (South). Ugartilok, in other words, Utgardaloki, "Loki of the outer enclosure," appears in the *Eddas*, where he is a giant with magical expertise; under the name Skrymir he uses his spells to take advantage of the god Thor.

📖 *Picatrix* III, 9; Munich, Germany, Bavarian National Library, ms. Clm 849, folio 63 v° passim.

NAMES OF THE VIRGIN: Spells, invocations, and charms often send appeals to the Virgin Mary, especially for births. For example, in the *Sachet accoucheur* (Aymar, 340), we can read: *Mary. Rebecca. Seffora. Susanna. Abigea. Esecrael. Salome,* names that are merely those of women who play a role in the scriptures. The *Liber iuratus* (fourteenth century) provides the following list of names for the Virgin Mary:

> *namque maria genitrix, mater, sponsa, filia, theoton, virga, vas, balsamus, nubes, ros, pacifica, princeps, regina aurora, imperatrix, domina, ancilla, ortus, fons, puteus, vita, via, semita, splendor, stella aurea, lumen, luna, fenestra vitrea, ianua, porta, velum cella, domus, hospitium, capsa, templum, aula, tabernaculum, manua, ciuitas, liber, stola, flumen, pons, vna malum, granatum femina, nutrix, mulier, turris, nauis, redemtrix, liberatrix, amica, thalamus, vallis, cinamomum, turtur, columba, lilium, rosa, consolatio, portus, spes, salus, gloria, fundamentum, vera peccatorum medicina, sacrarium, spiritus, sancti, radix, iesse, antidotum, recreatrix, syon, puella, miser[a]trix.*

The *Enchiridion Leonis Pape* proceeds with the Virgin in the same manner as with God (see Names of God entry), and collects names and adjectives applied to Mary.

Via, Virgo, Vita, Flos (flower), Nubes (clouds), Regina, Theateontola Cedra (aromatic like cedar), Imperatrix, Pacifica, Domina (mistress), Terra, Hortus (garden), Fons (spring, fountain), Puteus (wells), Aurora, Luna, Sol, Aries, Porta, Domus et Templum (house and temple), Beata (blessed), Gloriosa, Pia (pious), Aula (royal house), Principium, Finis, Schola (school), Scala (ladder), Stella (star), Ancilla Domini (servant of the Lord), Uva (cluster), Vinea (vine), Turris (tower), Navis (ship), Redemptrix, Liberatrix, Arca (chest), Thalamus (chamber), Cynnamomum (true cinnamon), Generatio, Homo, Foemina, Amica, Vallis (valley), Turtur (turtle dove), Mulier (woman), Vulva, Turba, Spina, Liber (book), Pulchra (beautiful), Pharetra (quiver), Mater, Speciosa (beautiful), Albula (whitish), Formosa (beautiful), Benedicta, Rosa, Janua (door), Cibus, Cruditas, Columba Gravata (lead-footed dove), Tabernaculum, Magna.

In the Spanish edition of the *Enchiridion Leonis Pape*, the list is as follows:

VITAE † Virgen † Flor † Nube † Reina † Toda Silenciosa † Emperatriz † Pacífica † Inmaculada † Señora † Nacimiento † Fuente † Mujer † Aurora † Luna † Gloriosa † Piadosa † Estrella + Madre † Viña † Redentora † Libertadora † la Rosa † Azucena † Alana † Senda † Escala † Puerta del Cielo † Lecho † Amiga † Piedra Preciosa † Espina † Paloma † Virgen Maria.

Romanian folk traditions provide a list of seventy-two names for "the Mother of God."

NOCTAR RAIBON BIRANTHER: When carved on a talisman, these words compelled an individual to reveal his secrets and plots against you or your friends. The talisman would be placed over the right ear and its matching ring on the little finger of the left hand. Saying the words *Noctar Raibon,* then after pausing, *Biranther,* would cause a genie to appear. Speaking the word *Noctar* would cause him to bring forth the person whose secrets you wish to learn. If there are several spirits, it is necessary to use *Zelander,* and to send them back *ô Solem.*

📖 *Trésor,* 177b.

NON TRADAS: To prevent a rifle from shooting straight, it is necessary, according to a grimoire from the end of the eighteenth century, to speak the following phrase while your left leg is crossed over your right leg:

Non tradas Dominum nostrum Jesum Christum mather. Amen.

Sometimes *mather* is replaced by *mathon;* the spell has also been corrupted into *Non tradas Dominus nostras jesuras Christum.*

In the Vaud canton of Switzerland in the early nineteenth century, this was the prescribed spell: "To raise the fire from the barrel. *Non tradas Dominum nostras jesuras;* Christ my hand. The left leg must be crossed over right when doing this."

📖 *Enchiridion* 1663, 170; *Enchiridion* (Spanish), Nombres de la purisima Virgen Maria. las solteras que los llevaren encima no se veran jamas enga ñadas de sus novios; ahuyenta las tentaciones de la carne y es de gran virtud para evitar el aborto y malos par tos en las casadas; Hervé, 357; Deonna, "À L'Escalade," 123ff. For more on the magic properties of crossing the legs, see Hoffmann-Krayer and Bächtold-Staübli, vol. 1 col. 1012–16; and Cartojan, 104–06.

N. Y. MILLA. OL'ME. FFARS. D. D. ADON: For protection against curses and enchantments, all one needs is to carry a *bref* with these *caracteres* on his person: *N. Y. Milla. Ol'me. Ffars. D. D. Adon. ay.mi.pp.re.mi.K.ra.x.bi.x.lis.Amen. Adonai* and *mirabilis* are visible in this spell. The two *d*'s should mean *deus deus.*

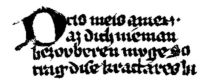

📖 Heidelberg, Germany, University Library, Cpg 214, folio 46c.

OAX MAX WAX: Spell used in Norway to hold a bird or other flying creature fast—in other words, to paralyze it.

Variants: *oax moax voax; ax : max : vaax.*

📖 Bang, no. 1354c.

OBES ORBIRIO: To heal eyestrain and other ocular pains, in the ninth century these *caracteres* would be written on virgin parchment and attached to the patient's forehead.

📖 Saint Gall, codex 751; Heim, 564.

ΟΓΟΡΟ ΟΧΦ. Ε.Γ.Ε.Ι.: This spell sends demons fleeing. It is used to keep them away from lunatics.

📖 Önnerfors, 36.

OCURIA: The first word of a magical enchantment spell on a tablet discovered in Byzacena province (Roman Tunisia). It opens and ends the spell.

Ocuria anoχ oton barnion formione efecebul.

The adjuration of the demon, "whoever it is," is followed by another spell:

Ιαω οι ον ια ιαα ιω ιωε οοριvω α ηια

📖 Audollent, 405–8.

ODRUS † ODRUS † ODRUS EDRUSIA HENSELL: This phrase is intended to provide protection from fevers.

📖 Heidelberg, Germany, University Library, Cpg 267, folio 14 v°.

OFANO, OBLAMO, OSPERGO: These three words form the closing of a prayer requesting the reduction of a fracture or the healing of a wound.

 📖 *Egyptian Secrets* II, 82.

† O FEBRIS, OMNI LAUDE COLENDA: In the fifteenth-century Tyrol, this would be written on a bread crust to cure fever:

> † *O febris, omni laude colenda, o languor sanitatis et gaudy* †
> *Ascribendas nox pax max*

 📖 Zingerle, 175.

O FFUSA: This is the opening of a spell that makes it possible to dull the blades of swords (in the name of the Father, and so on).

> *O ffusa + o Amplustra + o geninistra in nomine patris et f. e. s. S. Amen . . .*

 📖 Bang, no. 1161.

OGER † SUGER †: These magic words are dissolved in water that is given to a woman in labor to facilitate a birth.

 ✦ *Ogor.*
 📖 Braekman, no. 53.

OGGO. † and B. I. o. p. n. GG† [ ] O [ ] z. v. c. a. o. p. n. G. t. o. l.: To win the love of a man or woman, these *caracteres* must be written on virgin parchment, in uppercase and lowercase letters exactly as seen, along with the subject of desire's name, then worn or carried everyday. The brackets indicate the place for symbols that we could not reproduce.

 📖 Aymar, 346.

OGLA: see *Agla*.

 📖 Franz II, 397.

OGOOEEE LO: A late-eighteenth-century Swiss grimoire provides this strange phrase, "in order to fight with anger," which includes the symbol of Venus. It must be worn or otherwise carried on one's person: *oGooeee lo ce 9 ♀ vo766 IGIG 66.*

📖 Hervé, 364.

OGOR SECOR VAGOR: This phrase appeared in *Saint Anne's Charm,* whose purpose is to ease childbirth.

✦ *Oger.*
📖 Hunt, 361.

O. H. R.: Toward the end of the eighteenth century, these letters would be written in one's own blood, then worn over one's stomach. They afforded protection against all wounds.

o. h. R. o. b. h. l. a. o. z. g. f. m.
a. b. b. h. b. b

📖 Hervé, 363.

O HÛDIS: To part a man and woman and inspire enmity between them, two hollow wax figurines are crafted bearing their names, and a mixture based on black cat and pig bile, among other things, is prepared. This concoction is then poured down the mouth of the man's effigy. A second mixture is prepared consisting of fat and black dog bile that is then poured in until it covers the hollow of the shoulder blade. The chest of the male figure is then pierced with a needle while the caster says:

O Hûdis, 'Amjâlûs, Halwânîs, Bîhawâras.

The operation is repeated for the female figurine (see *Adnâlîs*) with another mixture, then both effigies are suffumigated while the curse is formulated.

📖 *Gâyat al-Hakîm,* 269–71.

ΩHTI Ω ΣI: In the fifth century, people would heal migraines by writing on a parchment: *ωhti ω σι aa loti poca zonie ho ωaΛΥΡΙΖε.* The text does not say what was done next, but other such prescriptions inform us that the parchment was attached around the head.

📖 Pseudo Theodore, 30ff., 314,

O I P U L U: This word would halt a nosebleed when written on tree bark with the blood flow. It can be found in these two forms: *O. I. P. U. L. O* in 1847 and *O : I : P : U : L : O* in 1885. The Rhineland doctor G. S. Bäumler indicated in 1736 that some people wrote these letters on the forehead of someone suffering from a hemorrhage, using a straw dipped in the patient's blood. In 1643, Jean Agricola did the same. The phrase can also be found noted as *OIPULK* and *OPVLVS*.

📖 Bang, no. 1056.

OKILIM KARIPATA: These are the opening words to a spell for dismissing spirits. Once the following spell has been read, the spirits become invisible and the master can leave his circle after a benediction:

> *Okilim Karipata Prince Amabosar lugosto horitus kikaym lutintos Parsas.*

📖 Herpentil, *Grimoires*, 285.

OMIS: This word is one of five featured in an Italian therapy against worms. *Omis* is written on the patient's head, *Et Manuel* over the right nipple, *sonos* on the thigh, *gob* on the right knee, and *Vermis* on the right foot.

Another fourteenth-century manuscript offers this variation: *Ono* on the forehead, *manovello* on the chest, *manasti* on the hand, *gobo* on the knee, and *vermi* on the foot.

📖 Amati, 31; Giannini, 32.

OMNIS SPIRITUS: To drive away spirits that are haunting a house, the following extracts from the Bible, written out on virgin parchment, are placed at the dwelling's four corners:

> *Omnis spiritus laudet Dominum, Mosen habent et prophetas, Exurgat Deus & dissipentur.*

> [May all that draws breath praise God (Psalm 150:6); They have Moses and the prophets (Luke 16:29); May God lift up and scatter (Psalm 68:1).]

📖 Scot, Book XII, chapter 14.

ON: This word is said to be the first name of God. In Greek *o ὤν* means "he that is." It is commonly found in Greek charms, mainly the long enchantment spells such as: *lampsoure othikalak aiphnosabao steseon uellaphonta sankiste chphuris on.*

In the Middle Ages, *On* was featured in weather spells and in conjurations of epilepsy such as:

+ *On confortat + panton durat quod tedet + detragrammaton reconciliat quod discordat.*

On was also used in spells for banishing fever in thirteenth-century England. It needed to be written on the patient's hand on the first day, like this: + *on Pater + on Filius + on Spiritus Sanctus.* On the second day, this phrase was required: + *on ovis + on aries + on angnus*, and on the third, this was written on the patient's hand: + *on leo + on vitulus + on vermis*. In lists of divine names, *On* is almost always present. An example of a list of this nature can be seen in this love spell:

On, onon, aneo, femiton, socumon, os sabaoth, adonai, el, ely, elyon, agla, tetragrammaton, akana, agya, egessie, alphano.

In the thirteenth century, *On* also appeared in a spell for relieving a toothache: + *on + in + in + in + on + bon + bin + bin + bon.* This phrase must be repeated three times over the ailing tooth, then written down and hung around the patient's neck.

A zodiac amulet featuring the sign of Taurus described by the Pseudo–Arnaldus de Villanova (1235–1311) bore *On. Joseph. Oytheon* at its center, encircled by *Benedictum sit nomen Domini Jesu Christi* (blessed be the name of Jesus Christ). This amulet affords protection against all eye disorders.

þ *Christus vincit.*

 📖 Franz II, 87, 101, 503; Ohrt II, 32, 118; Thiers I, 355; Braekman, no. 361; Hunt, 96; Pseudo–Arnaldus de Villanova, *Opera*, folio 302 r°; Ogden, 46.

ONAÏM PERANTES RASONASTOS: These words should be carved on a ring with a round, multifaceted setting. They permit the wearer to find treasure.

 📖 *Trésor,* 176b.

ON † JHESUS † ON † LEO † ON † FILIUS: This spell offers a remedy against fever. The caster takes three sacrificial wafers and writes this phrase on the outer rim of the back of the first one, with †A†G†L†A in the middle. †on†omg†on†aries†on†agnus† is written on the border of the second, with †te†tra†gra†ma†ton† in the center, and the third has †on†pater†on†gloria†on†mundus† on one side and *Jhesus nazarenus † crucifixus † Rex † judeorum † sit medicina mei* on the back. The spell also requires that five Our Fathers and five Hail Marys be recited each day.

📖 London, British Library, Royal 12 G IV, folio 175 v°.

† ON LONA ONU ONI ONE ONUS ONI ONE ONUS: To heal all kinds of fevers in thirteenth-century Provence, it was recommended that this spell be written on virgin parchment, have three masses said over it, then wear it around the neck.

📖 Cambridge, England, Cambridge University, ms. R. 14.30, folio 146 r°.

ONYSOMA † EPYN † SEGOK †: This phrase is part of a spell used to drive away a spirit or dismiss one that has been summoned. The caster must say:

Onysoma † Epyn † Segok † Satany † Degony † Eparygon † Galligonon † Zogogen † Ferstigon †

📖 *Verus Jesuitarvm libellus.*

ORISONS: These prayers to pagan gods and even to planetary angels and demons were gradually replaced by Christian magic orisons, which are still called "apotropaic prayers." The oldest ones are the Celtic *Loricae* (Breastplates). These are invocations listing the parts of the body and requesting the blessing of heaven or some saint to provide them with protection. The "Lorica," a poem, which is attributed to the Venerable Bede, opens like this: "May Gabriel be my breastplate, Michael my baldric, Raphael my shield, Uriel my protector, Rumiel my defender..."

Clerics composed the orisons—they can be found in books of hours and psalters—with the help of extracts from the Holy Scriptures and canticles, with which they often mixed in Kabbalistic spells and words. A prayer could be created by taking a biblical passage for a reference. For example, with the help of *Jesus autem transiens,* travelers could be provided with some sound protection.

On an amulet that was made to provide protection from all evils (currently housed in Geneva), there is an orison crafted this way with phrases taken from the Apostles' Creed and from the Gospel of Saint John, and others phrases such as *Christus vincit* and *Crux Christi*. This orison duplicates the *Orison of Seven Words,* attributed to the Venerable Bede, which offered complete protection to its bearer, including prevention of death without confession. Reginald Scot (circa 1538–1599) reproduced a number of orisons in his *Discoverie of Witchcraft,* published in 1584, like the one below:

¶ Saie first the praiers of the Angels euerie daie, for the space of seauen daies.

Michael.	☉
Gabriel.	☽
Samael.	♂
Raphael.	☿
Sadiel.	♃
Anael.	♀
Cassiel.	♄

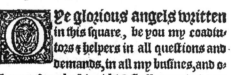

Ye glorious angels written in this square, be you my coadiutors & helpers in all questions and demands, in all my busines, and other causes, by him which shall come to iudge the quicke and the dead, and the world by fier.

O angeli gloriosi in hac quadra scripti, estote coadiutores & auxiliatores in omnibus quæstionibus & interrogationibus, in omnibus negotijs, cæterísque causis, per eum qui venturus est iudicare viuos & mortuos, & mundum per ignem.

¶ Saie this praier fasting, called
* *Regina lingua.*

✠ Lemaat ✠ solmaat ✠ elmay ✠ gezagra ✠ raamaasin ✠ eziere go ✠ mial ✠ egziephiaz ✠ Iosamin ✠ sabach ✠ ha ✠ aem ✠ re ✠ b ✠ e sepha ✠ sephar ✠ ramar ✠ semoit ✠ lemaio ✠ pheralon ✠ amic ✠ phin ✠ gergoin ✠ letos ✠ Amin ✠ amin ✠.

Among the most widespread orisons, I should mention the *Sacrosanctae et individuae Trinitati,* which was condemned by theologians, the orison of Saint Anthony for finding lost or misplaced objects, that of Saint Apolline for healing toothaches (this one was written on a support material to be held between the teeth), Bede's orison for protection from shipwrecks, and that of Saint Gerald against perils at sea. There is also Adam's orison against wounds and the one of Saint Cyprianus to make it "so that no unclean spirit, nor stain or rift, nor evil eye, nor evil tongue, nor any persecution can harm us." Others would include Saint Augustine's orison for protection against intrigues and the hatred of others, and the orison of the four evangelists for protection from wounds of the evil spirit, night phantoms, and all perils and accidents, and so forth. Some orisons carry indications of their origin; for example, the *Very Precious Orison,* "found in the tomb of Jesus Christ," requests the Virgin Mary to ask her son to grant its bearer assurance that he shall not die "neither of injustice, nor in prison, nor unconfessed." The most famous orison remains that of Pope Leo III, which is an amazing phylactery promising total protection. The collection made on the Sunday of the Octave of Christmas, *Omnipotens sempiterne Deus,* is used as an orison bearing a request to avoid death unconfessed. The pericope from the Gospel of John (1:1–14) also serves this purpose and must be recited three times when passing close to enemies. The *Enchiridion Leonis Pape* appears as a collection of a large number of magic orisons.

> Omnps semptn dr
> cuius spu totum
> corpus ecclesiae scifica
> tur & regitur: exaudi
> nos pro universis ordini
> bus supplicantes ut gratiae
> tuae munere ab omnibus
> tibi gradibus fideliter
> serviatur· per d nrm

The *Liber Iuratus,* a Solomonic grimoire first mentioned in the thirteenth century, includes many orisons that can be partially seen again in the *Ars notoria* (thirteenth century).

The Our Father prayer was also recited backward, especially in necromancy. In the nineteenth century, Jón Árnason took a narrative from magic books that explained what was necessary to do to awaken a dead person and bring him or her back in order to use the person as an "emissary" (*sendingr*) or as a zombie (*upvakningr,* which means "awakened one"):

> Runes must be carved on a cylinder (a piece of round wood) and the carver must then take these two things into the cemetery at midnight where he will head to the tomb of his choice, although he would be wiser to attack the smaller ones (graves). He must then place the cylinder on top of the grave and roll it forward and back over it while reciting the Our Father backward from the sheet (on which it was written) and, in addition, several magic spells that few people know except for sorcerers.

> During this time the revenant will be rising up slowly, because this does not occur quickly, and revenants will be begging the caster greatly: "let me rest in peace." (Árnason, I, 318)

In a spell against a thief we can read: *Dnaa. Gilleh. Go Nøs, Redaf Dug,* in other words, *Gud fader, søn og hellig aand* (God the Father, the Son, and the Holy Ghost). An extremely corrupted Apostle's Creed that includes some pieces from the Our Father is regarded as a magical spell: *Kredor nijande potamen Amen,* and so forth.

Orisons can also be found in the Kabbalistic scriptures, such as, for example, the Prayer of Vihi Noam, credited to the Rabbi Isaac Luria and transmitted in the *Sepher shimmush tehillim* (thirteenth century). It was used during times of plague. It is composed of the forty-one sacred names from Psalm 68 and must be recited seven times a day.

ואא Veaa	אלמ Alm	בשי Bichi	יבע Iba	ויכ Wich	יכע Ika	אעו Aau	וני Veni
מיי Mii	תמל Tmol	ואל Veal	כתצ Ktaz	ילו Ilu	מהב Mehob	ימי Imi	בכה Becha
אימ Im	רתכ Retak	בתו Betu	ליר Lir	ומא Uma	ימא Ima	מיצ Miz	מבי Mebi
עכי Aki	לכד Lakad	מול Mil	יבכ Ibak	רול Rul	לתא Leta	עשמ Ascham	
עאב Aab	שיו Schiu	אכי Aki	בחו Bechu	כוכ Kuck	ותת Vetat	רעש Raasch	פתכ Petasch
						יאוב Jaub	אוא Aua

It was combined with the drawing of a golden candlestick made from these names:

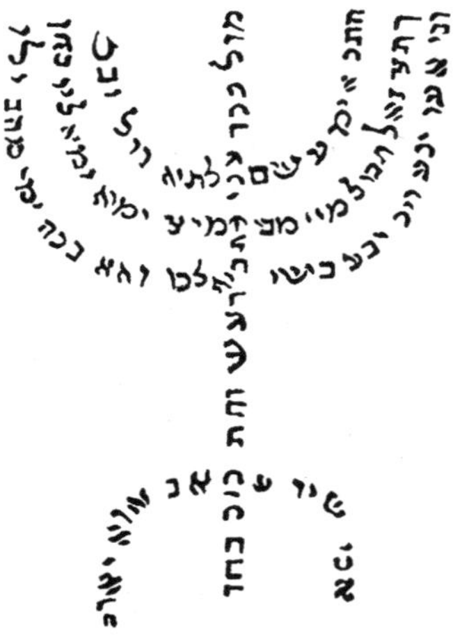

To end, it was necessary to recite verses 21 to 28 from chapter 12 of Exodus.

The literature diffused by peddlers contributed to the spread of orisons, as shown by a small booklet of twelve pages, *Le médecin des pauvres, ou recueil de prières pour le soulagement des maux d'estomac, charbon, pustule, fièvres, plaie, &c,* (Doctor of the Poor, or Prayer Book for the Relief of Stomachache, Coal, Pustule, Fevers, Wound, etc.), from the Blue Library of Troyes [a famous collection of popular literature from the Middle Ages—*Trans.*].

 📖 L. Gougaud, "Etudes sur les *Loricae* celtiques et sur les prières qui s'en approchent," 1 (1911): 265–81; 2 (1912): 33–41, 101–27; Gougaud, *Dévotions et pratiques religieuses du moyen âge;* Rézeau, *Les prières aux saints en français à la fin du moyen âge;* Le Blant, "De l'ancienne croyance à des moyens secrets de défier la torture," 289–300; Leroquais, vol. 1, 151; Leroquais, vol. 2, 237–41; Saintyves; Bang, no. 1339, 1377, 1451; Pedrosa, J. M. *Entre la magia y la religion, oraciones, conjuros, ensalmos.* Sendoa: Gipuzkoa, 2000.

ORSA – FORSA – FORSMA: To awaken love, write these words on a red apple with one's name and in one's own blood. One can also write *S iop f g li—* on a piece of bread to give to the desired individual to eat.

 📖 BaK, no. 65.

ORTUS † MORTUUS † CRISTUS † SURREXIT: These words must be written on nine sage leaves to cure an invalid of fever. The patient must eat three a day for three days in a row.

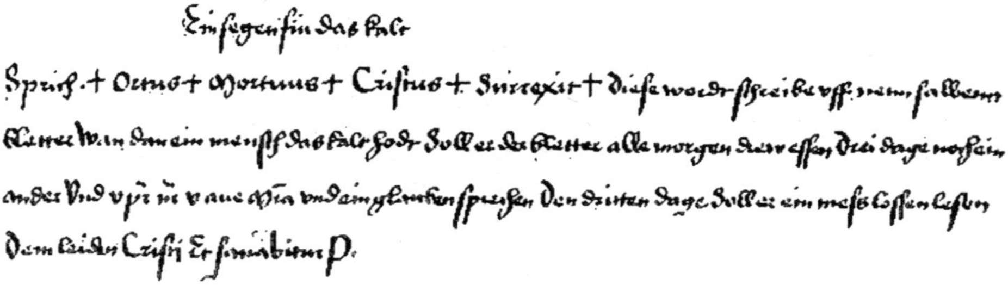

[handwritten manuscript text]

 ✦ *Christus natus, Jesus natus.*
 📖 Heidelberg, Germany, University Library, Cpg 267, folio 11 r°. Marzell, 199.

OS NON COMMINUETIS EX EO: This spell, which is drawn from the Gospel of John (19:36), is supposed to relieve a toothache.

📖 Ohrt I, no. 443.

OSO OSI OSIAN: To prevent a viper from biting you, these words should be spoken aloud when it is seen, after which it can even be held in your hands. A Dresden manuscript indicates that a serpent taker should go into the forest with a flute made from a cat bone and stand inside a circle in which + *o sy* + *o sy* + *o sya* + *tetragrammaton* + *Sabaoth* has been written. When he plays, all the vipers there will be drawn to him. Once they have all gathered together, he speaks the spell of conjuration.

> + *o sy* + *o sy* + *o sya,* you diabolical snake without salvation, listen and stay as tranquil as the water of the Jordan in which Saint John baptized the Christ, our Lord, + *o sy* + *o sy* + *o* you diabolical serpent, *Thetragramaton gea Sabaoth Emanuel.*

This is followed by a spell inviting the reptile to spit out its venom, then the thirteenth verse from Psalm 90; the phrase is then repeated and the spell is closed with *Tetragramathon Adonay Alpha et Omega.* After a second spell, the snake is invited to abandon its venom in the name of *Ely Eloy.* In the sixteenth-century Tyrol, *Osia* was repeated three times and accompanied by a curse intended to paralyze the serpent (Siller, s.v. "Osia"). In the *Merveilleux Secrets du Petit Albert,* the spell is read as *Osy, Osya, Osy,* and we are told that snakes will plug one ear with the end of their tail and press the other tight against the ground in order not to hear it. Thus stupefied they are incapable of causing any harm to humans.

Hispanic variant: *Osi Osoa.*

Italian variant: *ausi osià ausi.*

Dutch variant: *osi † osi † osi † ave admissive serpens stes in verbis die sicut ab ea in Jordano cum Johannes Xristum baptizavit † tetragramaton † adonay † alpha † et o †*

📖 Ohrt II, 119; Schönbach, 25ff.; Werner, no. 36, 204; Gallée, 452; *Libro de segretto e di magia,* 4.

OSTHARIMAN VISANTIPAROS NOCTATUR: These words are spoken aloud to direct the infernal powers against those one wishes to harm, and their effects are banished by *Abibale Necum*.

📖 *Trésor*, 184a–b.

OSURMY + DELMUSAN + ATALSLOYM +: To conjure inferior spirits, the *Grimorium verum* (book III) gives this spell:

> Osurmy + Delmusan + Atalsloym + Charusihoa + Melany + Liamintho + Colehon + Paron + Madoin + Merloy + Bulerator + Donmedo + Hone + Peloym + Ibasil + Meon + Alymdrictels + Person + Crisolay + Lemon Sessle Nidar Horiel Peunt + Halmon + Asophiel + Ilnostreon + Baniel + Vermias + Slevor + Noelma + Dorsamot + Lhavala + Omor Framgam + Beldor + Dragin + Viens, N.

OTA: A magic rune word translated as "terror." It has been found on sixth century bracteates. On one it is combined with *Alu* (see entry), which could refer to its function as an amulet.

📖 Fingerlin, Fischer, and Düwel, "Alu und ota."

Ô TAROT NISTA XATROS: When carved on a ring, these words make it possible to read the thoughts of individuals near the wearer and to see what is taking place inside a house without entering. It requires blowing on the ring while saying: *Ô Tarot Nezael Estarnas Tantarez*. To encourage someone, one says: *Nista Saper Vinos,* and for causing harm to one's enemies: *Xatros Nifer Roxas Tortos. Tarot* is most likely a corruption of Astaroth.

📖 *Trésor*, 180a–b.

OTHINEL PHAREL: In a ritual that is intended to permit an individual to make his way instantly to wherever he wishes to go and that relies on the herbs of the seven planets, the caster addresses Pharel, a demon or angel, by using this spell:

> *Othinel Pharel Clemosiel Pharel. Andromaniel Pharel.*

He then names the place he wishes to go. The other names besides Pharel designate either his assistants or are descriptive terms that have been given the appearance of angelic names with the addition of the suffix *–el*.

📖 Braekman, no. 250.

OUBAIX: To heal ophthalmia, this word should be written on virgin parchment and hung around the neck using the chain from a weaving loom. The same results can be obtained, according to Marcellus of Bordeaux (fourth century), with the word *phurphuran* (jujuran) read (φυρφυραν).

📖 Marcellus VIII, 56ff.

† OX † ROX † RONEN † UPERNINEN PATERNAM: This spell from 1350 was believed to offer protection against gout.

📖 Ohrt II, 119.

OXILA ENGLABIS PROMODUM: This is a spell from the *Gran Grimorio*. It is used to compel obedience from Guland, the spirit of Saturday. Although the spirits for the different days of the week appear in *Le veritable dragon noir et la poule noire*, these words do not appear there.

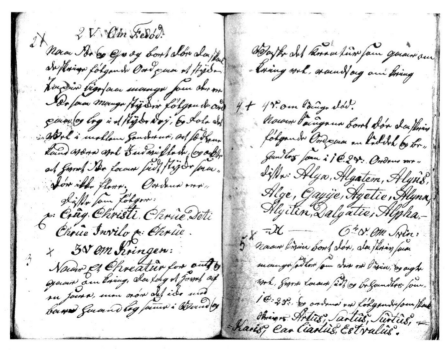

From the Black Book of Jeløen (Norway)

P A: According to Pliny the Elder, the consul Servilius Noniamus wore an amulet around his neck that bore these two Greek letters that in fact represent the Egyptian sun god Ra.

📖 Pliny, XXVIII, 5.

P A. B PB. A. PE.: This is an old charm written in Old German that carries a recipe for freeing a patient from a worm that will cause his or her teeth to fall out.

P a. b pb. a. pe. f. p. pf. e. pi. k. pk. i. po. p. pp. o. pu. x. px. u.

"Draw a dot behind P a ., two behind pe .., three behind pi .·., four behind pu ::, and five :·:. Then write on four sacrificial wafers:

> \+ *hely* == *heloy*.
> ++ heloe. ++ heloen.
> ++ ye. ++ ya.
> ++ sabaoth. ++ adonay+

while inserting the name of the patient on two or three of these hosts."

📖 *Zeitschrift für deutsches Altertum* 11, 437.

PACHAY † PATRE † ADONNAY: This is the beginning of an orison intended to bespell all kinds of weapons. It must be written down, then worn or otherwise carried on one's person. In addition to the names of God, the orison contains common Christian phrases such as *Jesus autem transiens* and *verbum caro factum est,* and it ends with † *Pacisdes* †††.

📖 Hervé, 362.

† PAGA † CHAGA † PAGULA † CHAGULA † PAGULA: These words should be written on a *bref,* then attached around the

neck of a man or animal. They offer protection against rabid dog bites.
📖 *Egyptian Secrets* II, 48.

† PAL † PAL † PAL: If this is written on the right palm of the person bleeding, using that same spilt blood, the hemorrhaging will be stopped.
📖 Hunt, 361.

PALINDROME: Since earliest antiquity, magic has expressed its fondness for magical words that are palindromes, which can be read either right to left or left to right, or anagrammatic words, which have the same letters in rearranged order. Greece provides a slew of examples, such as the following:

IAEOBAPHRENEMOUNOTHILARIKRIPHIAEYEAIP
IRKIRALITHONUOMENERPHABOEAI

Armand Delatte notes, "Angagrammatical phrases, which are made for circular inscriptions modeled on the serpent ouroboros, are an image of the sun's course." Attilio Mastrocinque informs us that a "magical papyrus describes the rite by which a person can be compelled to do or not do something. One takes a piece of hieratic papyrus or a strip of lead and an iron ring, then uses a feather to draw the inside and outside circles of the ring on the papyrus or strip of lead. Inside the band of the ring that has been thus drawn, a long magic inscription is written and inside the inner circle a rectangle of magic words is drawn. With them is written: May this thing not be done so long as the ring remains buried. The papyrus or lead is folded over the ring and bound shut, then placed in an abandoned spring or the grave of someone who died prematurely." The same papyrus, he adds, still held the drawing of a curse tablet of this time and displayed this palindrome:

ΙΑΕΩΒΑΦΡΕΝΕΜΟΥΝΟΘΙΛΑΡΙΚΡΙΦΙΑΕΥΕΑΙΦΙΡΚΙΡ
ΑΛΙΘΟΝΥΟΜΕΝΕΡΦΑΒΩΕΑΙ

📖 Betz, ed., 332; Delatte, "Études sur la magie grecque," 28; Mastrocinque.

PALLIUM. CRISCIUM. CONFAME. SIGNALE. SIGNE. SIGNIKADE: To heal someone bitten by a snake, it is necessary to write this on a piece of cheese that the victim is then given to eat.
📖 Utrecht, the Netherlands, University Library, ms. 1355, folio 48 r°.

PANCA PASCA CACARAT: In eighteenth-century Romania, to heal snakebite, the following spell was written on a glass, which was then washed with water or wine that the bitten person should drink:

Panca pasca cacarat poca poi tocosora panca paca caca panca rata.

Emanuela Timotin notes, "In his work on magic medicine, Candrea also analyzed several oral incantations, consisting of obscure words, which in some ways are similar to ours. I will cite the words, for which Candrea suggests a Western origin: Cararate/ Conopate/ Netie/ Congapate/ Corban; Pog conopago/ Cara gana carga/ Cararata pune."

📖 Bucharest, Romanian Academy Library, ms. rom. BAR 1517, f. 42 v°; Candrea, 340ff.

† PANTHON † GRATON † MURITON: This is the beginning of a spell that allows one to gain the power of invisibility from the three fairies Milia, Achilia, and Sibylia. The ritual involves being washed and possessing a candle made from virgin wax that is lit using the embers from a fire used to boil water in the middle of the room where the ritual takes place. Holding the candle in the right hand, the caster says this spell:

✠ *Panthon* ✠ *Graton* ✠ *Muriton* ✠ *Bisecognaton* ✠ *Siston* ✠ *Diaton* ✠ *Maton* ✠ *Tetragrammaton* ✠ *Agla* ✠ *Agarion* ✠ *Tegra* ✠ *Pentessaron* ✠ *Tendicata* ✠

Then, before the summoning, he says:

✠ *Sorthie* ✠ *Sorthia* ✠ *Sorthios* ✠ *Milia* ✠ *Achilia* ✠ *Sibylia* ✠ *in nomine patris, & filii, & spiritus sancti, Amen.*

Three beautiful young women will appear and give a ring to the caster. The first two words must be a variation on the word *Pantocrator* ("Almighty"), which has been divided into two words.

📖 Scot, Book XV, chapter 10.

PARA FARA GARA: This was a spell used in the Vosges region of France during the nineteenth century to get a thorn out of one's finger. This charm of four verses/worms evokes Saint John and Saint Nicholas.

📖 Laisnel de la Salle, 334.

PARA PARA PARA: To make yourself invisible for twenty-four hours, you must take off whatever clothes you are wearing and "draw" these signs at the same time. They are called "signs" because they are written in Greek letters (παραπαραπαρα).

📖 Ohrt II, 120.

PARTITI SUNT: To bewitch the cards and win at gambling, this spell is used while making the sign of the cross three times. The spell's opening is taken from the Bible (John 19:24, Psalms 22:18: *Partiti sunt vestimenta mea sibi, et in vestem meam miserunt sortem* ["They have shared my clothing and drawn lots for them"]), but with errors, and it also calls on demons, mainly Belzebuth, whose name has been corrupted into Oelzeut.

> *Partiti sunt vetimenta ema, miserut contra me ad incarte clea a fili a Eniol, Liebce, Braya, Braguesca, and Oelzut.*

📖 Werner, no. 37, 204.

PATUS, ARNNEPE, REMU: The spell that follows is written to protect one from curses and should be buried beneath the stable:

> *Patus, Arnnepe, Remu operantus, innomune, Paves, et, Spiritus Sanstye, Amen.*

Innomune and the words that follow are a distortion of "in the name of the father" and so on. The first three words are probably the names of saints: Paul, Remy, and, perhaps, Arnold.

📖 Bang, no. 1096.

PAVTE FOMAGAS EMANUEL DERENUS: When written on a slip of paper that one carries on his person, this spell protects one against bewitchment.

📖 Espeland, no. 8.

P ++ M COGA ♓ III: To unmask a thief, these signs would be carved on a piece of cheese that the suspect was given to eat. If he were truly guilty, he would be unable to swallow it.

📖 Bang, no. 1146.

P. ☒. B. PARAG. CP. EX. I. MIN. Y. 3. RD. Y. N.: To treat colic, draw these *caracteres,* then place them over or bind them to the patient's chest.

 📖 Braekman, no. 30.

PAX: This word, which shares nothing in common with the Latin *pax* (peace) except the consonance, can be found in countless magic spells. In the twelfth century this particular spell was written down to facilitate childbirth:

† *Christus* † *pax* † *Christus* † *pax* † *Christus* † *pax* † *Christus in utero* †

The term can be found in the fourteenth-century Norwegian charm *Pax Max Vax,* then again around 1800 in *Pax, Max / udred strax / Max, Max* for protection against theft.

Against quartan fever one would take three leaves of sage and write † *pater vita* on the first, † *filius pax* on the second, and † *spiritus remedium* on the third. They were then given to the patient to eat.

To win at cards, one must take the blood of a black dog and write *Pax Max urnax* with it on his left hand. Some variants are *Mahx, Pahx Paters Delix Spiritus Sali* and *Max phax Patris Diliux Spiritus Falax.* As for *vax pax Dax,* it has been an extremely common spell since around 1650. Here are three other uses of *Pax:*

- To cause a piece of property that has been stolen to return, write *Pax, Pox, Bizax* and give it to the thief to eat.
- To learn the identity of someone who has robbed you, it is necessary to write this on a piece of cheese: *Pax* † *Dax* † † *Emax* †††. The robber will be unable to ingest it. A variant of this same prescription suggests: *Max pax Firax urgux Exqeidax Arare-lingstram Tuam Fasie Dolore* †, accompanied by three Our Fathers.

- To prevent someone from shooting at you, it is necessary to say *PAX SAX SARAX* while looking in the barrel of the rifle.

  📖 Franz II, 202; Scot, Book XII, chapter 18; P. Spano, *Volgarizzamento del "trattato della cura degli occhi,"* Bologna, Italy: 1873, 51; Bang, no. 1058, no. 1060, no. 1061, no. 1062, no. 1063; Schulz, 302; *Egyptian Secrets* II, 33; Zingerle, 174ff.

PEANRO PETOSEN TANETDO: With these malefic and "Chaldean" words (*palabras caldeas*), one could prevent a man from urinating or ejaculating.

📖 Werner, no. 38, 204.

P.E.C.P.E.N.D.X.A.G.J.N.M.: An English spell, these *caracteres* must be written on two sheets of parchment for protection against hemorrhages. If one wishes to seek proof of the efficacy of this spell, inscribe it on a knife, then stab a pig with it; the pig will not bleed. The phrase can be found in another charm of this same country in which, to stop bleeding, it is necessary to place the writing on the patient's belly. The spell has been abbreviated to *pe. n. m. x. a. s. z. i. ii. Iii.*

The following variant has also been encountered: *p.g.c.p.e.v.o.x.a.g.z.* These *caracteres* are reputed to bring a stop to all blood loss. They are written on a piece of parchment that is bound to both thighs.

📖 Cambridge, England, Cambridge University, Trinity College, ms. O.2.13, folio 105 r°; Hunt, 96, 124.

PELA AMON OLE SATORUM LENTUM OVINS: To make an individual dance against his or her will, one must write these words on a piece of paper with bat's blood and place it beneath the doorsill of his or her home.

📖 Bang, no. 1141.

† PER CHRISTUM †: In the fifteenth century, for halting an overly long menstruation, this liturgical spell would be written on a piece of paper that was then placed on the woman's head:

† *per christum* † *cum christo* † *in christo.*

📖 Munich, Germany, Bavarian National Library, Cgm 723, folio 222 r°.

PERGAMA: This is the opening of the spell † *pergama* † *perga* † *pergamata* † *abraham* † *alume* † *zorobantur,* which should be written on paper or parchment, then tied beneath the belly of a horse suffering from worms.

📖 Braekman, no. 206.

PERLO: To prevent ever being bewitched, it is necessary to write and carry these words on one's person: + *Perlo* + *Amasus* + *Emanuel* + *2 Doremus.* The spell appears to be truncated because there is another serving the same purpose that appears in the form of *Porto Hamasias F Emanuel F doremus. Doremus. Doremus* must be *D* + *oremus,* meaning "let us pray to God."

📖 Bang, no. 1098.

PHALAY: Repeating this word three times will allow one to get a favorable judgment in a trial.

📖 *Grand Grimoire,* 56.

PHARMAKOYS: Written in Greek letters, this word forms part of a healing ritual intended to treat kidney pains. Before bathing, one must pour some oil in one's left hand and say *Pharmakoys* three times, then rub oneself with the oil. The Greek word *pharmakon* and the Latin word *pharmacum* both indicated the remedy as well as the potion and the spell. In the Middle Ages one of the words used for *witch* was *pharmaceutria.* In Romanian, the word *farmec,* which seems to have been in use since the sixteenth century, means "enchantment, spell, curse, charm."

📖 Önnerfors, 18.

PHATTU: Magic word appearing in an orison providing protection against any evil action. The person recites five Our Fathers and five Hail Marys; then recites a charm appealing to Christ's wounds, the four crowns of heaven, and the four evangelists; then he swallows the following words inspired by the Gospel of John: *Est principio, est in principio, est in verbum, Deum et tu phattu.*

📖 Honorius, 66ff.

PHILACRATES: If one wishes to become invisible, he must take, under the waxing moon, a piece of virgin parchment and write the words that follow with the blood of a bat: *Philacrates fabigata gorguides garon plaraka stelpa,* then draw certain *caracteres* and wrap it all in another parchment, and so on.

📖 Braekman, no. 243.

PHNÔ EAI IABÔCH (Φνω εαι Ιαβωχ): These are magic words, which were believed to be Egyptian, that were used to consecrate a ring that when worn makes its bearer invincible and invulnerable to all dangers, everywhere and at all times. After invoking the all-powerful God, these words are spoken with the addition of names of God in Hebrew (*Adonaï, Sabaoth*), Greek (*o panton monarchos Basileus* [oh king, who rules alone over all things]), and Parthian (*Ouertó pantothunata*), and it ends with *Iaô Sabaoth Abrasax.*

📖 PGM III, 74–76.

PHTA HRA IÈ: The opening of a Greek invocation that accompanies a request for assistance amid mortal perils. The plea is addressed to a god whose secret name is revealed here:

> *Phta hra iè Phta oun emècha erôchth Barôch thorchtha thôm chai eouch archandabar ôeaeô ynéôch èra ôn egôph bom phta athabrasia Abriasoth barbarbelôcha barbariaôch*
>
> [Φδα Ρα ιη Φδα ουν εμηχα ερωχδ βαρωχ δορχδα δομ χαιεουχ αρχανδβαρ ωεαεω ννηωχ ηρα ων ηγωφ βομ Θδα αδαβρασια Αβριασοδ βαρβαρβελωχα βαρβαιαω]
>
> The text closes with *Ablathangalba.*

📖 PGM II, 68ff.

PICATRIX: The title of a magic treatise translated from Arabic into Castilian, then Latin by order of Alfonso X the Wise, King of Castille, and finished in 1256.

The Arabic text titled *Gâyat al-Hakîm* (The Goal of the Wise), with the underlying implication "in magic," is mistakenly attributed to the mathematician and astronomer Maslama ibn Ahmad al-Madjritî (died circa 1005–1008). It is a tenth-century compilation of around two hundred books on the esoteric sciences, written in the Middle East during the ninth and tenth centuries by the Sabeans. It is a treatise of the orisons with which to address the spirits of the planets, their images, and magic rings, and reproduces many *caracteres* and figures.

This work had considerable impact, and its influence can be seen in the work of Peter d'Abano, then among the alchemists and occultists of the sixteenth century. It enjoyed great success into the seventeenth century. For example, Heinrich Cornelius Agrippa and Marsilio Ficino used it. An anonymous translation into French of only the first two books was made in the eighteenth century, three manuscripts of which are still in existence, one at the National Library and the other two at the Arsenal Library. There are also three known translations of the *Gâyat al-Hakîm* in Hebrew.

✦ *Abrutim, Acriuz, Bahâhajûs, Beheymerez, Deytuz, Gagneytania, Hantaraceret, Haphot, Harmum, Hendeb, Heyerim, Kardîlâs, Neforuz, Rhibarim, Seraphie, Ye Deluz.*

📖 See *Picatrix;* For the Arabic text, see *Gâyat al-Hakîm;* Boudet, Caiozzo, and Weill-Parot.

P I M T C S M: This is the abbreviation of Christ's words, *Pater, in manus tuas commendo spitirum meum* (Father, into your hand I commit my spirit), taken from the Gospel of Luke (23:46). It is commonly used on Christian amulets. These words form part of the *Orison of Seven Words,* attributed to Bede, which ensures protection against all evils and prevents an individual from dying without making his final confession.

PIRAN CACAFAS (πειραν κακαφας): To protect your eyes from all ills, these words should be carved on jasper, with a lizard floating on its belly, and this phylactery should be carried on one's person. The jasper can also be mounted on a ring that, if loaned, will heal ophthalmia. The Greek texts of this prescription carry ΧΟΓΘΕΣΟΓ'ΛΕ, a variant of the Latin manuscripts: κοβοβας.

📖 *Cyranides,* II, Z.

PIRON † PUPICON † DIRON: See *Gon † Bon † Ron †.*

PIX, NIX, NOX: The spell that features these three words was first mentioned by Cesarius of Heisterbach in his book *Dialogue on Miracles* (XII, 1). These particular terms designate torments. The complete spell is: *Pix, nix, nox, vermis, flagra, vincula, pus, pudor, horror.* It perhaps derives from a Greek list of demons: Ραξ Ριξ Ρηξ.

P.N.B.: In the fifteenth century when a woman had heavy menstrual periods she was given bullhorn shredded into wine and was made to carry a note on which was written: *P.N.B.C.P.X.A.O.P.I.L. In nomine patris et fily et spiritus sancti.*
 📖 Zingerle, 177.

P.N.T.C.O.T.O.T.I.G.P.P.T.ET 2 S: To stop a woman's bleeding, this spell should be written on a piece of parchment and placed on her chest. For a man, this parchment should be placed over his heart with this inscription: *p.n.p.a.s.5.x.a.es.a'.a.n'.z.e.ey'.*
 📖 Braekman, no. 20.

PORO. POTA. VERO ZEBERA: To banish fever, the person must take an apple, cut it into three pieces in the name of the Father, the Son, and the Holy Ghost, draw a cross on each piece, and then write:

> *Poro. Pota. Vero zebera. Maraim baraym. Paraclytus spiritus vincit. Christus regnat. Christus imperat.*

> [*Poro. Pota. Vero zebera. Maraim baraym.* The Paraclete spirit vanquishes, Christ rules, Christ commands.]

The patient must be urged to ingest one piece of the apple a day for three days.
 📖 Haust, 123ff.

PORO, POTA, ZABA, ZARO, ZARAI: These words are spoken while brewing a beverage that is given to someone to drink whom a serpent or other "worm" has jabbed. Another close spell (see *Poro. Pota. Vero zebera*) that comes from the same source is used to treat fever. *Poro* could well be the anagram of *Pater te oro*, "Father, I beg you."

The Royal Manuscript 12 B.XXV from the British Library suggests another reading: *Porro Porro Poto Zelo Zelo Zebeta Arra Array Praclitus* (folio 62 v°).

📖 Hunt, 75.

PORTO HAMASIAS F EMANUEL F DORENUS: These words offer protection from curses and evil spells when written on paper and carried on one's person.

✦ *Perlo.*
📖 BBE, 13.

P P P: The beginning of the text on a Christian amulet for travelers, which was recorded in sixteenth-century England. It is recommended that "it must never be spoken but carried."

p p p c g e g a q q est p t I k a b g l k 2 a x t g t b a m g 2 4 2 1 qp x c g k q a 9 9 p o q q r

The downstroke of the first two *p*'s is barred, and the *q* from the sequence "2 4 2 1" represents *quem*.

📖 Scot, Book XII, chapter 9.

P P z F z S S: Common abbreviation in the grimoires for "in the name of the Father, the Son, and the Holy Ghost." The *z* represents *and*.

✠ PRAX ✠ MAX DEUS I MAX ✠: These words appear in the body of a spell intended to cure the victim of a rabid dog bite.

O rex gloria Iesu Christe, veni cum pace. In nomine patris max, in nomine filii max, in nomine spiritus sancti prax: Gasper, Melchior, Balthasar ✠ prax ✠ max ✠ Deus I max ✠.

📖 Scot, Book XII, chapter 14.

PRINCES OF HELL: Lucifer, Belial, Astaroht, Satanas, Anumbes, Dryttianus, Drakeus.

✦ *Names of demons.*
📖 BBE, 27.

PRIOL FOLFAT FROFALL. GT. C. H. + F. T. G. A. T TZ TT:
This spell will make a love charm effective. It was recorded by Christian Heuschkhel, a forester of Neustadt s/Orla in Thuringia, in Germany, who lived during the eighteenth century.
📖 Peuckert, *Pansophie*, 386.

PRITAG † STROLAG † BRYSA † BORA †:
To stop a nosebleed, these words would be written on something that was then attached beneath the nose of the person who was bleeding.
📖 Ohrt II, 100.

PRORSUS MORTUUS DIREA KATHOCA:
It was believed in the fifteenth century that these words could heal snakebite. They followed a curse that addressed the reptile as a "serf of the devil." This spell is derived from *Ortus, mortuus*.
📖 Munich, Germany, Bavarian National Library, ms. Clm 27105, folio 77 v°.

P. R. Q. F. R. P. P. T. T. A P R. N.:
The magical *caracteres* from an eighteenth-century charm of protection against hits and bladed weapons. They must be written in bat's blood and attached to the arm.
📖 Peuckert, *Pansophie*, 386.

PSALMS:
Out of all Christian texts, the Psalms were the most used in magic, often accompanied by magical *caracteres*. We can see that the Jewish influence was quite significant if we refer to the *Sepher Shimmush Tehillim*, a treatise on the use of the Psalms taken from the practical Kabbalah, written in the thirteenth century by Shem Tov Ben Isaac of Tortosa. Let's first take a look at the uses gleaned from those Psalms that were used by themselves, with the understanding that this overview will only provide a representative sampling of the many uses.

First, Psalm 8 is used to ensure that a child's birth is easy; then Psalm 12 is used against thieves; Psalm 15 against the evil eye, Psalm 22 for not getting lost; Psalm 26 for planting vineyards and for good fortune; Psalm 34 to be freed of the necessities and to prevent wine from going sour; Psalm 24 for sleeping; Psalm 25 for dispelling evil spells; Psalm 35 for aiding childbirth; Psalm 36 to destroy an enemy; Psalm 38 against bad dreams; Psalm 42 to send enemies fleeing; Psalm 50 to recover stolen property (same thing with Psalm 119), to make oneself invisible, and to stop blood loss; Psalm 56 to banish fear of animals; Psalm 57 for banishing enchantments; Psalm 58 for impotence; Psalm 73 to have one's wishes granted; Psalm 84 to gain luck; Psalm 91 for conjuring serpents away; and Psalm 130 for unmasking a thief. Psalm 90 was used into the twentieth century as a phylactery as it forms a breastplate around one. It will be recalled that Psalm 109 (108) was greatly used as a curse because it is an imprecatory psalm.

These are the magical virtues of the Psalms when combined with magic *caracteres:* Psalm 2 for repelling bad moods, Psalm 5 for getting a loan, Psalms 9 and 14 for introducing oneself to a king or prince, Psalm 10 for destroying the house of an enemy, Psalm 16 for avoiding scandal and discord, Psalm 18 for a rapid birth, Psalm 19 for gaining the favor of one's lord, Psalms 20 and 81 to ensure a warm welcome, Psalm 21 for giving one no call to dread evil people, Psalm 28 for healing lunatics, Psalms 17 and 29 for disease and healing, Psalm 30 for prisoners, Psalm 32 against female sterility, Psalm 39 against false labor, Psalm 52 for inspiring the dread of all, Psalm 60 for having one's love reciprocated, Psalm 61 for scattering one's enemies, Psalm 63 for defeating one's enemy, Psalm 68 for mollifying one's enemy, Psalm 80 for staunching blood flow, and Psalm 85 to ensure that the wine is good.

In the sixteenth century, Reginald Scot mentioned a means of taking action against witches. It required the backward recitation of the words from the following verses of the Psalms: *Domine Deux noster* (8:10), *Dominus illuminatio mea, Domine exaudi orationem meam* (101, 2), and *Deus laudem meam ne tacueris* (108:2), after having crafted a volt (*voult*) and suffumigating it with a rotten bone. According to *The Lesser Key of Solomon,* when the virgin wax intended for magic workings is consecrated, it is necessary to recite nineteen psalms along with a conjuration. Iron objects require seven psalms and a prayer, while all virgin parchment needs is a spell followed by Psalm 72.

The best examples of the use of the Psalms for magical purposes are from a fifteenth-century Florentine manuscript in which ninety psalms are cited (illustrations below), and a grimoire with the title *Secrets of*

Saint Gertrude, whose recipes were falsely attributed to this thirteenth-century Cistercian nun, and another grimoire titled The *6th and 7th Books of Moses,* which includes an appendix on "the use and efficacy of the Psalms and their various purposes." These texts combine *caracteres* with the Psalms.

For its part, the *Sepher Shimmush Tehillim* indicates which verses of the Psalms to write and the divine name necessary to add to each one. Here are several examples. Against a premature birth, the first four verses of the first Psalm are combined this way to *Ashray* (happy), *L* (step), *Yatzliah* (will succeed), and *Derech* (route). The second Psalm is used against the dangers of a storm at sea, the third against back pain and headaches, the sixth against all eye disorders, the tenth against unclean spirits, the forty-fourth provides protection from one's enemies, the fifty-eighth prevents a dog who is attacking someone from doing him any harm, and so on.

Extracts from the psalms are also found on pentacles, especially in the tradition of *The Lesser Key of Solomon.*

Psalm 23:7   Psalms 69:23, and 135:16   Psalm 116:16ff.

📖 *Clavicules* II, 17–19; Florence, Italy, Laurentian Library, ms. Plut. 89, Sup. 38; Godfrey Selig, trans. *Sepher Shimmush Tehillim or Use of the Psalms for the Physical Welfare of Man. A Fragment Out of the Practical Kabbalah.*; Dürig, "Die Verwendung des sogenannten Fluchpsalms 108 (109) im Volksglauben und in der Liturgie," 1–84; Aubigné, *L'Escalade,* appendix § IV, 28 (amulet representing Psalm 57).

† P. T. K. V. C. P. P. Q. Q. Q. N.: If someone hates you and you want him to fear you, you must write these letters on an animal hide and place it near his head while he is sleeping.

📖 Braekman, no. 235.

P XX: These are the first magical *caracteres* of a series accompanied by Kabbalistic signs that form an amulet against serpent venom, poisons, betrayals, and evil spells.

$$P\ XX\ O + V\ \Upsilon\ L3 + A + \text{\textcircled{?}} + M\ A + + 1\ Z + 6\ X\ X\ X$$

Variants: *[handwritten variants]*

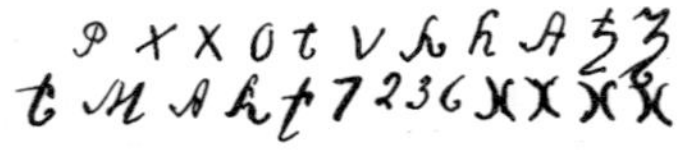

It is possible that *P* would be the Greek *rho* and *X* the Greek *chi*; *PXX* would then represent Christ.

📖 Bang, no. 1104; Horsley and Waterhouse, 211–30.

ΦΕΥΓΕ: In the fourth century to heal a sty, the individual would prick it with the end of nine barley grains while saying each time:

φευγε φευγε, χρείων σε διχει

📖 Marcellus VIII, 193.

Φυρφαραν: This word, when written on virgin parchment and attached to one's person with a string, was believed to cure rheum during the fourth century.

📖 Marcellus VIII, 56

P459, F1392, C49947p92, 582, F3662: Encrypted spell that reads like this: "To corrupt a girl, you must say and carry on your person while touching her hand with your own, the following words: *Bestarbesto, corrumpat viscera cujus mulieris.*"

📖 *Secrets magiques pour l'amour,* no. XXVII.

QAMLA: The first word in a long spell that is described as a "very useful prayer," whose purpose is not given. It must be written on a piece of paper, then hung around the individual's neck with a silk ribbon.

Qamla Clebsin Luo f lesmo optime Pilium Faut apta Sant Filionna nostra Rum.

The ending seems to be a corruption of *apta sunt filiorum nostrorum*. The presence of *apta* would indicate that it involves binding something or someone.

✦ *Qvinta*.
 Bang, no. 1174b.

Q F: This is the abbreviation of *quid faciunt*, the last of Christ's words: *Ignosce illis quia nesciunt quid faciunt* (Forgive them for they know not what they do), taken from the Gospel of Luke (23:34). This is another phrase that forms part of Bede's *Orison of Seven Words* (or attributed to him), which ensures protection against all misfortune and prevents an individual from dying unconfessed.

Q. H. N. C. F. A. RE.: This is a typical amulet spell that is found on a Latin charm intended to facilitate childbirth.
 Franz II, 201.

† Q. P. X. T. G. Y. H.: In fourteenth-century France, in order to learn if someone would recover from illness, this would be written on an egg that had been laid on the day when the illness began: it would be peeled the next day, and if it was found to be healthy, that meant that the patient would be cured.
 Paris, National Library, ms. Latin 8654 B.

Q.T.P.M.: Abbreviation of *qui tollit peccata mundi* (who takes on the sins of the world) that appears on a Spanish amulet that is supposed to spare its owner from catastrophes.

📖 *Gran Grimorio*, 1746.

QVINTA: This is the lead-in to the spell *Qvinta Cerbumluo Climu optima Pellium opta faut filliorum nostra*, which must be written on a slip of paper that is next dipped into the blood of a billy goat in which a snake's head has been placed. It is used as a lure for fish.

The variants unfortunately do not make any more sense, but a request for good fishing in Latin can be made out in them.

1 (1750)	2 (1822)	3 (1800)
Qvinta, Corbula, Olium Optima sunt. Siliorum nostra †.	*Qvento, Cerbulono, Liurne Optim, pillium, opta Sant Tillierum, Nostra*	*Quitta cerbunt volimus optima piscium, exte sunt filiorum nose.*

4 (1800)	5 (1700)	6 (1780)
Pelium, Qvinta cerbo in lies Climo optime Natranum	*Nolimun Optima Primum, esta, sunt, Silicrum, Nostra*	*Cgumlo Cleboin Luo Flome optimia Pilium fleut apla samt filiorma Nostrarum*

These corruptions offer a good example of a charm transmitted orally.

📖 Bang, no. 1174.

QUOSUM SINOBIA ZENNI TANTUS LECT VERI: To stop the pain of a toothache, it is necessary to write these words on a piece of paper and attach it to the jaw.

📖 *Egyptian Secrets* I, 173.

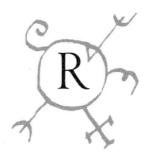

† R A B H Q †: These are the opening *caracteres* for a spell that works against ulcers in both humans and animals. The entire spell (see below) is written on a piece of paper that is then placed over the painful area.

† *R a b h q* † *H a s b a* † *E b n L H*
a † *K a c K a a b u l a* † *K a s H a S*
† *a* † *a o* † *b* † *o* † † † *o* †

📖 *Egyptian Secrets* I, 212.

RABI HABI GABI: To heal intermittent fever, these words are written on a piece of bread that is then eaten. It is almost certainly a variant of *Habi Dabi*. Also see *Abia, Dabi,* and *Habere*.

📖 Ohrt II, 123.

RABUN RATTACU FLUXA MAX PARVENECH: To uncover a thief's identity, these words are written on a piece of cheese that is then given to the suspected individual to eat. If the person cannot swallow it, that is proof of his or her guilt.

📖 Bang, no. 1065.

RACK SMACK STRACK: This is a magic spell for treating fractures that dates from the end of the Middle Ages. It can be deciphered as "pull, stick together, hold!"

📖 Heidelberg, Germany, University Library, Cpg 267, folio 77 r°.

RADITUS OSTRATA ERIMAS: By owning a talisman engraved with these words and by saying the spell *Raditus Polastrien Terpanau Ostrata Pericatur Erimas,* one can be transported to wherever one wishes to go.

📖 *Trésor,* 179b.

† RAERE † REDUCAT † RAROUT † JESUS † MOMATHYS: This phrase was used in Holland as part of *Saint Hubert's Charm* to heal skin rashes and inflammations.

📖 Van Haver, no. 59.

RANGARUA GAUERBAT: In order to prevent a burn from becoming infected, people would repeat these words three times, lick the burn three times, then spit.

📖 Önnerfors, 34.

RANMIGAN ADONAI: This is the beginning of a spell against diarrhea that was contained in a letter brought to Rome by an angel—perhaps one of the three archangels. This is a very long spell that also requests the assistance of Saint Veronica (Beronice).

Ranmigan adonai. eltheos. mur. O ineffabile. omiginan. midannian. misane. dimas. mode. mida. memagar. em. Orta min. sigmone. Beronice. irritas. uenas. quasi dulap. fervor. fruxantis. guinis. siccatur. fla fracta. frigula. mirgui etsihdon. segulta. frautantur. arno. midomnis. abar vetlio. sydone. multo. saccula. pp pppp sother. sother. Miserere mei Deus. Deus mi. AMHN. Alleluiah. Alleluiah.

Ranmigan adonai is the corrupted form of the Hebrew *rav magen*, "powerful shield;" *eltheos*, a compound word, is a mixture of this language with Greek, and means "God God." Thanks to a Dutch manuscript from the fifteenth century, we know that *sigmone* means "blood" (*sanguis*). The sequence *Beronice . . . siccatur* has been deciphered as "Veronica, you have irritated the veins like a pain[?]; the boiling of the flowing blood has dried up." Other variations of this incantation are used against bleedings and the plague.

♦ *Ka.*
📖 Storms, no. 35; Berthoin-Mathieu, 146.

RAPA. R. TARN. TETRAGRAMMATEN ANGELI: This spell from the *Livret de Romain* closes with I.N.R.I., a blessing intended to paralyze firearms and other weapons. The caster asks the aid of Jesus, the Three Magi, the four evangelists, and Saint Uriel.

📖 *Grimoires*, no. 268.

RATALIBUS: A reductive spell for the elderly when they suffer from a toothache. The word is copied over and over with a letter subtracted each time. This is then finished with the following inscription:

R + ✖ NB + + + iii

The symbol represents the animal that is gnawing on the teeth and causing the pain. Oddly enough, it is strongly reminiscent of a figure from *The Lesser Key of Solomon*. But other grimoires, such as the *Kvam Grimoire,* for example, show only the reductive spell.

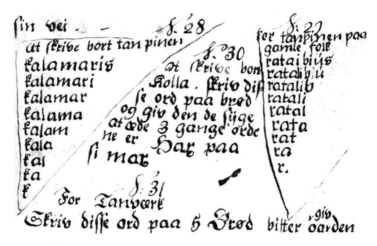

📖 Espeland, no. 29.

RAT PAT CAT: It was once believed that no one could be defeated at cards if he wrote these words with the blood of a black dog.

📖 BBE, 89.

RATOR: First in a series of ten names featured in a fifteenth-century incantation for inspiring the love of a woman, and also reputed to sow fears and terror (*nomina pauentia et trementia*).

Rator. Lampoy. Despan. Brulo. Dronoth. Maloqui. Satola. Gelbid. Mascifin. Nartim. Lodoni.

The texts do not make it possible to know whether these are the names of spirits or magic words.

📖 *Liber incantationum,* folio 10 v°.

† RAY † ROY † LAMITABAT † CASSAMUS: To prevent dogs from barking, this spell must be spoken in a place where there are crosses.

Variant: *† Roy † oy † lamitabat † cassamus.*

📖 Ghent, Belgium, University Library, ms. 1021 A, folio 145 r°; Braekman, no. 228.

RECABUSTIRA: This is the first word in a reductive spell that is reduced one syllable at a time, not one letter.

Recabustira, Cabustira, Bustira, Tira, Ra, A.

The spell was used to materialize the magic carpet necessary for the interrogation of spirits, after the recitation of a prayer that began with *Agla,* which was repeated three times. At the end of the ritual, *Recabustira* and the other syllables were repeated three times, with the addition of *Karkahita, Kahita, Hita, Ta, a.* The answers to the questions asked of the spirits would then be obtained.

📖 *Clavicules* I, 13.

REDUCTIVE SPELL: To cause a disease to retreat and thus heal the patient, the caster takes a word, most often a palindrome—a long one preferably—and reduces it by subtracting a letter from it each day until it is no more than an initial. An example of this can be seen on this fifth-century tablet that holds a charm for calming anger. It is a palindrome accompanied by a cluster of twelve magical names to its right.

The Kabbalistic term *Abracadabra* is one of the oldest examples of such a reductive phrase. Appearing as early as the eleventh century BCE, it was inscribed on an amulet in Greek letters spelling *a ba ga da*. *Abracadabra* was used in 1790 against cold fever, as was *ALMgata*, not to mention *Catanomare* (in 1789). Around 1777–1789, we find *Katalibus, Kalamaris, Cattatibusantrakus* and *Ratalibus*, and *TANVERKKU* in 1815, and *Horiandus* in 1850 to be used for a toothache. Around 1830, *Aur(a)tabul* (*Auratabuk*) made it possible to bind a robber.

```
ERÊKISITHPHÊARARACHARARAÊPITHISIKÉRE
 RÊKISITHPHÊARARACHARARAÊPHTHISIKÊR
  ÊKISITHPHÊARARACHARARAÊPITHISIKÊ
   KISITHPHÊARARACHARARAÊPHTHISIK
    ISITHPHÊARARACHARARAÊPHTHISI
     SIKÊREARARACHARARAÊPHTHIS
      IKÊREARARACHARARAÊPHTHI
       KÊREARARACHARARAÊPHTH
        PHÊARARACHARARAÊPH
         ÊARARACHARARAÊ
          ARARACHARARA
           RARACHARARA
            ARACHARAR
             ACHARA
              RCHAR
               A
```

```
              OPL.
         OMURTILOPLÊX
        EXANAKERÔNITHA
         LAMPSAMERÔ
         LAMPSAMAZÔN
          BASUMIAO
        OPLOMURTILOPLÊX
           ANACHAZA
        EXANAKERONITHA
          ANAXARNAXA
        KERASPHAKERÔNAS
       PHAMETATHASMAXARANA
        BASUMIAÔIAKINTHO
```

📖 Bang, no. 1043–54.

REGNAB † SADAY: These words appear in a charm intended to free one from persecution and unfair trials, and to allow one to remain at liberty when facing criminal charges. The powers whose assistance is invoked include, among others, the archangels, the angels, the cherubs, then all the saints. Following the invocation, this is said:

Amedam † Austis † Memor † Gedita † Eleison † Igion † Frigam † Fides † Valey † Unis † Regnab † Sasay † Afios Athanatos.

📖 *Enchiridion* (Spanish), Oracion misteriosa para librarse de persecuciones, procesos jnjustos y salir bien librado en causas crjminales.

REMAN: To compel the devil to appear before him, the caster would draw a circle at a crossroads, in which he drew a cross with the names of the Trinity on it, on three successive Thursday mornings. This word would be drawn each time.

📖 Ohrt I, no. 987.

RESTIA CLASTA: In the nineteenth century, for removing all kinds of curses, it was necessary to take a sheep's heart, pierce it with nails, then hang it from the chimney while saying: *Restia clasta, avarro, chasta, castadia, dara, N.*

Then one said over the sheep's body: *Il nye et bovuite.* In this way one was able to get a grip on the heart of a sorcerer, who would come to ask for mercy.

📖 *Le médecin des pauvres.*

RETTEREN SALIBAT HISATER CRATARES: To recognize plants and minerals and to know their medicinal properties, one would carry a talisman carved with these four words; they would also be spoken in the presence of the patient.

📖 *Trésor,* 182a.

REX. PAX. NAX.: This spell, which can be found in an eleventh-century English charm against migraines, must be written on the jaw of a person suffering from a toothache, and he or she will be cured. In Holland, the spell was written this way in the fifteenth century: *rex pax nox in filio Dei.* In Germany, it was written as *REX, PAX, MAX, PRO* with a nail from a horseshoe on three roads. This nail would then be hammered into a wall, and the individual would suffer no more from a toothache as long as the nail remained there. What is at work in this spell is the transfer of the problem into something else, a common action in folk medicine.

📖 Munich, Germany, Bavarian National Library, Cgm 92, folio 7c; Heidelberg, Germany, University Library, Cpg 267, folio 14 v°; Storms, no. 51; London, British Library, Harley 585, folio 184 r°; Braekman, no. 118; Baldinger, "Aberglaube und Volksmedizin in der Zahnheilkunde"; Gallée, 459.

RHIBARIM RIBHARIM CAYPHARIM CAYPHARIM DYAPHARIM DYAFORIM: This spell forms part of a complex ritual that takes place when the moon is in Taurus. This phrase must be repeated twenty times. Its purpose is to compel the appearance of a man to whom the caster will address his request, and the example that illustrates the ritual depicts a pauper who, thanks to the ritual, discovers a treasure. In the Arab source text, the spell reads this way: *Rabqar rabqâr 'iqâm taqfûr taqfûr.*

📖 *Picatrix* IV, 3; *Gâyat al-Hakîm*, 310.

RIBALD: This is one of the three words to speak aloud when knotting the britches' laces, in other words cursing a man with sexual impotence. *Ribald* is said when making the first knot while also making the sign of the cross. *Notal* is the word for the second knot, also accompanied by a sign of the cross, and finally *Vanarbi* for the third knot. It also requires the sign of the cross. This action must be performed at a certain time during Mass. It should be noted that *ribald* means "debauched!"

📖 Thiers IV, 582, 585.

RITAS OMBAS ZAMARATH: These words are used to acquire knowledge of the art or science in which one would like to shine. To transmit it to another, one says: *Ombas serpitas Quitathar Zamarath.*

📖 *Trésor*, 181a–b.

R. O. A. V A G X W: For deliverance from all misfortunes, God's aid is requested with the series of following *caracteres:*

R. O. A. V A G X w Grammata Thrachotin S Palleo Zobola sa Rex on thiothr.

The first two words refer to Tetragrammaton, the last to Sother.

📖 Aymar, 327.

ROKES ZOTOAS: To win at games of chance, one uses a die on which *Rokes Zotoas Xatanitos Pilatus Tulitas* has been carved, and it is sufficient to just speak these five words aloud.

 📖 *Trésor,* 183b–84a.

RØYSEHAMPIS RABIS: To win at cards, take a cat, cut a notch in its ear in the name of the devil, and with its blood, write these words on your left hand with a new quill.

 📖 Bang, no. 1133.

R R T. F. A. A. Q F. O. Q. Q. B. .V.: An Icelandic manuscript provides these *caracteres,* with the explanation, "If you want your enemy to fear you, carry these signs in your left hand!"

 📖 Saemundsson, no. 2.

RUBRIES RISCAS MELONES: A spell for conjuring demon attacks.

 📖 Heim, 551.

RUN RAS: To win a woman's love and fill her with desire to come to you, say:

Run Ras Paxifarmo
Granduras Denclifaq, Panta Silante

 One adds, "I conjure you by the four winds, by the ember and the coal, and by the devil Cojuelo, and by all the demons . . ." *Granduras* and so forth probably designate the winds. Cojuelo is a legendary demon of Castilian tradition, the limping devil who was quite popular in the seventeenth century. He can be seen mainly in the writings of Miguel de Cervantes and those of Velez de Guevera (1641).

 📖 Werner, no. 41, 205.

RUSIRIAB: This word forms part of the spell *Rusiriab* † *Sidrach* † *Phaas* † *Smisorich* † *Misael* † *Misach* † *Hertz vil din Ortz Amen.* To protect the house from fire, it would be inscribed on lead and placed at the four corners of the dwelling. It is common knowledge that these areas of the house were sacred to the household spirits that allegedly resided there. The German words *Hertz vil din Ortz* make no sense. It is easy to see that an idiom foreign to the scribe was incorporated into magic words by then. In the seventeenth century, the spell read like this:

Ruaiab † *sidrach* † *Srhaas* † *smisach* † *Misaell* † *misach* † *smitz vie Mels* † *Amen.*

We can recognize highly corrupted forms of the name of only one child in the furnace mentioned in the Bible (Daniel 3:51–90). Here the German can be translated as "melt away like fat!"

📖 Bang, no. 1088, 1297, 1305, 1195 (only one man is mentioned); Ohrt II, 124; Franz II, 375, 484.

S

SABOR. † SELES. † SELAS.: These are the opening words of a spell that says if a person wishes to have no fear of thieves and brigands, and to prevent any harm befalling him at their hands, "he should carry these three names" on his person:

Sabor. † seles. † selas. † bo. † N. V. [. . .] TetragrammatoN

It should probably be taken as meaning the first three words.

📖 Aymar, 346.

SADAIJ AMARA ELON PHENETON: When the Hebrews left Egypt, Moses caused manna to rain from heaven and water to gush out of the rock by using these words, among which we can recognize names of God:

Sadaij amara elon pheneton eloij eneij ebeoel messias ijahe vebu hejiane, ijananel elijon.

They should be used when an individual finds himself in great distress or when he wishes to perform wonders. *Sadaij* is the Hebrew *shaddaï* (שדי), meaning "all-powerful" and *elon* must be *elyon* (עליון), "supreme."

📖 *Semiphoras* II, 7.

SADAY HAYLOCS LUCAS ELACYUNS JACONY: These are the opening words that are inscribed on the forehead of the high priest Aaron when he speaks to the Creator. They have the power to ensure that all one's wishes are granted.

Saday haylocs Lucas elacyuns jacony hasihaia yeinino, sep, actitas barne lud doneny eya iebu reu, vaha, vailia, eye. Vie hahya hoya saya salna hahai, cuci yaya. Elenehel, na vena; setua.

📖 *Semiphoras* II, 5.

SADIES SATANI AGIR FONS TORIBUS: If an individual wishes to discover a treasure, he should make his way to the place where he believes one can be found and speak these words while striking the ground three times with his left heel, then do it again, three times in a row.

📖 Honorius, 103.

SAGAROTH: This is the beginning of a spell that is presented as a "remedy by the prayers and orisons of Pope Leo III," but which does not appear in that individual's *Enchiridion*.

> *Sagaroth † Aspanidore † paatia † vra jodion † Samacron † Fondon Aspargon Alamar Bourgavis Veniat. Serebonis,* one adds the word that has been made flesh and dwelt among us.

📖 *Le médecin des pauvres.*

S A M A: For a miller to always have grain to grind, he should write the following on lead and conceal in a secret hole in the mill:

> *S A M A ω ε ρ α υ z ε λ α Kηxes ampes rabs rors Kiend blode profinize.*

The spell combines Latin, Greek, and Danish, and is completely incomprehensible.

📖 Ohrt II, 125.

SANCITAN SANAMIEL SAMAFOELIS: To win the love of a young woman, you must whisper these words in her ear.

📖 Brussels, Royal Library, ms. IV 9588, fifteenth century, folio 12 r°.

SANGUET † CHRISTI † SIT † INTER † TE † ET ME †: In the Vaud canton of Switzerland during the eighteenth century, this spell was alleged to have the power to stop an enemy if spoken aloud.

📖 Hervé, 365.

SANTIKAPOUPIWAÏEIMONTIRAKAKARA: An Egyptian book of hermetic medicine conserved in London passed down this spell "against the Asian disease as the Cretans call it." It must be spoken aloud over a vase containing urine and another liquid.

📖 Lexa I, 66.

SAOS DRAOS DIDIMOS: An eighteenth- or nineteenth-century manuscript in the Romanian Academy Library in Bucharest gives this spell against fevers:

> *Saos draos didimos*
> *Saos draos didimos*
> *Saos draos didimos*

📖 Bucharest, Romanian Academy Library, ms. BAR 1123, folio 36 v°.

SARAIOUA SARAPHAEL: To reveal the identity of a thief, a person should write *saraioua* on a crust of bread and *saraphael* on a piece of cheese. The guilty individual will be unable to eat either.

Variant: sarson Sampson.
📖 Franz II, 336.

SARBASMISARAB: A magic word used with *caracteres* to bewitch horses and prevent them from winning races. The opisthographic tablet (written on both sides) was discovered in Hadrumetum, a port of Roman Africa.

Sarbasmisarah ⊕ θ ỿ Ƶ ᙠ ⊁ ⊃ ỿ

📖 Audollent, 378–80.

SARITAP PERMISOX OTTARIM: These words make it possible to open any lock without a key and to prevent any kind of detention. They must be engraved on a talisman whose ring must touch the lock at the time this spell is spoken.

📖 *Trésor,* 180a.

SATAN ADAMA: These two words provide the first two lines of the following magic square, which has been connected to the Knights Templar:

> S A T A N
> A D A M A
> T A B A T
> A D A M A
> N A T A S

SATOJ(R): The magic square *Sator Arepo Tenet Opera Rotas* was used to protect livestock from all evil spells. In Poland the following spell would be written on a black tablet or paper, then hung in barns or stables:

SATOJ(R)
AREPO
TENET
OPERA
ROTAS

It was also used to halt fire: it would be written down, then cast into the fire. It was used against rabies, and, in the following form when written on three sheets of paper that the patient would ingest over three days, it would cause fever to drop:

SATAR
APIRA
TITIT
ARIPA
RATAS

Very widespread in Europe, the spell has countless corrupted variants, such as these listed by Daiva Vaitkevičienė:

+ SATOR + AREPO TENET OPERA + ROTAS +	S+A+T+O+R A+R+E+P+O T+E+N+E+T O+P+E+R+A R+O+T+A+S	Sator apero tenet orepa rotas	R A T A S A R E P A T E N E T A P E R A S A T A R
s. o. t. o. r. o. p. e. r. o. t. e. p. e. t. o. r. e. p. o. r. o. t. o. s.	Sotor Opero tenet Orepo rotas	s. o. t. o. r. o. p. e. r. o. t. e. p. e. t. o. r. e. p. o. r. o. t. o. s.	X SATUR X AREPA TEVET APERA X RUTAS X

Satar Apira Titit Aripa Ratas	SATAR APIRA TITIT ARIPA RATAS	SATAR ARIPA TINIT APIRA RATAS	+++++ Sator +++++ arepo +++++ tenet +++++ opera +++++ rotas

SATOJ(R)
AREPO
TENET
OPERA
ROTAS

📖 Vaitkevičienė, no. 1376–92, 1533, 1625 (spell from Lithuania), 1377 (spell from Poland).

SATOR: The first recorded instance of the spell *Sator Arepo Tenet Opera Rotas* dates back to the year 70 AD. It was found in a Christian church in Pompeii. However, it was reversed and depicted in the following form: *ROTAS / OPERA / TENET / AREPO / SATOR*. It also appeared on other buildings elsewhere, such as among the graffiti of Bonaguil Castle (Perigord region of France).

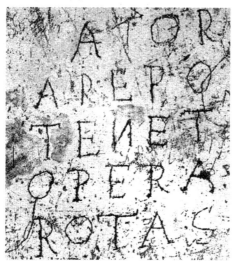

The spell gave rise to a slew of possible interpretations, which can be found in the study by Harald Fuchs that has the merit of demonstrating that the spell contains a cross formed by *TENET* in the center of the square, which I will show by putting those letters in bold:

S A **T** O R
A R **E** P O
T E N E T
O P **E** R A
R O **T** A S

This has been interpreted to mean, "The laborer Arepo carefully guided the plow," "The worker holds the wheels, the sower the plow," "With his chest the sower maintains the wheels (of the world), his work," and many other things that have no relationship to the spell's use. An abbreviation for a monastic precept was read into it (*SAT ORARE POTENter ET OPERAre RatiO TuA Sit*) by those who had forgotten that the spell had been in use long before the formulation of this precept! It was generally accepted that *Sator* designated God insomuch as the begetter of gods and men (*deorum genitor atque hominum sator*), and an exhaustive search was made for its meaning by those who had forgotten that a magic spell is encrypted and its users certainly never sought to penetrate its secret. Undoubtedly its obscure nature was regarded, as in many other cases, as a guarantee of its efficacy.

In fact, the magic square conceals the name of God. It is enough to replace the letters by their place number in the alphabet, then add together the two figures of the results to prove:

SATOR	19	1	20	15	18	= 73	7 + 3 = 10
AREPO	1	18	5	16	15	= 55	5 + 5 = 10
TENET	20	5	14	5	20	= 64	6 + 4 = 10
OPERA	15	16	5	18	1	= 55	5 + 5 = 10
ROTAS	18	15	20	1	19	= 73	7 + 3 = 10
	= 73	55	64	55	73		

The sum of the two figures resulting from the addition is 10, no matter in what direction it is read. Zero does not count, as today when the proof is made by 9, and thus the answer remains 1, in other words the One, the Only, God. And if any shred of doubt remains, the fact that *TENET* forms a cross in the center of the square should lift that doubt. Let's now take a look in what domains this spell was employed.

† *sator. Arepo. tenet. Opera. Rotas* can be read in an eleventh-century Christian charm intended to provide an easy childbirth. Another one, found in a manuscript of the *Letter of Hippocrates* (thirteenth century) indicates that "this text should be attached to the belly of the woman in labor:"

Maria peperit Christum † *Anna Mariam* † *Elisabeth Johannem* † *Celina Remigium* † *sator* † *arepo* † *tenet* † *opere* † *rotas*

A third charm, in Middle English and Latin, placed *rotas* after several Christian phrases.

Christus † *vincit* † *Christus* † *regnat* † *Christus* † *imperat* † *Christus* † *te* † *vocat* † *mundas* † *te* † *gaudet* [. . .] † *a* † *g* † *l* † *a* † *alpha* † *et o* †

In another incantation, dating from the fifteenth century and intended to drive away the storm demon, the spell appears twice. First it appears following a citation of the antiphon *O clauis David,* one of the seven antiphons of the Christian vigil, then after the incantation, strictly speaking, that expels the demon from inhabited areas.

1. *O clauis David et sceptrum domus Israel, qui aperis et nemo claudit, claudis et nemo aperit. Tetragrammaton. Alleluia. Sator Arepo Tenet Opera Rotas.*

[O key of David and scepter of the house of Israel, you who open what one can close and close what one can open. Tetragrammaton . . .]

Then comes the conjuration:

2. *Coniuro te, demon, per deum unum . . .*

[I conjure you, demon, by the one God . . .]

3. † *Sator Arepo Tenet Opera Rotas.* † *Crux est uerum signum.* † *Crux est reparacio* † *per hoc signum crucis fuge demon* † *Regia nosaan et gyran . . .*

[Sator . . . The cross is the true symbol, the cross is reparation, by this sign flee demon . . .]

We do not know the meaning of the last three words, and we presume that *Regia,* the word before them, would be *Ragi El,* "the firmament of God," and that the last one would designate an angel assigned to the month of Kislev, third month of the ecclesiastical year and the ninth month of the Hebrew civil calendar.

In *The Lesser Key of Solomon, Sator* opens an incantation intended to acquire grace and love, and it is represented on the second pentacle of Saturn, who is good against adversity and is most specifically used to lessen the pride of spirits.

In 1743, Duke Ernst August of Saxony Weimar ordered that all wooden dishes that had already been used be saved in every village. He commanded that an arrow be drawn on each, along with *Sator* and so forth, as well as drawing figures on it on a Friday when the moon was waning between eleven and twelve o'clock, with fresh ink and a new quill. If fire broke out, the dish should be cast into it, in the name of God, and repeated three times, for the fire to go out.

An eighteenth-century grimoire known as the *Romanus Büchlein* (Booklet of Romain) recommended the use of this spell to extinguish a fire without water. All one had to do was write it on both sides of a plate, then toss the plate into the fire. A little later, the spell was given to livestock in their food to protect them from witches and devils. In the nineteenth century, the magic square would be written on a piece of paper, then swallowed for protection against the consequences of a bite from a rabid dog. It also protected one from all kinds of fever if rubbed on one's body. Our spell was corrupted into *Arebrodas* (*Areb[o] rodas*) and carried, written as follows, to protect against dog bites:

Arebrodas
Rebrodas
Ebrodas
Brodas
Rodas
Odas
Das
As

In 1768, it was recommended that a piece of paper on which *Sator* and so forth had been written be glued to the main door of the house. Any thief who looked at the door would be unable to go any farther until this paper had been torn apart. Oddly enough, an entry door to a house in Grenoble shows the magic square on its upper panel.

In 1793, this spell was used in Norway in coscinomancy (divination with a strainer or sieve). In Switzerland, the spell's power was increased by writing it with a needle that had been used to sew a dead person's shroud. In Prussia, the twenty-five letters of the spell were mixed with bread and given to a person under enchantment to eat to break the spell. This had to be eaten for nine days in succession.

In his analysis of the spell, Josef Massenkeil observed that the hardest word to understand is *Arepo*, which is most likely a code. In his Romanian fieldwork, Felix Karlinger collected some extremely interesting information. His informant revealed that "the word should never be spoken aloud and is written in Greek; it includes a hidden meaning that can be read as *apero*. However, *Apero* is a Spanish word and means something close to harness or saddle. One is therefore harnessing the demon, and saddles it without its notice." The magic square should be written on the ground with consecrated chalk that has come from a specific location. To conjure a demon and obtain answers to the questions asked of it, one dances on the letters, beginning with the one in the center and moving in a spiral to end on the letter R, on the right hand side of the top of the square, while chanting certain phrases. To send the demon away, the same operation is performed in the opposite direction.

In the documents contained in the *Sachet accoucheur,* we can find pentacles with the complete spell, but *Sator* appears separately in the list of divine names and descriptive phrases.

† *Agios* † *Sator* † *Helyas* † *Hemanuel* † *orc adonay athanatos* † *otheos* † *Pentaton* † *fons,* † *sapientia* † *virtus* † *paraclitus* † . . .

I would also like to point out a passage from a Leiden manuscript dating from the thirteenth or fourteenth century in which we can read:

Rotas adrepotenat opera sator. Sator adrepotenat opera rotas.

The spell can be found carved on three seventeenth-century rings. The first offers protection against swords, the second from indignity and debauchery, and the third from the anger of the high and mighty and persecution by evil people.

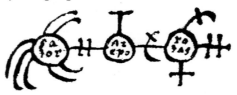

One hundred years later it worked against colic if written this way:

S † a † t † o † r, A † r † e † p † o †
T † e † n † e † t, O † p † e † r † a †
R † o † t † a s

To protect one's animals or people from harmful breezes and pestilences, this spell would be attached to them on a Friday before sunrise at an odd-numbered hour:

SATOR
AREPO
TENET
OPERA
ROTAS
† J † C † S † H S b y 1 S a n n e t.
U S M m a t e r o n n y † S b a b e 2
S †

To learn if a woman was a witch, it was necessary to write:

S A T O R †
Crux Jesu Christi mild epos
A R E P O †
Crux Jesu Christi Mesopos
T E N E T †
Crux Jesu Christi Habenepos
O P E R A
R O T A S

Then cull some Saint John's wort into the piece of paper and enclose the spell and herb in a piece of leather to carry on your person.

Corruptions: *Sacred Magic or the Book of Abraham the Mage* proposes *Salom Arepo Lemel Opera Molas* to win the love of a pope, emperor, or king. The spell can be found in an 1820 grimoire, written as *SatoD Ajebo Teret Obera Roeas!*

📖 Hunt, 98ff., 133; Franz II, 94–95; *Clavicules de Salomon* I, 15, 60, 67; Leiden, Netherlands, University Library, codex Scaligerianus 28; *Galdrakver*, 35–36.; Secret 2, 291; Schulz, 198; *Egyptian Secrets* II, 332; Mowat, 41–68. A bibliography of the old studies and various interpretations of the spell can be found in Fuchs "Die Herkunft der Satorformel," 28–54; Karlinger, 300–303; Massenkeil, 145–50; Cf. Frischbier, 23; Bang, 581; Tettau and Temme, 270; *Romanus=Büchlein vor Gott der Herr bewahre meine Seele, meinen Aus=und Eingang; von nun an bis in alle Ewigkeit, Amen. Halleluja* (Venice, Italy: n.d.), 7, which I (Lecouteux) translated in *The Book of Grimoires*, 191–208; BaK, 86; Coulon, 64 (to facilitate childbirth).

† † † SATORA ROBOTE NETABE RATOTTA. S. †: These words, which are the ending to a prayer, should be spoken when one's feet are in pain. We can recognize an extremely corrupted version of the *Sator Arepo* spell in *Sator arobo tenet abera totta!*

📖 *Egyptian Secrets* II, 76.

SAULE: To banish the effects of firearms, one speaks Christ's words to Saul backward: *Saule, Saule, qui de persequeris?* (Saul, Saul, why do you persecute me?), while adding words that Jean-Baptiste Thiers tells us have no meaning, and he does not tell us what they are.

📖 Thiers I, 365.

SAX, AMON, SAX, ABRASAX: Spell used in Egypt to interrogate the moon; after rubbing your eyes with green and black makeup and then climbing to the roof of your house, this spell must be repeated seven or nine times while this astral body is full.

📖 Lexa I, 86.

SCEABOLES, ARBARON, ELOHI: This is the opening of a spell featured in a working "of experiment with invisibility." It must be spoken within one's heart in a tone of devotion before beginning the operation. The context indicates that it must involve the names of spirits conjured in the name of God (Elohim), as somewhat later, the caster addresses Almiras, "the master of invisibility," and his ministers.

📖 *Clavicula*, 51.

SCHEVA: This magic word forms part of a recipe for winning the love of an individual, as passed down by the *Petit Albert*.

> You shall go on a Friday morning before sunrise to an orchard and harvest from a tree the most beautiful apple you can find; then you shall write your first and last name in your own blood on a small piece of white paper, and on the following line, the first and last name of the person whose love you seek, and you shall try to have three of his or her hairs, which you shall combine with three of your own and use to tie the small note you have written with another on which only the *Scheva* appears, also written in your own blood, then you shall cut the apple in half, remove the seeds, and in their place you shall put the two notes bound with the hairs, and with two small pointed sticks from a green myrtle branch, you will neatly put the two halves back together and dry it in an oven until it has become hard and without any moisture like the dried apples of Lent; you shall next wrap it in laurel leaves and myrtle leaves, and try to place it beneath the head of the bed in which the beloved individual sleeps, without his or her notice, and in a short while, she or he shall show you signs of love.

Scheva is accompanied by this figure.

The Lesser Key of Solomon is the source of this passage, but the word used there is *Sebeva*.

> *Ecris avec de ton sang, ton nom a rebours un autre ou tu aura. Ecrit le nom de celle que tu aime, et un autre ou sera ecrit les mots et caracteres qui suivent* **SCHEVA ♀** *et aiant joint ces trois billets ensemble*

Scheva can also be found in a Colombian charm intended to destroy the potency of a rival in love.

📖 *Petit Albert*, 17ff; Werner, no. 12, 199.

S D S: In Byzantium, John the Baptist and Jesus Christ were invoked against third- and fourth-degree fevers, as well as diurnal and nocturnal fevers, by asking that the patient be delivered from them thanks to the spell:

ς Δ ς μ ϕ β θ. *Ili Ili lama savachthani.*

The phrase, "My God, why have you forsaken me," can be recognized here, preceded by *caracteres* (see *Ely, Hely*).

📖 Tselikas, 75.

S . D . S . F . S.: This is the beginning of a long series of *caracteres* that accompany a complex operation whose purpose is to find a lost object. The caster must hold a new knife in either his right or left hand and set down a *bref* containing the following group:

📖 Heidelberg, Germany, University Library, Cpg 214, folio 55 v°.

SEME(H)T. SEGHEHALT. RAGNAHT.: These are some of the opening words of the nineteenth magical orison from the *Liber iuratus*.

semeht uel semet. seghehalt. ragnaht. reloymal. haguliaz. exhator. hanthomos. lezen. saccail. marab. briamathon. lephez. hiesacco. themay. salaihel. agessomagy. arothatamal.

✦ *Liber iuratus.*
📖 *Liber iuratus*, chap. 29.

SEMESEILAM: It is thought that this word derives from a Hebrew expression meaning "sun of the world" or "eternal sun," or even from the Aramaic *shemi shelam*, "peace is my name." A tablet found in Carthage says, "Semeseilam, the god that illuminates and darkens the world."

📖 Wünsch, no. 4, 248ff.

SEMIPHORAS/SHEHAMPHORAS: This is the title of a grimoire on the unspeakable name of God formed from seventy-two Hebrew letters taken from verses 19–21 in the fourth book of Exodus. It appeared in German in 1686 and was attributed to Solomon. The name is taken from the Hebrew *Shem ha-mephorash* (שם המפורש). In a straight line from the Kabbalah, it uses the numerical value of the letters to find all the divine names. These names are composed of seventy-two groups of three letters, each being the name of an angel. Among other things, this grimoire offers instructions on how to address the elements, spirits, the dead, and so on through two series of magic words. In the *Lemegeton*, the first book of *The Lesser Key of Solomon*, *shehamphoras* designate seventy-two demons, but this most likely means *daimons* in the Greek sense of the term.

The *Liber incantationum* devotes a note to what it calls "*semiforas,* the great name that was written on Aaron's forehead" (folio 106 v°–107 r°).

The first book of *Liber iuratus* (see that entry) provides a version of the *Semiphoras* and adds the name of the angels bearing this "great name of God."

✦ *Abtan, Eliaon, Holomaati, Jod, Lagumen, Letamnin, Lyacham, Maya, Micrato, Saday, Sadaj, Yane, Yeseraye.*

📖 *Semiphoras,* Schäuble edition, 298; Kohler, 19–32; Eisler, 157–59.

SENAPOS ESTAMOS NOTARIN: Carved on a talismanic ring, these words subjugate genies and abort any plans being laid against you. When using the talisman, you say: *Senapos Terfita Estamos Pertifer Notarin.*

📖 *Trésor,* 180a–b.

SENOZAN GORGORA GOBERDON: A prisoner seeking to escape should write these words on a piece of birch bark.

📖 Werner, no. 42, 205.

SEPA † SEPAGA † SEPAGOGA: According to Johann Weyer (*Opera Omnia* V, 8), this spell will stop bleeding. It was used in sixteenth-century England to stop hemorrhages, as in the following charm:

> ✠ *Sepa* ✠ *Sepaga* ✠ *sepagoga* ✠ *sta sanguis in nomine patris* ✠ *podendi* ✠ *& filij* ✠ *podera* ✠ *& spiritus sancti* ✠ *pandorica* ✠ *pax tecum. Amen.*

The reader will note the variation on *podendi* (meaning *potenti,* in other words "all-powerful"); *pandorica* would appear to be derived from *pantocrator,* which has the same meaning.

📖 Scot, Book XII, chapter 18.

SERAPHIE SERAPHIE: This spell is part of a complex ritual that takes place when the moon is in Scorpio, and it requires two earthen incense burners filled with water, a sacrifice, and fire. Its purpose is to cause the appearance of "a man to whom the caster will make his request, and who will fulfill it." The Arab source text presents the spell as: *Šarâfihâ šarâfihâ.*

📖 *Picatrix* IV, 9; *Gâyat al-Hakîm,* 315.

SESENGENBARPHARANGÊS: This term is a *vox mystica* that is associated with the sun and quite common in Greek charms. It is found in spells featuring *Abrasax, Adônai, barbaratham, cheloumbra, Barouch* (blessed), and *Iaô,* as in a love charm written on a lead tablet found in Egypt that dates back to the fourth century.

📖 PGM III, 109ff.; IV, 1805; V, 351, 365; VII, 645–50; Gager, 99, 269.

† SEUS † DEUS † GRATIUS: This is a spell used in Denmark to bind a thief. It is used four times in this charm, which mentions Jesus's encounter with the four thieves. It punctuates the three following conjurations:

> † *Seus* † *deus* † *gratius.* Freeze fast as stone and count for me every blade of grass growing on earth! † *Seus* † *deus* † *gratius.* Freeze fast as stone and count for me all the stars in heaven! † *Seus* † *deus* † *gratius.* Freeze fast as stone and count for me every grain of sand on the shores of the sea! † *Seus* † *deus* † *gratius.*

Seus most likely represents *sanctus*. It will be noted that the charm imposes an impossible task on the robber; it so happens the same strategy is used every time one wishes to rid himself of a spirit or prevent one from approaching. Other variants use poppy seeds or peas to be counted.

📖 Ohrt I, no. 916.

SEVEN SLEEPERS OF EPHESUS: This refers to the legend of Malcus, Maximinus, Martinus, Dionysius, Johannes, Serapion, and Constantine, citizens of Ephesus who sought refuge in a cave of Mount Selyon to escape persecution, a legend that was spread thanks to Gregory of Tours. Insomniacs could find sleep by writing their names on a slip of paper that they placed beneath their pillow. This note also protected them from fever. To cure quartan fever, their names were written down, then dissolved in holy water, which was then given to the patient to drink. They were also invoked against demons, in much the same way as were God, the Virgin Mary, the apostles, and even elves, as in the following Latin charm:

In the name of the Father, the Son, and the Holy Ghost. Amen. I conjure you elves, and all kinds of nocturnal and diurnal demons, by the Father, the Son, the Holy Ghost, and the indivisible Trinity, by the intercession of the blessed still virginal Mary, by the prayers of the prophets, by the merits of the patriarchs, by the suffrages of angels and archangels, by the intervention of the apostles, by the passion of the martyrs, by the faith of the confessors, by the intercession of all the saints, by the seven sleepers whose names are Malchus, Maximinianus, Dionisus, Johannes, Constantinus, Séraphion, and Martinianus, by the name of Sunday that is blessed through the centuries, + *A+G+L+A,* so that you cannot harm or inflict any evil on this servant of God, N., whether he is sleeping or awake. +*Christus vicit* + *Christus regnat* + *Christus imperat* + may Christ bless us and protect us from all evil. Amen. (London, British Library, Sloane 963, folios 9 r°–v°)

In sixteenth-century Iceland, the seven sleepers appear in an epistle that is used to overcome the madness sent by an evil spell caster to afflict someone.

📖 Braekman, no. 111, 262; Hunt, 89; Franz, II, 480–82; Stockholm, Royal Library, ms. XIV in kl. 4°, folio 103; Heidelberg, Germany, University Library, Cpg 267, folio 12 r°; *Galdrakver,* 51; *Acta Sanctorum* July VI, 375–97; Bonser, "The Seven Sleepers of Ephesus"; *Grimoires,* no. 30, 115; Storms, no. 37–38.

SHOURIN, SHOURAN: The beginning of a Coptic spell that must be spoken while preparing a love potion intended to steal the heart of the woman who drinks it.

Shourin, Shouran, Shoutaban, Eibones, Sharsaben.

After the spell, the caster adds: *Klinmas, Klinmas, Masklin.*

📖 Lexa I, 101.

SICILIA: The name of a fever, regarded as a sister of Elia, Vellea, Suffocalia, Commonia, Genia, and Eema. These names vary wildly according to the manuscripts.

Ylia, Sayculia, Violetta, Suppocalia (suffocalia), Senye, Deneya,

Emyta; Parlya (Paralysia), Reptilia, Fugalia, Astrata, Ruta, Ignata; Daliola, Vestalia, Fugalia, Superalia, Affrega, Lilia, Ligalia; Illia, Reptilia, Folia, Suffagalia, Affrica, Filica, Loena or Ignea.

Each name represents a particular ailment, as shown by a twelfth-century German manuscript in which we find: *Nessia, Nagedo, Stechedo, Troppho, Crampho, Gigihte, Paralisis.*

Nagedo is coined from the word *nagen* ("to gnaw, erode"), *Troppho* from *tropfen* ("to drip"), *Crampho* means "cramp," and *Gigihte* means "gout."

✦ *Gylloy, Names of demons.*

📖 London, British Library, Sloane 140; Sloane 389; Sloane 405; Sloane 2948, folio 22 r°; Ohrt I, no. 1143; Engelbert, Abbey Library, ms. 3/2 (twelfth century), flyleaf.

SICLIS PICHE TICLIS: When a mirror is used for a divinatory operation (catoptromancy), the caster should go to a remote place and draw a circle on whose rim these words are written:

siclis. piche. ticlis. noturas. baruch. cortex. garym. buent. hismuie. haruel. fuganes. fortym. fermal. faruc. cornalis. bosuo. zelades. pasapa. phirpa. tirph.

Then the caster speaks a conjuration asking God to illuminate the mirror, while demanding the intercession of the three children in the furnace (Sydrac, Mysaach, Abdenago), the three kings (Caspar, Balthasar, Melchior), and the three patriarchs (Abraham, Isaac, Jacob), and the operation is concluded with a spell that blends Christian and pagan elements: "And by the name of he who calls himself theoden, lien, elyon, uergiton, Christus dieu fort, Emanuel, Caspar, Caspan, Caspar, corpion, asmal." Then many things appear in the mirror.

📖 *Liber incantationum,* folio 39 v°–40 v°.

SIESNBRA FIAT: To discover a thief's identity, the following words were written on a piece of paper that was placed under a heavy stone for three Thursday nights, then had water spread on top of it:

Siesnbra fiat Tacit Nameium Dempus alligeum Tinut.

The whole thing has been interpreted as forming a phrase asking for the thief to be bound in God's name.

📖 BBE, 75.

SILA ADONA ELOHIM: These three Hebrew names for God (I have been unable to identify the first) are used to bind a thief from a distance. They accompany a ritual in which one must spin around in a circle three times and draw three crosses.

The variant *Sila Adong Elohim* appears in another charm that serves the same purpose but opens with these words: "Our Lord Jesus Christ told his disciples, 'What I bind in heaven shall be bound on earth, and what I unbind on earth shall be unbound in heaven in the name of (†††) *Sila Adong Elohim.*'"

📖 Ohrt I, no. 920, 1294.

SILLOMONDUS: To be the victor over the strongest adversary in a brawl, it is necessary to carry a small slip of paper on which is written:

> *Sillomondus et hæritid*
> *Filli honstus nobis*
> *Coriander Cordo*
> *tempus alliqvo*
> *tugarij motan*
> *Commidatibus*

📖 Bang, no. 1084.

SIMSVM: A magic word formed from the initials of six planets (Saturn, Jupiter, Mars, Sun, Venus, Mercury) that is used on jewels for crafting amulets.

SINISTRÆ PAX PAXAS EBULE: To compel a young woman to dance, most certainly against her will, one must write these words on cheese or wax, which is then placed beneath her doorsill.

📖 Ohrt, II, 126.

SION † MARON † SAPHERT †: This is the closing phrase in a charm of protection against thieves.

📖 Hunt, 94.

S IOPG F G LI: To inspire the love of a young woman, this phrase is written on a piece of bread that is given to her to eat.

📖 BaK, no. 65.

SI ORGOME GACERITIS SIRITE: By saying these words, one can prevent a rifle from firing (eighteenth century).
 📖 Hervé, 357.

SIRAS ETAR BESANAS: These words must be spoken aloud when using a talisman (a ring) to conjure the heavenly and infernal powers.
 📖 *Trésor,* 175b.

SITIO: Words spoken by Christ while on the cross ("I am thirsty"), taken from the Gospel of John (19:28). These words were reused in the *Orison of Seven Words,* attributed to Bede. This orison guarantees one protection against all kinds of misfortune, including death without confession.
 ✦ *Orisons.*

S K H: A post-Byzantine-period charm tells us that when someone has a terrifying enemy, he should recite the entire Psalm 24, write the following *caracteres* on a piece of paper, and invoke the archangels to send them fleeing: σχ δχ πε λε κ ψ λι κλ ψ χχ.
 📖 Tselikas, 74ff.

S M K L: To counter the knotting of the britches' laces, which prevents couples from enjoying sexual relations, one should recite the entire Apostles' Creed, then, on three pieces of paper, write, "The Christ was born, the Christ was crucified, the Christ was resurrected and delivered Adam and Eve from bondage. Lord Jesus Christ our God, Son, and Word of the living God, crush and break the shackles and bonds holding your servant N. σ μ κ λ σ μ μ τα φ β θ, *Amen.*

The writing of the first page should be diluted in water that the couple should then drink. The husband then places the second page by his right thigh, and the third one is placed beneath the couple's pillow.
 📖 Tselikas, 76ff.

SOLAM S. TATTLER S. ECHOGARTNER GEMATAR: These *caracteres* form part of the manufacturing of a magic mirror that allows one to see everything. It is buried at the fork of two roads at an odd-numbered hour and so on. It is also recommended that a cat or dog be made to look in the mirror first. This prescription matches a very hardy belief of an earlier time, according to which a person could lose his or her soul by looking into a brand new mirror, or if one allowed oneself to be reflected too long in a cheval glass, one would see the devil appear in it.

 📖 *Egyptian Secrets* II, 116.

✠ ✠ ✠ **SORTHIE, SURTHIA, SORTHIOS:** As part of a long procedure intended to summon a spirit to appear in a crystal, the caster drew two circles and had to write these words on parchment under a new moon during the hour when Jupiter, the sun, and the moon were in one of the signs of the zodiac such as Cancer, Sagittarius, or Pisces. He then had to wear it over his chest. The spirit who entered the crystal was then charged with the task of seeking out Sibylia, "the beautiful blessed virgin," who would enter the second circle and answer any question asked of her.

She will appear dressed in white and give a ring to the caster, who will slip it on to his finger and become invisible. He can verify this by looking into a mirror; he will see nothing in it.

 See also *Panthon* ✠ *Graton,* because Sibylia is part of a group of three fairies.

 📖 Scot, Book XV, chapter 10.

SOUTRAM UBARSINENS: With these words, genies will come to transport one wherever he wishes to go. To travel vast distances, one says *Saram,* and to return, *Rabiam.*

📖 *Trésor,* 174b.

S. Q. R. P.: This is the beginning of a larger series of letters on an amulet for stopping blood loss. It was necessary to write these letters on virgin parchment and then hang it around the person's neck:

S. q. r. p. r. tz. os. t. q. e. t. o. a. c. ge. e. h. x. cta . serenisa.

📖 Aymar, 346.

S. S. S.S. † Z.: This is a very long charm addressed to Jesus for protection against all weapons, "be they sharp or firearms, of wood, metal, wood, and fire": S. S. S.S. †Z. †† Z. † C. S. † K. A. C. T. U. A. H. O. U. .C. H. H. The list was intended to encompass all possibilities.

📖 Spamer, 344ff.

S S S X: To counter all manner of curses and ills, the Greeks would recite the entire Apostle's Creed, request, while making the sign of the cross, that all demons be destroyed, then repeat Saint Cyprian's prayer to be protected from "all illnesses, the female demon, unlucky hours, the night, infernal, air-dwelling, or noon demon, and from all ghosts." The Gospel of Matthew came next, with an invocation of the power of the sign of the cross and a request for aid.

> May the holy angel Sabaoth be before me, Michael at my right, Gabriel at my left, and Raphael on my head! May Uriel and Misaël assist me, Cherubim and Seraphim, powers of almighty God, attach and restrain my enemies that have cast themselves upon me, N., servant of God. Make me a shepherd and them my flock! May they find themselves before me blind, mute, and paralyzed, hunchbacked, and incapable of speaking . . .

The conjuration continues with the evocation of various weapons and a request for protection addressed to Jesus Christ, the Virgin, Saint Constantine, and Saint Helen, then closes with:

Amen ς ς ς Χ ε δ π θ ο π ς θ α u τ η ο β η π τ.

The text of an amulet crafted for the same purpose is given as a conclusion (cf. Berthoin-Mathieu).

📖 Tselikas, 79.

STAPHULÉ (ΣΤΑΦΥΛΗ): This word, which means "bunch of grapes" and "uvula," is carved on a lapis lazuli amulet conserved at the National Library of France in the form of a cluster, which corresponds with the format of reductive spells.

ΣΤΑΦΥΛΗ
ΤΑΦΥΛΗ
ΑΦΥΛΗ
ΦΥΛΗ
ΥΛΗ
ΛΗ
Η

📖 Sambon, 112.

† STOEXHOR † ABALAY †: The opening of an orison to recite before going to bed in order to have a vision of the "celestial palace, God in all his glory, the nine orders of angels, and the company of the blessed spirits."

† *stoexhor* † *abalay* † *scyystalgaona* † *fullarite* † *kesphiomoma* † *remiare* † *baceda* † *canona* † *onlepot* †

✦ *Liber iuratus.*
📖 *Liber iuratus,* chap. 101.

STOMEN CALCOS: In an English incantation for a nosebleed, which dates from around 1100, we find the transcription of part of a Greek prayer: "*Stomen calcos stomen metatofu,*" which means, "Let's maintain ourselves appropriately, let's be respectful!" It must be written in the shape of a cross on the patient's forehead. A medical codex from the eighth or ninth century offers this variant: *Stomen kalaos stomen metaphow.*

📖 Storms, no. 54; Berthoin-Mathieu, 216; Singer, 258–60.

SUBUL: A magic word that is used in a charm to stop a hemorrhage.
  📖 Albertus Magnus, *Being the Approved, Verified, Sympathetic and Natural Egyptian Secrets,* 32.

SUMUS OXO: In the summoning of the spirits of the week of the Italian *Gran Grimorio,* the caster uses a spell that contains these words to compel their obedience:

> *Oxila Somus oxo*, for Surgat, spirit of Sunday;
> *Alexo Somus Oxo*, for Lucifer;
> *Lixalo Somus oxo*, for Frimost, spirit of Tuesday.

Although the spirits of the days of the week are included in *Le véritable dragon noir et la poule noire,* these spells are not mentioned.

✦ *Kailos, Musso.*

SUPILILIE: To win a young woman's love, write the following spell on your left hand, then clap your hands:

> *Supililie Farer garislia Sacra* [a heart should be drawn here]
> *Ordinia Venta Venta urum Camiter Spen San Fattus Sarum.*

📖 Bang, no. 1124.

SURGUR: If blood is flowing out of the right nostril, this word should be spoken over the left side.
  📖 Pseudo Theodore, 10ff., 276 (fifth century).

SUSTUS FUSTUS FRATIS: For protection against rabies, write these words and then give them to dogs.
  📖 Ohrt II, 127.

SWORD BREVET: Around 1780, this *brevet* (short note) was carried to provide protection against attacks and to ensure victory in brawls. It explicitly states, "No sword, axe, or knife can bite you when you have this *brevet* on your person."

Sole mando oasiluta Sabra Spesis	*Sole Mando Oscilutas Saba Spesis*
Fera habat Tabenta Jasa Sanar	*Sera habat Tabenta Doza Sanas*

Qvadua dimas pulmoruno
Famaseise Sapas Crema alfunt
Debmus Seara Seraslos alo
Seurata Cabi Lolulos in Nomine
Ne Matris Sieuts Spiritus Amen

Qvadua Dimas Pulmonorumfamma
Seicef-esapas Crema Alfuit
Debæmus Seara Sierasla volo
Seuroto—Babi Colubos
Je Nominematris Silius Spiritus Amen

Around 1830, it was believed necessary to write these words on paper with bat blood. The Latin has been corrupted beyond repair and only the end of the text is identifiable (*In nomine patris,* and so on). Dimas is Dismas, the good thief, whose name has been passed down to posterity by the Gospel of Nicodemus.

📖 BBE, 59: s.v. "Sverd breev"; Bang, no. 1084b; Grambo, "Formler for døyving av sverd. En motivanalyse."

S. X. S. 4. 9. X. S. N. V. W. U. D.!: This series of *caracteres* closes a charm against *caillebottières,* which is the term for witches who steal milk from a distance. It was discovered in 1906 during the demolition of a stable. It was hidden in the threshold beam.

📖 Spamer, 96.

SZ / V / D / X / C / K: To win a young woman's love, one must write these *caracteres* on an apple in such a way that she doesn't see them, then have her eat the fruit.

Variant: *v. d. x. c. k. h.*
📖 Braekman, no. 349.

TALIY: A magic word that must be repeated three times in the *Conjuration of the Shepherd's Star,* in order to obtain the love of a young woman.

📖 *Secrets magiques pour l'amour,* no. LIX, 47.

TANTALE PIE: To stop a nosebleed, the following spell is written on three laurel leaves that are then washed in leek juice that is then given to the patient to drink:

Tantale pie, pie Tantale, Tantale pie.

📖 Pseudo Theodore, 10ff., 276 (fifth century).

TASCA MASCAS VENAS OMNES: When combined with an adynaton, this spell heals a nosebleed.

📖 Pseudo Vegetius, iv, 26.

TATAI TATYT: To find love, these words would be written down, then carried on one's person. This may be a borrowing from the *Toto Aiti Aitai* of the *Enchiridion Leonis Pape.*

Variant: *Jatai Jyt.*

📖 Ohrt II, 128.

TAU/THAU: This last letter of the Hebrew alphabet, which was quickly confused with the Greek *tau* (the Latin *T*), was transformed into a *caractere* and a magic symbol. It was also cited in the Bible (Ezekiel 9:4, 6; Job 31:3, 5). In his *History of the Franks* (IV, 5) Gregory of Tours recounts how the *tau* appeared on the walls of houses and churches when an epidemic of the inguinal plague was raging in the Arles region. This sign was given an apotropaic value in the Middle Ages in the belief that it provided protection against pestilence. The cross of Caravaca, for example, is topped with a Latin inscription that reads, "By the virtue of this Tau. With which the son of Israel is designated, may our God free us of contagion! Son of God, take pity on me!" This cross provides protection from calamities, most importantly storms. *Domine Tau libera me, In nomine Patris,* and so on. The *tau* is described as a "venerable symbol of the holy letter" (*Clavicula*, 17).

✦ *Arcum conteret.*

TAX. MOAX. VOAX: See *Minate.*

† TE † E † R † 9 † G † A † M † N † E † N †: This way of writing *Tetragrammaton* can be found in a fifteenth-century Dutch spell for relieving a toothache. The deformation of the name changes the perspective: we are leaving the Christian world for that of pagan magic.

✦ *Fetra; Tetragrammaton.*
📖 Braekman, no. 116.

TEGNETA ABODONIKA: This is the beginning of a summoning of evil spirits that was used in Sweden around 1870. It is accompanied by *caracteres.*

> *Tegneta abodonika ärepa Salonia Rotas Belial, Belsebuleb Luciferdiabolus asonans avec tous les artifices des hommes qui leur sont soumis ont été apaisés au nom du Père, au nom de Dieu le Père, au nom du Fils de Dieu et au nom du Saint-Esprit de Dieu, Amen.*

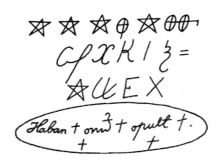

We can recognize disfigured fragments of the spell *Sator Arepo Tenet Opera Rotas,* presented in a different order.

📖 BaK, no. 56.

† TEL † BEL † QUEL † CARO † MORS † AQUA: To not be put to the question [euphemism for torture at the hands of the Inquisition—*Trans.*], this spell was used during the seventeenth century.

📖 *Enchiridion* (anno 1663), 166.

TENTA SORTEM OVIS: To win the love of a woman, it is necessary to take the yolk from an egg laid on Holy Friday and three drops of blood from your left little finger, place this on red-hot ash, crush it into powder, and give it to her to eat or drink while saying this spell three times.

📖 *Secrets magiques pour l'amour*, no. XXXI.

† TEN THURAN, TEN APHRODITEN: This spell is attached to the door to provide protection to a house and its inhabitants. It opens with: "The door, Aphrodite," then the goddess's name is repeated, reduced one letter each time:

† Ten Thuran, Ten Aphroditen	† Τὴν θύραν, τὴν Ἀφρδιτην
phroditen	φροδιτην
roditen	ροδιτην
oditen	οδιτην
diten	διτην
iten	ιτην
ten	την
en	ην
n	ν

The letters are arranged to depict a cross.

📖 PGM II, 189.

TERA. TERA. TERA.: This is the beginning of a spell that is intended to prevent or heal dysentery.

Tera. tera. tera. testis. contera. taberna. gise. ges. mande. leis. bois. eis. andies. mandies. moab. lib. lebes

The closing phrase of this spell is: *Eax. filiax. artifex. Amen.* While several Latin words are identifiable, the whole of the spell makes no sense. It seems, though, that one needs to touch the ground in order to transfer the disease to it.

◆ *Eax, Ire.*
📖 Berthoin-Mathieu, 193; Storms, no. 68.

TERIX. CONTERIX. PETRONIX. PETRONISSA. TERIX: According to a thirteenth-century manuscript, these are the words the angel allegedly spoke to Mary during the Annunciation. With them, an entity called "worm" is summoned in order to prevent it from devouring you or biting flesh and bone. This spell is also effective against migraines and the "flying gout," a name for a parasite.
📖 Berlin, Prussian State Library, Latin ms., quart. 2, folio 25 r°.

TERRA, FARRA, GARRA: If a man approaches a dog while holding his left testicle in his hand, then spins around while saying these words, the animal will not bark.
📖 *Ritual of High Magic.*

TERRA PESTEM TENERE SALENE: To treat gout, it was believed necessary in the eighteenth century to say the following spell nine times while fasting, then spit on and rub the afflicted limb with volatile alkali for seven days.

terra pestem tenere salene, salene, salene manete his hirè pedibus

📖 D'Abano, 94.

TETRAGRAMMATON (τετράγραμματον): The term *tetragrammaton* means "God in four letters." In a fourteenth-century herbal benediction, these are expressed as: *Joth, Ey, Way, He* (יהוה), meaning Jehova. Isidore of Seville wrote this as: *joth he vau he* in the sixth century. According to other exegetes, it would be: *Joem, sai, neot, he,* or else the first four letters from the beginning of the Jewish morning prayer: *aleph, beth, lamed,* and *aleph.* The Jews are alleged to have said "Adonai the ineffable tetragrammaton *YHWH*" (Yahwe). The writer of the *Sachet accoucheur* rendered this ineffable name of God as *V.I.O.O(n). H.V.A.V.,* before interpreting it as *ioth,* meaning "beginning"; *he,* meaning "just"; *vau,* meaning "life"; and *neth,* "passion."

The *tetragrammaton* is used for fevers when written on a sacred wafer as follows: † *te* †*tra* †*gra* † *ma* † *ton* (Hunt, 360). A sixteenth-century

Italian charm against quartan, tertian, and constant fevers closes with this spell: *Agios, tragmaton ataneatam Samuel e Manuel, Hyesus primus novissimus agessia agios, fiat fiat fiat. Amen.*

These other spellings can also be found: *tetragramacio, trenagramaton, tetagraamaton, Fetra gramalum, Tara gramaton, Tera gramator, grammata Trachotin.*

✦ *Fetra; Tragta gramontetta.*

📖 Franz I, 409; Isidore of Seville VII, 1, 16; Kohler, 19–32; Lauterbach, 39–67.

THEBAL: This magic word appears in countless medieval spells. For protection from cramps, it is necessary to write this on a parchment: + *Thebal + Ech + Guth + Et + Guthanay,* and carry it on your person (England, fifteenth century). A manuscript from the cathedral library of Canterbury contains a splendid incantation against cramps. It requires that one take a piece of parchment, make the sign of the cross over it like this: ›*III,* then write:

> + *Thebal + Guthe + Guthanay + in nomine patris + et filij + et spiritus sancti Amen + IRe nazarenus + Maria + Johannes + Michael + Gabriel + Raphael + verbo carum factum est +*

Next, the parchment must be folded in such a way that none of the letters on it can be seen. "There can be no doubt that he who bears it with honesty and reverence in the name of all-powerful God, will be saved. This charm (*iste carmen*) possesses great power thanks to God who gave words, stones, and plants their virtues. It must be used secretly so that everyone does not learn of it and cause this gift of God to lose its strength." In the eleventh century, we find it in a protection charm against dwarves. It is necessary to say: *thebal guttatim aurum et thus de.* + *albra Iesus.* + *alabra Iesus* + *Galabra Iesus,* then write on three waffles: *THEBAL GUTTA*. The beginning of the spell is reminiscent of Isaiah 60:6 (All from Sheba will come, bearing gold and incense; *omnes de Saba venient, aurum et thus deferentes*). *Thebal* has also been compared with the Hebrew word for healing, *thehalah*. For protection from gout around 1350, individuals would carry a *bref* with: *Tepal guth gutta Niteas Ne ganim guspas.*

In October 1904, a gold ring with a square section, which was dated to the last third of the thirteenth century, was discovered in Donauwörth, Bavaria. The inscription it bears exhibits a clear kinship with the one above:

+ *GVGGVGBALTEBANI* + *ALPHA &* ω
+ *EHERAVELAGAIHAEHRA* + *ENORAYA.* ω
+ *GVT* + *GVNANIA* + *ADOSDE.B.E.L* ω
+ *MELCHAAGLA* + *AQTVO LCLO M O—OI*

In it we find *Agla,* combined with *Melcha,* "a very sacred name." A Munich manuscript informs us that "whoever bears it on their person shall be delivered from all peril."

The word *THEBALGVTGVTANI,* sometimes written in Greek letters, as is the case on a ring found in 1846 (+ ΘΗΒΑΛΓVΘΓVΘΑΝΙ), is extremely frequent on magic rings, like those discovered in the Wiltshire region (*Debal gut Gudani*), Glamorganshire (ΘΗΒΑΛΓΥΘΓΥΘΑΝΙ), Rockingham (*Guttu: gutta: madros, adros / Thebat: adros: adros*), Rome (*AΩGVTGVT THEBAL GVTTANI*), and Petrossa (*GVTANI OD HAILAG*). Comparison with a Latin charm against cramps or spasms suggests that the ring adorned with this word protects the wearer from this affliction. A ring was discovered southeast of Jutland that bore:

† *TH | EB | AL | GV | VT | HA N |*

Carved on the rim of a fifteenth-century talismanic ring discovered in the Worcestershire region of England, we find: + *THEABIGVTHVTHANI*. One side of a silver brooch reads:

EZERA. EZERA. ERAVERAGAN + *GUGVRALTERANI. ALPHA Et.* Ω.

On the other side this inscription appears:

+*AOTVUNO OIO MO OOIO AV.*

On the square section of a ring found near Amiens, France, in 1763, the following long spell appears:

+ OE GUTA + SAGRA + HOGOGRA + IOTHE + HENAVEAET + OCCINOMOC + ON + IKC + HOGOTE + BANGUES + ALPHA 71B + ANA + EENETON + AIRIE + OIRA +ALGA + OMEGA + ADONAI + HEIERNATHOI + GEBAL + GUTGUTTA + IEOTHIN

📖 London, British Library, Sloane 56, folio 7 r°; Hunt, 348; Berthoin-Mathieu, 154, 492ff.; Storms, no. 78; Ohrt II, 128; Harmening, "Zur Morphologie magischer Inschriften," 67–80; Mély, 342–53; King, 25–34, 149–57, 225–35; Evans, 123. (The Evans book focuses particularly on England.)

THEON, HALTANAGON, HARAMALON: This is the opening to the magic phrase in a thirteenth-century orison requesting that God give us wisdom.

Theon, Haltanagon, Haramalon, Zamoyma, Chamasal, Jeconamril, Harionatar, Jechomagol, Gela Magos, Kemolihot, Kamanatar, Hariomolatar, Hanaces, Velonionathar, Azoroy, Jezabali. By these holy and glorious mysteries, by these precious offices, the virtue and knowledge of God, correct my beginnings, Zembar, Henoranat, Grenatayl, Samzatam, Jecornazay.

✦ *Ars notoria.*
📖 *Ars notoria*, 72; *Liber iuratus*, chap. 64.

THEOS: This is the lead-in of the eleventh magic orison from the *Liber iuratus*. It allows the speaker to obtain a divine vision.

Theos † megale † patir † ymos † hebrel † habobel † hecoy † haley † helyhot † hety † hebiot † letiel † iezey † sadam † salaseey † salatial † salatelli † samel † sadamiel † saday † helgyon † helliel † lemegos † mitron † megos † myheon † legmes † muthon † michoyn † heel † hesely † iecor † granal † semhel † semobzhat † semeltha † samay † geth † gehel † rasahanay † gelgemana †

semana † *harasymihon* † *salepatir* † *selapati* † *ragion* † *saletha* †
thurigium † *hepatir* † *vsion* † *hatamas* † *hetanas* † *harayn.*

Hepatir is the Greek *ho pater,* "father."

It is identical to a word close to the terms of an orison that is good for the memory, this term being encrypted as follows:

m : m :: r:. . m (memoriam)

When one wishes to study, it is necessary to say *lemach, lemoch, salmalsaach,* and so on. One says *Theos patir beherenos* to invoke God's angels, notably *Eliphat, Nasay,* and so on, and to ask the Lord to illuminate one's consciousness and strengthen one's intelligence. It is easy to see that God the Father (*Theos patir*) is being turned to for the request expressed by *behere,* which remains incomprehensible.

We find *Theos. Patir. behemnos. lehernnyos. behenny* in other orisons (no.s 14 and 16).

📖 *Liber iuratus,* chap. 46; Franz II, 259ff.

THEOS PATER VEHEMENS: When a magical operation is begun beneath a new moon, prayers are addressed to God with requests for his aid in purifying consciousness and strengthening understanding in order to remember what the individual has learned from the following orison:

Theos Pater vehemens; God of the angels, I implore and invoke you by your very holy angels, Eliphamasay, Gelomiros, Gedo bonay, Saranana, Elomnia.

✦ *Ars notoria.*
📖 *Ars notoria,* 117.

THEZAY LEMACH OSSANLOMACH AZABATH: This is the opening of an extremely long thirteenth-century incantation contained in an orison whose purpose is to endow the student of the liberal arts with wisdom.

Thezay lemach ossanlomach azabath azach azare gessemon relaame azathabelial biliarsonor tintingote amussiton sebamay halbuchyre gemaybe redayl hermayl textossepha pamphilos Cytrogoomon bapada lampdayochim yochyle tahencior yastamor

Sadomegol gyeleiton zomagon Somasgei baltea achetom gegerametos halyphala semean utangelsemon barya therica getraman sechalmata balnat hariynos haylos halos genegat gemnegal saneyalaix samartaix camael satabmal simalena gaycyah salmancha sabanon salmalsay silimacroton zegasme bacherietas zemethim theameabal gezorabal craton henna glungh hariagil parimegos zamariel leozomach rex maleosia mission zebmay aliaox gemois sazayl neomagil Xe Xe Sepha caphamal azeton gezain holhanhihala semeanay gehosynon caryacta gemyazan zeamphalachin zegelaman hathanatos, semach gerorabat syrnosyel, halaboem hebalor halebech ruos sabor ydelmasan falior sabor megiozgoz neyather pharamshe forantes saza mogh schampeton sadomthe nepotz minaba zanon suafnezenon inhancon maninas gereuran gethamayh passamoth theon beth sathamac hamolnera galsemariach nechomnan regnali phaga messyym demogempta teremegarz salmachaon alpibanon balon septzurz sapremo sapiazte baryon aria usyon sameszion sepha athmiti sobonan Armissiton tintingit telo ylon usyon, Amen.

There are several identifiable words such as *beth*, which could be either the letter of the Hebrew alphabet or "the dwelling," (בית־אל); or the Greek *cratos*, meaning "powerful."

✦ *Ars notoria;* "Azay lemach."
📖 *Ars notoria*, 105ff.

THIGAT: In twelfth-century England, a spell that opened with this word was used to heal invalids. The body of the spell continued with invocations of the crosses of Saints Matthew, Mark, Luke, and John. This obscure spell takes the following form:

Thigat. Thigat. Thigat. calicat. Archlo. cluel. Sades. Achodes. Arde. et hercleno. Abaioth. ArcocugtiA. Arcu. ArcuA. fulgura. sophuinit. ni. cofuedi. necutes cuteri. nicuram. Thefalnegal. Uflem. archa. Cunhunelaja.

Several words are identifiable, but the meaning of the whole thing escapes us. Furthermore, the copyists of the time do not seem to have grasped what they were reading: *Abaioth*—which could be *abba ioth*, "father of the beginning"—has become *Nonanaioth, cunhunelaja, tuxuncula,* and the words no longer appear to be divided in the same way.

📖 Storms, no. 70, no. 71 (another variant).

THREE KINGS: The use of the names of the Three Magi or Three Kings was allegedly the recommendation of Pope John XXII (1276–1277). Extremely popular, the names Gaspar, Melchior, and Balthazar can be found in magic texts everywhere. Their Hebrew names (Galgalat, Magalath, and Sarachim) as well as their Greek names (Apellus, Amerus, and Damasiu) are not used in Western spells.

According to Pope John XXII, to fight epilepsy, it is necessary to write their names on parchment and hang it around the ailing individual's neck. The accepted phrasing is: "He who bears these names: Melchior, † Pabtizar † Caspar is by the grace of Christ delivered from the falling sickness." Their names are also effective for bleeding. Another prescription combines their names with those of God (*Messias, Sother, Emmanuel,* and so on), and this kind of charm can be found in countless manuscripts.

Their names help facilitate childbirth when connected with the *Charm of Saint Suzanne* and the phrases *Christus natus, Christus vincit,* and so on. When combined with *Ananizapta,* the names of God, and *Jesus autem transiens,* the Three Kings provide protection against the plague. When combined with the names of the evangelists and *Christus vincit,* and so on, they protect one from all misfortunes. If they are coupled with Saint Felicity and the three men in the furnace, they provide protection against all one's enemies.

The initials of their names (CBM) provide protection to houses.

Casper Ψ Balsar Ψ Melchior
Ψ Jesus   Ψ meus Rex Judæorum
Ψ Jesus   antem transiens per
medium horum ibat
reborum Ψ dei Ψ de se gras   a
Adam   Elias

The abbreviation "Cabane," with an *N* for the *M* in Melchior, was used as a baptismal name into the fifteenth century.

In the twelfth century, Gaspar, Melchior, and Balthazar were the patron saints of travelers. If their names were used in combination with the Apostles' Creed, the Trinity, and *Jesus autem transiens* (Luke 4:30), a person could travel in complete security. They were invoked to prevent fatigue from walking, for example, by writing the phrase: "May the three mage kings, C. M. B., be my road companions," on three slips of paper that were attached to the hollows of the traveler's knees. In the fifteenth century the charm said: *Caspar me ducat, Balthasar me regat, Melchior me salvet, et ad vitam aeternam me perducant* ("May Caspar lead me, Balthazar guide me, Melchior save me, and may they lead me to eternal life"). The following spell against disease was carried like an amulet:

+ *Melchior* + *Pabtizar portans hec nomina* + *Caspar*
Solvitur a morbo Christi pietate caduco

[By bearing these names, one will be protected from the falling sickness by the grace of Christ.]

The physician Bernard of Gordon (died before 1330) indicated that this spell needed to be repeated in an epileptic's ear three times in succession, and he would be healed. On the back of a Scottish brooch dating from the fifteenth century, the name of the three kings is accompanied by the word *consummatum*.

Over the course of time, the three kings gained the reputation of being able to offer protection against thieves, bad weather, and fire, and their image was borne with the phrase: *Sancti tres reges Gaspar, Melchior, Balthasar, orate pro nobis, nunc et in hora mortis nostrae* ("Three holy kings Gaspar, Melchior, Balthazar, pray for us now and at the hour of our death"), according to Jean-Baptiste Thiers. When a horse was being shod, this phrase was whispered in its ear to keep it still: *Caspar te tenet, Balthasar te liget, Melchior te ducat* ("May Caspar hold you, Balthazar bind you, Melchior lead you"), and a cross was drawn on its forehead each time.

In a compilation known as the *Ritual of High Magic,* mistakenly attributed to Heinrich Cornelius Agrippa, the names of the three kings were used to ensure accurate shooting. The phrase, "Gaspard, Balthazard, Melchior, guide my bullet to the animal I wish to slay," was written on a small piece of paper, which was then used as wadding, and these words were repeated when one fired the weapon.

We can also find the name of the three kings in a spell carved on a gold ring that dates from around 1500: *burabariaberioraaiabaltesar.*

They are invoked in the *Conjuration of the Shepherd's Star* when one wishes to obtain what he desires from a woman. The conjuration ends with the phrase: *Cave! Cave! Cave! Ecce enim veritatem dilexisti. Incerta et occulta sapientia tua manifestasti mihi* ("Look out! Look out! Look out! Indeed, you have loved truth. Show me your uncertain and hidden science").

If one writes the names of the Three Magi on three laurel leaves on the eve of King's Day and slips them in the shape of a cross beneath the headboard of one's bed, one will see the man or woman one will marry in a dream.

In the nineteenth century, houses were given protection with the help of the names of the mage kings, as shown by this photograph of a house in the Salzach Valley in upper Austria:

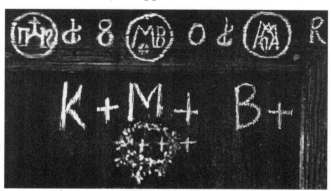

Variants include: *Jaspar, Casber, Caspar, Kasper; Baptizar, Balcer, Bathasar, Walthesar; Melkior, Milcorium.*

✦ CBM.

📖 Braekman, 36; Franz II, 226–28, 266ff., 268, 505; Bernard of Gordon, *Lilium medicinae*, II, 25, pp. 376–77; Ohrt I, no. 229ff. (against epilepsy), no. 269 (against intermittent fever, with *Christus vincit* et *consummatum est*), no. 600-605 (against fire), no. 777, no. 1090; no. 1263 (*bref*); London, British Library, Sloane 3285, folio 25 r°; Braekman, no. 49, no. 234, no. 272, no. 277; Thiers I, 357; Ohrt II, 96; *Grimoires*, no. 268 (to render guns and weapons inoperable); Honorius, 54, 71; Van Haver, no. 1029 (in a witchcraft conjuration); Bartsch, *Sagen, Märchen und*

Gebräuche, vol. 2, no. 2060; *Secrets magiques pour l'amour,* no. XLII, no. LXII; Coulon, 44 (against epilepsy).

TIECON, LELELOTH, PATRON: To manufacture a beverage effective against the Lenten disease, one takes plants that are steeped in beer, to which holy water is added. The entire concoction is then boiled while invoking the four evangelists, and the invocation is sealed with this spell. The three words come from an ancient Hebrew phrase that scholars have translated as meaning, "Resist the night like a guardian spirit!"

 📖 Storms, no. 33; Berthoin-Mathieu, 66.

TIN BIB ELITHI: To enjoy sexual relations with no risk, these words (τιν βιβ ηλιϑι) should be written on a piece of hide in which the end of a fox limb has been wrapped. The Greek manuscripts of the *Cyranides* offer: T'IN BI'B H'ΛΙΘΙ.

 📖 *Cyranides,* II, Ω.

† T † Ω A: For protection against a dwarf, these *caracteres* must be written on one's arm, celandine crushed into beer, invocations made to Saint Machutus and Saint Victoricus, then this written along one's arm:

$$+ \tau + P + \tau + N + \omega + \tau + UI + M + \omega A.$$

Then the saints are again invoked while repeating the action with the celandine. *UI* and *M* are surely designations for the two saints, and *ω A* for God.

 📖 Storms, no. 44; Bethouin-Matthieu, 126.

TONUCHO: To make oneself invisible, one must craft a gold ring in the moon's ninth house and set in it a yellow stone on which is carved the *caractere* seen below; beneath the stone, the word *Tonucho* is placed, written on virgin parchment with the blood of a white dove and perfumed with orange peel.

 📖 London, British Library, Lansdowne 1202, 4to, folio 173.

TOOGRAS: To awaken love, it is recommended that these letters be written on one's hand before sunrise.
- BaK, no. 66.

TOPINOCH: To defeat one's enemies, one should craft a gold ring in the moon's tenth house and set in it a yellow stone on which is carved the *caractere* seen below; this word is placed beneath the stone, written on virgin parchment with the blood of a white dove.

- London, British Library, Lansdowne 1202, 4to, folio 176.

TORAX: In a charm against a migraine, a spell that is constructed from the meeting of Jesus with the doleful Saint Peter, Christ states that the individual who bears the following will no longer know suffering:

> † *Agios* †*Agios* † *Agios* † *Pater. Aue. Credo. Torax Calamite. Torax Rubee. Torax Liquide. Omnes Gumme.*

Torax seems to be a reference to storax or styrax (balsam), a resinous tree that provides a balm.
- London, British Library, Sloane 2457, folio 19 v°.

TORUM CULTIN, CULTORUM, BULTIN, BULTOTUM: An individual known as Father Girard recommended saying these words while blowing one's nose or while kissing the woman whose love one desires, in order to win enjoyment of that love.
- Honorius, *Grimoire of Pope Honorius*, 69.

TOTO, AITI, AITAI: These are magic words from the orison *Pax Domini*, provided by Pope Leo XIII. They summon divine protection for the one who says them.
- *Enchiridion*, 73.

TRAGTA, GRAMONTETTA, ANGTELA †††: This is the closing spell from the *Charm of the Three Flowers*, which are three roses in this instance, whose purpose is to "freeze in its tracks" game or any other animal. The animal is named and bewitched to no longer move "by the four elements of the sky," and is it "forbidden to run or to leap" before *tragta* and so on is spoken. Here we can recognize *Tetragrammaton*, literally camouflaged by the letters that have no recognizable source (*ta*) and those that have been divided.

📖 *Egyptian Secrets* III, 189; Spamer, 357.

TRIANGLE: In ancient Greek magic, a plentiful number of spells were written in the shape of a triangle. Formations of words into a triangle were called "wings" (*peruges, pterugômata, kardiai*). F. Dornseiff notes that these formations go back to a Pythagorean tradition, and R. Kotansky observes that they treat words like additions. A charm asking Serapis to free a certain Artemidora from illness prescribes:

A
EE
HHH
IIII
OOOOO
YYYYYY
ΩΩΩΩΩΩΩ

The point of the triangle also can be on the bottom, as on carved stones for inspiring love, as well as on a curse tablet against circus chariot drivers, discovered in Rome; the word *eulamô*, "eternity," is inscribed as follows:

ΕΥΛΑΜΩ
ΥΛΑΜΩ
ΛΑΜΩ
ΑΜΩ
ΜΩ
Ω

In his *Liber medicinalis* (verses 935–39), Quintus Serenus Sammonicus prescribed the writing of *Abracadabra* on parchment and wearing it around the neck when stricken with demitertian fever.

📖 PGM XVIIa, 1–25; XXXVI, 115–33, 231–55; XXXIX, 1–21; Dornseiff, 58ff.; Mastrocinque.

TRIX TRAX FILILAX: This spell is to be written on a new leaf and carried when one wishes to win at cards.

 📖 Ohrt II, 129.

TRO ETANATOR: This is the opening of a long spell intended to prevent anyone from harming one's livestock.

> *Tro Etanator Durich Pinaopentye Jalamut Lidfutter Jyepichminför Qvur prœit † Gaaba † Bel Pelmilgano Kapmatgelbeg kapamatgalle Japmat.*

 📖 Ohrt II, 129.

T R X O V T V T T T V T O T: For protection from one's enemies, around 1800 it was recommended that an individual carry on his person a piece of paper on which these letters were written.

 📖 BaK, no. 74.

TUDICHA STELPHA: To procure a horse, it is necessary to inscribe the following words at twilight on the door of an empty house, "in the way of the Hebrews" (*more hebrayco*), with the blood of a bat:

> *tudicha stelpha alpha drato mariodo ypation.*

When the horse appears, place your left foot in the stirrup while speaking a conjuration addressed to the Creator of heaven and Earth. The text says that the sign of the cross should not be made and that the animal's bridle should be buried when the horse is not being ridden. When one wants to use the horse again, the conjuration is repeated with the addition of *Kastelya, Elogo, Yetas.*

 📖 *Liber incantationum,* folio 36 r°–v°.

TURAN ESTANOS FUZA: These words make one virtuous when they are spoken three times while holding a talisman on which they are carved in one's right hand, at eye level. If one says *Vazotas Testanar* while raising the talisman over one's head, the words bestow on one all kinds of talents, "and one will see the production of miracles."

 📖 *Trésor,* 181b.

TURBAN EROBAL INFINITUS EST: This spell appears in an enchantment ritual that also refers to *Gamilaren uxtos bohot*. The first two words are most likely the names of demons.

Variants: *Turban Kereba (Kerebal, Kerobal) infinitus.*

📖 Werner, no. 43, 205.

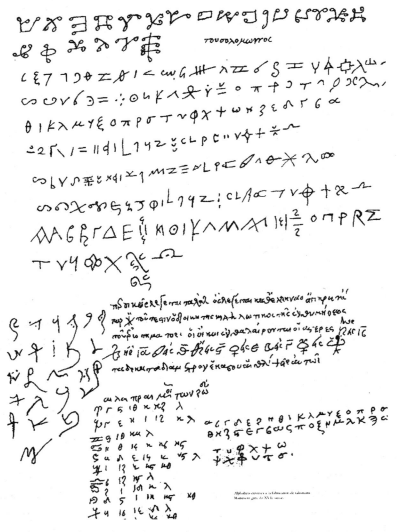

Secret alphabets
Vienna, National Library, Cod. Phil. Gr. 108, folio 3702 (sixteenth century)

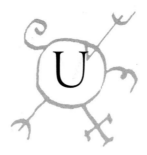

UAX PAX DEAX: These are three names of God (*Via, Pax, Deus*) used in an epistle that allows one to master the madness sent by an evil spell caster to afflict someone.

 📖 *Galdrakver*, 51.

URIEL + SERAPH + JOSATA: To summon Uriel so that he might help the conjurer to read the future, the *Grimorium verum* (book III) provides the summoning spell: *Uriel + Seraph + Josata + Ablati + Agla + Caila*. The four words that God spoke to Moses are added to this: *Josta + Agla + Caila + Ablati*.

URINI BURINI BLICTEUM: A trouble-free childbirth can be granted thanks to this incantation.

 📖 Braekman, no. 51.

USION/USYON: This is a title of God that recurs frequently in charms, incantations, and orisons, and on amulets. The term is a corruption of the Greek *ousion* (οὐσιον), "substance, essence," and was Latinized into *usion* in medieval lexicons.

 ✦ *Names of God*.

USION. JOTH. HETH: An amulet with a zodiac motif, this time that of Aquarius. It was described in a text attributed (probably falsely) to the doctor and astrologer Pseudo–Arnaldus de Villanova (1235–1311). It carries these three words encircled by the phrase, "Here is the Lamb of God who takes away the sins of the world," in Latin. It offers protection from blood diseases and disorders affecting the eyes. Joth (י) and Heth (ח) are the names of two Hebrew letters, the second of which can be interpreted to mean "life." The word *usion*, or *usyon*, recurs frequently in lists of divine names.

 📖 Pseudo–Arnaldus de Villanova, *Opera*, folio 302 r°.

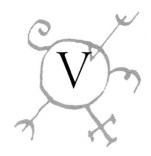

VAHOS, A NOSTRO NOXIO BAY GLOY APON AGIA AGIOS ISCHYROS: Adam is supposed to have uttered these words when at the border of limbo or by the banks of the Acheron. If they are carried when going to war or while traveling, the individual can never be wounded or killed, according to Jean-Baptiste Thiers and the *Enchiridion Leonis Pape*. *Agia agios* mimics the liturgical hymn "Trisagion," and *ischyros* means "strong."

 Enchiridion, 75.

VALANDA JACEM RAFIT: To escape an assault or attack, this phrase should be written on a small slip of paper to be worn around the neck:

 Valanda jacem rafit massif excorbis anter valganda zazar.

 Honorius, 102ff.

VALCANDAZAZAS ADONAY: These are the words with which the *Orison of Adam* opens. The first part of this text is simply a long list of the names of God. *Valcandazazas* must be an appeal to the deity.

 Enchiridion, 75.

VASSIS ATATLOS: The following spell was used for a variety of purposes:

 Vassis atatlos vesul etcremus, verbo san hergo dibolia herbonos.

To cause another person to suffer, the caster worked while fasting on the final Friday of the month. He took a piece of lard, stuck it full of pins while saying these words, then placed it between two blessed branches used to make a cross. The item was then buried in a wild area.

To destroy a curse and see who cast the evil spell, one took an ani-

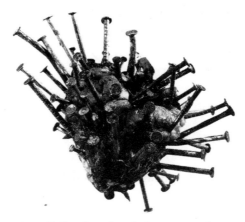

mal heart and stuck it full of nails while saying these words with each one. The heart was then placed in a pot with camphor and three drops of holy water, then boiled from 11:30 to one hour past midnight. The pot was then buried in fallow ground. To avert an evil encounter, the spell was abbreviated to *Against you, verbo san Diboliâ herbonos.*

📖 *Dragon noir,* 156–58.

V. C. E.: To compel someone to fall in love with you, you must write these letters on a piece of paper with blood from a pigeon that was bled on a Friday, then roll the paper up and place it "inside a fatty figure." Place coral on the paper and dry the figure in the sun, wrap it in taffeta, then wear it for nine days over your heart. If you succeed in convincing the desired woman to kiss the paper, you will win her love.

📖 *Secrets magiques pour l'amour,* 22ff.

VEIDE, ROUGAN, RADA, BAGABIUS: When one says this with his knee and wrist flat on the ground while turning over and then getting back up without touching anything with the left wrist, one or several people will be brought to an abrupt halt, says the *Ritual of High Magic,* mistakenly attributed to Heinrich Cornelius Agrippa.

VEJE EIGIE JEWJ: This is from a Dutch spell for healing a burn. It is necessary to write a long series of letters and place it over the injury. If the pain is too intense for an individual to do it himself, another person can do it. See page 330 for the complete spell.

Veje eigie jewj
B d t laar E get bee
S t a n h h Z g
Uj ké J he je get
Jee Jenj bnoxi
J J Ge

📖 Van Haver, no. 114.

VEL: This magic word appears in a spell against fever dating from the tenth or eleventh century. It can be found in *L'Antidotaire de l'âme* (Collection of Antidotes for the Soul) by Guglielmo da Saliceto, an Italian doctor of Bologna, in a fourteenth century blessing for plants, and finally in the work by J. B Thiers. It forms part of an incomprehensible spell that has been subjected to endless corruption: *La velere rare rari,* "what the tongues of the living are incapable of explaining," as one ancient commentary describes it. It is also claimed that Adam allegedly implored and bent God to his will by speaking the sacred name *Lavelerarerari.*

📖 Heim, 551; Thiers I, 354; IV, 54.

VENI FORAS: A common spell in charms for ensuring a trouble-free birth. It is often combined with other spells, as can be seen in this example:

in nomine patris lazarus et filij veni foras
et speritus scantus christus te uocat
† christus † stonat †
issus predicat † christus regnat † erex † arex †
rymex † chrsti eleyzon † eeeeeeee †

✦ Birth, Erex, Exi foras.
📖 Ohrt II, 130.

VERBUM CARO FACTUM EST: This passage from the Gospel of John appears frequently in magic practices. An amulet described by the Pseudo–Arnaldus de Villanova (1235–1311) carries the phrase: *Verbum caro factum est et habitavit in nobis* on its rim, surrounding the words: *Alpha, Oméga* and *Sanctus Petrus* in the center. This phylactery offers protection against lightning, storms, floods, violent winds, and pestilences. It must be made from very pure gold that has been melted down on the fifteenth day of the month of April while reciting certain psalms. The carving of the front side must be made when the moon is in Cancer or Leo, and the reverse side when this astral body is in Aries.

A fifteenth-century exemplum says this: "The travelers were pursuing their journey one day when a violent storm burst out that they were unable to escape. The lightning struck and killed one of them, then took a second victim shortly afterward. The third in his terror suddenly recalled the words of God and said: 'The Word made flesh.' He then heard a voice asking: 'Why didn't you kill him?' 'I couldn't,' responded another voice, 'because he spoke the words of salvation, the Word made flesh.'"

 📖 Pseudo–Arnaldus de Villanova, *Opera*, folio 301 v°; Klapper, no. 114, 324.

VERONICA: See *Beronix*.

VGALE HAMICATA: This is the beginning of a magic orison when one "cleans the carpet for addressing the Intelligences to learn the answer to whatever things one wishes to know." After addressing the archangels of the four cardinal points and after the recitation of a first orison that was opened with a quadruple *Agla*, one said: *Vgale hamicata, umsa, terata, ye dah ma baxasoxa un hora hime sere.*

 📖 *Clavicules, Les véritable clavicules de Solomon*, 76.

VINCIT LEO DE TRIBU JUDA, RADIX DAUIT: This is a fragment of a very common spell that consists of a passage from John (4:5) and another from Revelation (5:5): *Ecce crucem Domini, fugite partes adverse! Vicit leo de tribu Iuda, radix Dauid* ("Behold the cross of the Lord, flee opposing parties! The lion of the tribe of Judah has triumphed, David's offshoot"). With or without *alleluia* as an ending, these words generally reinforce other more pagan phrases for driving away shivering and fevers, the disease called *dysiaticum*, the opaque spot over the eye, and both male and female elves. They are also used to banish thunder and lightning. In the grimoire from Vinje, Norway, the phrase reads: † *De viro vicit leo* † *de tribis Judae,* and it facilitates childbirth. The spell is also in the *Geraldus falconarius* (thirteenth century), in a treatise on horse care for protection against worms, in a Liège medical book, and on the Stavelot triptych. Combined with other Christian elements, the phrase is used to send demons fleeing. Today it is used to remove enchantments from livestock and more generally to dispel curses.

 📖 Franz II, 87, 165, 200; Berthoin-Mathieu, 62, 202; Ohrt I, no. 332, no. 1080, no. 1259; Vinje, no. 14; Abeele, "De arend bezweren"; Hunt, 81; Camus 2002, 276, 296.

VOLACTI, ADA, NOLA, APRISON: A Norwegian ritual in use around 1790 for blinding a thief in one eye featured this phrase in a spell that was followed by an invocation of nine demons.

 📖 Bang, no. 1376b.

VOLG: To cure vertigo, you must craft a seal of gold, iron, and silver during the hour of Mars on the day of Jupiter when the moon is in the sign of Aries. On one side of the seal, carve: *Volg νωρχα γεγδαυχω Arnilot*, and on the other: *Ζελλα Ζωνδεαγ*. This seal should be worn accompanied by other remedies.

 📖 *Archidoxis magica,* I, 17.

VOLO ET VONO BAPTISTA SANCTA AGALA TUM EST: To destroy an enchantment cast on animals, salt is cast over the bewitched victims while saying these words. *Tum est* represents *consumatum est,* here with the meaning of *fiat,* and *Agala* is nothing less than *Agla* transformed into a saint!

 📖 Honorius, 91ff.

VOS K E H R MANRARET HOSI Z 1 ° Y β G HAKL λ: To get the better of one's enemies, one must tear the dewclaw from a hen's foot, then write these letters with it. The thing on which these letters are written must then be carried on one's person.

 ✦ *V.V.M.A.X.*
 📖 Ohrt II, 130.

† **VRIEL TOBIEL BRAC:** Inscription carved on a thirteenth-century gold ring discovered in Denmark. The names of two angels are combined with a magic word.

📖 Ohrt II, 129.

V R S V S M V: The *Benediction of Saint Benedict* was once used as an amulet. Abbreviations of this benediction were inscribed on medals or crosses with the inclusion of words from Matthew 4:10 ("Get thee behind me, Satan").

			Variant
VRSVSMV	VRSVSMV	*Vade retro Satana,*	*Vade retro Satanas Ne*
SMQLIVB	SMQLIVB	*umquam suade mihi*	*(umquam) suade mihi*
CSSML	CSSML	*vana Sunt moda quae*	*vana Sunt mala quae*
NDSMD	NDSMD	*libas ipse venena bibas*	*libas, Ipse venena bibas*
		crux sacra sit mihi lux	*crux sacra sit mihi lux*
		Non draco sit mihi dux	*Non draco sit mihi dux*

["Get thee behind me, Satan! You shall not convince me to do evil; whatever you show me is evil, drink your own poison! May the sacred cross be my light! May the devil not be my guide."]

A precise arrangement is respected when doing this. The first sentence occupies the border of the amulet, the second is written in the shape of a cross, then the four words *Crux Sancti Patris Benedicti* are written in the four corners. This amulet works against the evil spells of sorcerers and the snares set by demons; it also protects animals and is used to free the possessed. A manuscript bearing this benediction and instructions in the ways to use the Cross of Saint Benedict was found in the Bavarian monastery of Metten in 1647. The cross was worn on a very long chain, it was dipped into the water one drank and the water used to bathe, and it was affixed to the front door of the home or buried beneath the threshold. Sometimes the reverse side of the cross bears the twenty-five letters of *Zacharias's Benediction*.

The variant *Vade retro Satanas et omnis angele nociue percuciens* drives storms away. This "benediction" made its way into France around 1741, where it was published under the title *The Effects and Virtues of the Cross or Medal of the High Patriarch Saint Benedict. Augmented with the Benediction and Prayers. Extracts from the German Printers*, with the following information noted: "Paris: Chez Pierre de Bats, bookseller of the Palace, in the image of Saint Francis, DCC XLI. With permission." The text describes how the medallion's virtues were discovered.

> In the year 1647, while hunting witches in Bavaria and even having executed several in the town of Straubingen, several of them during their interrogations confessed to the judges that their spells had no effects on the people or animals of Nattreumbec Castle, neighbor to Metten Abbey of the Benedictine Order, because of several holy medallions in places that they identified. These, in fact, were found, but no one, not even the witches, could decipher the *caracteres* engraved upon them, until an ancient manuscript was discovered in the library of this abbey that provided complete illumination. A full report on this was made to the Duke of Bavaria, who, wishing to learn this for himself, had the medals and manuscripts brought to the town of Ingolstadt and from there to Munich. After comparing the one with the other, he assured all that one could use these medallions profitably without any hint of errors or superstition, and had a written account drawn up of his findings.

The 1741 printing notes:

> Rumors of this discovery spread throughout the land, and everyone wanted to have one of these medallions. One was obliged to make several, which were blessed by the monks of the order and produced wonderful effects, primarily against charms and evil spells, as reported by those who used them either by wearing them at their necks or by dipping them in water that was given to the bewitched animals to drink. . . .

The effects of this medallion are:

1. Wherever this medallion is present, it drives all manner of curses, bindings, evil spells, and other diabolical effects out of the human body.
2. It prevents any witches, sorcerers, enchanters, or magicians from entering the places where this medal is present or approaching the people who possess it.
3. It is a good, quick remedy for helping animals infected and poisoned by some curse, evil spell, or other unknown ill to grow larger.
4. Several women in labor who were unable to deliver immediately gave birth once one of these medallions was hung around their neck while invoking Saint Benedict.
5. This holy medallion is a guaranteed remedy for creatures infected by a demon; by wearing it they will possess full peace and self-assurance.

✦ + Z + *Dia.*

📖 Villiers, 81ff.; Franz II, 107.

V.V.M.A.X.O.G.S.T.H.12N.Z.J.H.4: To overcome one's enemies, one must take the dewclaw from a living rooster's right foot and carry it on one's person along with these letters.

Variant: *V : H : M : A : Xo : p. S : F : H : I : N : L : J. X: 4: 1:.*

✦ *Volo et Vono.*

📖 Bang, no. 1143, no. 1167.

Et fera sechew le tout dans un four après la Sortie du pain, jusqu'à ce qu'il se puisse reduire en poudre et jetteras cette poudre dans le passage de la personne, ou en jetteras sur elle et tu verras merveille mais sois bien Exact aux Caractères.

Autre pour le même Sujet

Environ le douzieme Septembre jour et heure de venus tu feras ou feras faire une Medaille de Cuivre rouge et sur icelle graveras ou fera gravew d'un côté ces Caractères ⟨◁⟩ ♂ ♀ **A** et de l'autre côté ces parolles **IEOVA AE NONNA**, ce que étant fait tu les garderas pour le besoin. qui est de la pendre à ton col par un cordon qui ait servi a la personne que tu desire, et tous les matins pendant tout le mois d'octobre avant Soleil levé tu iras a sa porte et diras les parolles Suivantes

From *The Lesser Key of Solomon*

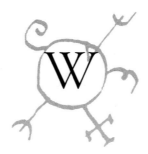

† WARAGEN † DITAGEN † SARAGON: To heal a toothache in the Netherlands, this would be written on a piece of bread that is given to the person suffering from the toothache to eat.
  📖 Braekman, no. 121.

WERBOM DEI MANET METERUNUM: When written on a door, these words can halt a fire. They mean, "May the divine word remain eternally." In 1780, the variant *Erbum Manetine Ferumen † Norien † Asion †* was used. The phrase is preceded by two Kabbalistic symbols, and the first two words are topped with a cross. It had to be inscribed on a piece of lead to be cast into the fire, which would then stop burning.
  Variants: *4erbum Die manet me Fre runen; I Erbum die manet Me Terunem.*
  📖 Bang, no. 1082.

W. G.: This is the abbreviation of the angelic salutation in the Dutch charm, *Weest gegroet Maria* ("I salute you, Mary").

W H W B E: This is the opening to a spell against a toothache that is part of a "notebook of secret recipes" compiled by Christian Heuschkhel, a forester of Neustadt an der Orla in Thuringia, in Germany, who lived during the eighteenth century. The full spell is written as follows:

W H W B E
sV V H H SS
W E A H CB

with the person's name added. The full thing is then buried beneath the rain gutter. This spot is, among other things, a spot where spirits reside and a choice place for communication with the beyond.
  📖 Peuckert, *Pansophie,* 386.

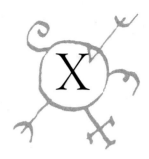

X. C. I. T. A. X. E. X. XY. X. A.. X. PÖVEAS. SPIVIUS: To hit someone repeatedly from a distance, this is written with chalk on a piece of clothing, which is then hung from an image of the person to be struck, but it is necessary to know the name of one's target.

📖 Spamer, 366.

7:X,C,X,O,X,V,B,X: To be loved, this spell should be written down and carried on one's person:

> *7:X,C,X,O,X,V,B,X*
> *S+,X,1X, ob[?]m*
> *X.30,X Ol: Z:S:3X4X [?] 106*

📖 Vaitkevičienė, no. 1634 (spell from Poland).

XF IOX: To enjoy the favor of one's patron, a person should write and carry:

> *XF IOX, Foraun[?] x Flior*
> *x Atatnreg[?] x: w imię patrix*
> *x str.F ily x*

📖 Vaitkevičienė, no. 1633 (spell from Poland).

X M Γ: A Greek abbreviation used in childbirth charms. These are the initials for the words of the phrase, "Mary gave birth to Jesus," *CMG* in Latin. A very beautiful Greek spell uses it for another purpose, and it provides us with a splendid illustration of how Christianity and paganism were often blended together.

> *X M Γ Or Or phor phor Iao Sabaoth Adonai Eloe Salaman Tarchei demon. I bind you, scorpion of Artemis, 315 times. Protect this house and those that dwell in it from all misfortunes, the evil*

eye *of the aerial spirits, illness, the bite of scorpions and serpents, by the virtue of the name of the supreme God. Enrouro pades aaaaaa Bainchoooch mariii iii. Protect me, Lord, true son of David, born of the holy virgin, Mary, holy and supreme God of the holy spirit. Praise be upon you, heavenly king. Amen. A†Ω A†Ω IXΘΥΣ* (*ichthus* means "fish, an early symbol of Christianity").

Bainchoooch may be an Egyptian invocation that was transformed into a deity or spirit on curse tablets and amulets.

📖 PGM II, 189; Youtie and Bonner, 57.

X M O Θ X A P † † ε A 4 λ A L X Z V 8 V ν: If you were to wear or otherwise carry these *caracteres* on your person around the year 1650, no one could cause you any harm. *X* has been decoded as Christus, and *O Θ* has been interpreted as *o Theos,* meaning "God."

📖 Ohrt II, 130.

X O H O: For protection against bullets, the long spell of which this phrase is a part was used in the Swiss canton of Vaud during the

thirteenth century. It was necessary to write a long encrypted spell accompanied by figures.

📖 Hervé, 360.

XO XO: This is the beginning of a very long series of *caracteres* that form the heart of a charm against wounds that features the legend of a King Sero, who was made invulnerable thanks to these magic symbols:

XO XO XZ X H X V X J X B D X F X K X M X 11 X W X 9 X ss X n X VV VV X L X P X S X n X y v X x X a Y R X H D H 11 o o x D X C X S X r X H X Y F X 9 eleison pax, recent pax Christi.

It is still not certain if the *X*'s are the letter of the alphabet in representations of Saint Andrew's Cross. *P* probably means "protégé," and *S* is likely either *salua* or *sanctifica*.

📖 Spamer, 334.

XP: This is a common abbreviation for Christus in spells.

📖 Horsley and Waterhouse, 211–30.

X 3 P N ALIGELL: To make yourself invulnerable, it is necessary to write this spell on a piece of paper and carry it on your person.

📖 Schulz, 191, 638 (footnote).

X S: To prevent dogs from catching rabies, the Silesians traced the following on a slice of buttered bread with a needle:

X	S	X	M	X
6	X	6	X	5
X	SSS	C	X	6
O	X	SSS	C	X

They then cut the bread into three pieces, which were then given to dogs to eat, in the name of God.

📖 Drechsler, 2, 291.

† XTUS VINCIT: See *Christus vincit*.
 📖 Van Haver, no. 449.

XX: To obtain the favors of one's lord or king, or some other individual, or to meet that person, it was believed necessary in eleventh-century England to carry a note bearing a text that opened with this series of letters:

XX. h. d. e. o. e. o. o. e. e. e. laf. d. R. U. fi. ð. f.p.Λ. x. Box. Nux. In the name of the King Father. M. per x.xix. xcs. xh. ih.

Deo. eo. deeo. lafdruel. bepax. box. nux. bu. An nom du Père roi de Marie. ihs. xpc. mon seigneur. ihc. + boni fia senioribus H. hrintur her letus contra me. hee. Larrhibus. Excitatio pacis inter virum et mulierum. A.B. et alfa tibi reddit vota fructu leta lita tota tauta vel tellus vel ade virescit.

There are two spells, with the start of the second detectable by *Deo*, and the second obviously a simple variant of the first as it contains the same *caracteres*. The sequence *boni fia senioribus*, because the last word is incorrect (*seniores*) can be understood as, "May the Elders become good." The sequence of *excitatio . . . mulierum*, "plea for peace between men and women," corresponds to the purpose of the spell. *Tibi . . . fructu* suggests that an offering of fruit be made. *Per x.xix. xcs. xh. ih* represents an abbreviated variant of Christ.
 📖 Berthoin-Mathieu, 498–503; Storms, no. 69.

XΣ: An abbreviation for Christos found frequently in Greek texts. In a Coptic healing spell it is repeated eight times, preceded by four crosses and accompanied by an abbreviated form of the Apostles' Creed and the staurogram (from the Greek σταυρος, "stake," "cross"), which differs from the Christogram, or monogram of Christ, formed of the Greek letters *X* and *P*. The text says, "Christ appeared, Christ suffered, Christ died, Christ resurrected, Christ was carried up [to heaven], Christ is king, Christ save us, who birthed Gennaia, from all burning fever and daily cold sweats, daily, already, already, quick, quick," followed by †††††††.
 📖 Boswinkel et al., eds., 98.

YAFAA: In a conjuration meant to procure good understanding between a man and a woman, who will be named, an image is made in yellow bronze or yellow wax, then dyed green, and the individual then addresses God while recalling the harmony he established between Adam and Eve, Jacob and Rachael, Michael and Gabriel. He then conjures the angels with these words:

yafaa safaa alleya hayala haya halix hayul ataya hytoia saffebata colfossol remlestar.

Finally the image is buried in a spot where the man and woman are in the habit of walking.

📖 *Liber incantationum,* folio 89 r°–v°.

YANE MARE SYAM: When Moses made the bronze serpent and destroyed the golden calf, his staff bore the following text:

Yane mare syam, abyl alia, nano, hya actenal tijogas ijana, eloim ija nehn ijane hay ijanehu, abijaco mea.

These words have the virtue of driving off all magic and all misfortunes.

📖 *Semiphoras* II, 6.

YAO: A variant of Ιαω found in Coptic charms. One example can be seen in a manuscript that contains a long curse by a certain Jacob, who wants revenge on a family whom he asks God, the angels, and so forth to strike down.

Adonaï, Eloë, Eloi, Eloi, Eloi, Eloi, Yao, Yao, Yao, Yao, Sabaoath, Emanuel, el, el, el, el, el, el, el, Emanuel, Michaël, Gabriel, Raphaël, Rakouël, Souriël, Anaël, Ananaël, Fanouël, Fremouël, Abrasaxsax.

As in Greek magic prescriptions, the curse concludes with a series of sounds:

B. A. A. A. A. A. A. A. E. E. E. E. E. E. E. E. E. É. É. É. É. É. É. É. I. I. I. I. I. I. I. O. O. O. O. O. O. O. Y. Y. Y. Y. Y. Y. Y. Ô. Ô. Ô. Ô. Ô. Ô. Ô.

✦ *Iaô.*

📖 Lexa I, 106ff.

Y. B. A.: These *caracteres* must be written with blood in extremely tiny script on the navel of a woman in labor so that she can deliver her baby.

📖 Braekman, no. 46.

YE DELUZ MENYDEZ: To win a woman's love, a dish should be prepared that contains coagulated hare's blood, wolf's blood, liquid mutton fat, amber, musk, camphor, and the blood of the one seeking the woman's affections. The entire concoction is heated, then blended with drink, meat, or fowl. One then casts a little incense and galbanum into the fire, and when it begins smoking, says: "*Ye Deluz, Menydez, Catrudiz, Mebduliz, Huenehenilez,* I disturb the heart and spirit of the woman N by the virtue of these spirits and this concoction," and then ends by saying: "*Hueheyulyez, Heyediz, Cayimuz, Hendeliz.*" If this does not work, the blood of the person asking is replaced with that of his heart's desire, while saying: "*Adyeruz, Metayruz, Beryudez, Fardaruz*" during suffumigations, then the spirits Vemedeyz, Audurez, Meyurneyz, and Sandaruz are invoked. The preparation is given to the coveted woman to eat, and a new suffumigation is made while speaking these names: *Hamurez, Heydurehiz, Heldemiz, Hermeniz.*

Here are the instructions from the *Gâyat al-Hakîm*, the Arabic source of the *Picatrix*:

1. *O Dîlûs, Ahîdâs, Batrûdalîs, Bandûlîs, Wajâgîlâs*
2. *Adirûs, Bâtîrûs, Barjûdîs, Fardarûs*
3. *Anamûrâs, Habwâlûs, Fânîs, Badrûlâs*
4. *Hânûdîs, Mahrijâs, Tidûras, Umîrûs*

📖 *Picatrix* III, 10; *Gâyat al-Hakîm*, 262ff.

YESERAYE: This is the second *Semiphoras of Solomon,* which Adam received from the angels with whom he was conversing. It translates as "God without beginning or end." It should be spoken aloud only when addressing the angels at the time one wishes answers to his questions and for his wishes to be granted (*Semiphoras*).

YETAYROZ: In an operation for winning the love of women, a suffumigation is made by the caster while saying: *Yetayroz, Maharahetym, Faytoliz, Andararuz.*

The four spirits are invoked. The woman the caster desires is then smeared (if possible, says the text) with an oil consisting of several ingredients (musk, amber, hare's blood . . .). The *Gâyat al-Hakîm,* which is the original Arabic source for this text in the *Picatrix,* offers this instruction: *Jâtirûs, Fihârîs, Fitûlîs, Andarawâs.*

📖 *Picatrix* III, 10, 12; *Gâyat al-Hakîm,* 264.

† YGOS.: To learn whether a patient will recover, one takes an egg that a hen laid on the very day the patient was stricken by the illness, and writes on it with wax: *† YGOS. S. FF. X. G. Y. X. G. 9.* Then the egg is placed in front of the door and left there overnight in the open air. The egg is opened on the following day. If blood comes out, the patient shall die. Another very similar spell (*.i. so. S. p. q. x. s. y. s. 9. o.*), which has the same purpose and most likely the same source, adds that the patient should be given wine with mugwort to drink.

📖 Hunt, 139.

YRYRR: The beginning of a magic word carved on a sixteenth-century ring now housed in Bern, Switzerland:

YRYRRAGVTVBERALTERAMIALPLAEZERAE.

Some corrupted Italian words can be made out in this spell word (*altera mi al plaezerae/piacere*).

📖 King, 229; Evans, 123.

YSA. BASA. OLEA. BASOLEA.: This spell is the opening to a blessing for gardens. It is intended to drive away worms while the vegetables are being watered with holy water. *Ysa* is simply the Greek *Isa,* "Jesus."

📖 Franz II, 168.

YVE: According to the *Liber incantationum* (folio 63 r°–64 v°), Moses heard this name of God (Yahweh) and spoke it aloud. This word can be found in a list of biblical figures—Noah, Abraham, Jacob, Aaron, Joshua, Solomon, Ely—who had received the revelation of the God names Genery, Joth, Eyaserie, Anathematon, Sabaoth, Oristion, Eloy, Artifontice, Yephaton, Arbitros, Elyon, Adonay, Pantheon, Arimon, Geremon, Yegeron, Ysiston, Anabona, Egyryon, Patheon, Eya, Gabaon, Pantraton, Symayon...

Variants: *Yvex, VX.*

Zacharias's Benediction

ZAARE ZAARE: The *Picatrix* mentions a Moor who treated scorpion bites and performed miracles with the help of the following magic words:

> *zaare zaare raam zaare zaare fedem bohorim borayn nesfis albune fedraza affetihe taututa tanyn zabahat aylatricyn haurane rahannie ayn latumine queue acatyery nimieri quibari yehuyha nuyym latrityn hamtauery vueryn catuhe cahuene cenhe beyne.*

These words must be written in seven lines. Some maintained it must be done on the first day of Jupiter's month, while others said the month did not matter. The author adds, "Take care not to make mistakes on these names, their forms and their figures, for fear of bringing error down upon them." This advice was obviously difficult to follow, and the written forms of spells like this are routinely corrupted over the centuries.

A cleric did note in the margin of one manuscript that the spell could be written this way:

> *caare zaare raam zaare fegem boorim vabarayn nense albime fedrata offetihe traveuta tannin tribalat aylatricyn haurauc rahaune ayn latumine quene atatyeri miniery quibarii yehaybary ymlateyoyn hanitanerii veveryn cahuene theonhe beyne* † † (Paris manuscript).

A scholar has also noted that these same words were recorded differently in another book:

> *caare zare regem boorum vabara yn nefx albune federata effocye tantuca canyn cabahut ay latricyn haurane rahannye ayn lataminie quene acatyery mynery quibari yehuy kanny ym latricin hamtaveri verieryn catuhe canene tenothe beyne.*

📖 *Picatrix* I, v, 27.

ZANATOS PROCUL ZEBBI: To heal bullet wounds, one must rinse his mouth and cleanse his teeth with eau-de-vie, then rose water, then wash the wound, kneel, and say these words, followed by, "Man is born, man dies, Hypapanti heal this wound by the power of the firmament *Carnisprivium, Carempremium, Caramentrant.*" The phrase "man is born" borrows the *Christus natus* model, and Hypapanti remains a mystery; is it a demon, a person, or an angel? As for the three names for Lent that refer to Carnival, they seem to be used because of their sonorous nature. *Zanatos* is most likely a corruption of *sanat nos* (heal us).

📖 Van Haver, no. 362.

ZARA . ZAI . DEZEVAL: A spell carved in a magic ring found on the Glamorgan coast in Scotland. Inside the ring is this inscription: + *DEBAL . GUT . GUTTANI.*

📖 Evans, 23.

ZARAII ZALMAII DALMAII: When a magic spell requires the use of parchment or incense, these materials can be exorcised with these words to ensure their purity:

> *Zarii Zalmaii Dalmaii Adonai Anaphaxeton Cedrion Cripon Prion Anaraiton Elion Octinomon Zevanion Alazaion Zedeon Agala On Yod He Vau He Artor Dinotor.*

Then the caster recites Psalms 72, 117, and 134, as well as the *Benedicite omnia opera*. According to the text, this spell contains the names of angels, but it is easy to recognize a good many Hebrew names of God (Adonai, Agla, Yaweh, Elion *(עליון*, "supreme"), in it.

◆ *Thebal.*

📖 *Clavicules* II, 17.

ZARI ZARO PATROS: The beginning of the closing spell in an Italian charm for healing snakebite: *Zari zaro patros hemanuhel paraclitus.*

📖 Baldelli, 456.

Z. B. A. C. I. D. N. † X † ro : ooooo—oooo—ooooo— ࿓: To win love, one must draw these *caracteres* on virgin parchment and then carry it on one's person.

📖 Aymar, 346.

+ Z + DIA + BIZ + SAB + ZHGF + BFRS: Since the sixteenth century, a compilation of Biblical verses written in an abbreviated form has been known by the name of *Zacharias's Benediction*. These initials correspond to:

Z: *zelus domus tuae liberat me;*
D: *Deus, Deus meus expelle pestem;*
I: *in manus tuas* (Luke 23:46);
A: *ante coelum et terram Deus erat;*
B: *bonum est praestolari auxilium Dei* (Jeremiah 3:26);
I: *inclinabo cor meum* (Psalms 112, 119);
Z: *zelavi super iniquos* (Psalms 3, 72);
S: *salus tua ego sum;*
A: *abyssus abyssum invocat* (Psalms 8, 41);
B: *beatus vir qui sperat in Domino* (Psalms 5, 39);
Z: *zelus honoris Dei convertat me;*
H: *haeccine reddis Domine populo stulte* (Deuteronomy 32:6);
G: *gutturi meo et faucibus meis adhaerat lingua mea* (Psalms 6, 136);
F: *factae sunt tenebrae* (Luke 23:44);
B: *beatus vir qui non respexerit in vanitates;*
F: *factus est Deus in refugium mihi* (Psalms 22, 93);
R: *respice in me Domine* (Psalms 1, 21);
S: *salus mea tu es* (Jeremiah 17:14).

"May the zeal of your house free me!
O God, my God, drive off the plague!
Into your hands, O Lord, I commend my spirit.
God existed before heaven and earth.
It is good to await in silence the help of God (so that he may drive the plague away from me).
I wish my heart to be inclined (to respect your precepts).
(I saw the sinners in peace) and unjust men annoy me.
I am your savior.
Abyss calls to abyss.
Blessed be he who places his hope in the Lord!
May I be full of zeal for God (before I die)!
[Here is a dubious passage.]
May my tongue stick to my palate (if I so not praise thee)!
Darkness shall spread (o'er the entire earth at your death).
Blessed be he who seeks not vanities!
The Lord is my refuge.
Look at me, Lord (my God Adonaï)!
You are my salvation (heal me and I shall be healed)!"

This benediction is also written on a cross in the two following ways:

One wears or carries on one's person the note on which these initials have been written as protection against the plague and a variety of other ills. The crosses here indicate that the sentences or orisons begin with *crux Christi*.

I have found a slightly altered version of this benediction in a spell intended to prevent anyone from stealing from you.

EE: † Z. † D. I. A. † B. † Z. † S. A. B. Z. † H. V. W. F. † B. E. R. S. † † †

It is necessary to write this on a staff that is placed close to one's belongings. The alteration appears to be the result of a flawed reading of the spell, as depicted on the cross above. In the nineteenth century, it was not rare for the names of family members to be inscribed on this amulet. Additions concerning the cross are also visible; there is even a mistake as, on the second bar of the cross, the *I* is read as † and glossed as *crux Christi defendi nos,* and so on.

📖 *Egyptian Secrets* II, 106.

† Z·I·N· † A†B I Z † S. A. B † Z † H. Z. E. Ł BEAS L: These *caracteres* are used to provide protection against the plague. They must be written on a piece of paper that is then tied to the right hand.

These letters can also be written on a silver ring that is worn on the left finger.

The manuscript indicates that these letters were found in a pillar of a Greek monastery and that they performed wondrous things: a vine that was infested with worms and would only produce green grapes, then would quickly wither, was cured when these letters were attached to it.

📖 Bucharest, Romanian Academy, BAR 1698, folio 34 v°.

ZINUPT: This is the first word of a spell that is intended to cure a horse that sprained its leg. It is necessary to write + *zinupt* + *anta* + *peranta* + *anta* + on a piece of parchment that is then attached to the afflicted limb.

✦ *Ante.*
📖 Hunt, 96.

2 Z KRUX CHRISTI KRUX DALI KRUX IURI LO KRUZ Z: This spell is written on paper that is then given to livestock in their feed as protection against an epizootic disease. Bang provides a spell dating from 1750 that ends with this variation: *Crux Jurilo Crux i Z.*

📖 Espeland, § 14; Bang, no. 1147.

ZOAR: When written in Greek letters on a parchment after having picked a certain herb beneath a waxing moon, then placed in a cloth that is tied with a linen thread to the head of someone suffering from headache, this word possesses healing virtues.

📖 Önnerfors, 2.

ZORAMI ZAITUX ELASTOT: Magic words to speak for summoning a genie to perform your work or halt that of others. They are spoken after placing a talisman on your left side while naked.

📖 *Trésor,* 178a.

Z. P. V. 4 † 2: In the fifteenth century these *caracteres* were part of the ending of a spell against *caillebottières,* the term for witches who stole milk from a distance: *Z. p. v. 4 † 2 † 7 † L X m † ε † probatum est.* This charm made it possible to strike the thief where she stood.

📖 Spamer, 362.

† ZUNO † NINERE: Repeated three times, this spell is supposed to offer protection against curses, and it follows a prayer addressed to "Mary's child," Jesus, in other words.

📖 Braekman, no. 378.

This piece of jasper discovered in Egypt bears the following inscription:
iaêio uôêiê êôiii
Michaêl Rephaêl Gabriêl Ouriêl
Aieê
sêmea kenteu konteu kengeu kêrideu darunkô lukuêxi
semeseilam lathramaphta iô iô iô iê iê iê iiiiiiiiiii aêaêaê aaaiai eiô
psinôtherthernô

APPENDIX ONE

USE OF *CARACTERES* IN MAGIC

The signs called *caracteres* are components of magic spells, but they do not permit the standard arrangement called for in a dictionary. Here then are several spells that describe what needs to be drawn and why.

ASTROLOGICAL SIGNS

1.

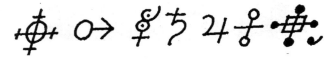

These signs are written with the blood from a white cock's comb on a wand that had been harvested on the evening of a holy Thursday or a Sunday morning before sunrise. It was believed in early-eighteenth-century Sweden that when a wand of this nature passed over a spot where treasure had been hidden, it would twist of its own accord in its holder's hand. These *caracteres* each represent a planet.

📖 BaK, no. 67.

2.

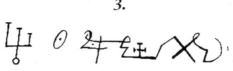

In order to gain wisdom or knowledge of the future, it is necessary to write these "Wittemberg letters" with the blood of a rooster. Then they must be placed beneath the seeker's left side when he goes to bed. That is when revelations of what will occur in the months to come will arrive. The term "Wittemberg letters" is an allusion to the most widespread and best-known grimoire in the Scandinavian countries, the *Cyprianus kunstbok* (Grimoire of Cyprian), which is said to have been discovered in the Wittemberg Academy in Germany around 1520 according to some, and 1722 according to others. It is a manuscript on parchment that was sealed inside a marble strongbox.

 📖 BaK, no. 69.

3.

To have all your wishes granted, you must scrupulously perform a ritual featuring a mole's heart, honey, a piece of paper that is burned, and the expression of the wish, along with these *caracteres*. From left to right, we have the symbols of Jupiter, the sun, and the archangel Michael. The source of these *caracteres* is Peter d'Abano, most likely passed on by Heinrich Cornelius Agrippa's *Occult Philosophy*, a trace of which can be found in the *Cyprianus* (Scandinavian grimoires). They should be compared to the following figure.

 📖 Bang, no. 1175.

4.

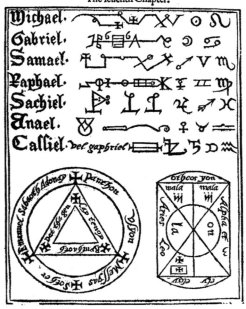

"Write these letters or *caracteres* with your blood on a laurel leaf, then bury it beneath the door of the girl or woman." This is one of the recipes from *Secrets magiques pour l'amour en nombre de octante et trois* (no. XXV).

RUNES

5.

To win the love of a young woman when waving hello, it is necessary to make these signs on one's hands with saliva, while fasting. She must be greeted with the right hand.

📖 Saemundsson, 7.

6.

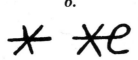

To cause your enemy fear when he sees you, you should write these letters on a piece of oak and wear it between your breasts—this detail indicates that this prescription is addressed to women—and it is necessary that you see your enemy before he or she spies you. This final recommendation generally applies to an encounter with a wolf, which will lose its "voice" if a human sees it first.

📖 Saemundsson, 8.

7.

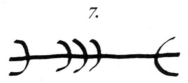

To protect a home from unclean spirits, this rune is carved over the entrance door with a pointed piece of juniper or silver.

📖 Hólmavík, Iceland. Strandagaldur Museum of Icelandic Sorcery and Witchcraft.

8.

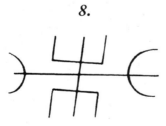

To calm anger, draw a rune on the forehead with one's index finger of the left hand, literally speaking, "with the finger to lick," and say, "I am wearing a helm of terror [*Ægishjálmr*] between my eyes. Vanish wrath, enmity stop! May every man become as good to me as Mary was good to her blessed son when she found him on the flagstone of victory. In the name of the Father and the Son and the Holy Ghost." In Germanic mythology, the dragon Fafnir was the owner of the helm of terror before Siegfried took it from him. In *sigurhellinu* (the flagstone of victory), I have chosen to translate *hella* as "flagstone," for while the word also means "mountain, flat stone, tile, cavern," I believe the allusion it may be making here is to when Jesus gave wise answers to the sages in the temple. But we should also keep in mind Jesus's meeting with Satan on the mountain in the desert. Jesus refused to give in to Satan's temptations, which is also a victory.

📖 Saemundsson, 41.

9.

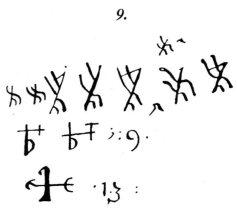

Here is a charm titled "Runes against the Winds of the Stomach," or *fretrúnir*, meaning stomach gases, which calls on Germanic deities at the same time as God and the devils.

> Write these letters on a white calf hide with your blood. Take dog's blood and say: I carve [write] eight gods, nine harsh spirits, thirteen trolls, so that each torment your stomach with excrements and diarrhea, and that all torment your stomach with astounding eruptions of wind. Let your *etalons* [studs/standards] perish, your intestines burst, let your [stomach] wind never calm neither by day or night. You must be driven completely mad and made the enemy of Loki who of all the gods is the most malicious. In the name of our Lord, the Spirit, the Creator, Odin, Thor, the Savior, Freyr, Freyja, Oper, Satan, Belsebub, help us, powerful god, who protects your believers, Uteos, Morss, Noht, Vitales." Uteos is a corruption of *o theos* (o God), Morss is most likely the Latin *mors* (death), and Noht is the night. We have not been able to identify Oper, who was fit in between the gods and the devils.

📖 Saemundsson, 44.

10.

Whosoever carries this group of signs on their person can have no wrong done to them that day, and their enemies shall have no power over them.

 📖 Saemundsson, 8.

11.

If men or women bear these signs on their person, nothing can harm them. Neither sword, nor any of their enemies, nor poison in their mouth or food shall have that power. This must be carved and carried on one's person, and men shall only love you the more.

 📖 Saemundsson, 12.

12.

Carve this and bear it on you, says the charm, and you shall only be better loved.

 📖 Saemundsson, 14.

13.

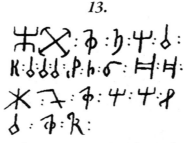

To escape all that is evil, it is necessary to bear these letters on your person. In this way no one shall be able to harm you, nor shall any sword, torment, serpents, or poison in food or drink have that power. These twenty-four runes [pictured above] were read as follows:

D h m p s s a h h o h h d d m m o s d k

📖 Saemundsson, 17.

14.

It was believed in seventeenth-century Iceland that your enemies shall dread you when you bear these signs (runes) on your person.

📖 Saemundsson, 18.

15.

To win the love of the desired individual, these signs (runes) are written on a sacred wafer or on a fish, which is then given to the one whose love is sought to eat.

📖 cf. Saemundsson, 27.

16.

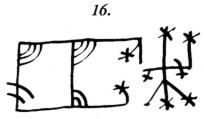

To kill someone, it is necessary to draw these runes on a piece of paper that is then thrown over the hoof prints of one's enemy's horse; if any of his animals steps on it, the caster's foe will die.

 📖 Hólmavík, Museum of Icelandic Sorcery and Witchcraft, Strandagaldur, Galdrasyning á Ströndum.

17.

To obtain the love of a woman, one must write this on one's right hand with one's blood on a Friday morning before sunrise. These *caracteres* seem to be a variant of arborescent runes and would correspond to three þ called "thorns."

 📖 Bang, no. 1128.

18.

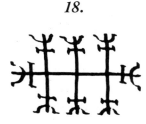

This rune offers protection against all magic and sorcery. It must be drawn on a seal's shoulder blade with mouse blood, then carried on one's person.

 📖 Hólmavík, Museum of Icelandic Sorcery and Witchcraft, Strandagaldur, Galdrasyning á Ströndum.

19.

Around 1627, in order to protect one's farm from any damage, it was believed necessary to write this letter on a rowan tree when the sun was shining at noon, and it was then necessary to walk around the farm three times clockwise, then three times counterclockwise, then stop at the rowan saplings, where one had to write and sharpen the dog roses (wild roses), then place the rowan and dog roses at the animals' gate.

 Saemundsson, 29.

20.

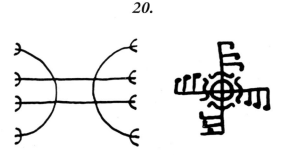

To be victorious at battle, you must keep these two runes in your shoes: Gapaldur under the heel of the right foot, Ginfaxi beneath the toes of your left foot. While looking at the waxing moon, cut a piece of sod with the knife you use to eat with, sprinkle it with your blood, place it in your shoe, and say, "Ginfaxi under the heel/Gapandi on the toe/work like before/there is great need for it now."

 Hólmavík, Museum of Icelandic Sorcery and Witchcraft, Strandagaldur, Galdrasyning á Ströndum.

SCANDINAVIAN *CARACTERES*
21.

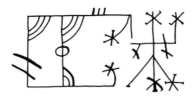

One should write this letter on a piece of paper, then cast it wherever one's horse goes; if it hurts you when you have done no wrong, then all your domestic animals shall die; hide the writing wherever the horse goes.

 Saemundsson, 30.

22.

If one wishes to be feared by one's enemies, this sign should be worn under one's left hand.

 Saemundsson, 15.

23.

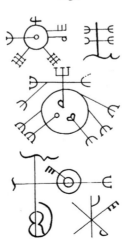

To cause a man to fall asleep, write these letters on an alder chip and place it beneath his head. He shall most surely sleep until this chip is removed from his presence.

📖 Saemundsson, 32.

24.

This figure is part of a 1281 spell against theft. Write these letters in a vase made of ash wood, put water in it, add flour and yarrow, and say, "By the [supernatural] force of the plant and the power of the letter, I desire that the thief be shown to me in the water." Write these names on a whale bone with the spells of the giants and say, "Odin, Loki, Frey, Baldur, Mardur, Týr, Birgir, Hænir, Freyja, Gefjun, Gusta, and all those who built Valhalla and who have been building since the origin of the world. Make it so I obtain what I desire." Odin is the master of the gods of the Scandinavian pantheon. Baldur is his son and Freya his wife, while Hænir is a minor deity about whom little is known. Gefjun is a giant, as Gusta most surely is as well: his name is taken from the noun *gust,* which means a "blast of air." Birgir has a name that speaks volumes: "he who helps."

📖 Saemundsson, 32; Lecouteux, *Dictionnaire de mythologie germanique,* 2nd ed.

25.

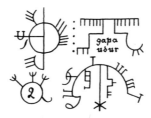

In 1554, in order to enchant a woman so that she could not harm you or steal from you, it was necessary to contrive a hole in the floor of the place where she spent her time and place blood from a giant's spear inside it. The term used, *jötungeirablod,* is a compound of three words: *jötunn* meaning giant; *geirr,* "spear," and *blód,* "blood." This could be translated as meaning the blood taken from a giant by a spear. Outside the hole, it was necessary to write your name and these letters. "A little earth and man three times baptized [*man priteypta*], leaf, distress, hops, and a very long time [eternity?], and you read these curses there." It is Ronald Grambo to whom we owe thanks for being the first to translate the *hapax legomenon man priteypta. Teypta* is the past participle of the verb *deypa,* "baptized," and *pris* means "three times." This sibylline enumeration remains a puzzle to this day.

📖 Saemundsson, 34.

26.

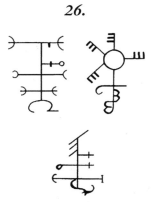

These signs accompany a very curious recommendation: "Write this over a man's footprints and he shall come to you and vomit like a madman.

📖 Saemundsson, 35.

27.

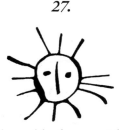

"Do you wish to learn who robbed you with the aid of sorcery? Take a small thorny shrub and carry it in such a way that you shall not lose it. Next, take a small copper peg and a copper hammer. Let the staff that has been made injure the thief; also cast this peg into his right eye and say at the same time: *In Buskan Lucanus Stafurinn.*" These may be two demon names; the last word means "sign, letter, stick." This phrase should probably be translated as "by the stick or sign of Buskan Lucanus." This extremely obscure procedure becomes more comprehensible when it is known that it requires the drawing of an eye, which the individual then damages.

📖 Saemundsson, 44.

28.

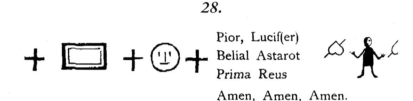

These figures were used around 1780 to discover the identity of a thief in the water.

📖 Bang, no. 1381d.

29.

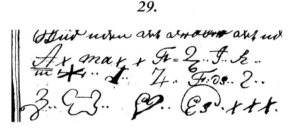

Magic *caracteres* intended to paralyze a bird or animal.

📖 Bang, no. 1354b.

30.

He who carries this "sign" on his person shall never drown.

📖 Hólmavík, Museum of Icelandic Sorcery and Witchcraft, Strandagaldur, Galdrasyning á Ströndum.

31.

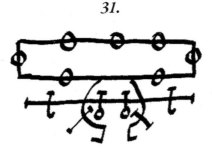

To ensure your sheep bear twins, you must draw this sign on sheep dung with a mouse's rib using crow's blood on a basalt flagstone, then burn the dung on the threshold of the sheepfold so that the smoke covers the flock. This must all be done on Saint John's Day.
 📖 Hólmavík, Museum of Icelandic Sorcery and Witchcraft, Strandagaldur, Galdrasyning á Ströndum.

32.

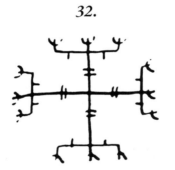

To win the love of a young woman, draw this sign on bread or cheese that you then make sure she eats.
 📖 Hólmavík, Museum of Icelandic Sorcery and Witchcraft, Strandagaldur, Galdrasyning á Ströndum.

33.

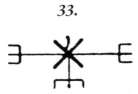

To win the love of a woman, write this sign on the palm of your right hand with blood drawn from the tip of your left thumb, take her hand, and say, "My hand is in yours, and my will overcomes you. May your bones burn if you do not love me as much as I love you. May these words be as impassioned and potent as eternity! May all magic and sorcery push your spirit to love me, and may all the dwellers of the higher world help me in this!"

 📖 Hólmavík, Museum of Icelandic Sorcery and Witchcraft, Strandagaldur, Galdrasyning á Ströndum.

34.

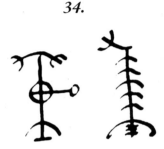

To avoid being robbed, this first sign must be carved during the day and the second at night on the inside of the lid of the chest inside of which one stores his wealth. These *caracteres* are called, respectively, Blood Bull and Earth Bull (Blóðuxi, Molduxi).

 📖 Hólmavík, Museum of Icelandic Sorcery and Witchcraft, Strandagaldur, Galdrasyning á Ströndum.

35.

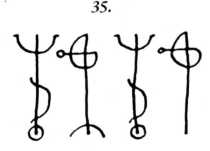

To dream of what you desire, these signs must be inscribed on silver or white leather on Saint John's Night.

 📖 Hólmavík, Museum of Icelandic Sorcery and Witchcraft, Strandagaldur, Galdrasyning á Ströndum.

36.

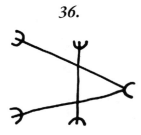

To win a legal case, you should draw this sign on lignite, color it with blood from your nose, and keep it over your chest. If the person is fearful of losing in court, he should keep another on his back, and he will win, even if his cause is unjust.

📖 Reykjavík, ms. Lbs 4375, folio 8 v°.

37.

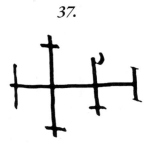

If a cow shows blood in her milk, carve this sign on a piece of oak and milk the animal above it.

📖 Hólmavík, Museum of Icelandic Sorcery and Witchcraft, Strandagaldur, Galdrasyning á Ströndum.

38.

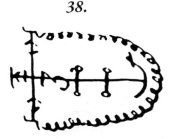

If your livestock is accident prone, carve this sign on oak, bury it, and guide your flock to walk over it.

📖 Hólmavík, Museum of Icelandic Sorcery and Witchcraft, Strandagaldur, Galdrasyning á Ströndum.

39.

To make sure your sheep are docile, when the sun rises, take a juniper or willow branch that is growing facing eastward, carve this sign on it, then have your animals walk over it in summer and beneath it in winter.

 📖 Hólmavík, Museum of Icelandic Sorcery and Witchcraft, Strandagaldur, Galdrasyning á Ströndum.

40.

To protect one's sheep from drowning, this sign would be carved on the horn of the oldest ram.

 📖 Hólmavík, Museum of Icelandic Sorcery and Witchcraft, Strandagaldur, Galdrasyning á Ströndum.

41.

USE OF *CARACTERES* IN MAGIC 371

To avoid being robbed, carve this sign on the door casing and make the sign of the cross with your left hand.

 📖 Hólmavík, Museum of Icelandic Sorcery and Witchcraft, Strandagaldur, Galdrasyning á Ströndum.

42.

To avoid becoming the victim of theft, place this sign beneath the threshold, and the robber will be obstructed from entering the house.

 📖 Hólmavík, Museum of Icelandic Sorcery and Witchcraft, Strandagaldur, Galdrasyning á Ströndum.

43.

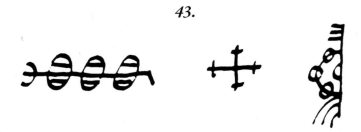

To become a good fighter, draw this sign using a human bone on the shoe or big toe of the leg you use to fight while facing northwest and saying, "I send the devil into the chest and bones of my foe, in the name of Thor and Odin."

 📖 Hólmavík, Museum of Icelandic Sorcery and Witchcraft, Strandagaldur, Galdrasyning á Ströndum.

44.

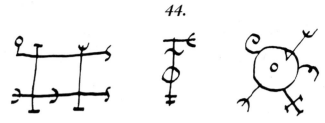

To ensure the docility of your sheep, carve this sign on a piece of stunted oak and bury it beneath the threshold of the sheepfold with your signature.

 📖 Hólmavík, Museum of Icelandic Sorcery and Witchcraft, Strandagaldur, Galdrasyning á Ströndum.

GREEK *CARACTERES*

45.

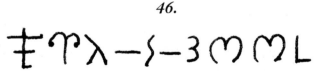

Engraved on a gold strip with a bronze stylus and worn in one's sandals, these *caracteres* allow the wearer to be victorious. The recipe specifies that they can also be attached to a boat or a horse.

 📖 PGM VII, 919–24; PGM: Preisendanz I, 40.

46.

To win someone's favor or friendship, one took a mugwort or pasithea root and carved these signs on it, then carried it on his or her person. All those whose eyes fell on this individual could not help but love him or her.

 📖 PGM XII, 397–400; Preisendanz I, 83.

47.

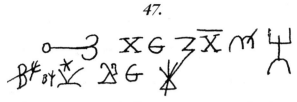

Caracteres to be written in chalk on a magic circle during an operation in order to be protected. Wearing a cat's tail on his head, the caster would turn toward the sun on the fifth hour and recite a long incantation.

📖 PGM VII, 846–61; Preisendanz I, 37.

48.

πατήρ, υἱόc, μήτηρ

πν(εῦμ)α ΑΩ ἅγιον

Ἀβραcάξ

This figure accompanied a prayer asking God to protect someone named Aria from the shivering caused by cold and fever. It translates as, "Father, Son, Mother, Holy Ghost ΑΩ Abrasax."

📖 Preisendanz I, 192.

49.

> *Iaô Sabaoth Adonay akrammachammarei*
> *aô Sabaoth Adonay akrammachammarei*
> *ô Sabaoth Adonay akrammachammarei*
> *Abrasax.*

This is the text on an amulet against fever. It must be written on clean paper and worn or carried.

📖 Preisendanz I, 10.

50.

ABRASAX

Written in scarlet, this would be worn around the temples, to combat a migraine.

📖 PGM VII, 201ff.

51.

To ensure a horse wins a race, this sign would be inscribed on its hooves with a bronze stylus. The person would then add, "Grant me success, friendship, celebrity, and the favor of the stadium."

📖 PGM VII, 390–93; Preisendanz I, 390.

52.

⳽ ⊠ ⊛ ✳ ⳽ ʊ ⇀ ⋒ ⵉ ⊼ ⊗ ⅁ / BACHYCH ⵉⵉ ≣ ⊔ ⎕ AALOUGIKI ELŌAI BAIN- CHŌŌŌCH ⋻ ⊱ ⟨ 3 ⟩ ⊠ ⳽ ୧ · ⎟⎟ EULAMŌ PHNOUBENE EIZOCHOR MOBOR PHŌ CHORBA ZACHEI ANACHIA ჶ K ⟊ ⟡ ⟆ ι ß PHŌRPHORBA PHŌRBORBA SEMESILAM ARCHENTECHTHA ASCHELIDONĒL

To bind and subjugate, one would take a lead water pipe and cut a strip from it, on which he would carve these *caracteres* and names:

Βαχυχ, ααλουγικι Ἐλωαι Βανχωωωχ, ευλαμο φνουβενε ειξχορ μοβορ φω χορβα ξαχει ανχια.

📖 PGM VII, 396–404; Preisendanz I, 397–404.

53.

ΑΘΑΘΛααΒΖαΤΙΖΒ. The charm that contains these *caracteres* is called "night revelations." The spell called for a hoopoe's heart, myrrh, and the *caracteres* written on a sheet of papyrus with the magic name. The heart was then wrapped inside the papyrus, and it was placed on the sex organ of a woman, who would then respond to any questions.

 📖 PGM VII, 411–16; Preisendanz I, 413–17.

54.

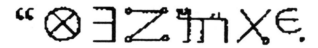

To create a binding, these *caracteres* would be carved on a strip of tin with a bronze stylus before dawn, accompanied by the names: 'χρημιλλον' Μουλοχ καμπυ χρη ωφθω Μασκελλ-λόγος Ἐρηκισφθη Ἰαβεξβυθ, then it was cast into the sea while asking the gods to hold fast the targeted individual.

 📖 PGM VII, 417–22; Preisendanz I, 418–22.

55.

DAMNIPPE PĒPĒ ŌŌ LYKYXUVHYCH NN CHYCH XYKYL PSCH ŌŌ ĒPĒP ĒPP INMAD

These *caracteres* accompany a love spell that is intended to bring the woman one desires to him, even if she refuses. They are preceded by: ΔΑΜΝΙΠΠΗ ΠΗΠΗ.

 📖 PGM XVIIa, 1–25; Preisendanz I, 138.

56.

This is a text for an amulet to be written on a strip of gold, silver, or tin, or a sheet of papyrus for protection from ghosts and demons, illness, and suffering. It contains the name and power of the great god: *Kméphis, Chphyris, Iaô, ow, Aión, Iaeó, Baphrênêmoun, othilarikriphi-aêuêai phirkira, lithanuome, nerphabôêai.*

📖 PGM VII, 579–90; Preisendanz I, 26.

57.

Caracteres accompanying a love spell. They are carved on a tin tablet with a copper nail from a sunken ship, and the following magic words are added to them: ιχαναρμεθω χαcαρ.

📖 PGM VII, 462–66; Preisendanz I, 21.

58.

By drawing the figure of a person holding a torch in his right hand and a knife in his left, with a scarab beneath his feet, and beneath that a snake that is biting its own tail (Ouroboros), one obtains a counterspell.

📖 PGM VII, 178–87.

59.

⊗ЄPT⊗AP⊗PL.

To heal tenderness of the breasts, it is necessary to draw these signs on a parchment of hyena hide with black ink and to carry it on one's person.

📖 PGM VII, 208–9.

60.

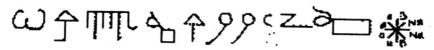

To cure a scorpion bite, these *caracteres* are drawn on a sheet of papyrus that is used to wrap the wound.

📖 PGM VII, 193–96.

61.

TKΛΓ˝Ч⊗AKYATЄYTЄOPШI

An amulet of protection against coughs. These *caracteres* are drawn on parchment made from hyena hide and then worn around the neck.

📖 PGM VII, 206ff.

62.

"ḷPȣ⌐◯†◯sssss⊞⌐⌐ʃP̣J°₣ṿḶJX⊠BZH
EREKISIPHTHEARARCHARAEPHTHISIKERE."

Accompanied by a sacrifice, these *caracteres* are written on a silver tablet on which incense is placed. This makes it possible to win the favor of the people and the mob, but the magic only works for an individual persecuted by demons.

📖 PGM XXXVI, 275–83.

63.

This is used to make someone ill. One writes it with weasel's blood on a triangular pot, which is then buried in the house. Fairly obscure, the text for this curse appears to indicate that a figurine is made and placed inside the pot, which is then filled with water before totally covering it up.

📖 PGM CXXIV, 1–43.

64.

These *caracteres* are carved on tablets holding a Latin curse that were found in Hadrumetum. The tablets were intended to cause chariot drivers and their horses to fall during races in the arena. On no. 276 and no. 277, the *caracteres* are repeated, whereas on no. 278, their second mention is replaced on the other side by:

It should be noted that the enchantment is centered around three verbs: *cadere*, "to fall," *vertere*, "to overturn," and *frangere*, "to break." In no. 276, the first word is repeated twenty-nine times, the second, seven times, and the third, twice. We most often find the pair *cadat vertat* (five times at the beginning of the spell) and *cadat frangant* once. In the broken tablet, no. 277, only *cadat vertat* is used, whereas in the opening of no. 278, we have *cadat vertat frangat* three times and *cadat frangat vertat* once.

📖 Audollent, 386–89.

USE OF *CARACTERES* IN MAGIC 379

ENGLISH *CARACTERES*
65.

Write in paper these characters following, on the saturdaie, in the houre of ☽, and laie it where thou thinkest treasure to be : if there be anie, the paper will burne, else not. And these be the characters.

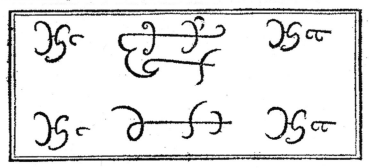

To discover a treasure, one must inscribe these *caracteres* on paper on a Saturday, then place it where one believes the treasure to be. If it is there, the paper will burst into flames.

📖 Scot, Book XV, chapter 10.

שם　　　　　　　　　　　　　　　　　　שם

Alphabeta sunt septem.

	1	2	3	4	5	6	7
א							
ב							
ג							
ד							
ה							
ו							
ז							
ח							
ט							
י							
כך							
ל							
מם							
נן							
ס							
ע							
פף							
צץ							
ק							
ר							
ש							
ת							

hæc de Numismatibus Hebraicis, & Hebræo-Christianis dicta sint satis

APPENDIX TWO

CRYPTOGRAPHY

1. On the facing page are alphabets commonly used in medieval grimoires, according to Athanasius Kircher.

    The *caracteres* in columns two to seven originally represented astral figures marked by two small circles and connected with lines, which subsequently became secret alphabets.

2. Alphabet from a fifteenth-century Italian manuscript:

📖 Omont, 253–58.

3. The first and second alphabet of Solomon, according to Blaise de Vigenère.

📖 Vigenère.

4. The alphabet of Antonio de Fantis, a sixteenth-century esotericist.

5. The two alphabets of Apollonius of Tyana, the first coined from Greek, the second from Hebrew.

6. A Gothic alphabet used by the Scandinavians.

7. Alphabet used in the grimoire of Stavanger, Norway, (Oslo University, Norwegian Folklore Collection, NB *Svartebok fra Stavanger*).

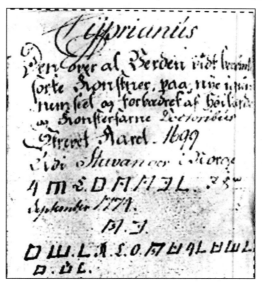

8. A grid for encrypting through the use of runes and substitutions.

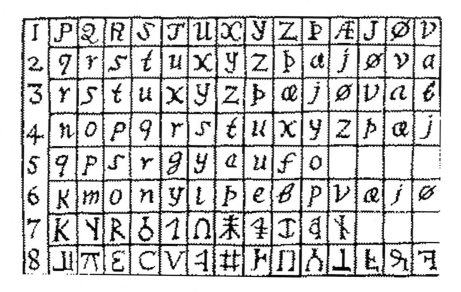

APPENDIX THREE

LIST OF MAGIC WORDS APPEARING IN THE SPELLS

The table below indicates in which spell the principal magical word can be found.

MAGICAL WORD	NAME OF SPELL	MAGICAL WORD	NAME OF SPELL
Abachasis to Alamar		**Alas to Arabor**	
A		Alas	Dismas
Abachasis	Kaijda	Aleono	Hall
Abodonika	Tegneta	Algadena	Dismas
Abraxat	Hoerbae	Aligell	X 3 P
Abyzou	Gylloy	Allocax	A Π
Adochy	E †	Aloscora	Nameit
Adong	Sila	Amon	Pela
Adrepotenat	Sator	Amorona	Ele
Adromaniel	Othinel	Amplustra	O fusa
Æratin	Heabor	Anabonac	Hoscaraa
Afesorcherin	Yarebidera	Anglobis	Kailos
Ageltor	Hafel	Aoldominum	Bede
Aglanas	Dismas	Aphonidos	Lasgaroth
Aitai	Toto	Aprision	Volacti
Alamar	Lasgaroth	Arabor	Arols

MAGICAL WORD	NAME OF SPELL	MAGICAL WORD	NAME OF SPELL
Arnnepe to Borsibs		**Brabarasaba to Cuttar**	
Arnnepe	Patus	Brabarasaba	Abara
Arpagon	Lasgaroth	Brac	Vriel
Artamati	Hall	Briora	Bastam
Artesie	Alga	Brixa	Barto
Arthimei	Alga	Brorithire	Neptalnabus
Artifex	Eax	Brysa	Pritag
Asasus	Arols	Bulbotum	Torum
Asion	Werbom	Burgum	Mergastor
Athloger	Habor	**C**	
Atocora	Nave	Calia	Achit
Avalapiis	Kalipiis	Camita	Supililie
Avalcentom	Abla	Cardon	Gon
Avestia	Names of the Demons	Castan	Iran
Ayalo	Holomaati	Cat	Rat
Ayrata	FF Lale	Cayhaeçar	Laceyleçun
B		Ceccentimos	Ele
Bactrus	Baetra	Chamasal	Theon
Bagabius	Veide	Cherib	Dis
Baracha	Hoscaraa	Clebsin	Qamla
Basolea	Ysa	Cletemati	Hell
Beherenos	Theos	Cnitas	Inquintas
Bekahu	Holomaati	Coblamot	Araba
Bele	Ele	Cocorerstu	Bell
Beley	Ele	Colate	Guarac
Berig	Buri	Con	Ecce
Bessiabato	Abhz	Condion	Lasgaroth
Biß	Hall	Conterix	Terix
Blicteum	Urini	Corantrix	Neon
Blode	Sama	Corbula	Qvinta
Boetite	Hoerbae	Coriander	Sillomondus
Borcay	Tinira	Cunhunelaja	Thigat
Borsibs	Diston	Cuttar	Araba

LIST OF MAGIC WORDS APPEARING IN THE SPELLS

MAGICAL WORD	NAME OF SPELL	MAGICAL WORD	NAME OF SPELL
Cymopum to Ezonorum		**F to Giennem**	
Cygmopum	Ky	**F**	
D		F	Werbom
Dabulb	Dis	Fagiam	Elo
Dali	Z Crux	Ferstigon	Onysoma
Dali	2 Z	Ffars	N. Y.
Dicapron	Cheilei	Fiilkout	Axtu
Diesla	Hosala	Fikka	Da Sa
Dinotor	Zaraii	Filiax	Eax
Direa	Prorsus	Fililax	Trix
Divernas	In tes	Firar	E†
Don	Ecce	Firax	Max
Dorenus	Porto	Firin	Lagumen
Dorsa	Jorsa	Flax	Massa
Dragor	Alga	Florit	Hell
Dutter	Janna	Fondon	Lasgaroth
E		Fokoram	Narkados
Ebule	Sinistræ	Fomagas	Pavte
Ecgitar	Abhz	Forsma	Orsa
Echogartner	Solam	Franest	Dufa
Ecriger	Fratter	Frofall	Priol
Effrecga	Agla	Froha	Aha
Ehur	Ele	**G**	
Eleona	Hell	Gaaba	Tro Etanator
Elion	Droch	Gagar	Massa
Elmay	Lemaac	Galligonon	Terra
Eoraya	Thebal	Garislia	Supililie
Eparygon	Onysoma	Garon	Philacrates
Erfratus	Futus	Gebali	Stant
Esbrey	Didai	Gematar	Solam
Esem	Droch	Geronay	Names of God
Exgvedia	Neguba	Gestas	Dismas
Exqeidax	Pax	Gheter	Boro
Ezonorum	Eløn	Giennem	Guarac

MAGICAL WORD	NAME OF SPELL	MAGICAL WORD	NAME OF SPELL
Gievfe to Iavgellaym		*Iegal to Lume*	
Gievfe	Hax	Iegal	Megal
Gimum	Kalepiis	Imaholite	Cara; Chimrat
Gleon	B.O.K.	Imax	Max
Gomeret	Kailos	Ista	Huat
Gomson	Kaijda	Itadoch	Augusti
Gorgides	Philacrates	Iuri	2 Z
Gottzo	Arill	**J**	
Gramenkios	Dedra	Jadon	Gon
Grammata	R.O.A.	Jameth	Nave
Grantem	Elo	Jer	Janna
Graton	Diston	Jechomagol	Theon
Grax	Job	Jezabali	Theon
Greem	Afriass	Jurilo	ZZ
Grichema	MWst	Jyepichminför	Tro Etanator
Gruba	Job	**K**	
Guthanay	Thebal	Kafter	Iram
Guttatim	Thebal	Kamanatar	Theon
H		Kaminaka	Jakepta
Habi	Dabi	Kanali	In navsitus
Hamasias	Porto	Kant	Ereret
Hariomolatar	Theon	Kathoka	Prorsus
Hatamas	Theos	Kefer	Mathrebeton
Hecas	Gebali	Kemolihot	Theon
Hedas	Gebali	Kien	Dedra
Hensell	Odrus	Kikaym	Okilim
Herbonos	Vassis	Kout	Futus
Hoccayethos	Ele	**L**	
Hondendion	Martificion	Lakom	Hax
Horepta	Jakepta	Lamacron	Lasgaroth
Hosi	Vos k	Lavatosorin	Lagumen
I		Lemach	Theos
Iabôch	Phnô	Lentum	Pela
Iaias	Ieppel	Lugosto	Okilim
Iavgellaym	Lagumen	Lume	Ellieue

LIST OF MAGIC WORDS APPEARING IN THE SPELLS

MAGICAL WORD	NAME OF SPELL	MAGICAL WORD	NAME OF SPELL
Lutinto to Morche		**Nanay to Piron**	
Lutinto	Okilim	**N**	
M		Nanay	Ele
Magola	Ago	Nay	E†
Magubula	Mala	Nazir	† Loy
Magula	Job	Nebandat	Minate
Malasinala	Hyla	Nemos	Aros
Malmort	Kalepiis	Nenonamini	Eulogumen
Manraret	Vos k	Netabe	Sator
Maratarikin	Arato	Ninere	Zuno
Massa	Hola	Nobalutz	For
Matanor	Bassor	Nordor	Neon
Materonny	Sator	**O**	
Mefenecon	Ele	Obrigat	Abrido
Meillum	Ellieue	Octinomon	Zaraii
Mematus	Nameit	Oga	P ††
Mesepos	Sator	Oigan	Ka
Mesonor	Hoscaraa	Ol'ma	N. Y.
Meterunum	Werbom	Omel	Araba
Metoro	Mersus	Ominigan	Ka
Miesrom	Abla	Orbl	Maxis
Mildepos	Sator	Ospergo	Ofano
Milla	N. Y.	Ovins	Pela
Momcethys	Raere	**P**	
Morbor	Neon	Pagula	Paga
Morche	Achit	Parsas	Okilim
Mesonor	Hoscaraa	Parvenech	Rabun
Meterunum	Werbom	Patir	Theos
Metoro	Mersus	Pelmilgano	Tro Etanator
Miesrom	Abla	Penta	Asta
Mildepos	Sator	Petronix	Terix
Milla	N. Y.	Pharel	Othinel
Momcethys	Raere	Phebas	Gebali
Morbor	Neon	Pirella	Eras
Morche	Achit	Piron	On

MAGICAL WORD	NAME OF SPELL	MAGICAL WORD	NAME OF SPELL
Plaraka to Sarson		**Sartus to Syola**	
Plaraka	Philacrates	Sartus	Artus
Pliata	Dufa	Sathonich	Micrato
Plons	E †	Satorum	Pela
Porus	Næsi	Sarax	Pax
Pöveas	X. C. i.	Segehalt	Semeht
Pupicon	On	Segem	Achit
Q		Segok	Onysoma
Qvara	Milkefe	Selama	Baro
Qvisen	Milkefe	Seles, Sellas	Sabor
Qvoddealde	Indomo	Sepagoga	Sepa
R		Seratamier	Kalepiis
Raepy	Micrato	Sicalos	Tinira
Rafit	Valanda	Simma	Kalepiis
Ragium	Lamed	Sinefor	Neon
Ragnaht	Semeht	Sinobia	Quosum
Ragon	Merida	Sipia	Agerin; Ageron
Ranx	Arex	Sirite	Si orgome
Ratotta	Sator	Sirosio	Tinira
Rattacu	Rabun	Skdomin	Ereret
Rauex	MW st	Smarthagon	Mercurion
Redugbit	Abria	Smisorich	Rusiriab
Refoa	Agla	Sobath	Hell; L.Bian
Reqvision	Martificion	Sorchistin	Job pax
Ron	Ecce	Sorebex	Kailos
Rougan	Veide	Spatbus	Ereret
Ruaiab	Rusiriab	Spivius	X. C. i.
S		Srus	Afriass
Sabira	Ele	Stalon	Mersus
Sagata	Agata	Stelpa	Philacrates
Salmalsaach	Theos	Strassus	Cinium
Salonia	Tegneta	Strolag	Pritag
Samafoelis	Sancitan	Subratum	Abhz
Saphert	Sion	Sutagon	Aragon
Sarson	Saraouia	Syola	Dedra

LIST OF MAGIC WORDS APPEARING IN THE SPELLS

MAGICAL WORD	NAME OF SPELL	MAGICAL WORD	NAME OF SPELL
Tahebal to Vranatum		**Wax to Zyriffen**	
T		**W**	
Tahebal	Boro	Wax	Oax
Tamar	E †	Waystou	Chamacha
Tarchei	XMG	**X**	
Tattler	Solam	Xaaja	Afriass
Tax	Minate	Xfol	Mathrebeton
Terumen	Erbum	**Y**	
Thefalnegal	Thigat	Ytumba	Abremonte
Thrachotin	R.O.A.	**Z**	
Thurigium	Theos	Zaboha	Ada
Tibri	Gebare	Zabulantes	Albo
Tifrat	Heyerim	Zalmaii	Zaraii
Timus	Ca Ta	Zamary	Kados
Tinut	Siesnbru	Zamoyma	Theon
Toribus	Sadies	Zarai	Poro
Trahu	Job pax	Zazar	Adibaga;
Transonie	Albo		Valanda
Tridag	Gebare	Zebere	Poro Pota
U		Zenni	Quosum
Uperninen	† Ox	Zerobantes	Job
Urat	Lasgaroth	Zeut	Kados
Utum	Hum	Zezyphulos	Narcados
V		Zimi	Kados
Vagor	Ogor	Zin	Maya
Valata	Nam	Zobola	R.O.A.
Venibbeth	Metatron	Zogogen	Onysoma
Vins	In tes	Zonen	Ox
Vitalot	Milant	Zulphi	Kados
Vort	Haber	Zyriffen	Narcados
Vranatum	Eli		

Conjuration of the Devil

BIBLIOGRAPHY

RARE MANUSCRIPTS

Basel, Switzerland. University Library, ms. B. VII. 30.
Berlin, Germany. Prussian State Library, ms. lat., Quart. 2.
Brussells, Belgium. Royal Library, ms. IV 9588.
Bucharest, Romania. Romanian Academy Library, ms. 4458; ms. 4743.
Cambridge, England. Cambridge University, Corpus Christi College ms. 367.
Cambridge, England. Cambridge University, Trinity College, ms. O.2.13.
Dresden, Germany. Saxon State and University Library, ms. M. 206.
Einsiedeln, Switzerland. Einsiedeln Abbey Library, ms. 731.
Engelbert, Germany. Abbey Library, ms. 3/2 twelfth century.
Florence, Italy. Laurentian Library, Plut. 89 sup. 38.
Ghent, Belgium. University Library, ms. 1021 A.
Gotha, Germany. Ducal Library, ms. Chart.
Heidelberg, Germany. University Library, Cpg 214; Cpg 267; Cpg 268; Cpg 367; Cpg 369; Cpg 478.
Karlsruhe, Germany. Baden State Library, Donaueschingen 792.
Leiden, the Netherlands. Codex Scaligerianus 28.
Leipzig, Germany. Municipal Library, C.M. 66; *Magio de furto,* ms. C.M.
British Library, Arundel 2558; Arundel 36674; Harley 273; Harley 585; Lansdowne 1202; Royal 12 B.XXV; Royal 12 G IV; Royal 17 A xlii; Sloane 56; Sloane 73; Sloane 121; Sloane 122; Sloane 140; Sloane 389; Sloane 405; Sloane 962; Sloane 963; Sloane 1315; Sloane 2187; Sloane 2457; Sloane 2584; Sloane 2948; Sloane 3160; Sloane 3285.
Munich, Germany. Bavarian National Library, Clm 849.
New Haven, Connecticut. Yale University Library, Mellon MS 1.
Oslo, Norway. National Library, Ms. 8° 10, *Cyprianus,* copied around 1790; Ms.

8° 81, *Cyprianus formaning,* copied circa 1650–1700 by Tinn, in Telemark, discovered in 1868; Ms. 4° 279, *Extract aus dem Cyprianus,* 18 pages, circa 1700; Ms. 8° 640a, *Cyprianus frikonst udgivet udi Aaret 1719,* 10 + 1 pages, by Galgum, in the Romedal, circa 1780; Ms. 8° 640e, *Cyprianus Rette Fri Kounster ud Given og Trokt udi Witten Bergh Anno 1509,* printed in Wittemburg in 1509, 34 pages, by Moland, in the Telemark; Ms. 4° 832, *Cyprianus den over ald verden viit berømte Sorte Konstner . . . Stravanger I Norge anno 1699,* 53 pages, circa 1750; Ms. 8° 2062, *Den anden Del af Cypriania skrifter,* 8 pages, 6–8, circa 1790–1800, discovered in Vingrom, Faberg Parish; Ms. 8° 3136, *Cyprianus' Trekandt. Ret forklaring holdende inde formaninger og frie Konster Iligemaade Konste bog og Charactererne Datum von Wittenberg 1707,* copied 1760; *Svartebok fra Fron*; *Svartebok fra Jeløya*; *Svartebok fra Stavanger.*

Oxford, England. Oxford University, Bodleian Library, Rawlinson C. 668.

Paris, France. National Library, ms. Latin 8654 B; new Latin acquisition 7743.

Princeton, New Jersey. Princeton University, Garret 80.

Reykjavik, Iceland. National Library, lbs 4375.

Rouen, France. Municipal Library, ms. 1407.

Saint Gallen, Switzerland. Abbey of Saint Gall, codex 751; ms. 878.

Sankt Florian, Austria. Abbey Library, Codex Flor. XI 467.

Stockholm, Sweden. Royal Library, ms. XIV in kl. 4°.

Trondheim, Norway. Gunnerus Library, XA HA, Qv. 62, *Cyprianus eller Swart-Bogen med Anmækninger til Oplysning anførte of tilsatte af Chr. Hammer,* dated April 17, 1793, 55 pages; LibR, Oct. 5342, *Cyprianus eller Svartebogen. Forfattet av Cyprianus fra Antiokhia Fortale av Willum Stephanson,* Trondheim, 1798, 48 pages; GO, Ky2f8 Cyp, *Mester Cyprianus eller Svartbogen. Forfattet av Cyprianus fra Antiokhia,* Lillehammer, printed by M. Urdal, 1850.

Utrecht, the Netherlands, University Library, Ms. 1355, 16°.

Vienna, Austria. National Library, Codex 3071; Cod. Phil. Gr. 108.

BOOKS, STUDIES, AND REFERENCE WORKS

Bolded entries are listed in accordance with the abbreviation used in the main text of the dictionary.

Abeele, Baudouin van den. "De arend bezweren. Magie in de middeleeuwse valkerijtraktaten." *Madoc* 11 (1997): 66–75.

Abraham a Sancta Clara. *Huy! und Pfuy! der Welt.* Würzburg: Franz Hertzen, 1725.

Acta sanctorum. Antwerp and Brussels: Société des Bollandistes, 1642–1940. 68 vols.

Addabbo, Anna Maria, "Carmen magico e carmen religioso." *Civiltà classica e Cristiana* 12 (1991): 11–27.

———. ""La formule magico-mediche dal latino ai dialetti italiani." *Atti e memorie dell'Accademia Toscana di Scienze e Lettere "La Colombaria"* 56, n.s. 42 (1991): 103–26.

Agrippa, Heinrich Cornelius. *De Occulta Philosophia Libri Tres.* Cologne, 1533.

———. "*Les oeuvres magiques de Henri-Corneille Agrippa par Pierre d'Aban, latin et français, avec des secrets occultes.* Liège, 1788.

———. "*Opera.* 2 vols. Lyon: M. & G. Beringen, n.d., ca. 1600.

Agrippa d'Aubigne, Louis Dufour-Vernes, and Eugène Ritter. *L'Escalade: Recit tiré de l'Histoire universelle et accompagné de documents nouveaus.* Geneva: H. Georg, 1884.

Allatius, Leo. *De templis Graecorum recentioribus.* Cologne: Jodocus Kalcovius, 1645.

Amati, Girolamo. *Ubbie, ciancioni e ciarpe del secolo XIV.* Bologna: Romagnoli, 1866.

Amundsen, Arne Bugge. *Svartebok fra Borge.* Sarpsborg, Norway: Borgarsyssel Museum, 1987.

———. "A Genre in the Making: The First Study of Charms in Norway." In *The Power of Words: Studies on Charms and Charming in Europe*, edited by J. Kapaló, E. Pócs, and W. Ryan. Budapest: Central European University Press, 2012.

Anglo, Ricardo Argentino. *De praestigiis et incantationibvs daemonvm et necromanticorvm.* Basel: R. Silver, 1568.

Anonymous. *Antidotarium Bruxellense* [same edition as the *Pseudo Théodore*]. Edited by Valentin Rose. Leipzig: Teubner, 1894.

Antidotarium Bruxellense. Edited by Valentin Rose. Leipzig: Teubner, 1894.

Anzeiger fur Kunde der deuschen Vorzeit 3, 279.

Apocalypse XXI in *Biblia sacra juxta vulgatam clementinam.* Paris: Desclée & Soc., 1947.

Archidoxis magica: in vol. 14 of *Theophrastus von Hohenheim gennant Paracelsus, sämtliche Werke,* edited by Karl Sudhoff. Munich and Berlin: Oldenbourg, 1933, 437–98. Cited by book and chapter.

Argentine, Richard. *De praestigiis et incantationibvs daemonvm et necromanticorvm.* Basel, 1568.

Árnason, Jón. *Íslenzkar þióðsögur og æfintýri*, vol. 1. Reykjavík: Þjóðsaga, 1954.

Arpe, Peter Friedrich. *De prodigiosis naturae et artis operibus talismanes et amuleta dictis*. Hamburg: Christian Liebezeit, 1717.

Ars notoria: *The Notory Art of Solomon Shewing the Cabanistical Key of Magical Operations.* Translated by Robert Turner. London: J. Cottrel, 1657.

L'Ars notoria au moyen âge. Introduction and critical edition by J. Véronèse. Florence: Micrologus Library, Salomon Latinus I, 2007.

Astori, Roberta. *Formule magische: Invocazioni, giuramenti, litanie, ligature, gesti rituali, filtri, incatesimi, lapidary dall'Antichità al Medioevo.* Milan: Mimesis, 2000.

Astromagia: Alfonso X el Sabio. *Astromagia (Ms Reg. Lat. 1283°)*, edited by Alfonso D'Agostino. Naples: Liguori, 1992.

Aubigné, Théodore-Agrippa d'. *L'Escalade: Récit tiré de l'Histoire universelle.* Edited by L. Dufour-Vernes and Eugène Ritter. Geneva: H. Georg, 1884.

Audollent, Augustus. *Defixionum tabellae quotquot innotuerunt tam in graecis Orientis quam in totius Occidentis partibus, praeter atticas in Corpore Inscriptionum Atticarum editas.* Paris: in aedibus A.Fontemoing, 1904.

Aymar, Alphonse. "Le sachet accoucheur et ses mystères. Contribution à l'étude du folklore de la Haute-Auvergne du XIIIe au XVIIIe siècles." *Annales du Midi* 38 (1926): 273–347.

Baader, Bernhard. *Volkssagen aud dem Lande Baden und den angrezenden Gegenden.* Karlsruhe: Verlag der Herder, 1851.

Bachter, Stephen. *Anleitung zum Aberglauben Zauberbücher und die Verbreitung magischen Wissens seit dem 18. Jahrhundert.* Dissertation, Hamburg University, 2006.

Bæksted, Anders. *Målruner og Troldruner.* Copenhagen: Gyldendal, 1952.

———. "*Runerne. Deres historie og brug.* Copenhagen: Gyldendal, 1943.

BaK: Klintberg, Bengt af. *Svenska trollformler.* Stockholm: Wahlström and Widstrand, 1965. Cited by spell number.

Baldelli, Ignazio. "Scongiuri cassinesi del secolo XIII." *Studi di filologia italiana* 14 (1956): 456.

Baldinger, Max. "Aberglaube und Volksmedizin in der Zahnheilkunde." in *Volksmedizin.* Series: Wege der Forschung LXIII. Edited by E. Grabner. Darmstadt: Wissenschaftl, 1967.

Balletto, Laura. *Medici e farmaci, scongiuri ed incatesimi, dieta e gastronomia nel medioevo genovese.* Genoa: Università di Genova, 1986.

Bang, Anton C. *Norske hexeformularer og magiske opskrifter.* New edition with foreword and registers by Velle Espeland. Oslo: Univeritetsforlaget, 2005. [1st ed. Kristiania (Oslo), 1901–1902]. Cited by spell number.

Banis, Victor J. *Charms, Spells, and Curses for the Millions.* San Bernardino: Borgo Press, 2007.

Barb, Alphonse A. "Abraxas-Studien." *Latomus* 28 (1957): 67–86.

Bartsch, Elmar. *Die Sachbeschwörungen der römischen Liturgie: Eine liturgiegeschichtliche und liturgietheologische Studie.* Münster/Westfalen: Aschendorff, 1967.

Bartsch, Karl. *Sagen, Märchen und Gebräuche aus Mecklenburg,* vol. 2. Vienna: Braumüller, 1880.

BBE: Rustad, Mary S., ed. and trans. *The Black Books of Elverum.* Lakeville, Minn.: Galde Press, 1999.

Beck, Paul. "Die Bibliothek eines Hexenmeisters." *Zeitschrift des Vereins für Volkskunde* 15 (1905): 412–24.

Beckers, Hartmut. "Eine spätmittelalterliche deutsche Anleitung zur Teufelsbeschwörung mit Runenschriftverwendung." *Zeitschrift für deutsches Altertum und Literatur* 113 (1984): 136–45.

Bernand, André. *Sorciers grecs.* Paris: Fayard, 1991.

Bernard of Gordon. *Lilium medicinae.* Frankfurt: Lucas Jenni, 1617.

Berschin, Walter. *Greek Letters and the Latin Middle Ages: From Jerome to Nicholas of Cusa.* Translated by Jerold C. Frakes. Washington, D.C.: Catholic University of America Press, 1988.

Berthoin-Mathieu, Anne. *Prescriptions magiques anglaises du Xe au XIIe siècle.* Paris: Association des miques anglaises du Xeof America Press, 1996.

Betz, Hans Dieter, ed. *The Greek Magical Papyri in Translation, Including the Demotic Spells.* Chicago: University of Chicago Press, 1986.

Biblia sacra juxta vulgatam clementinam. Paris: Desclee & Soc., 1947.

Biedermann, Hans. *Handlexikon der magischen Künste. Von der Spätantike bis zum 19. Jahrhundert.* Graz: Akademische Druck- und Verlagsanstalt, 1968.

Birlinger, Anton. *Volksthümliches aus Schwaben.* 2 vols. Freiburg-im-Breisgau: Herder, 1861–1862.

Bischoff, Bernard. *Übersicht über die nichtdiplomatischen Geheimschriften des Mittelalters.* Cologne: Böhlau, 1954.

———. "Paläographie des römischen Altertums und des abendländischen Mittelalters.* Berlin: Erich Schmidt, 1979.

Bissing, Friedrich Wilhelm von. "Ägyptische Knotenamulette." *Archiv für Religionswissenschaft* 8 (1905): 23–27.

Blau, Ludwig. *Das altjüdische Zauberwesen.* Budapest: Landes-Rabbinerschule, 1898.

Bohak, Gideon. *Ancient Jewish Magic: A History.* Cambridge, England: Cambridge University Press, 2008.

———. "Hebrew, Hebrew Everywhere: Notes on the Interpretation of *Voces Magicae*." In *Prayer, Magic, and the Stars in the Ancient and Late Antique World*, edited by Scott Noegel, Joel Walker, and Brannon Wheeler, pp. 69–82. Philadelphia: Penn State University Press, 2003.

Bonner, Campbell. *Studies in Magical Amulets, chiefly Graeco-Egyptian*. Ann Arbor: University of Michigan Press, 1950.

Bø, Olav. "Trollformlar." In *Kulturhistorisk leksikon for nordisk middelalder*, vol. 18, 674–78.

Bonser, Wilfrid. "The Seven Sleepers of Ephesus in Anglo-Saxon and Later Recipes." *Folklore* 56 (1945): 254–56.

Boswinkel Ernst et al., eds., *Textes grecs démotiques et bilingues (P. L. Bat. 19)*. Leiden: Brill, 1978.

Boudet, Jean-Patrice. "Le *who's who* démonologiques de la Renaissance et leur ancêtres médiévaux," *Médiévales* 44 (2003): 117–40.

———. "'Magie théurgique angélologie et vision béatifique dans le *Liber sanctus* attribuée à Honorius de Thèbes." *Mélanges de l'École Française de Rome: Moyen Âge* 114, no. 2 (2002): 851–90.

Boudet, Jean-Patrice, Henri Bresc, and Benoît Grévin, eds. *Les anges et la magie au moyen âge*. (= *Mélanges de l'École française de Rome: Moyen Âge* 114, no.2. [2002]).

Boudet, Jean-Patrice, Anna Caiozzo, and Nicolas Weill-Parot, eds. *Images et magie:* Picatrix *entre Orient et Occident*. Paris: Champion, 2011.

Boutet, Frédéric. *Dictionnaire des sciences occultes*. Paris: Librairie des Champs-Elysées, 1937.

Braekman, Willy Louis. *Middeleeuwse witte en zwart magie in het Nederlands taalgebied. Gecommentarieerd compendium van incantamenta tot einde 16de eeuw*. Ghent: Royal Academy, 1997. Cited by spell number.

Breteton, Georgina E., and Janet M. Ferrier. *Le Mesnagier de Oaris*. Translated by Karin Ueltschi. Paris: le livre de Poche (Lettres gothiques), 1994.

Brillet, Pascal, and Alain Moreau. *La magie, bibliographie générale*. Montpellier: Université de Montpellier III, 2000.

Browe, Peter. "Die Eucharistie als Zaubermittel." *Archiv für Kulturgeschichte* 20 (1930): 134–54.

Campbell, Thompson R. *Semitic Magic*. London: Luzac, 1908.

Camus 1990: Camus, Dominique. *Paroles magiques, secrets de guérison: les leveurs de maux aujourd'hui*. Paris: Imago, 1990.

Camus 2001: Camus, D. *Le livre des secrets. Les mots et les paroles qui guérissent*. Paris: Dervy, 2001.

Camus 2002: Camus, D. *Voyage au pays du magique. Enquête sur les voyants, guérisseurs, sorciers*, Paris: Imago, 2002.

Candrea, I. Aurel. *Folclorul medical roman comparat. Privire generala. Medicina magica*. Iasi, Romania: Polirom, 1999.

Cardan, Jerome. *De varietate rerum*. Basel: Sebastian Henri Petri, 1581.

Cartojan, Dalman N. *Cartile populare in literatura romaneasca*, vol. 2. Bucharest: N. G. Dossios, 1938.

Cherry, John. *The Middleham Jewel and Ring*. York, England: The Yorkshire Museum, 1994.

Chesnel, Marquis Adolphe de. *Dictionnaire des superstitions, erreurs et préjugés*. Vol. XX of the *Nouvelle encyclopédie théologique*. Paris: Abbé Migne, 1843.

Clavicula: Mathers, S. Liddell MacGregor, trans. *The Key of Solomon the King* (Clavicula Salomonis). London: Routledge and Kegal Paul, 1974. I have also used the edition revised and corrected by Joseph H. Peterson.

Claviculas: *Claviculas de Salomon*. Translated from Hebrew into Latin by the Rabbi Heboganzar, from Latin into French by Monsignor de Darvault, then into Castillan.

Clavicules: Les véritable clavicules de Salomon. Edited from the Lansdowne 1203 manuscript in the British Library by Joseph H. Peterson.

Clement of Alexandria. *Le pédagogue*. Translated by Claude Montdésert, Henri-Irénée Marrou, and Chantel Matray. Paris: Le Cerf, 1970 (Sources chrétiennes).

Coulon, Hyacinthe. "Curiosités de l'histoire des remèdes comprenant des recettes employées au moyen age dans le Cambrésis." *Mémoires de la Société d'Emulation de Cambrai* 47 (1892): 1–153.

Cyranides: Delatte, Louis, ed. *Textes latins et vieux français relatifs aux Cyranides*. Paris: E. Droz, 1942 (Bibliothèque de philosophie et lettres de l'Université de Liège XCIII).

D'Abano, Pierre. *Les œuvres magiques de Henri-Corneille Agrippa*. Rome: Approuvé par moi Sargaranas, 1744.

Dac, Pierre, and Francis Blanche. *Signé Furax*. [A radio drama]

Dalman, Gustaf H. *Der Gottesname Adonaj eine seine Geschichte*. Berlin: H. Reuther, 1889.

Dalton, Ormond M. *Catalogue of the Finger Rings in the British Museum*. London: British Museum, 1912.

Daniel, Robert W., and Franco Maltomini. *Supplementum magicum* I. Opladen, Germany: Westdeutscher Verlag, 1990.

Daniels, Cora Linn, and Charles McClellan Stevans, eds. *Encyclopaedia of*

Superstitions, Folklore, and the Occult Sciences of the World. 3 vols. Chicago and Milwaukee: J. H. Yewdale & Sons, 1903.

Das Geheimnis der heiligen Gertrudis durch Sophia, das Gespons unsers Herrn und Heilandes Jesu Christi, 1506. Reissued, in *Buch Jezira, Das das ist das grosse Buch der Bücher Moses; das sechste, das siebente, das zehnte und das elfte. Aus ältesten kabbalistischen Urkunden.* Berlin: E. Bartels, circa 1910.

Davidson, Gustav. *A Dictionary of Angels Including the Fallen Angels.* New York and London: The Free Press, 1967.

Delatte, Armand. *La catoptromancie grecque et ses dérivés.* Paris-Liège: E. Droz, 1932.

———. ""Études sur la magie grecque." *Musée Belge* 18 (1914): 5–96.

Delaurenti, Beatrice. *La puissance des mots "virtus verborum." Débats doctrinaux sur le pouvoir des incantations au moyen âge.* Paris: Cerf, 2007.

Deonna, Waldemar. "À L'Escalade de 1602: les billets du père Alexandre." *Schweizerisches Archiv für Volkskunde* 41 (1944): 73–105; 113–58.

———. "Abra, abraca. La croix talisman de Lausanne." *Geneva* 22 (1944): 115–37.

———. "Formules magiques: Christos propylaios ou Christus hic est." *Revue archéologique* 22, 5th series (1925): 64–74.

———. "Superstitions à Genève aux XVIIe et XVIIIe siècles," *Schweizerisches Archiv für Volkskunde* 43 (1946): 345.

———. "Talismans chrétiens." *Revue d'histoire des religions* 95 (1927): 19–42.

———. *Revue d'histoire vaudoise,* no. 23 (1926): 231.

Derolez, René. *Runica manuscripta: The English Traditions.* Bruges: De Tempel, 1954.

Descombes, René. *Les carrés magiques. Histoire et technique du carré magique, de l'antiquité aux recherches actuelles.* Paris: Vuibert, 2000.

Dick, Wilhelm, ed. *Die Gesta Romanorum nach der Innsbrucker Handschrift vom Jahre 1342.* Erlangen and Leipzig: A. Deichert and G. Böhme, 1890.

Dieterich, Albrecht. *Abraxas: Studien zur Religionsgeschichte des späteren Altertums.* Leipzig: B. G. Teubner, 1891.

Die wahre und hohe Beschwörung der heiligen Jungfrau und Abtissin Gertrudis. Capucine Monastery of Türkhein. Ed. in *Handschriftliche Schätze aus Kloster-Bibliotheken, umfassend sämtliche vierzig Hauptwerke über Magie, verborgene Kräfte, Offenbarungen und geheimste Wissenschaften.* Köln: Hammers Erben Erben, 1743.

Dornseiff, Franz. *Das Alphabet in Mystik und Magie.* 2nd ed. Leipzig: Teubner, 1925.

Doulet, Jean-Michel. *Quand les démons enlevaient les enfants: Les changelins, étude d'une figure mythique.* Paris: Presses de la Sorbonne, 2002.

Dragon rouge: *Le Dragon rouge, ou l'art de commander les esprits célestes, aériens, terrestres, infernaux avec le vrai secret de faire parler les morts, de gagner toutes les fois qu'on et aux lotteries, de découvrir les trésors cachés, etc.* Nismes, Belgium: Chez Gaude, Printer-Bookseller, 1823.

Drechsler, P. *Sitte, Brauch und Volksglaube in Schlesien*, 2 vols. Leipzig: B. G. Teubner, 1909.

Dumas, F. Ribadeau, ed. *Le véritable dragon noir et la poule noire.* Paris: French and European Publishers, 1972, 133–67.

Dürig, Walter. "Die Verwendung des sogenannten Fluchpsalms 108 (109) im Volksglauben und in der Liturgie." *Münchener theologische Zeitschrift* 27 (1976): 1–84.

Düwel, Klaus. "Buchstabenmagie und Alphabetzauber: Zu den Inschriften der Goldbrakteaten und ihrer Funktion als Amulette." *Frühmittelalterliche Studien* 22 (1988): 70–110.

———. "Le rune como segni magici." *Annali sezione germanica* 1–3, n.s. II (1992): 7–23.

———. *Runen.* Stuttgart: Sammlung Metzler, 1983.

Egyptian Secrets: Magnus, Albertus. *Ägyptische Geheimnisse, bewährte und approbirte sympathetische und natürliche egyptische Geheimnisse für Menschen und Vieh.* 4 booklets. Braband, the Netherlands: n.d. I have numbered the spells. www.esotericarchives.com/moses/egyptian.htm (accessed March 9, 2015).

Magnus, Albertus. *Being the Approved, Verified, Sympathetic and Natural Egyptian Secrets, or White and Black Art for Man and Beast.* Chicago: Egyptian Publishing Co., n.d.

Eis, Gerhard. *Altdeutsche Zaubersprüche.* Berlin: Walter de Gruyter, 1964.

Eisler, Robert. "Le mystère du Schem Hammephorash." *Revue des études juives* 82 (1926), 157–59.

Eliade, Mircea. "Adam, le Christ et la mandragore." In *Mélanges d'histoire des religions offerts à Henri-Charles Puech.* Paris: Presses Universitaires de France, 1974.

Elliott, R. W. V. "Runic Mythology: The Legacy of the Futhark." *Bamberger Beiträge zur englischen Spachwissenschaft* 15 (1984): 37–50.

———. "Runes, Yews, and Magic." *Speculum* 32 (1957): 250–61.

———. *Runes: An Introduction.* Manchester, U.K..: Manchester University Press, 1989.

Enchiridion: Pope Leo III. *Enchiridion Leonis Pape* (Pope Leo's Enchiridion). Rome, 1848. Reissued in Dumas, F. Ribadeau. *Grimoires et rituels magiques.* Paris, 1972, 45–93.

Enchiridion (Spanish): *Enchiridion Leonis Papae. San Leon, papa iii de este nombre, reunio y puso en orden las oraciones de este libro, sacadas todas ellas de nuestra santa madre iglesia, y las envio al emperador carlo magno, acompanadas de la siguiente carta.* Rome, 1740.

Espeland, Velle. *Svartbok frå Gudbrandsdalen.* Norsk Folkeminnelags Skrifter 110. Oslo, Bergen, Tromsø, Norway: Universitetsforlaget, 1974.

Evans, Joan. *Magical Jewels of the Middle Ages and the Renaissance Particularly in England.* Oxford: Clarendon Press, 1922.

Faggioto, Marta. "Aspeti della religiosità contadina nella diocesi di Padova alla metà del quattrocento: scongiuri e pratiche magiche." *Quaderni di storia religiosa* XIV (2007): 235–78.

Fanger, Claire, ed. *Conjuring Spirits: Texts and Traditions of Medieval Ritual Magic.* Stroud, England: Sutton Publishing, 1998.

Fingerlin, Gerhard, Josef F. Fischer, and Klaus Düwel. "Alu und ota—Runenbeschriftete Münznachahmungen der Merowingerzeit aus Hüfingen." *Germania* 76 (1998): 781–822.

Flint, Valerie. *Witchcraft and Magic in Europe: Ancient Greece and Rome.* London: Athlone, 1999.

Flowers, Stephen E. *Runes and Magic: Magical Formulaic Elements in the Older Runic Tradition.* New York, Bern, Switzerland, and Frankfurt: Peter Lang, 1986.

Franz, Adolph. *Die kirchlichen Benediktionen in Mittelalter.* 2 vols. Graz: Herder, 1909.

Frischbier, Hermann. *Hexenspruch und Hexenbann, Ein Beitrag zur Geschichte des Aberglaubens in der Provinz Preussen.* Berlin: Verlag Adolph Enslin, 1870.

Frommann, Johann Christian. *Treatise on Fascination.* Nuremberg: Endtertus, 1675.

Fuchs, Harald. "Die Herkunft der Satorformel." *Schweizerisches Archiv für Volkskunde* 47 (1951): 28–54.

Gager, John G. *Curse Tablets and Binding Spells from the Ancient World.* New York and Oxford, England: Oxford University Press, 1992.

Galdrakver. 2 vols. Reykjavik, 2004. Volume 1 is a facsimile of the manuscript; volume 2 contains transcription and translations.

Gallée, Johan Hendrik. "Segensprüche." *Germania* 32 (1887): 454.

Gaster, Moses. "Romanian Spells." *Romanian Bird and Beast Stories.* London: Sidgwick and Jackson, 1915.

Gâyat al-Hakîm (**The Goal of the Wise**): *Picatrix, Das Ziel des Weisen von Pseudo-Magritti*. Ritter, Hellmut, and Martin Plessner, trans. London: Warburg Institute, 1962 (Studies of the Warburg Institute 27).

Giannini, G. *Una raccolta di segreti e di pratiche superstizione fatto de un popolano fiorentino des secolo XIV*. Cittá di Castello, 1838.

Goldsmid, Edmund, ed. *A Treatise of Magic Incantations*. Edinburgh: Private printing, 1886. Translated from the Latin of Christianus Pazig, circa 1700.

Gollancz, Hermann. *The Book of Protection, Being a Collection of Charms Now Edited for the First Time from Syrian Manuscripts with Translation, Introduction, and Notes*. London: Oxford University Press, 1912.

Gordon, Bernard, *Lilium medicinae*, Frankfurt: Erasmus Kempffer, 1617.

Gougaud, L. "Etudes sur les *Loricae* celtiques et sur les prières qui s'en approchent." *Bulletin d'ancienne littérature et archéologie chrétiennes* 1 (1911): 265–81; 2 (1912): 33–41, 101–27.

———. *Dévotions et pratiques religieuses du moyen âge*. Paris: Desclée de Brouwer, 1925.

Graf, F. *Gottesnähe und Schadenzauber. Die Magie in der griechisch-römischen Antike*. Munich: C. H. Beck, 1996.

———. *La magie dans l'antiquité gréco-romaine. Idéologie et pratique*. Collection Histoire. Paris: Belles Lettres, 1994.

Grambo, Ronald. "A Catalogue of Nordic Charms—Some Reflections." *NIF Newsletter* 2, no. 19 (1977).

———. "Norske kjærestevarsler." *Maal og minne* (1966).

———. *Norske trolleformler og magiske ritualer*. Oslo, Bergen, and Tromsø, Norway, 1984.

———. "Formler for døyving av sverd. En motivanalyse." *Maal og Minne* (1989a): 1–2, 39–55.

———. "Guddommers navn. Magi og ordets makt." *Folkeminner* 59 (2012): 10–20.

Graesse, J. G. *Bibliotheca magica et pneumatica*. Leipzig: Wilhelm Engelmann, 1843.

Gran Grimorio: *Gran grimorio del Papa Honorius*. Rome: 1760. Spanish translation of the *Grimoire of Pope Honorius*. https://sites.google.com/site/leersindescargar/ocultismo/el-gran-grimorio-papa-honorio.

Grand Grimoire: *Il Grand Grimoire con la Clavicola di Salomone*. L'Arcano Incantatore, 2002. Italian translation: www.esotericarchives.com/solomon/Il_Grand_Grimoire.pdf (accessed March 11, 2015).

Gray, Douglas. "The Five Wounds of Our Lord." *Notes and Queries*, vol. 10, no. 208 (1963).

Greenfield, Rochard P. H. "Saint Sisinnios, the Archangel Michael and the Female Demon Gylou: The Typology of the Greek Literary Stories." *Byzantina* 15 (1989): 83–142.

Gregory of Tours. *A History of the Franks.*

Grévin, Benoît, and J. Véronèse. "Guddomers navn. Magi og ordets makt." *Folkeminner* 59 (2012).

———. "Les 'caractères' magiques au Moyen Âge (XIIe–XIVe siècle)." *Bibliothèque de l'École des Chartres* 162 (2004): 305–79.

Grimoires: Lecouteux, Claude. *Le livre des grimoires.* Paris: Imago, 2005. Translated into English by Jon E. Graham. *The Book of Grimoires: The Secret Grammar of Magic.* Rochester, Vt.: Inner Traditions, 2013.

Hampp, Irmgard. *Beschwörung—Segen—Gebet. Untersuchungen zum Zauberspruch aus dem Bereich der Volksheilkunde.* Stuttgart, Germany: Silberburg, 1961. (Veröffentlichungen des Staatl. Amts für Denkmalpflege, Stuttgart. Reihe C: Volkskunde. Band 1).

Harmening, Dieter. *Zauberei im Abendland. Vom Anteil der Gelehrten am Wahn der Leute. Skizzen zur Geschichte des Aberglaubens.* Würzburg: Quellen and Forschungen zur Europ. Ethnologie X, 1991. For magic rings, see 87–103.

———. "Das magische Wort." *Perspektiven der Philosophie, Neues Jahrbuch* 23 (1997): 365–85.

———. *Wörterbuch des Aberglaubens.* Stuttgart: Reclam, 2005.

———. "Zur Morphologie magischer Inschriften." *Jahrbuch für Volkskunde* (1978): 67–80.

Harrauer, C. *Meliouchios. Studien zur Entwicklung religiöser Vorstellungen in griechischen synkretistschen Zaubertexten.* Vienna: Wiener Studien, Beiheft 1, Arbeiten zur antiken Religionsgeschichte 1, 1987.

Hasdeu, Bogdan Petriceicu. *Cuvente den batrani,* vol. II, *Cãrtile poporane ale romanilor in secolul XVI in legatura cu literature poprana cea nescrisa. Studiu de filologie comparative.* Bucharest: Editura didactica si pedagogica, 1879.

Hausmann, L., and L. Kriss-Rettenbeck. *Amulett und Talisman: Erscheinungsform und Geschichte.* Munich, Germany: G. D. W. Callwey, 1977.

Haust, J. *Médicinaire liégeois du XIIIe siècle et médicinaire namurois du XVe siècle.* Académie royale de Langue et Littérature française, textes anciens 4. Brussells: Liège, 1941.

Heim, R. "Incanta magica graeca latina." *Jahrbücher für classische Philologie* 19 (1893): 463-576.

Heimliche Offenbarung St. Gertrudis von Nivel aud Brabant, 1504. In *Handschriftliche Schätze aus Kloster-Bibliotheken, umfassend sämtliche vier-*

zig *Hauptwerke über Magie, verborgene Kräfte, Offenbarungen und geheimste Wissenschaften.* Köln: Hammers Erben Erben, 1743.

Herjulfsdottir, Ritwa. *Jungfru Maria möter ormen—om formlers tolkningar.* Gothenburg: Gothenburg University, 2008.

Herpentil, Joseph Anton. *Des hochwürdigen Herpentils, der Gesellschaft Jesu Priester, kurzer Begriff der übernatürlichen schwarzen Magie, enthaltend Beschwörungen und Namen der mächtigen Geister und deren Siegeln, oder das Buch der stärksten Geister, eröffnend die großen Heimlichkeiten aller Heimlichkeiten.* Salzburg, 1519. Translated by C. Lecouteux, *Le Livre des Grimoires.* 3rd ed. Paris: Imago, 2005.

Herter, Hans. "Böse Dämonen im frügrieschen Volksglauben." *Rheinisches Jahrbuch für Volkskunde* 1 (1950): 117–43.

Hervé, Georges. "Superstitions populaires suisses concernant les armes, le tir, la guerre, les blessures." *Revue anthropologique* 26 (1916): 351–65.

Heurgren, Paul, ed. *Salomoniska magiska konster. Utdrag ur en westboprests svartkonstböcker.* Meddelanden från Örebro Läns Museum VII. Örebro, Sweden, 1918.

Heyl, Johann Adolf. *Volkssagen, Bräuche und Meinungen aus Tirol.* Brixen, Italy: Gerolds, 1897.

Hoffmann-Krayer, Eduard, and Hanns Bächtold-Staübli. *Handwörterbuch des deutschen Aberglaubens,* 10 vols. Berlin: Walter de Gruyter, 1927.

Holthausen, F. "Rezepte, Segen und Zaubersprüche aus zwei Stockholmer Handschriften." *Anglia* 19 (1897): 75–88.

Honko, Lauri. *Krankeitsprojektile: Untersuchung über eine urtümliche Krankheitserklärung.* Helsinki: Suomalainen Tiedeakatemia, 1967.

Honorius: Honorius, Pope. *Le livre des conjurations.* Rome: Trajectoire, 1670. Reissue, Paris: Éditions Magnard, 2001.

Hörmann, Ludvig von. *Das Tiroler Bauernjahr, Jahreszeiten in den Alpen.* Innsbruck: Wagner, 1899.

Horsley, G. H. R., and Elisabeth Ruth Waterhouse. "The Greek Nomen Sacrum XP in Some Latin and Old English Manuscripts." *Scriptorium* 38 (1984): 211–30.

Horst, Georg Conrad. *Zauber-Bibliothek von Zauberei, Theurgie und Mantik Zauberern, Hexen und Hexenprocessen.* Mainz: Kupferberg, 1821.

Hunt, Tony. *Popular Medicine in 13th Century England, Introduction and Texts.* Cambridge, England: D. S. Brewer, 1994.

Isidore of Seville. *Etymologiae* VII. Stephen Barney, W. J. Lewis, J. A. Beach and Oliver Berghof, *The Etymologies of Isidore of Seville.* Cambridge, England: Cambridge University Press, 2006.

Jacobus de Voragine. *La légende dorée (Legenda aurea, vers 1261–1266)*, trad. sous la dir. d'Alain Boureau, Gallimard, 2004 (coll. "La Pléiade").

Jacoby, Adolf. "Die Zauberbücher vom Mittelalter bis zur Neuzeit, ihre Sammlung und Bearbeitung." *Mitteilungen der Schlesischen Gesellschaft für Volkskunde* 31 (1931).

Jenkinson, Francis John Henry, *The Hisperica famina*, Cambridge, England: Cambridge University Press, 1908.

Johannes de Sacrobosco. *Sphaera mundi noviter recognita cum commentariis*. Venice: F. Renner de Hailbrun, 1478.

Jónsson, Finnur. *Historia ecclesiastica Islandiæ*, vol. 2. Copenhagen: Salicath, 1774.

Joret, Charles. "Les incantations botaniques." *Romania* 17 (1888): 337–54.

Josephus Flavius. *The Antiquities of the Jews* II. Translated by William Whiston, 2013: www.gutenberg.org/files/2848/2848-h/2848-h.htm.

Julliard, André. "Gestes et paroles populaires du malheur: Pratiques médicales magiques et sorcellerie dans les sociétés rurales contemporaines de la Bresse et du Bugey (Ain)." Thesis, *Paris Descartes University* (Paris V), 1985.

Kahane, Henry Renée, and Angelina Pietrangeli. "Picatrix and the Talismans." *Romance Philology* 19 (1966): 574–93.

Kaimakis, Dimitris V., ed. *Die Kyraniden*. Meisenheim and Glan: Anton Hain, 1976. (Beiträge zur klassischen Philologie), 76.

Karlinger, Felix. "Anmerkung zu AREPO." *Österreichische Zeitschrift für Volkskunde* 82 (1979): 300–303.

Kieckhefer, Richard. *Forbidden Rites: A Necromancer's Manual of the Fifteenth Century*. University Park: Penn State University Press, 1998.

———. *Magic in the Middle Ages*. Cambridge, Mass.: Cambridge University Press, 1989.

King, Charles W. "Talismans and Amulets." *Archaeological Journal* 101 (1869): 25–34; 144–235.

Klapper, Joseph. *Erzaählungen des Mittellalters*. Wroclaw, Poland: M & H Marcus, 1914.

Kohler, Kaufmann. "The Tetragrammaton (Shem ham-M'forah) and Its Uses." *Journal of Jewish Lore and Philosophy* I, 1909, 19–32.

Kornreuther, Johannes. *Fünf Bücher der Schwarzen Magie: Geister, Siegel und Beschwörungen von Kornreuther, Herpentil, Scotus und Dee*, edited by Christian Eberstein. Norderstedt: Book on Demand GmbH, 2011.

———. *Magia ordinis artium et scientiarum abtrusarum*. Welcome Library, ms. 253, 1515.

Kotansky, Roy, "Incantations and Prayers on Inscribed Greek Amulets." In *Magika Hiera: Ancient Greek Magic and Religion*, edited by Christopher A. Faraone and Dirk Obbink. Oxford, England: Oxford University Press, 1991.

———. *Greek Magic Amulets: The Inscribed Gold, Silver, Copper, and Bronze Lamellae. Part I: Published Texts of Known Provenance.* Opladen, Germany: Westdeutscher, 1994.

Kronfeld, Ernst Moritz. *Der Krieg im Aberglauben und im Volksglauben.* Munich: Schmidt, 1915.

Kruse, Britta-Juliane. *Verborgene Heilkünste. Geschichte der Frauenmedizin im Spätmittelalter.* Berlin: De Gruyter, 1996.

Laisnel de la Salle, Germain. *Croyances et légendes du centre de la France: souvenirs du vieux temps, coutumes et traditions populaires,* 2 vols. Paris, 1875–1881.

Lancaster, W. T., and W. P. Baildon, eds. *The Coucher Book of the Cistercian Abbey of Kirkstall, in the West Riding of the County of York.* London: Publications of the Thoresby Society 8, 1904.

Lang, Benedek. *Unlocked Books: Manuscripts of Learned Magic in the Medieval Libraries of Central Europe.* University Park: Penn State University Press, 1974. Reprinted, 2010.

Lauterbach, Jacob Z. "Substitutes for the Tetragrammaton." *Proceedings of the American Academy for Jewish Research* (1931): 39–67.

Le Blant, Edmond. "De l'ancienne croyance à des moyens secrets de défier la torture." *Mémoires de l'Institut Nationale de France* 34 (1892): 289–300.

———. "Le premier chapitre de saint Jean et la croyance à ses vertus secretes." *Revue archéologique* 25 (1894).

Le Blevec, Daniel. "Pharmacopée populaire en comtat venaissin: les recettes du notaire Jean Vital (1395)." *Razo* 4 (1984): 127–31.

Lebrun, François. *Se soigner autrefois: Médecins, saints et sorciers aux XVIIe et XVIIIe Siècles.* Paris: Seuil, 1983.

Leclerc, H. "Œil (le mauvais œil)." In *Dictionnaire des antiquités grecques et romaines.* Edited by Charles Victor Daremberg and Edmond Saglio. Paris: 1936. Vol. XII/2, col., 1936–1943.

Lecouteux, Claude. "Agla. Remarques sur un mot magiques." In *Le secret d'Odin, Mélanges pour Régis Boyer.* Edited by Marc Auchet, 19–34. Nancy, France: PUN, 2001.

———. "Agla, sator. Quelques remarques sur les charmes médicaux du moyen âge." *Nouvelle plume: Revue d'études mythologiques et symboliques* 2 (Nagoya 2001): 19–34.

———. *Charmes, conjurations et bénédictions: lexique et formules.* Essais sur le Moyen Âge 17. Paris: Champion, 1996.

———. *Dictionnaire de mythologie germanique.* 3rd ed. Paris: Imago, 2014.

———. *Le livre des amulettes et talismans.* Paris: Imago, 2004. Translated into English by Jon E. Graham as *The High Magic of Talismans and Amulets.* Rochester, Vt.: Inner Traditions, 2014.

———. *The Book of Grimoires.* Rochester, Vt.: Inner Traditions, 2013.

———. "La médecine magique au Moyen Âge." In *Guérir l'âme et le corps: au-delà des médecines habituelles,* edited by P. Wallon, 176–87. Paris: Albin-Michel, 2000.

———. "Magie médiévale." *Les temps médiévaux* 9 (August–September 2003): 26–29.

Léger, Louis. *La Bulgarie.* Paris: Le Cerf, 1883.

Legran, Alexandre. *Les sortileges de la science.* Paris: Andréal Librairie, 1898.

Leroquais, Victor. *Les livres d'heures manuscrits de la Bibliothèque Nationale,* vols. 1 and 2. Paris: Imprimerie Nationale, 1927.

Lexa, François. *La Magie dans l'Égypte ancienne,* vol. 1. Paris: Librairie orientaliste Paul Geuthner, 1925.

Le médecin des pauvres, ou recueil de prières pour le soulagement des maux d'estomac, charbon, pustule, fièvres, plaie, &c (Doctor of the Poor, or Prayer Book for the Relief of Stomachache, Coal, Pustule, Fevers, Wound, etc.). Mâcon, France: Imprimerie Romand, 1875.

Libellus St. Gertrudis. In *Handschriftliche Schätze aus Kloster-Bibliotheken, umfassend sämtliche vierzig Hauptwerke über Magie, verborgene Kräfte, Offenbarungen und geheimste Wissenschaften.* Köln: Hammers Erben Erben, 1743.

Liber incantationum, exorcismorum et fascinationum varium (Book of Incantations). Munich, Germany, Bavarian National Library, ms. Clm 849.

Liber iuratus (Book of Consecrations): Hedegård, Gösta. *Liber Iuratus Honorii: A Critical Edition of the Latin Version of the Sworn Book of Honorius.* Stockholm: Studia Latina Stockholmiensia 48, 2002.

Libro de segretto e di magia. Private manuscript never published.

Lidka, J., ed. and trans. *Liber de ymaginibus planetarum* (The Book of Angels, Rings, Characters, and Images of the Planets). In *Conjuring Spirits: Texts and Traditions of Medieval Ritual Magic,* edited by Claire Fanger, 50–65. Stroud, England: Sutton, 1998.

Lindqvist, Adolf N. *En Isländsk svartkonstbók från 1500-talet.* Uppsala: Appelberg, 1921.

Marcellus: Niedermann, Maximilian, and Eduard Liechtenhan, eds. *Marcelli de medicamentis liber.* Corpus Medicorum Latinorum 5. Berlin: Academie-Verlag, 1968. Cited by book and chapter.

Martinez, David G. *Michigan Papyri XVI: A Greek Love Charm from Egypt (P. Mich. 757).* Ann Arbor: University of Michigan Press, 1991.

Massenkeil, Josef. "AREPO. Ein Beitrag zur Aufhellung des Satoranagramms." *Österreichische Zeitschrift für Volkskunde* 82 (1979): 145–50.

Maurer, Konrad von. *Isländische Volkssagen der Gegenwart.* Leipzig: Märchen and Gebräuche, 1860.

Marzell, Heinrich. *Geschichte und Volkskunde der deutschen Heilpflanzen.* Darmstadt, Germany, 1967.

Mastrocinque, Attilio. "Metamorfosi di Kronos su una gemma di Bologna." In *Gemme gnostiche e cultura ellenistica,* edited by A. Mastrocinque. Bologna: Pàtron editore, 2002.

———. "Le pouvoir de l'écriture dans la magie." Cahiers "Mondes anciens" 1 (2010). http://mondesanciens.revues.org/index168.html (accessed March 12, 2015).

McKinnell, John, and Rudolf Simek. *Runes, Magic, and Religion: A Sourcebook.* Vienna: Fassbaender, 2004.

Mély, Ferdinand de. "Inscriptions talismaniques." *Bulletin de la Société des Antiquaires de France* (1916): 342–53.

Meyer, Pau. "De quelques manuscrits de la collection Libri à Florence." *Romania* 14 (1885): 528.

Mirecki, Paul, and Marvin Meyer. *Magic and Ritual in the Ancient World.* Leiden: Brill, 2002.

Mone, Franz Joseph. "Beschwörung und Segen." *Anzeiger für Kunde des deutschen Mittelalters* 3 (1834): 277–90.

Mondino, Gianmarco. "Un' antica orazione salvifica: L'Epistola diu Leone III a Carlo Magno." *Panorami-Vallate Alpine* 82 (2010): 28–33.

Mowat, Commandant, M. H. "Le plus ancien carré de mots: Sator Arepo Tenet Opera Rotas." *Mémoires de la Société des Antiquaires de France* 4, 7th series (1905): 41–68.

Müllenhoff, Karl. *Sagen, Märchen und Lieder der Herzogsthümer Schleswig, Holstein und Lauenburg.* Kiel: Schwers, 1845.

Musset, Lucien. *Introduction à la runologie.* Paris: Aubier-Montaigne, 1976.

Nielsen, Karl Martin. "Runen und Magie. Ein forschungs Überblick." *Frühmittelalterliche Studien* 19 (1985): 75–97.

Niggermeyer, J. H. *Beschwörungsformeln aus dem "Buch der Geheimnisse."*

Judaistische Texte und Studien 3. Hildesheim: Georg Olms Verlag, 1975.
Noegel, Scott, Joel Walker, and Brannon Wheeler. *Prayer, Magic, and the Stars in the Ancient and Late Antique World*. Philadelphia: Penn State University Press, 2003.
Østberg, Kristian. *Svartboka*. Oslo: Steenske Forlag, 1925.
Ogden, David. "*Voces magicae*: Letters, Shapes and Images," in *Witchcraft and Magic in Europe: Ancient Greece and Rome*, edited by Valerie Flint. London: Athlone Press, 1999.
Ohl des Marais, Albert. "Le chiffre 4, talisman contre la peste." *Bulletin de la Société Philomatique Vosgienne* 62 (1937): 195–99.
Ohrt, Ferdinand. *Danmarks trylleformler*, 2 vols. Copenhagen: Christiana, 1921. Vol. I: *Innleding og tekst* is cited by spell number. Vol. II: *Efterhast og lanformler* is cited by page number.
———. *Fluchtafel und Wettersegen*. Helsinki: FF Communications 86, 1929.
———. "Trylleord." *Fremmede og danske danmarks folkeminder* 25 (1922).
Ohrvik, Ane. "Conceptualizing Knowledge in Early Modern Norway. A Study of Paratexts in Norwegian Black Books." Thesis, University of Oslo, 2011. Includes a catalog of grimoires, 195–309.
Oikonomidis, D. B. "H G ellw eiV thn kai roumanikhn naograin." *Laographia* 30 (1975–1976): 246–78.
Olsan, Lea T. "The Arcus Charms and Christian Magic." *Neophilologus* 73 (1989): 438–47.
———. "The Inscription of Charms in Anglo-Saxon Manuscripts." *Oral Tradition* 14 (1999): 401–19.
———. "Latin Charms of Medieval England: Verbal Healing in a Christian Oral Tradition." *Oral Tradition* 7 (1992): 116–42.
Olsen, Magnus. *Om troldruner*. Fordomtima, Skriftserie II. Uppsala: Akademiska Bokhandein, 1917.
Oman, Charles Chichele. *Catalogue of Rings*. London: Adam and Charles Black, 1930.
Omont, Henri. "Un traité de physique et d'alchimie." *Bibliothèque de l'Ecole des Chartres* 58 (1897): 253–58.
Önnerfors, Alf. "Iatromagische Beschwörungen in der 'Physica Plinii Sangallensis.'" *Eranos* 83 (1985): 235–52.
———. "Zaubersprüche in Texten der römischen und frühmittelalterlichen Medizin." In *Études de médecine romaine*, edited by G. Sabbah, 506ff. Saint-Étienne: Presses Universitaires de Saint-Étienne, 1989.
Origen: *Traité d'Origène Contre Celse*, Amsterdam: Chez Henry Desbordes, 1700.

Page, Ray I. "Anglo-Saxon Runes and Magic." *British Archaeological Association Journal* 27 (1964): 14–31.

Panzer, Friedrich. *Beiträge zur deutschen Mythologie,* vol. II. Munich: Literarisch-artistische Anstalt, 1855.

Patera, Maria. "Exorcismes et phylacteries byzantins: Écrire, énoncer les noms du démon." *Cahiers Mondes anciens,* vol. I (2010).

Pedrosa, José Manuel. *Entre la magia y la religion, oraciones, conjuros, ensalmos.* Sendoa: Gipuzkoa, 2000.

Perdrizet, Paul. *Negotium perambulans in tenebris. Études de démonologie greèco-orientale.* Strasbourg, France: Istra, 1992.

Peterson, Erik. "Engel- und Dämonennamen: Nomina Barbara. " *Rheinisches Museum* Neue Folge, 75 (1926): 393–481.

Petit Albert: *Petit Albert. Secrets merveilleux de la magie naturelle et cabalistique du Petit Albert.* Lyon: Héritiers de Beringos fratres, 1782.

Petropoulos, John. *Greek Magic: Ancient, Medieval, and Modern.* London: Routledge, 2008.

Petzold, Leander, ed. *Magie und Religion.* Wege der Forschung 337. Darmstadt: WBG, 1978.

Peuckert, Will-Erich. "Die ägyptischen Geheimnisse." *ARV* 10 (1954): 40–96.

———. *Pansophie, Ein Versuch zur Geschichte der weissen und scharzen Magie.* Berlin: Erich Schmidt Verlag, 1956.

PGM: Preisendanz, Karl, and Albert Henrichs, eds. *Papyri Graecae Magicae. Die Griechischen Zauberpapyri.* 2nd ed. 2 vols. Stuttgart: B. G. Teubner, 1973–1974.

Picatrix: Pingree, David, ed. *Picatrix: The Latin Version of the Ghayat al-Hakîm.* London: 1986. Bakhouche, Béatrice, Frederic Fauquier, and Brigitte Pérez-Jean, trans. *Picatrix, un traité de magie médiéval. Miroir du Moyen Âge.* Translation of the Latin text. Turnhout, Belgium: Brepols, 2003.

Atallah, Hashem. *Picatrix: The Goal of the Wise.* 2 vols. Seattle, Wash.: Ouroboros Press, 2002–2008.

Pingree, David. "Some of the Sources of the *Ghâyat al-Hakîm.*" *Journal of the Warburg and Courtauld Institutes* 43 (1980): 1–15.

Pio, Louis. *Cyprianus: Inde holder mange adskillige viddenschabe.* Copenhagen: Immanuel Rée, 1870.

Pliny. *Natural History* XXVIII. *C. Plini secondi Naturalis historiae libri XXXVII.* Edited by Ludovicus Janus, 5 vols. Leipzig: B. G. Teubner, 1870-1878. Cited by book and chapter.

Pluquet, François-André-Adrien. *Mémoires pour servir à l'histoire des égarements de l'esprit humain par rapport à la religion chrétienne,* vol. 1. Paris: Dualpha, 1764.

Pourrat, Henri. *Trésor des contes,* vol. 2. Paris: Omnibus, 2009.

Pradel, Fritz. *Griechische und süditalienische Gebete, Beschwörungen und Rezepte des Mittelalters.* Religiongeschichtliche Versuche und Vorabeiten 3/3. Giessen: Töpelmann, 1907.

Pseudo–Arnaldus de Villanova. *Opera.* Lyon, France: François Fradin, 1509.

Pseudo-Théodore: Rose, Valentin, ed. *Theodori Prisciani Euporiston libri III cum physicorum fragmento et addimentis Pseudo-Theodoreis.* Leipzig: B. G. Teubner, 1894.

Pseudo-Vegetius: Lommatzsch, Ernst, ed. *P. Vegeti Renati digestorum artis mulomedicinae libri.* Leipzig: B. G. Teubner, 1903.

Rabelais, François. *Gargantua and Pantagruel,* 4 vols. Paris: Jean de Bonnot, 1995.

———. *The Works of Francis Rabelais,* vol. 2. London: Lackington, Allen, and Co., 1807.

Rava-Cordier, I. "Un recueil provençal d'exempla du XIIIe siècle." *Provence historique* 159 (1989).

Registro dei morti della parrocchia di Groscavallo, Groscavallo, 1779.

Rézeau, Pierre. *Les prières aux saints en français à la fin du moyen âge.* Geneva: Publications romanes et françaises CLXVI, 1983.

Renou, Jean de. *Œuvres pharmaceutiques.* Lyon: Chez Antoine Chard, 1626.

Romano, Franca. "Guaritrici tradizionali nel Bresciano." *Lares* 48/4 (1982): 521–43.

Roper, Jonathan. *Charms and Charming in Europe.* Hampshire, New York: Palgrave Macmillan, 2004.

———. *English Verbal Charms.* Helsinki: 2005 (FFC 288).

Roscher, Wilhelm Heinrich. *Über Alter, Ursprung und Bedeutung der Hippokratischen Schrift von der Siebenzahl.* Leipzig: B. G. Teubner, 1911.

Rosetti A. "De quelques traits caractéristiques de la langue des formules roumaines de sorcellerie." In *XIV Congresso Internazionale di Linguistica e Filologia Romanza, Napoli Aprile 1974* (Naples: 1977), 559–67.

Rowling, J. K. *Harry Potter and the Half-Blood Prince.* London: Bloomsbury, 2005.

Ruff, Margarethe. *Zauberpraktiken als Lebenshilfe: Magie im Alltag vom Mittelalter bis heute.* Frankfurt: Campus Verlag, 2003.

Rutebeuf. *Le Miracle de Théophile* (The Miracle of Théophile). Edited by Achille Jubinal. Paris: É. Pannier, 1838.

Ryan, William F. *The Boathouse at Midnight*. University Park: Penn State University Press, 1999.
Saemundsson, Matthiás Viðar. *Galdrar á Íslandi. Íslenzk galdrabók*. Reykjavik: Almenna, 1992.
Saintyves, Pierre. *Les grimoires à oraisons magiques*. Paris: Nourry, 1926.
Sallmann, Jean-Michel, ed. *Dictionnaire historique de la magie et des sciences occultes*. Paris: Le Livre de Poche (La Pochotèque), 2006.
Saltveit, Laurits. "Litt mer om laukaR og alu." *Maal og minne* (1992): 150–56.
Sambon, Arthur. "La bague à travers les âges." *Le Musée* 6 (1909): 112.
Schäfer, Peter, and Hans G. Kippenberg. "Jewish Magical Literature in Late Antiquity and Early Middle Ages." *Journal of Jewish Studies* 41 (1990): 75–91.
Schneegans, Heinrich. "Sizilianische Gebete und Rezepte in griechischer Umschrift." *Zeitschrift für romanische philologie* 32 (1908).
Schäuble, Johann. *Das Kloster. Weltlich und geistlich. Meist aus der ältern deutschen Volks-, Wunder-, Curiositäten-, und vorzugsweise komischen Literatur*, 12 vols. Stuttgart: Otto Wigand, 1845–1849.
Schmidt, Johan Georg. *Die gestriegelte Rockenphilosophie*. 2 vols. Chemnitz: Conrad Stössein, 1718–1722.
Schneider, Wolfgang. *Lexikon alchemistisch-pharmazeutischer Symbole*. Weinheim: Verlag Chemie, 1962.
Schönbach, A. E. "Eine Auslese altdeutscher Segensformeln." *Analecta Graecensia. Fechtschrift zur 42. Versammlung deutscher Philologen und Schulmänner in Wien*. Graz: Verlagbuchhandlung der Styria, 1893.
Schönwerth, Franz. *Aus der Oberpfalz. Sitten und Sagen,* 3 vols. Augsburg: Rieger, 1857.
Schulz, Monika. *Magie oder die Wiederherstellung der Ordnung*. Beiträge zur europäischen Ethnologie und Folklore 5. Berlin: Peter Lang, 2001.
Scot, Reginald. *Discoverie of Witchcraft,* Books XII and XV. London: Elliot Stock Pages, 1584. Cited by book and chapter.
Sébillot, Paul, *Le Folklore de la France*, 3 vols. 2d ed. Paris: Maisonneuve et Larose, 1968.
Secrets magiques pour l'amour en nombre de octante et trois. Charmes, conjurations, sortilèges et talsimans. Paris: Académie des bibliophiles, 1868.
Seligman, Siegfried. "Ananisapta und Sator." *Hessische Blätter für Volkskunde* 20 (1921): 1–25.
———. *Der böse Blick und Verwandtes. Ein Beitrag zur Geschichte des Aberglaubens aller Zeiten und Völker*. Berlin: H. Barsdorf, 1910.
———. *The History of Magic*. New York: Pantheon, 1948.

Semiphoras: *Semiphoras Salomonis Regis.* Wesel, Duisburg, and Leipzig, Germany: Andreas Luppius, 1686. Republished in Johann Schäuble, *Das Kloster. Weltlich und geistlich. Meist aus der ältern deutschen Volks-, Wunder-, Curiositäten-, und vorzugsweise komischen Literatur.* Vol. 3, 289–329. Stuttgart and Leipzig, Germany, 1845–1849.

Sheldon, Suzanne Eastman. *Middle English and Latin Charms, Amulets, and Talismans from Vernacular Manuscripts.* Dissertation, Tulane University, 1978.

Siller, Max. "Zauberspruch und Hexenprozeß. Die Rolle des Zauberspruchs in den Zauber- und Hexenprozessen Tirols." In *Tradition und Entwicklung. Festschrift Eugen Thurnher,* edited by Werner M. Bauer, Achim Masser, and Guntram Plangg, 127–54. Innsbruck: Innsbrucker Beiträge zur Kulturwissenschaft. Germanistische Reihe 14, 1982.

Singer, Charles and Dorothy Singer. "On a Greek Charm Used in England in the 12th Century." *Annals of Medical History* 1 (1917): 258–60.

Spamer, A. *Romanusbüchlein. Historisch-philologischer Kommentar zu einem deutschen Zauberbuch.* Berlin: Veröffentlichungen des Instituts für deutsche Volkskunde 17, 1958.

Sprenger, James, and Heinrich Institoris. *Malleus maleficarum.* Speyer: Peter Drach, 1487.

Stevens, William Oliver. *The Cross in the Life and Literature of the Anglo-Saxon.* New York: Yale University Press, 1904.

Storms, Godfrod. *Anglo-Saxon Magic.* The Hague: Martinus Nijhoff, 1948.

Stübe, Rudolf. *Jüdisch-babylonische Zaubertexte.* Halle: J. Krause, 1895.

Stürzl, E. "Die christlichen Elemente in den altenglischen Zaubersegen." *Die Sprache* VI (1960): 75–93.

Talos, Ion. *Gândirea magico-religioasa la Romani, dictionary.* Bucharest: Editura Enciclopedica, 2001.

———. *Petit dictionnaire de mythologie roumaine,* s.v. "Avestiţa." Grenoble: ELLUG, 2002.

Tettau, Wilhelm Johanne Albert von, and J. D. H. Temme. *Die Volkssagen Ostpreussens, Littauens und Westpreussens.* Berlin: Nicolai, 1837.

Thiers, Jean-Baptiste. *Traité des superstitions selon l'ecriture sainte, les décrets des conciles et les sentiments des saints pères et des théologiens.* Paris: A. Dezallier, 1679. Also published in 4 vols., Avignon: L. Chambeau, 1777.

Thomas, Keith. *Religion and the Decline of Magic: Studies in Popular beliefs in Sixteenth and Seventeenth Century England.* Oxford, UK: Oxford University Press: 1971.

Thorndike, Lynn. *The History of Magic and Experimental Science during the*

First Thirteen Centuries of Our Era. 8 vols. New York: Columbia University Press, 1923–1934.

Timotin, Emanuela. "Les charmes roumains manuscrits. Évolution et transmission d'un savoir traditionnel aux XVIIe-XIXe siècles." Thesis, Grenoble III, 2009.

———. "*Irodia doamna zânelor. Notes sur les fees roumaines et leur cohort fantastique*," in *Les Entre-Mondes: Les vivants, les morts*, edited by K. Ueltschi and M. White-Le Goff, 179–94. Paris: Klincksieck, 2009.

———. "Limba descântecelor românești." Thesis, Bucharest, 2007. Includes a file containing eighty-three Romanian charms.

———. "Queen of the Fairies and Biblical Queen. Notes of the Romanian Herodias." *Acta Ethnographica Hungarica* 64 (2009): 363–76.

Trachtenberg, Joshua. *Jewish Magic and Superstition*. New York: Behrman's Jewish Book House, 1939.

Trésor: Le génie et le trésor vu viellard des pyramides, veritable science des talismans. In *Grimoires et rituels magiques*, edited by F. Ribadeau Dumas, 170–202. Paris: Belfond, 1972.

Tselikas, Agamemnon. "Spells and Exorcisms in Three Post-Byzantine Manuscripts," in *Greek Magic, Ancient, Medieval, and Modern*, edited by John Petropoulos, 72–81. London: Routledge, 2008.

Vaitkevičienė, Daiva. *Lietuvių užkalbėjimai: Gydymo formulės* (Lithuanian Verbal Healing Charms). Vilnius: Lietuvių literatūros ir tautosakos institutas, 2009.

Van Haver, Jozef. *Nederlanse incantatieliteratuur. Een gecommentarieerd compendium van Nederlandse besweringsformules*. Ghent: Koninklijke Vlaamse Academie voor Taal-en Letterkunde, 1964.

Venerable Bede, The. "Lorica." *The Hisperica famina*. Edited by Francis John Henry Jenkinson. Cambridge: Cambridge University Press, 1908.

Vernaleken, Theodor. *Mythen und Bräuche des Volkes in Österreich*. Vienna: Wilhelm Braumüller, 1859.

Véronèse, Julien, ed. *L'Ars notoria au moyen âge*. Florence: Sismel, 2007.

Verus Jesuitarvm Libellus Sev fortissima coactio et constrictio omnium malorum Spirituum cujuscunque generis, conditionis, status vel officii sint. et conjuratio fortissima et probatissima in usielem Huic est annixa CYPRIANI CITATIO ANGELORVM, ejusque Conjuratio Spiritus, qui thesaurum abscondidit, una cum illorum Dismissione. Paris, 1508.

Vigenère, Blaise de. *Traicte des chiffres ov secretes maniere d'escrire*. Paris: Chez Abel L'Angelier, 1586.

Villiers, Elisabeth. *Amuleti, talismani, ed alter cose misteriosi*. Milan: Hoepli Editore, 1989.

Vinje: Garstein, Oskar. *Den eldste svartebok fra norsk middelalder*. Oslo: Solum Forlag, 1993.

Wackernagel, Wilhelm. *Altdeutsche Predigten und Gebete aus Handschriften*. Basel: Richter, 1876.

Waegeman, Maryse. *Amulet and Alphabet: Magical Amulets in the First Book of Cyranides*. Amsterdam: J. C. Gieben, 1987.

Waite, Arthur Edward. *The Book of Ceremonial Magic*. London: Rebman, 1911.

Wallberger, Johann. *Berühmtes Zauberbuch oder aufrichtige Entdeckung bewährter ungemeiner Geheimnisse*. Frankfurt and Leipzig, 1760.

Werner, Reinhold. "Nichtspanische Sprachelmente magischer Formeln in volkstümlicher kolumbianischer Literatur." In *Europäsche Volksliteratur. Festschrift für Felix Karlinger*. Edited by Dieter Messner, 194–207. Vienna: Verlag des österreichischen Museums für Volkskunde, 1980 (Raabser Märchen-Reihe, 4). 1980.

Wesselski, Albert. *Hokuspokus oder geborener Narr ist unheilbar*. Prague: A. Haase, 1926.

Wessely, Karl. *Ephesia grammata aus Papyrusrollen, Inschriften, Gemmen*. Vienna: A. Pichlers Witwe and Sohn, 1886.

Weyer, Johann. *Cinq livres de l'imposture des diables, des enchantements et sorcelleries*. Paris: Jacques du Puys, 1570.

———. *Opera Omnia*, Editio nova et hactenus desiderata, Amstelodami: Apud Petrum van den Berge, 1660. I. *De praestigiis daemonum et incantationibus ac veneficiis libri sex. Ab acutore seies aucti et recogoniti, justa exemplar Basilense* 1583; II. *Liber apologeticus et Pseudomonarchia daemonum*; III. *De lamiis liber, et De commentitiis iejuniis*; IV. *De ira morbo, ejusdem curatione philosophica, medica et theological liber*; V. *Observationes medicae rariores quibus accredit, Liber secundus, nunc demun et germanico idomate, in latinum translatus*.

Wickersheimer, Ernest. *Manuscrits latins de médecine des bibliothèques françaises antérieurs au XIIe siècle: Les manuscrits latins de médecine du haut moyen âge dans les bibliothèques de France*: Paris: CNRS, 1966.

Wipf, K. A., "Die Zaubersprüche im Althochdeutschen." *Numen* XXII (1975): 42–69.

Wünsch, Richard. *Antike Fluchtafeln*, no. 3–4, 248ff. Bonn: Marcus and Weber, 1912.

———. "Deisidaimoniaka." *Archiv für Religionswissenschaft* 12 (1909): 37–41.

Württembergisches Jahrbuch. Stuttgart: W. Kohlhammer, 1980.

Youtie, H. C., and Campbell Bonner. "Two Curse Tablets from Beisan." *Transactions of the American Philological Society* 68 (1937): 57.

Zingerle, Ignaz Vinzenz. "Segen und Heilmittel aus einer Wolfsthurner Handschrift des XV. Jahrhunderts." *Zeitschrift der Vereins für Volkskunde* 1 (1891): 172–77; 315–24.

———. *Sitten, Bräuche und Meinungen des Tiroler Volkes.* Innsbruck: 1871.

Zeitschrift für deutsches Altertum 11 (1859): 437.

TEXTS ONLINE

Anglo-Saxon Charms

University of Hawaii. Anglo-Saxon Charms. www2.hawaii.edu/~kjolly/unc.htm (accessed March 9, 2015).

Ars Notoria

Scribd. Ars Notoria 13th Century Latin. www.scribd.com/doc/59159587/ars-notoria-13th-Century-Latin (accessed March 9, 2015).

Germany

Galdorcraeft. Mittekalterliche Zaubersprüche. www.galdorcraeft.de (accessed March 9, 2015).

Greece

Open Library. Audollent, August. *Defixionum tabellae quotquot innotuerunt in graecis orientis quam in totius Occidentis partibus, praeter atticas in corpore inscriptionum atticarum.* http://openlibrary.org/books/OL20622270M/Defixionum_tabellae_quotquot_innotuerunt_tam_in_Graecis–Orientis_quam_in_totius_Occidentis (accessed March 9, 2015).

Hermetic. Papyri Graecae Magicae. www.hermetic.com/pgm (accessed March 9, 2015).

Grimoire Collections

Esoteric Archives. Twilit Grotto: Archives of Western Esoterica. www.esotericarchives.com/esoteric.htm (accessed March 9, 2015).

Iceland

www.galdrasyning.is/index.php.
Digitale Bibliothek–München. *Liber incantationum, exorcismorum et fascinationum variarum.* http://daten.digitale-sammlungen.de/~db/0003/bsb00037155/images (accessed March 9, 2015).

Norway

www.edd.uio.no/ikos/svarteboker/svarteboker
www.hf.uio.no/ikos/tjenester/samlinger/norsk-folkeminnesamling/svarteboeker/det-digitale-arkivet/
www.ess.uio.no/ikos/svarteboker/svarteboker.html.
www.hf.uio.no/ikos/tjenester/samlinger/morsk folkeminnesamling/svarteboeker/det-digitale-arkivet.